THE JACKSON ADR HANDBOOK

THE JACKSON ADR HANDBOOK

SECOND EDITION

SUSAN BLAKE

JULIE BROWNE

STUART SIME

Editorial Advisory Board

Lord Neuberger of Abbotsbury (Co-Chair)
Lord Clarke of Stone-cum-Ebony (Co-Chair)
His Honour Judge Philip Bartle QC
Peter Causton, The Law Society
Andrew Goodman, Convenor, Standing Conference of Mediation Advocates
District Judge Margaret Langley, Judicial College DR Committee
Colin Manning, Chairman, The Bar Council ADR Panel
Master Victoria McCloud
Sir Vivian Ramsey
Tim Wallis
Sir Alan Ward, Chairman, Civil Mediation Council
William Wood QC, Civil Justice Council

Endorsed by

The Judicial College
The Civil Justice Council
The Civil Mediation Council

OXFORD
UNIVERSITY PRESS

OXFORD

UNIVERSITY PRESS

Great Clarendon Street, Oxford, OX2 6DP,
United Kingdom

Oxford University Press is a department of the University of Oxford.
It furthers the University's objective of excellence in research, scholarship,
and education by publishing worldwide. Oxford is a registered trade mark of
Oxford University Press in the UK and in certain other countries

© Susan Blake, Julie Browne, and Stuart Sime 2016

The moral rights of the authors have been asserted

First Edition published in 2013
Second Edition published in 2016

Impression: 1

Published in the United States of America by Oxford University Press
198 Madison Avenue, New York, NY 10016, United States of America

British Library Cataloguing in Publication Data
Data available

Library of Congress Control Number: 2016944784

ISBN 978–0–19–878319–0

Printed in Great Britain by
Bell & Bain Ltd., Glasgow

FOREWORD TO THE FIRST EDITION

In 1976, Professor Frank Sander of Harvard University breathed new life into our interest in Alternative Dispute Resolution (ADR). The development of ADR in both the United States and in England and Wales can be traced to his pioneering work.[1] It informed the Woolf Reforms and the Civil Procedure Rules, just as it ultimately informed the conclusions which Sir Rupert Jackson expressed in his Costs Review. As a consequence of Professor Sander's work and the commitment of ADR practitioners and those involved in the reform of civil justice, ADR is now a well-established part of every lawyer's practice. If there was ever any doubt that the consensual settlement of disputes—facilitated through the use of ADR—served the public interest, it has been laid to rest. Consensual settlement—whether facilitated through informal negotiation, a structured mediation, early neutral evaluation, or any other such means—is an essential aspect of any civil society. The effective promotion of ADR is unquestionably in the public interest.

This book is one of the latest offsprings of Professor Sander's work. It is the direct result of Sir Rupert Jackson's recommendation in his Costs Review that there should be 'a single authoritative handbook, explaining clearly and concisely what ADR is (without either "hype" or jargon) and giving details of all reputable providers of mediation'. It is properly authoritative. It is readily accessible. I cannot commend it more highly. Thanks to the tireless work carried out by Tim Wallis on behalf of the Civil Justice Council, the vision of the authors, and Oxford University Press's commitment, a book of genuinely high quality has been produced; a book which I have no doubt at all will soon realize Sir Rupert's expectation that the ADR Handbook— this book—should be as tried and trusted as the White Book and the Green Book. This book deserves to be the first and only port of call for every student of ADR, irrespective of whether they are a litigant, a law student, a lawyer, or a judge. I am sure that it will be.

Lord Dyson
Master of the Rolls
January 2013

---

[1] F Sander, 'Varieties of Dispute Processing' (1976) 70 *Federal Rules Decisions* 111.

PREFACE TO THE SECOND EDITION

The production of this handbook was one of the recommendations by Sir Rupert Jackson in his review of civil litigation costs. He saw the need for a 'single authoritative handbook, explaining clearly and concisely what ADR is'. In the three years since the first edition, this handbook has attained recognition by the courts and by practitioners as a major authority on the practice and procedure of ADR. It is frequently cited in court, as well as being used as a source of information for lawyers and clients. We therefore believe that Sir Rupert's recommendation has been achieved.

The time has come for a new edition to take account of changes and to ensure that the handbook maintains its reputation. Originally, it was suggested that it might be produced on an annual basis. Whilst there have been developments every year, these have not justified the production of a new edition. Rather, a three-year cycle for new editions has proved to be appropriate. This allows for new cases and approaches to ADR to be included to reflect important changes, without taking away the familiarity of a trusted and well-thumbed reference book.

Whilst the focus has, again, been on ADR, the book covers all other non-adjudicative alternatives including negotiation, expert evaluation, mini trials, conciliation, and grievance procedures. These, often used in combination, can assist parties to realize the strengths and weaknesses of their positions and better understand the position of the other party, paving the way for a consensual solution to the dispute. Adjudicative methods such as arbitration, adjudication, and expert determination are also dealt with. They complete the range of options which are available to help parties to achieve an appropriate solution when a third party determination is necessary. However, it is often the case that prior to, or in parallel with, the adjudicative approach, parties will seek an agreed solution. The cost and time taken by the adjudicative methods often raise similar problems to litigation. The saving of that cost and time, together with the collateral benefits of achieving a solution which the parties have agreed, can be equally important in relation to adjudicative methods.

The timing of ADR is always an important factor, particularly where avoidance of expense and time is a major consideration. Timing forms a major section in the handbook, as does the choice of an ADR option. Taken together with the detailed consideration of the options, we believe the new edition will continue to maintain its position, as Sir Rupert envisaged, on the bookshelves of judges and litigators.

Whilst we played a small part in the production of the handbook together with other members of the Editorial Advisory Board, the hard work has been done by others. First and foremost are the authors, Susan Blake, Julie Browne, and Stuart Sime, who, despite their busy academic lives, have been able to use their specialist knowledge of ADR to make the necessary changes to update the chapters with, we hope, helpful suggestions from the Editorial Advisory Board. However, the handbook could not have been produced without the encouragement of Katie Hooper and the team at OUP, to whom we are very grateful. The Editorial Advisory Board now includes some new members, replacing the equally distinguished colleagues who have retired. Its members have also played their part in providing suggested areas for change. We are delighted, too, to have the continuing endorsement of three important organizations: The Judicial College, The Civil Mediation Council, and the Civil Justice Council. That endorsement is essential in ensuring the pre-eminence of the handbook and we thank them for their support.

We hope that the handbook and its companion website will continue to help judges, practitioners, and clients to better understand the ADR processes so that ADR will continue to fulfil its appropriate role in the litigation process. Whilst final determination of disputes is always available in the courts, the benefits achieved by the parties reaching a proper resolution of their disputes cannot be underestimated.

Finally, we encourage readers to make any suggestions or comments so that we can incorporate them into the next edition.

Tim Wallis
Vivian Ramsey

Online Resource Centre
A companion website providing further resources and updates is available at <http://www.oup.co.uk/companion/ADR2e>.

CONTENTS

2 INTERPLAY BETWEEN ADR, CPR, AND LITIGATION

3 NEGOTIATION

12. Negotiation and Joint Settlement Meetings

4 MEDIATION

6 OTHER ALTERNATIVE DISPUTE RESOLUTION OPTIONS AND THE INTERNATIONAL PERSPECTIVE

TABLE OF CASES

TABLE OF STATUTES

GLOSSARY AND ABBREVIATIONS

ABS	Alternative business structure. Options for the ownership and management of bodies providing legal services provided by the Legal Services Act 2007
ACAS	Advisory, Conciliation and Arbitration Service (in relation to employment matters)
ADR	Alternative Dispute Resolution (see 1.02 for meaning in this Handbook)
Adjudication	Adjudicative dispute resolution procedure providing a binding and relatively speedy decision, often adjusted to meet the needs of a specific industry
Adjudicative	A form of alternative dispute resolution in which the parties agree to engage a third party to make a decision in relation to the dispute
Agreement to mediate	A written agreement to engage in a mediation process (to be distinguished from an agreement recording terms at the end of a successful mediation)
AICA	Association of Independent Construction Adjudicators
APCM	Assessed Professionally Competent Mediator
Arbitral award	The decision made by a tribunal at the end of an arbitration
Arbitral Institution	An organization which administers arbitrations. It may publish its own institutional arbitration rules
Arbitration	Adjudicative dispute resolution process under which the parties agree to submit their dispute to an impartial tribunal appointed by a process agreed by the parties
Arbitration agreement	A written agreement between parties to carry out an arbitration
ATE	After the event, as in insurance taken out after the events giving rise to a dispute, but before liability or damages in relation to the events is established
BATNA	Best alternative to a negotiated agreement
BTE	Before the event, as in insurance taken out before events giving rise to a dispute
CAMS	Court of Appeal Mediation Scheme
CEDR	Centre for Effective Dispute Resolution
CFA	Conditional Fee Agreement under which the lawyer will be paid through a success fee if the case is won
CIA	Chartered Institute of Arbitrators
Claimant	Party bringing a claim, particularly in litigation or arbitration

CMC	Civil Mediation Council
Confidentiality	The duty not to disclose communications made in an attempt to settle a dispute. As appropriate, disclosure should not go beyond the parties, their lawyers and any third party engaged to take part in the settlement process
Court	In litigation this describes the tribunal appointed to decide the issues between the parties. In arbitration a court is usually a governing body of an arbitral institution usually with no judicial function
Court Settlement Process	A form of mediation provided by judges in the Construction and Technology Court
CPR	Civil Procedure Rules 1998 (SI 1998/3132), the procedural rules governing litigation in the High Court and county courts
CSP	Court Settlement Process
DBA	Damages Based Agreement under which a lawyer will be paid through a share in damages if the case is successful
Defendant	Party responding to a claim
Determiner	Expert or other person appointed to decide a matter referred to expert or neutral determination
eADR	Electronic ADR
ED	Expert determination
EE	Expert evaluation
EHRC	Equality and Human Rights Commission
ENE	Early neutral evaluation
ICC	International Chamber of Commerce
iDR	Internet dispute resolution
IMI	International Mediation Institute
Jordan order	An order requiring parties to file witness statements setting out why the use of ADR is thought to be unreasonable in a case
JSM	Joint settlement meeting, used for negotiation, particularly in personal injury cases
Litigation funding	The provision of funds by a third party to finance a party involved in a legal dispute
LSC	Legal Services Commission
Mediation	A non-adjudicative dispute resolution process under which the parties agree to try to reach a settlement of their dispute with the assistance of an independent third party using a process agreed by the parties
Mediation agreement	A written agreement between parties to carry out a mediation
MIAM	Mediation information assessment meeting
MSEO	Mediation Settlement Enforcement Order under which an agreement reached through mediation in a cross border dispute within the EU can be recorded in a court order
Non-adjudicative	A form of alternative dispute resolution in which agreement is reached by the parties
ODR	Online dispute resolution

Opening statement	An oral statement often made by a mediator and then by each party in the joint session often held at the start of a mediation
Party	A party to a civil dispute
Position statement	A written statement that may be provided by a party to a mediator setting out a position prior to a mediation
QOCS	Qualified one-way costs shifting applies in personal injury cases allowing a claimant to generally avoid the risk of paying the defendant's costs if a case is lost
Respondent	Party responding to a claim or application
SCCS	Small Claims Court Scheme
SCMS	Small Claims Mediation Scheme, a free scheme provided for lower value cases in county courts
Scott Schedule	Multi-column document used in construction disputes for setting out items in dispute with columns for responses by other parties and by the decision taker
Settlement	The terms agreed when a non-adjudicatory ADR process ends in agreement
SME	Small and medium enterprise
SRA	Solicitors Regulation Authority
TCC	Technology and Construction Court, a specialist court within the High Court
Tomlin Order	Consent order in litigation which stays a claim on terms set out in a schedule
Tribunal	Body appointed to determine a dispute
UNCITRAL	United Nations Commission on International Trade Law
Ungley order	An order requiring parties to consider ADR, and if a party thinks ADR unsuitable to be prepared to justify that view at the conclusion of any trial
WATNA	Worst alternative to a negotiated agreement

Part 1

GENERAL PRINCIPLES

1

GENERAL PRINCIPLES OF ADR

A The Importance of ADR

In the resolution of a civil dispute, anyone is entitled to a fair opportunity to **1.01** put their case, within a reasonable time, at a reasonable cost, and with appropriate independent input to ensure fairness. The quality of justice in the courts of England and Wales is very well respected. However, there are circumstances in which options other than litigation may be more cost effective, quicker, or flexible, while still resulting in a fair outcome. The potential litigant should be sufficiently aware of, and appropriately advised about, other options. Alternative dispute resolution (ADR) has a long and respected history in this jurisdiction. It has received increasing support from the Civil Procedure Rules 1998 and associated Practice Directions, the judiciary, and developments in government policy. We have reached the stage, not least following the introduction of the Jackson Reforms from 1 April 2013, when resolution through ADR processes needs to be given serious consideration as part of resolving almost any civil dispute, forming part of case and costs management. Rises in court fees and limits in the availability of legal aid funding are also making the potential use of ADR more attractive.

B The Definition of ADR

1.02 The term 'alternative dispute resolution' has no agreed definition. For the purpose of this Handbook, the phrase is used to cover the full range of alternatives to litigation potentially available to resolve a civil dispute. It therefore includes any option where: there is a dispute between two (or more) parties; that dispute relates to civil legal rights and/or duties; and the dispute could potentially be addressed through litigation. The process may or may not involve an independent third party. The parties to the dispute will have some control over the process and the decision taken, through agreeing the form the process should take, and in some circumstances the final outcome. The range of ADR options is set out in Chapter 2.

1.03 An ADR process may result in a binding decision being made by a third party (adjudicative) or by the parties themselves by agreement (non-adjudicative). There may be a relatively formal procedure (as in arbitration) or substantial flexibility (as in negotiation). The process may be paper-based, internet-based, or involve meetings. The process may be evaluative (with proposals for a fair outcome being made) or facilitative. Lawyers may advise in respect of the process, and may play a role in it. The process may be administered by a commercial or not-for-profit organization, and such organizations can be a very useful source of information.

C The Role of the Courts in the Use of ADR

1.04 The courts have played a very significant role in the development of the use of ADR.

- Since 1994 the Commercial Court has led developments with procedural guidance, requiring lawyers to consider with their clients and other parties the possibility of attempting to resolve a dispute using ADR, and to ensure parties are informed as to cost-effective dispute resolution options.[1] The commercial courts have also led developments in the use and wording of orders to support the use of ADR.
- Since 1995 the High Court has also provided guidance on the use of ADR, with judicial control of cases including the option to question legal representatives on whether the use of ADR had been discussed, or might assist in resolving or narrowing issues.[2]

---

[1] 'Practice Note: Commercial Court; Alternative Dispute Resolution' [1994] 1 All ER 34.
[2] 'High Court Practice Note (Civil Litigation: Case Management)' [1995] 1 All ER 385.

- In 1996 a pilot scheme in the Central London County Court offered time-limited voluntary mediation. Such pilot schemes led to nationwide provision through the HMCTS Small Claims Mediation Scheme, see 16.07–16.10.
- A voluntary mediation scheme attached to the Court of Appeal was established in 1997. The scheme developed successfully and from March 2012 as a pilot a significant range of appeals have been referred to mediation unless a judge orders otherwise, see 16.11–16.13.

Encouragement of the use of ADR is built into the Civil Procedure Rules 1998. The key elements are as follows, and they are developed in Chapters 8–11. **1.05**

- The overriding objective. This obliges the court to deal with a case justly and at proportionate cost.[3] Other elements of the objective, such as saving expense, and ensuring that cases are dealt with expeditiously, support the appropriate use of ADR.[4] The parties and their lawyers are under a duty to assist the court in furthering the overriding objective.[5]
- Pre-action requirements. There is an expectation that parties will consider the use of ADR prior to the issues of proceedings under the Practice Direction Pre-action Conduct and the Pre-action Protocols, see Chapter 8.
- The interim stages of litigation. Parties are expressly encouraged to cooperate with each other in the conduct of the proceedings, deciding promptly which issues need full investigation and trial. Judges should encourage the parties to use an ADR procedure if the court considers that to be appropriate, and facilitate the use of ADR, and help the parties to settle the whole or part of a case.[6] There is specific support for the use of ADR in the Civil Procedure Rules and the Court Guides, see Chapter 9.

D The Role of Judges in the Use of ADR

There is strong judicial support for the appropriate use of ADR. This has grown significantly since 1 April 2013 with the use of more proactive case management and costs management. Orders to support ADR are a robust approach readily granted and the potential use of ADR is more often considered by the court, within the use of costs sanctions where unreasonable failure to use ADR is shown. There is judicial support for a shift of ethos in litigation, with practitioners expected to bring a sense of proportion to litigation, trying to agree facts and issues, and not **1.06**

---

[3] CPR r 1.1 as amended by the Civil Procedure (Amendment) Rules 2013.
[4] CPR r 1.1(2).
[5] CPR r 1.3.
[6] CPR r 1.4(1) and r 1.4.2(e).

seeing a concession as weakness in the post-Jackson world.[7] Clear views that excessive and disproportionate costs bring no credit to litigation and should be avoided also support the use of ADR.[8]

1.07   Judicial support for ADR is shown through the Judicial College, the Civil Justice Council, and the application of the Civil Procedure Rules 1998. As examples of judicial endorsement, explored more fully in Chapters 9 and 11:

- 'All members of the legal profession who conduct litigation should now routinely consider with their clients whether their disputes are suitable for ADR.'[9]
- The use of ADR is seen as consistent with the overriding objective, potentially achieving a timely outcome for even a complex dispute.[10]
- Costs penalties may be imposed on a party who refuses to make reasonable use of an ADR process that could have been successful, even where that party goes on to win the case.[11] The obligation to make reasonable use of ADR has been expanded so that a failure to respond to a proposal that ADR be used may be treated as a refusal to engage in ADR.[12]
- 'Today, sufficient should be known about alternative dispute resolution to make the failure to adopt it, in particular when public money is involved, indefensible'.[13]
- Judges will provide robust and detailed guidance to parties in relation to the use of ADR.[14]
- Judges expect a party to raise any perceived obstacle to the use of ADR at the time so that it may be addressed, rather than raised later.[15]
- While acknowledging that a court cannot oblige truly unwilling parties to mediate, a judge will in an appropriate case make orders that give a strong steer towards mediation, perhaps with directions for speedy conduct of the case should that fail.[16]
- Judicial guidance may be given on how to implement ADR processes, for example as regards the basis upon which a judge may provide an early neutral evaluation to

---

[7] *Kazakhstan Kagazy Plc v Zhunus* [2015] EWHC 996 (Comm); *Gotch v Enelco Ltd* [2015] EWHC 1802 (TCC).

[8] *Ted Baker Plc v AXA Insurance Plc* [2014] EWHC 4178 (Comm); *Gilks v Hodgson* [2015] EWCA Civ 5.

[9] *Halsey v Milton Keynes NHS Trust* [2004] EWCA Civ 576.

[10] *Dyson v Leeds City Council* [2000] CP Rep 42 (per Lord Woolf).

[11] *Dunnett v Railtrack* [2002] 1 WLR 2434.

[12] *PGF II SA v OMFS Company 1 Limited* [2013] EWCA Civ 1288.

[13] *R (Cowl) v Plymouth City Council* [2002] 1 WLR 803 (per Lord Woolf); *Brewer v Mann* [2012] EWCA Civ 246 (per Rix LJ).

[14] *Brookfield Construction (UK) Limited v Mott Macdonald Limited* [2010] EWHC 659 (TCC) (per Coulson J).

[15] *PGF II SA v OMFS Company* [2012] EWHC 83 (TCC).

[16] *Bradley v Heslin* [2014] EWHC 3267 (Ch); *SM v DAM* [2014] EWHC 537.

assist in the resolution of a case where the parties have differing views as to their prospects of success and the parties ask for such an evaluation.[17]

There are numerous instances of judges stating specifically that ADR rather than litigation was the appropriate way to proceed with a case. **1.08**

- If a reasonable complaints or similar process is in place, litigation may be disproportionate.[18]
- In disputes between neighbours, settlement should often be preferred to incurring disproportionate costs.[19]
- Where allegations involve matters such as employment and possible harassment, litigation may not be the best way to address them.[20]
- In a complex dispute between individuals as regards interests in a property, litigation costs may be disproportionate to the sum in dispute.[21]
- Even in a relatively high value case, issues may not be best addressed through litigation relating to law and fact.[22]
- Complex litigation such as mesothelioma claims may be best addressed through ADR.[23]

There has also been support for the use of ADR in speeches made by senior judges, **1.09** including many of those made in relation to the implementation of the Jackson Review of Costs. For example, Lord Neuberger has described ADR as 'litigation's invaluable twin' and said:

> The … post-Woolf commitment to proportionality weaves ADR more tightly into the fabric of civil justice … it gives it a crucial role to play in dispute resolution. It does so not because it requires courts to divert cases from their formal adjudicative processes to ADR … It does so because it is an expression of our commitment to civil justice for the public good … Promoting and facilitating the use of ADR for those cases where it will be of genuine advantage to the parties, because of, for instance, its informality, the flexibility of its processes and the availability of remedies not available to the litigation process—is of benefit not only to those litigants but also to the justice system. It is of benefit because it ensures that only those cases which truly call for, truly require, formal adjudication utilise the limited resources available to the justice system.[24]

---

[17] *Seals v Williams* [2015] EWHC 1829 (Ch).
[18] *R v Hampshire County Council* [2009] EWHC 2537 (Admin).
[19] *Oliver v Symons* [2012] EWCA Civ 267 (per Elias LJ); *Faidi v Elliot Corporation* [2012] EWCA Civ 287 (per Jackson LJ); *Gilks v Hodgson* [2015] EWCA Civ 5.
[20] *Iqual v Dean Mason Solicitors* [2011] EWCA Civ 123.
[21] *Dibble v Pfluger* [2010] EWCA Civ 1005.
[22] *Uren v Corporate Leisure (UK) Ltd* [2011] EWCA Civ 66.
[23] *Dyson v Leeds City Council* [2000] CP Rep 42 (per Lord Woolf).
[24] The Fourth Keating Lecture, 2010, 'Equity, ADR, Arbitration and the Law: Different Dimensions of Justice' <http://www.judiciary.gov.uk/NR/rdonlyres/CBC3DC2C-DE43-43EC-8A02-3D3CADCB0442/0/mrkeatinglecture19052010.pdf>.

1.10   There are several areas still requiring development as regards the use of ADR. For example, what may be regarded as reasonable use of ADR in relation to a potential costs sanction remains a significant area for dispute at the costs stage. It is important both to clarify further what will be seen as reasonable use of ADR, and to ensure that where appropriate ADR is built into case and costs management.

E The Context of the Jackson Review of Costs

1.11   A key role in the ongoing development of civil dispute resolution has been played by the Review of Civil Litigation Costs carried out by Lord Justice Jackson.[25] While in his wide-ranging review of the litigation process, Lord Woolf expressed support for the encouragement of the resolution of disputes before they come to trial, and the role of the courts in encouraging and supporting this, reforms following his review did not lead to all the benefits in streamlining litigation and saving costs that Lord Woolf envisaged. [26]

1.12   A number of Lord Justice Jackson's proposals, most of which were implemented as a package from 1 April 2013, are now being seen to support the use of ADR. The extension of case management to include costs management,[27] and the introduction of cost budgets, can focus the minds of parties on costs and ensure that ADR options are sufficiently explored. In addition, greater costs transparency, and the revised test of 'proportionality', are helping to ensure that the cost effectiveness of ADR is better understood. Lord Justice Jackson has himself commented that costs management is encouraging early settlement through the exchange of costs information.[28] The courts are providing guidance on how a case management timetable can sensibly include flexibility for ADR.[29] It is hoped that encouraging the use of ADR through case management and budgeting will increasingly mean that reasonable use of ADR takes place during the resolution of the case, rather than being left for argument when costs are considered.

1.13   The Review of Civil Litigation Costs specifically supported the increased use of ADR.[30] Lord Justice Jackson concluded that 'ADR (particularly mediation) has a vital

---

[25] 'Review of Civil Litigation Costs: Final Report', published in January 2010, see <http://www.judiciary.gov.uk/publications-and-reports/review-of-civil-litigation-costs/reports/civil-litigation-costs-review-final-report>.

[26] 'Access to Justice: Final Report', July 1996 Chap 1 para 7(d).

[27] CPR Part 3, as amended by the Civil Procedure (Amendment) Rules 2013.

[28] 'Confronting Costs Management', Harbour Lecture May 2015, <https://www.judiciary.gov.uk/announcements/harbour-lecture-by-lord-justice-jackson-confronting-costs-management/>.

[29] *CIP Properties (AIPT) Ltd v Galliford Try Infrastructure Ltd* [2014] EWHC 3546 (TCC).

[30] 'Review of Civil Litigation Costs: Final Report', Chapter 36 and Recommendations 75 and 76.

role to play in reducing the costs of civil disputes, by fomenting the early settlement of cases. ADR is, however, under-used. Its potential benefits are not as widely known as they should be.' He stated that: 'There should be a serious campaign (a) to ensure that all litigation lawyers and judges are properly informed about the benefits which ADR can bring, and (b) to alert the public and small businesses to the benefits of ADR.'[31]

Lord Justice Jackson concluded that an authoritative handbook should be pre- **1.14** pared to explain clearly and concisely what ADR is. This Handbook was written in response to that recommendation, setting out the current law and practice in relation to the use of ADR in relation to civil claims in England and Wales,[32] and presented in a way that is designed to be reasonably comprehensive for the use of judges, lawyers, and court users. Key sources for further information and updating are available on the companion website. Points made in this Handbook have received judicial approval.[33]

The Interim and Final Reports of the Review of Civil Litigation Costs were substan- **1.15** tial documents based on significant research and consultation.[34] Both the research material and the series of Implementation Lectures remain valuable.[35] For example in the Eleventh Implementation Lecture, Lord Justice Jackson explained the importance of proactivity in relation to the use of ADR, and the need for explanations to be given for a failure to use ADR when appropriate.[36]

F Key Recent Developments

Many developments in the last few years underline the growing importance and **1.16** diversity of ADR.

- A number of successful bodies supporting and promoting the use of ADR have been established. Of particular note is the Civil Mediation Council, set up in 2003, which provides standards for training and practice.[37]

---

[31] 'Review of Civil Litigation Costs: Final Report', Recommendation 75.
[32] 'Review of Civil Litigation Costs: Final Report', Recommendation 76.
[33] *PGF II SA v OMFS Co 1 Ltd* [2014] 1 WLR 1386 (per Briggs LJ); *Northrop Grumman Mission Systems Europe Ltd v BAE Systems (Al Diriyah C41) Ltd* [2014] EWHC 3148 (TCC) (per Ramsey J).
[34] 'Review of Civil Litigation Costs: Interim Report', 'Review of Civil Litigation Costs: Final Report' see <http://www.judiciary.gov.uk/publications-and-reports/review-of-civil-litigation-costs/reports/civil-litigation-costs-review-final-report>.
[35] See <http://www.judiciary.gov.uk/publications-and-reports/review-of-civil-litigation-costs/lectures>.
[36] Eleventh Implementation Lecture 'The Role of Alternative Dispute Resolution in Furthering the Aims of the Civil Litigation Costs Review'.
[37] See <http://www.civilmediation.org>.

- From 1 April 2014 the Small Claims Mediation Service has provided mediation services free for many types of defended claims up to a value of £10,000, replacing a scheme set up in 2007. Parties can express willingness to be referred to the scheme, but cannot be forced to mediate.[38]
- A compulsory Mediation Information pilot scheme took place in the Central London, Birmingham, and Manchester County Courts, based on the Mediation Information and Assessment Meetings (MIAMs) used in family cases.[39] A separate pilot scheme for the use of mediation in relation to some types of case issued through the County Court Money Claims Centre was extended to 31 March 2014.[40] Lord Neuberger has proposed that the use of MIAMs should be extended to smaller civil cases, and that clauses proposing the use of mediation in the event of a dispute be more common in contracts.[41]
- European Union Directives and Regulations have supported the development of the use of ADR in relation to cross-border and to consumer disputes, see Chapter 21.
- The Civil Justice Council's Online Dispute Resolution Advisory Group published a report on Online Dispute Resolution for Low Value Civil Claims in February 2015, recommending the establishment of a new internet-based court service known as HM Online Court to assist in resolving civil disputes of a value less than £25,000, see Chapter 21.[42] The Civil Courts Structure Review being conducted by Lord Justice Briggs also considers an Online Court.
- There is an increase in the use of ADR to resolve costs disputes, and support services for costs ADR are available, including options such as early neutral evaluation or expert determination.
- There has been a substantial rise in the costs of bringing a civil action, both as regards issue and hearings. For example from 6 April 2015 a claim for between £10,000 and £200,000 has attracted an issue fee of 5 per cent of the value of the claim, with a fee of £10,000 for a claim above £200,000.[43] It is possible that fees may rise further. This makes it ever more important to consider the potential cost effectiveness of using ADR.
- The Institute of Family Law Arbitrators launched a Family Law Arbitration Scheme on 26 March 2012, providing a scheme under which family law disputes can be decided through a decision-making process that is within the control of

---

[38] CPR r 26.4A.
[39] Practice Direction 51H The Mediation Service Pilot Scheme.
[40] Practice Direction 51L The Second Mediation Service Pilot Scheme.
[41] <http://www.civilmediation.org/downloads/>.
[42] <www.judiciary.gov.uk/online-dispute-resolution/odr-report-february-2015/>.
[43] Civil and Family Court Fees from 6 April 2015, HM Courts and Tribunals Service, see <http://hmctsformfinder.justice.gov.uk/courtfinder/forms/ex050-eng.pdf>.

the parties.[44] The President of the Family Division has given guidance as regards the implementation of arbitral awards through consent orders in family cases.[45]

- From October 2015 CPR r 3.1 was amended to specify that case management powers can include the possibility of the judge hearing an early neutral evaluation with the aim of helping the parties to settle. It remains to be seen how this will work in practice.

Government policy has shown increasing support for ADR, expressing a belief that **1.17** 'access to justice for all parties depends on costs being proportionate and unnecessary cases being deterred'. There is a concern that 'cases are resolved too late, too expensively, with complex procedures and an adversarial climate imposing costs that sometimes dwarf the value of a contested claim'.[46] On 23 June 2011 the government issued a Dispute Resolution Commitment, strengthening an Alternative Dispute Resolution Pledge made in 2001. This requires all government departments and agencies to use alternatives such as mediation and arbitration whenever possible before taking a dispute to court.[47] The Lord Chancellor has expressed support for developing the use of online dispute resolution for small claims.[48] The Ministry of Justice issued 'Boundary Disputes: A Scoping Study' in January 2015. This recommends encouraging the use of mediation and expert determination as well as further improving court and tribunal procedure, with research showing reasonable success for mediation.

G The Success of ADR

Evidence of the success of ADR is relevant to persuading parties and lawyers to use **1.18** it. Research and statistics generally show good rates of success, and good levels of satisfaction for parties. For example, the Small Claims Mediation Scheme results in about 70 per cent of disputes being resolved, with high levels of satisfaction amongst parties. The Court of Appeal mediation scheme results in the resolution of about 40 per cent of cases that use the scheme. Success rates tend to be better where a party has voluntarily agreed to use ADR.

There are numerous independent research projects relating to the use and potential **1.19** success of ADR, some sponsored by the Ministry of Justice.[49] These studies include

---

[44] See <http://www.ifla.org.uk>.
[45] *S v S* [2014] EWHC 7 (Fam); *S v P (Settlement by Collaborative Law Process)* [2008] 2 FLR 2040.
[46] 'Solving Disputes in County Courts: Creating a Simpler, Quicker and More Proportionate System', see <http://www.justice.gov.uk/consultations/consultation-cp6-2011.htm>.
[47] See <http://www.justice.gov.uk/guidance/mediation/dispute-resolution-commitment.htm>.
[48] <https://www.gov.uk/government/speeches/what-does-a-one-nation-justice-policy-look-like>.
[49] See <http://www.justice.gov.uk/publications/research-and-analysis/moj> and http://asauk.org.uk/alternative-dispute-resolution/adr-research/>.

assessment of court-related mediation.[50] Some ADR service providers also carry out research and surveys.[51]

H Compulsion to Use ADR

1.20 The position has been reached where the use of ADR should be appropriately considered, and an unreasonable refusal to use ADR may be met with a costs penalty. This gives rise to the question whether a party could be compelled to use ADR rather than litigation, and in a few jurisdictions mediation has effectively been made compulsory in some circumstances. In England and Wales the position is that it is acceptable that regulations provide for the provision of information on and strong encouragement to use ADR so long as it is ultimately possible for a case to go to trial, see 9.06–9.14. The Jackson Review of Costs supported the view that mediation should not be compulsory, though a court will make its own objective judgment as to whether the use of ADR is reasonable in a particular case. It is important to distinguish the provision of information and support from compulsion to reach a settlement. It is not possible to compel a party to agree to a settlement in a non-adjudicative ADR process, though a party will normally be bound by the decision in a valid adjudicative ADR process that the party has agreed to. The Court of Appeal has commented on whether there should be some compulsion to use ADR where litigants in person proceed with litigation where this is not an objectively sensible option.[52]

I Regulation of ADR

1.21 There is no single statutory or regulatory framework for the use of ADR in England and Wales. The statutory framework for arbitration is provided by the Arbitration Act 1996, which provides for applications to be made to court in particular circumstances, see Chapter 25. While there is no single formal statutory or regulatory framework for mediation, there are statutory and regulatory frameworks for some kinds of complaints and conciliation processes, see Chapter 23.

---

[50] *Twisting Arms: Court Referred and Court Linked Mediation under Judicial Pressure. A Review of the Central London County Court Scheme* by Professor Hazel Genn and Professor Paul Fenn (Ministry of Justice Research Series, 2007); *Court-Based ADR Initiatives for Non-family Civil Disputes: The Commercial Court and the Court of Appeal* by Professor Hazel Genn (2002).

[51] See <http://www.cedr.com/docslib/TheMediatorAudit2014.pdf>.

[52] *Wright v Michael Wright Supplies Ltd* [2013] EWCA Civ 234.

There is no formal requirement that a person who performs an ADR service be **1.22** qualified in a particular way, though parties may be slow to use someone who does not have recognized training and experience. There are separate training and accreditation systems for arbitrators and for mediators. While the majority of arbitrators and mediators have a legal background many have other professional backgrounds. Training and accreditation for arbitrators is provided by the Chartered Institute of Arbitrators.[53] Arbitration service providers should be able to provide information about the training and experience of arbitrators, and may assist in finding an appropriate individual.

While there are no formal requirements for the training of mediators, the Civil **1.23** Mediation Council sets detailed standards for the training of mediators in line with European Union standards, and all organizations registered on the CMC website meet these. Many ADR organizations see standards as important and some of the larger providers set their own. Mediation services may be provided by courts, commercial providers, not-for-profit providers, solicitors' firms, or barristers' chambers. If the level of training and experience offered by an organization or individual is not sufficiently clear, details should be requested before a mediation agreement is entered into.

No single framework or body provides oversight of individuals offering services in **1.24** adjudication, expert determination, early neutral evaluation etc, though the larger ADR providers or a relevant professional organization may assist in finding a suitable individual. The training and experience of the individual should be sufficiently clear and appropriate before an ADR agreement is entered into. Experts in different fields may be subject to relevant professional codes of conduct.

As the use of ADR is by contractual agreement between the parties, ultimate over- **1.25** sight of agreements to use ADR, and settlements or awards resulting from an ADR process, lies with the courts. A claim relating to ADR might come to court for the purpose of enforcing a term requiring the use of ADR, an agreement to use ADR, a settlement resulting from an ADR process, or for dealing with a breach of a settlement reached through ADR, or in relation to a vitiating factor such as misrepresentation or fraud. It is important to note that the principles of without prejudice and confidentiality mean that a court will only look at a communication that is part of an ADR process in very limited circumstances, see Chapter 5. While a court will look at the original agreement to conduct ADR and any resulting settlement, it will not normally consider communications made during an ADR process.

---

[53] See <http://www.ciarb.org>.

J The International Context

1.26 As an ADR process takes place by agreement between the parties, there is no requirement for ADR to take place within a specific legal jurisdiction. If there are elements relating to more than one jurisdiction, the normal principles of conflict of laws in relation to contracts may apply. To provide a more certain structure, and to assist with enforcement, a number of international organizations provide for international ADR, but if one of these is not used some thought may need to be given to what law covers the ADR agreement and any ADR settlement. The regulatory framework for international arbitration is provided by international treaties, principally the New York Convention 1958, see 25.25.

1.27 Some regulatory oversight of mediation is provided within the European Union by the EU Directive on Mediation in Civil and Commercial Matters.[54] This encourages the use of mediation in cross-border disputes within the EU. The EU Code of Conduct for Mediators has been adopted by the CMC, see Chapter 17. Some harmonization of international standards in mediation is provided by the UNCITRAL Model Law on International Commercial Conciliation,[55] and through organizations such as the International Mediation Institute which sets international standards.[56]

---

[54] Directive 2008/52/EC.
[55] <http://www.uncitral.org/uncitral/en/uncitral_texts/arbitration/2002Model_conciliation. html>
[56] <http://www.imimediation.org/>

2

THE RANGE OF ADR OPTIONS

This chapter provides an overview of alternative dispute resolution options, outlin- **2.01** ing the key characteristics of each, and providing guidance on criteria for selection of an option. Further detail on most options can be found in later chapters of this book, or in relevant specialist works. Each option can only be used with the agreement of the parties, and the details of that agreement are often adaptable to meet the needs of an individual case. The role of a lawyer in advising on ADR options and criteria is developed in Chapter 4.

A Adjudicative Options

In adjudicative ADR an independent third party reaches an impartial deci- **2.02** sion on a dispute, but the process provides more flexibility and more privacy than litigation. The parties control the choice of process as it will be set up by a contractual agreement between them. This agreement will cover the form of the adjudicative process to be used, the person or body to carry out that process (or how that person is to be selected), and such other details as the parties choose to include. The parties can for example agree what material should be available to the third party, and what access to the decision maker each party should have. An adjudicative process may be subject to court oversight if the agreed process is not followed, or where the decision reached by the third party is tainted. Adjudicative ADR is most appropriate where the taking of an independent decision is important, but is not necessarily quick or inexpensive if the process selected is similar to a trial.

The key characteristics of the most common forms of adjudicative ADR are as fol- **2.03** lows. All these processes will be conducted in private and on a confidential basis.

Arbitration

An arbitration may be conducted by one or more arbitrators who will make a deci- **2.04** sion on the basis of what is submitted by the parties. The process to be followed will be agreed in advance by the parties, or can be delegated to the arbitrator, and many arbitration providers offer sample arbitration agreements and process rules. While arbitration may involve a hearing broadly similar to a trial, it may alternatively be conducted on the basis of written submissions. The use of arbitration is formally regulated in many jurisdictions, in England and Wales by the Arbitration Act 1996.

2.05 While arbitration is commonly used for commercial cases, it can also be appropriate in other areas where a decision by an independent third party without the full formality of litigation may be useful, and is for example increasingly used in family cases. Arbitration may also be used where the parties want a binding decision to be reached using a particular approach, for example applying sharia law.

2.06 The main attractions of arbitration are that:

- the parties can select an arbitrator with appropriate expertise and experience;
- the process is private, unlike a trial in open court;
- many aspects of the process can be tailored to the needs of a specific dispute;
- each party selects what material is submitted;
- the process can be relatively structured, if that is attractive to the parties;
- the process can be relatively simple and cost effective if the dispute is decided on the basis of written submissions rather than a hearing.

2.07 The potential drawbacks of arbitration are that:

- arbitration is not necessarily a cost-saving option if a process similar to trial is used;
- the parties will be bound by a third party decision, so control over the final decision is surrendered;
- an arbitration process cannot deal easily with a party who fails to cooperate, as an arbitrator will not have the wide powers of a judge as regards matters such as disclosure;
- the arbitrator needs to be selected with care as regards expertise, experience etc, to ensure the parties will have confidence in the award made.

Adjudication

2.08 Adjudication involves a neutral third party acting under an agreed process and reaching a decision on a dispute, or on specified issues. Adjudication is most likely to be appropriate in a specialist commercial field where the parties prefer a system adapted to the needs of their industry or business, see for example the process used for construction disputes in Chapter 26.

An adjudication process should be agreed between the parties in a binding form. **2.09**
Parties often agree in a commercial contract to be bound by a relevant adjudication process should there be a dispute. The process to be used may be laid down in advance in terms agreed by the industry, and/or by the body or person who provides the adjudication. The key elements of an adjudication process tend to be broadly similar to those for an arbitration, though they are often simpler. By agreement, the adjudication may lead to a binding decision, or to a decision that will only be binding if the parties agree to it, or if neither party appeals within a set period.

The potential benefits of adjudication are that the process can be carefully adjusted **2.10**
to meet specific commercial or other needs. The process tends to be more flexible and cost effective than arbitration, especially where the process is paper-based. The possible drawbacks are that adjudication is not necessarily low cost, and there may be difficulties if the adjudicator is not chosen with care. If the adjudication agreement does not provide that the adjudicator's decision will be final and binding on both parties, litigation or arbitration may still be necessary.

Expert determination

Many cases turn wholly or largely on issues requiring expert knowledge. Reliance **2.11**
on expert witnesses in litigation can be expensive and time consuming, and is controlled by the court, so there can be significant advantages in time and cost in agreeing to use an appropriate expert to make a binding decision on some or all issues in dispute. There are also advantages in terms of flexibility, though it is important that process and matters to be considered are clearly agreed in writing at the start of the process to avoid possible difficulties in relation to the outcome.[1]
One option is to appoint an expert to decide the outcome, if the only or main issues in the case require expert knowledge and a full adjudication procedure is not needed. An alternative is that an adjudication takes place, but with an expert assisting the adjudicator. A further option is that the parties each get a separate expert report and present them to an arbitrator or adjudicator for a decision. The main potential drawbacks are the possible cost of the process (although this should be less than litigation), and that the determination is normally binding even if it is flawed, eg by a mistake of fact. Even if a court encourages the use of an expert in ADR, the expert acts for the parties.[2] The process is considered in more detail in Chapter 24.

---

[1] *Shafi v Rutherford* [2014] EWCA Civ 1186; *Begum v Hossain* [2015] EWCA Civ 717; *Bruce v TTA Management Ltd* [2015] EWHC 936 (Ch).
[2] *Beauty Star Ltd v Janmohamed* [2014] EWCA Civ 451.

Other adjudicative options

2.12   Each of the above process options can be adapted to meet the needs of a case and of clients. For example, if a full arbitration may not be cost effective a paper-based option can be chosen. Alternatively, in 'baseball arbitration' an independent decision-maker is chosen and provided with an agreed summary of the case and a proposal for settlement from each party. The only power given to the third party is to decide which proposal is most reasonable, and should therefore provide the resolution to the dispute. Parties of necessity make realistic offers in an effort to be selected, and the decision is quick. This is not suitable for a dispute of any complexity, but can work if there are limited issues.

B Non-Adjudicative Options

2.13   In a non-adjudicative ADR process, the parties to a dispute retain control of both process and outcome. The process may be fairly fluid and involve only the parties/lawyers, as in a negotiation, or the process may be facilitated by a third party, as in mediation. The basis upon which any third party is involved is a matter of contract between the parties and the third party. Any settlement is a matter of a separate contractual agreement between the parties. The process is normally confidential, save for any need to enforce an agreed outcome. Non-adjudicative ADR is most appropriate where the parties wish to retain control over outcome as well as process.

Offer and acceptance

2.14   Offer and acceptance is the simplest form of non-adjudicative ADR. If an offer is accepted then an agreement is reached with the greatest possible saving of time and money. An offer can be made and accepted orally, but it is normally done in writing to ensure certainty as to the terms agreed. Normal contractual principles apply as regards whether an agreement is reached, and if so on what terms. It is vital to ensure that all terms are covered in the offer as it will form a binding resolution of the case if it is accepted. This approach is probably best suited to a case with a relatively limited number of issues to avoid any misunderstanding about the agreed terms. In a more complex case, exploration of an offer may lead to a further exchange of letters, and confusion as to terms may arise if this is not carefully controlled.

2.15   An offer made in an attempt to settle a dispute will be protected by without prejudice privilege, and therefore must be kept confidential and cannot be referred to in court, see 5.17–5.26. If the party may wish to be able to refer to the offer in relation to the court's discretion as to costs, it must expressly be made as an open offer, or 'without prejudice save as to costs'. To obtain the best potential advantages as regards costs the offer should comply with the terms of CPR Part 36, see 10.25–10.31.

Negotiation

Negotiation remains the most common form of dispute resolution. There is no set procedure, and the process may involve a very simple exchange between parties and/ or lawyers, or a more complex structured settlement meeting including the parties, see 12.16–12.17. **2.16**

The main potential advantages of negotiation are that: **2.17**

- it is very flexible and can be conducted by parties and/or by lawyers;
- it is relatively cost effective, as only a limited amount of special preparation may be required;
- clients retain complete control of the outcome through giving instructions, and approval of any agreement reached.

The main potential drawbacks of negotiation are that: **2.18**

- success depends to a significant extent on how well the case has been researched and analysed;
- success can depend on the skill of the negotiator, and the strategy and tactics employed;
- negotiation can lead to a relatively weak outcome for a client if the strengths of a case are not properly exploited;
- the relative informality of negotiation can lead to confusion as to process;
- a negotiation may fail if party expectations are unrealistic, or the parties are too entrenched.

Mediation

Mediation involves the use of a neutral third party who seeks to facilitate what is essentially a negotiation process to resolve a dispute. Various types of mediation service are available, and may be provided by the courts, by a commercial or not-for-profit organization, or by an individual. Normally parties will want to select a mediator with appropriate training and experience. **2.19**

A mediation service provider may offer a standard form of agreement and a standard process, and details are usually set out in a written agreement to mediate. Many mediations take up to a day, though a complex commercial mediation may last longer. **2.20**

In contrast, a small claim mediation is normally conducted by telephone within one hour. A mediation will be attended by the parties, and may also be attended by lawyers. There is provision for a judge in the Technology and Construction Court to act as a mediator through a court settlement process, see 16.24 –16.25. The details of the mediation process are covered in Chapters 13 to 15.

2.21   There will often be some contact with the mediator before the mediation, and preparation is important, often including preparation of document bundles and a written position statement. A mediation is normally conducted face to face, with a mix of joint meetings and separate meetings between the mediator and the parties with their lawyers. Commonly the process will start with a joint meeting of parties and lawyers with the mediator, with each side making an opening statement. It is then normal for each party to occupy a separate room, with the mediator visiting one party then the other to discuss issues and potential offers. If a potential settlement is reached there will normally be a joint final meeting to agree and sign written terms.

2.22   The main potential benefits of mediation are:

- a neutral third party can help a party to see the strengths and weaknesses of a case more clearly;
- a mediator can help parties step outside an adversarial framework and entrenched positions, so mediation may work where negotiation has failed;
- a mediator can make possible offers and concessions look more acceptable;
- a robust and experienced mediator can help to find a way forward even in a relatively intractable dispute;
- the structure of a mediation allows a lawyer and client time to review offers and options in a way that may not be possible in a negotiation;
- the flexibility of mediation can be used to advantage, for example letting a party make a statement about something of particular personal importance;
- mediation generally achieves good success rates and party satisfaction.

2.23   The main potential drawbacks of mediation are:

- success depends partly on the abilities of the mediator;
- mediation can increase costs if a case might have been resolved by negotiation, or if the mediation fails;
- mediation may need to be approached with skill by a mediator and by lawyers if a party tries to misuse the process, eg to get an unjustified offer in a weak case;
- mediation may not work if the parties are deeply antagonistic, or if adversarial positions are maintained in the face of reasonable settlement options;
- mediation can be more difficult where one or both parties are not represented, and/or not fully advised in advance.

Early neutral/expert evaluation

An early evaluation is a written assessment of some or all of the issues in a dispute **2.24**
by an independent third party. This may be appropriate where the case wholly or
largely turns on limited issues, particularly if those issues require expertise, and
the parties will respect the views of an agreed appropriate individual. The evaluation may relate to the whole dispute, to a specific point like the construction of a
contractual term, or to conflicting expert evidence. The written evaluation should
help each party to evaluate their own case and reach a resolution. The third party
may be an expert or an independent person with legal knowledge. The parties will
agree which issues are to be evaluated. There may be a hearing or the evaluation
may be done on paper. The report can include findings or provisional recommendations as requested by the parties. The Commercial Court and the Technology
and Construction Court both provide forms of ENE by a senior judge or lawyer,[3]
and this type of approach is becoming more widespread. The basis upon which a
judge may provide an early neutral evaluation to assist in the resolution of a case
where the parties have differing views as to their prospects of success could comprise
non-binding recommendations rather than a provisional judgment, with directions
providing for a consent order if the parties reach agreement.[4] This process is more
fully examined in Chapter 22.

The potential advantages are that an independent report may facilitate the early and **2.25**
cost-effective settlement of a case, or at least some of the issues, especially where
the third party has the confidence of the parties. An agreed evaluation can be less
time-consuming and expensive than mediation. The costs of using contested expert
evidence at trial may be avoided. Greatest benefit will be achieved if the evaluation is carried out as early as is reasonably possible, once the parties have sufficient
information to identify the issues to be addressed, and to brief the evaluator. ENE
can be useful where the parties are quite far apart on a particular issue of law or fact
with views that may become entrenched. Possible drawbacks are that work will be
required to agree what materials and issues are put to the evaluator, and success may
depend on the quality of the report produced.

Mini trial

A mini trial may be arranged to determine specific issues. The format is a **2.26**
matter of agreement between the parties as best suits the needs of a case. It

---

[3] *Admiralty and Commercial Courts Guide* Section G2, and the *Technology and Construction Court
Guide* Section 7.
[4] *Seals v Williams* [2015] EWHC 1829 (Ch).

might for example involve senior officers from the parties meeting together with an independent adviser. An ADR service provider can assist in appointing an independent adviser. Each side makes summary submissions, and the senior officers seek to reach an agreement. If they fail to do so the independent adviser may issue an opinion, following which the parties will again try to reach agreement.

Conciliation

2.27 The term conciliation has no single agreed meaning, though it normally involves a neutral third party. The conciliator might facilitate a negotiation between parties. Alternatively a conciliator might propose a decision if the parties cannot reach one, though this may be non-binding. In some instances if conciliation does not produce a final result another process may follow. A number of bodies offer conciliation services, probably the best known being the Advisory, Conciliation and Arbitration Service (ACAS). This process is further explored in Chapter 23. It is important to be clear what form conciliation will take before agreeing to it to assess potential advantages and drawbacks.

Complaint or grievance procedures

2.28 There are numerous processes for dealing with complaints or grievances, with most large organizations having internal processes which often provide for a person or body to look at a dispute or concern. The process may provide for some form of investigation, facilitation or decision-making. One example is the use of an ombudsman-type process. Some industries have developed special procedures to meet specific needs. For more detail see Chapter 23. A court may expect such a process to be used if it is potentially more cost effective than litigation,[5] but otherwise potential benefits and drawbacks will depend on the detail of the process.

Other options

2.29 It is possible to choose an option that combines the advantages and disadvantages of different ADR options. For example a 'med-arb' will comprise an agreement to mediate, but allowing the mediator to impose an outcome if the parties fail to reach agreement,[6] or in 'arb-med', the parties set up an arbitration, but the arbitrator may try to mediate an outcome before giving a decision. See 15.39–15.47.

---

[5] *R v Hampshire County Council* [2009] EWHC 2537 (Admin).
[6] *IDA Ltd v Southampton University* [2006] EWCA Civ 145.

C Motivations for the Use of ADR

The potential benefits of ADR are important to a party, to a lawyer advising a cli- **2.30**
ent, and to a judge reviewing case and cost management options. They may also be
relevant in persuading another party to agree to use ADR. The key potential benefits
will apply differently to each case, and each stage in a case.

Lower costs

The use of ADR will usually keep down the costs of resolving a dispute, particularly **2.31**
if the case is settled at a relatively early stage and if non-adjudicative ADR is used.
The potential advantage will decrease if ADR is not attempted until significant costs
have accumulated, if the ADR process fails, and/or if a potentially expensive form
of ADR is selected. A cost-benefit analysis might cover what key steps are needed
for an adequate and proportionate investigation of the case, and what form of ADR
with adequate prospects of success might be most cost effective.

Speed of settlement

Non-adjudicative ADR or expert determination can potentially take place very **2.32**
quickly, and soon after a dispute arises. There is less potential time advantage in
using arbitration, depending on the process agreed. Quick settlement can of itself
limit the indirect costs of dealing with a dispute, and the distraction and stress of
dealing with a dispute.

Choice of forum

In most forms of ADR the parties have a wide choice in selecting an arbitrator, **2.33**
mediator, or independent evaluator. This may be of particular value where the parties feel that the dispute calls for a particular type of expertise.

Control of process

An ADR process is subject to contractual agreement between the parties, and while **2.34**
many ADR providers use standard processes, the parties can agree options to suit
their needs. If an adjudicative ADR process is used, control of process will often pass
to the individual reaching a decision once the parties have agreed process.

Flexibility of process

Litigation involves standard stages, which may be an advantage, especially if secur- **2.35**
ing necessary evidence from another party is proving difficult. However set stages

can increase expense. In adjudicative ADR a more flexible process can be agreed, and in non-adjudicative ADR the process is normally very flexible.

Confidentiality

2.36   Court hearings are usually in public, so justice can be seen to be done. A party may prefer a more private process. Confidentiality can to some extent be protected in litigation, for example through a Tomlin order, but is more fully protected through ADR, which is a private process, protected by the 'without prejudice' principle, and confidentiality clauses in ADR agreements.

A wider range of issues/outcomes may be considered

2.37   The litigation process focuses on issues as defined by statements of case. A judge can only order a remedy that is within the powers of the court in relation to those issues. In an ADR process the parties can deal with any issues between them, and especially in a non-adjudicative process they can agree any terms they wish, even terms going outside the areas in dispute. ADR can provide a way of handling complex issues that cannot easily be reduced to statements of case.

Shared future interests may be protected

2.38   Litigation is often focused on taking decisions about past events, such as who was responsible for an accident. In some cases a future relationship may be just as important as the past. An ADR process may be more effective in preserving a relationship, and reaching a settlement that best reflects future interests.

Use of a problem-solving approach

2.39   Litigation is an adversarial process. This can have great strengths, but it can have drawbacks in deepening a rift between the parties and causing them to reach entrenched positions. An ADR process can be more constructive, and an experienced mediator will be able to use a range of techniques to help to move parties away from intransigence.

Risk management

2.40   In principle, a case with a chance of success of 51 per cent might proceed to litigation on the basis that it could be won, and if it were won reasonable and proportionate costs would be reimbursed. In litigation, risk may be managed by incurring additional expense in the hope of strengthening the case, but risk may be more directly and cost effectively controlled through constructive and proactive use of ADR.

D Criteria for the Selection of an ADR Option

If there is a good reason for using ADR, the following criteria may be relevant to selecting   **2.41**
the most appropriate form of ADR. Timing should also be considered, see Chapter 3.

How important is it to minimize costs?

In a relatively low value case, the need to keep costs proportionate may be key.   **2.42**
Court-based mediation may be free. If not a written offer may be cost effective.
Negotiation will often be cheaper than mediation. In a higher value case, negotiation, mediation, early neutral evaluation, or expert determination can be very cost
effective, if best adapted to the needs of the individual dispute.

How important is fast resolution?

If quick resolution is important, a non-adjudicative option such as negotiation or   **2.43**
mediation may be most effective. In an appropriate case, adjudication or expert
determination can also be completed relatively quickly. Early neutral evaluation
may at least help to narrow issues.

How much control does the party want?

A party can potentially have substantial control over any ADR process because ADR   **2.44**
is based on agreement. This is particularly the case in non-adjudicative ADR as settlement can only be reached by agreement. In an adjudicative option such as arbitration the party will not have control over the outcome, but will have some control
over forum and process.

What are the main objectives of the party?

Different objectives may be best achieved in different ways. If the main objec-   **2.45**
tive is to decide on an appropriate sum of compensation, any ADR process may
be appropriate. However non-pecuniary objectives may be best achieved in non-
adjudicative ADR such as mediation because of the degree of discussion between
the parties.

Is a future relationship important?

Where there is likely to be an ongoing relationship between the parties, for example   **2.46**
in a commercial or family dispute relationship, a non-adjudicative option is most
likely to produce a successful outcome, as terms can be fully discussed and any terms
thought desirable agreed.

Is the view of an expert important to key issues?

2.47 Where expert opinion is important to one or more of the main issues, early neutral evaluation or expert determination should be considered. If appropriate, the early neutral evaluation could be followed by negotiation or mediation. Using expert evidence in litigation is almost inevitably more expensive and time consuming.

Would neutral assistance be valuable?

2.48 Parties in an adversarial process may become entrenched or focused on 'winning' in ways that, objectively, do not suit their best interests. The parties may find it difficult to compromise. In such a case an adjudicative process may be the only option, but mediation with an effective mediator may also prove effective in helping a party to see the strengths and weaknesses of a case more objectively. The courts have stressed in several cases the value that a skilled mediator can bring, with an independent perspective that can cut through the positions taken by parties, identify middle ground, or propose new solutions.[7]

E When ADR may not be Appropriate

2.49 Almost any dispute can potentially be resolved through the use of ADR, save for cases involving public law rights. There are no categories of case in which ADR is always inappropriate, though there are circumstances in which it may not be suitable. A party may be able to show it was not unreasonable to refuse mediation if it would have wasted time and money and was unlikely to succeed,[8] but in many cases the court is more likely to see ADR as potentially useful and cost effective.[9] Possible problems may be addressed by careful selection of a type of ADR, and control of that process. The following factors may mean that ADR is not appropriate for a specific dispute.

The need for a precedent

2.50 Only a court judgment can provide a legal precedent, which may be an important concern if for example the case relates to the interpretation of a clause in a standard

---

[7] *Northrop Grumman Mission Systems Europe Ltd v BAE Systems (Al Diriyah C4I) Ltd* [2014] EWHC 3148 (TCC); *Garritt-Critchley v Ronnan* [2014] EWHC 1774 (Ch).

[8] *Uwug Ltd (in liquidation) v Ball* [2015] EWHC 74 (IPEC).

[9] *Northrop Grumman Mission Systems Europe Ltd v BAE Systems (Al Diriyah C4I) Ltd* [2014] EWHC 3148 (TCC).

form contract.[10] Concern has been expressed as to whether the growth of private ADR processes might undermine the development of legal precedent, and that the development of the common law depends on courts taking decisions which are reported. Unreported and confidential dispute resolution could cause the law to ossify, or develop in a way that lawyers could not easily track. Such concerns must be balanced against whether it is in the interests of a particular client to litigate rather than reach a settlement. There is a strong debate amongst practitioners and academics concerning the public interest in ensuring sufficient cases proceed to trial to develop law through precedents.[11]

The importance of a court order

There are some circumstances in which an outcome can only be achieved through a **2.51** court order. For example, for a declaration of legal rights or a technical order such as an amendment of the register of members of a company, court proceedings will be required. ADR may still assist in agreeing the terms of the order to be made.

The relevance of interim orders

The powers of a court to make interim orders, such as an interim injunction, may be **2.52** important in a particular case, and proceedings may need to be issued to secure a relevant order. However ADR may be used once appropriate interim orders have been made, or a court may in limited circumstances be able to make a relevant order prior to the issue of proceedings, or very soon after proceedings have been issued, to support ADR. An arbitrator may have some power to make relevant orders, or the parties may agree to something as a condition precedent for agreeing to the use of ADR.

Evidential rules are important

Rules providing for disclosure and the exchange of witness statements will be of **2.53** particular importance in some cases, especially where one party is not forthcoming in producing relevant information. However the level of pre-action disclosure should provide sufficient information for parties to evaluate a case. A judge may be prepared to order specific disclosure to support the use of ADR. Specific disclosure may take place voluntarily as a basis for agreeing to the use of an ADR process. The need for evidence may be more relevant to the timing of ADR rather than to whether it is appropriate at all.

---

[10] *McCook v Lobo* [2002] EWCA Civ 1760.
[11] Genn, H and Mulcahy, L 'The collective interest in private dispute resolution', Oxford Journal of Legal Studies Vol 33 No 1 (2013) pages 59–80.

The strength of a case

2.54 A client with a strong case may fear that agreeing to an ADR process may show weakness or necessitate the making of some concessions. There is authority that a party with a strong case may not act unreasonably in refusing ADR,[12] though in that case the effect of costs on the claimants was described as disastrous. A belief by a party that a case is strong must be objectively justifiable.[13] A belief by a party that his case is strong is only one factor and will not necessarily of itself justify a refusal to use ADR,[14] as the strength of a case can be put forcefully in an ADR process. If a party feels a case is strong then the most appropriate course may be to apply for summary judgment.

The complexity of the case

2.55 It might be thought that a case involving complex law needs a judge's decision, but complexity can lead to disproportionate costs, and the interests of a client may be better served in reaching a practical outcome through ADR. Complex facts may be appropriately considered in court, especially if cross-examination may be important. However there can be significant risks in taking a complex factual dispute to court, which may be controlled through ADR. The courts have stressed that it is not necessary to litigate simply because the law in an area is complex if this may lead to disproportionate costs.[15]

2.56 Complexity may arise from the number of parties in a case. The civil litigation rules provide structured ways for a number of parties to be engaged in a dispute, but litigation is not inevitable. An ADR process can be structured to involve a number of parties, with, for example, a mediation being structured to deal with a claim in stages, and/or to deal with potential parties in groups, see 16.30–16.47. The flexibility of ADR methods can be used imaginatively to address needs in a multiparty commercial or negligence case.[16]

High levels of animosity

2.57 High levels of animosity might suggest that a process based on agreement could not work, but animosity will not necessarily mean that litigation is an inevitable or best

---

[12] *Swain Mason v Mills & Reeve* [2012] EWCA Civ 498 (per Davis LJ).

[13] *ADS Aerospace Ltd v EMS Global Tracking Ltd* [2012] EWHC 2904 (TCC).

[14] *Burchell v Bollard* [2005] BLR 330; *Northrop Grumman Mission Systems Europe Ltd v BAE Systems (Al Diriyah C41) Ltd* [2014] EWHC 3148 (TCC).

[15] *Faidi v Elliot Corporation* [2012] EWCA Civ 287; *Oliver v Symons* [2012] EWCA Civ 267.

[16] *Channel Tunnel Group Ltd v Balfour Beatty Ltd* [1993] AC 334.

option. The introduction of robust impartiality in the form of a skilled mediator or a robust neutral evaluation by an expert may assist in reaching resolution.[17] ADR may be appropriate even if trust has broken down.[18]

Power imbalance

A non-adjudicative ADR process may not be appropriate where one party has sub-   **2.58**
stantially more resources than the other, or where one party may have improper control over the other, for example through domestic violence. This does not necessarily mean that litigation is the only option if a sufficiently strong third party can be involved in an ADR process to manage the imbalance.

Quasi-criminal allegations

Cases involving allegations such as fraud or libel may not be suitable for non-   **2.59**
adjudicative ADR. If cross-examination is key to the case, and/or judicial determination of a serious allegation is required then litigation may be necessary.

Having a day in court

The concept of having 'a day in court' can seem important to a party seeking vindi-   **2.60**
cation, but this may need to be placed clearly within the context of potential cost and the chances of success. An ADR process can be tailored to include the making of statements by the parties and independent decision-making.

Enforcement may be an issue

Non-adjudicative ADR processes often result in a settlement in contractual form,   **2.61**
and enforcement will rarely be an issue where the terms are clear and agreed. An adjudicative process might lead to enforcement difficulties if a party is not content with the decision given, though there is provision for the enforcement of arbitral awards. If enforcement might be an issue, ADR may be best used after issue of proceedings so the outcome can be recorded in a consent order that may be enforced more easily.

---

[17] *Garritt-Critchley v Ronnan* [2014] EWHC 1774 (Ch).
[18] *Wright v Michael Wright (Supplies) Ltd* [2013] EWCA Civ 234.

3

TIMING THE USE OF ADR IN RELATION TO THE PROGRESS OF A CASE

A The Importance of Timing

3.01 ADR can be used at any stage from the time a cause of action arises to appeal or the assessment of costs. To ensure the most strategic and cost effective use of ADR, timing may be a key issue. In addition to advising a client on timing, a lawyer may need to address a judge on timing in relation to an application for a stay, or in relation to case or costs management decisions. A judge considering an application may need to take a view not only on whether ADR should be attempted, but also at what stage it should be attempted. The overriding objective includes factors relevant to the timing of the use of ADR. Dealing with a case justly includes, so far as is practicable, ensuring that it is dealt with expeditiously, and dealing summarily with issues that do not need to be fully investigated and to go to trial.[1]

3.02 There have been various judicial comments on the importance of timing. Premature use of ADR can waste time and money if issues are not sufficiently clear. However, waiting until after the exchange of statements of case or disclosure before attempting ADR can mean that the attitudes of the parties have hardened and costs have grown to a level that threatens successful ADR.

- 'The trick in many cases was to identify the happy medium: the point when the detail of the claim and the response were known to both sides, but before the costs that had been incurred in reaching that stage were so great that a settlement was no longer possible.'[2]
- 'Experience suggests that many disputes ... are resolved before all material necessary for a trial is available ... the saving of costs ... is achieved ... by the parties

---

[1] CPR r 1.1(2), CPR r 1.4(2).
[2] *Nigel Witham Ltd v Smith* [2008] EWHC 12 (TCC) (Judge Peter Coulson QC).

being prepared to compromise without necessarily having as complete a picture of the other parties' case as would be available at trial.'[3]

- 'Identifying the best stage at which to mediate is a matter upon which experienced practitioners should advise by reference to the circumstances of the individual case.'[4]
- In several cases judges have commented strongly that settlement should have been attempted before embarking on litigation that led to disproportionate costs.[5]

There is not a single appropriate time to attempt ADR. A decision on timing may **3.03** be complex, with some factors favouring the use of ADR immediately, and others suggesting possible benefits in delay. It is quite possible that at any given time, ADR may be more attractive to one party than the other. A decision on the suitability and timing of ADR will rarely be taken once in a case, but the position should be kept under review as relevant factors change. In a case of any size there should be an ADR strategy alongside the litigation strategy. With the increased use of case and costs management it is becoming more common for ADR proposals to be used tactically, for example asking the court to require the other side to file a witness statement indicating why ADR is thought to be inappropriate.[6] A case may move between litigation and ADR options more than once. This fluidity is generally positive, but it is important to ensure that processes do not become confused.

- Records should be kept of what attempts have been made to use ADR, as such records may be relevant to an application for a sanction or for costs.
- A confusion of cross offers in relation to ADR without responses should be avoided as it can lead to difficulties in relation to a decision on costs.
- Communications made with a view to settlement are privileged,[7] but a statement made in an ambiguous context might be seen as an admission.

B Procedural Factors Relevant to Timing

Pre-selection of ADR

An advance commitment in a contract may provide for the timing of ADR. A clause **3.04** may set out a particular ADR method to be used, a body or person to be approached

---

[3] *PGF II SA v OMFS Company* [2012] EWHC 83 (TCC) (per Mr Recorder Furst QC).

[4] Eleventh Implementation Lecture 'The Role of Alternative Dispute Resolution in Furthering the Aims of the Civil Litigation Costs Review' (per Lord Justice Jackson), <http://www.judiciary.gov. uk/publications-and-reports/review-of-civil-litigation-costs/lectures>.

[5] *Faidi v Elliot Corporation* [2012] EWCA Civ 287 (per Jackson LJ); *Brewer v Mann* [2012] EWCA Civ 246 (per Rix LJ).

[6] *Wilson v Haden (t/a Clyne Farm Centre)* [2013] EWHC 1211 (QB).

[7] *The Dorchester Group Ltd v Kier Construction Ltd* [2015] EWHC 3051 (TCC).

to resolve any dispute, and/or it may specify steps aimed at resolution to be taken before litigation can be commenced. Provided the clause is sufficiently clear and is contractually binding, a court is likely to enforce the clause,[8] see 9.27–9.35. As an alternative to the wording of individual agreements, an organization may make a general commitment to use ADR where appropriate, as the government has done.[9]

3.05   Clauses providing for pre-selection of ADR have proved effective in relation to adjudicative processes,[10] steps prior to an adjudicative process,[11] expert determination,[12] and mediation,[13] but not where there was only a general expression of intention to use ADR,[14] or the issue related to taking an effective part in a non-adjudicative ADR process.[15] If there is a disagreement as to the effect of a clause the parties should try to agree the best way forward.[16] The potential advantages of pre-selecting ADR timing and steps are:

- it is easier to make an agreement to deal with a dispute constructively when a contract is made, rather than when a dispute has already arisen;
- it can provide more control as regards appropriate, cost-effective, and timely dispute resolution. Timescale and how costs will be met can be prescribed;
- pre-selection provides more certainty as to how any dispute can be settled, making litigation less likely;
- a specific body or person can be identified in advance to conduct ADR;
- it can make it easier to ensure confidentiality should any dispute arise;
- it can be easier to maintain a constructive approach to a dispute rather than risk dispute escalation.

The use of ADR at the pre-action stage

3.06   If there is no pre-agreement, the advantages of actively considering ADR at an early stage are:

- this will provide the best opportunity to save time and costs;

---

[8] *Cott UK Ltd v FE Barber Ltd* [1997] 3 All ER 540; *Holloway v Chancery Mead* [2007] EWHC 2495 (TCC); *Wah v Grant Thornton International Ltd* [2013] 1 All ER (Comm) 1226.

[9] See <http://www.justice.gov.uk/guidance/mediation/dispute-resolution-commitment.htm>.

[10] *Cape Durasteel Ltd v Rosser & Russell Building Services Ltd* [1995] 46 Con LR 75; *Herschel Engineering Ltd v Breen Property Ltd* [2000] 70 Con LR 1; *DGT Steel & Cladding Ltd v Cubitt Building & Interiors Ltd* [2007] BLR 371.

[11] *Emirates Trading Agency LLC v Prime Mineral Exports Private Ltd* [2015] 1 WLR 1145.

[12] *Channel Tunnel Group Ltd v Balfour Beatty Construction Ltd* [1993] AC 334.

[13] *Cable & Wireless v IBM* [2002] EWHC 2059 (Comm) (per Colman J).

[14] *Sulamerica CIA Nacional de Seguros SA v Enesa Engenharia SA* [2012] EWHC 42 (Comm).

[15] *Pitt v PHH Asset Management* [1993] 4 All ER 961; *Balfour Beatty Construction Northern Ltd v Modus Corovest (Blackpool) Ltd* [2008] EWHC 3029 (TCC); *Walford v Miles* [1992] 1 All ER 453.

[16] *Gotch v Enelco* [2015] EWHC 1802 (TCC).

- adjudicative ADR, such as arbitration, is effectively a direct alternative to litigation and should therefore normally be selected before steps are taken with regard to litigation;
- some non-adjudicative ADR, such as early neutral evaluation, is by its nature most effective if it is incorporated into a case reasonably quickly;
- ADR may assist in clarifying issues even if it does not lead to a final settlement;
- a constructive approach may help to ensure that the views of parties do not become entrenched.

The potential drawbacks of using ADR at too early a stage are: 3.07

- time and money may be wasted if the ADR process is not successful;
- an unsuccessful ADR process may exacerbate the dispute between the parties;
- it may be difficult to evaluate the case properly;
- the ADR process may be used tactically rather than as a genuine attempt to settle.

There are obligations to consider the use of ADR at the pre-action stage, which need   3.08
to be taken seriously as a failure to do so may be met with an adverse costs order.[17]
Essentially each party should consider and make or respond to a proposal for the
use of appropriate ADR at the pre-issue stage, or record reasons why ADR was not
appropriate, see 8.14–8.23.

On issue of proceedings

Pre-action requirements include a general need to review the position on ADR   3.09
before issuing proceedings, see 8.14–8.18. In any event the position in relation
to ADR will need to be reflected soon after issue in completing the Directions
Questionnaires.

Case and costs management and directions

Case management powers are directed to support the use of ADR in vari-   3.10
ous ways, see 9.20–9.24. The Directions Questionnaire (Small Claims Track)
includes guidance on trying to settle a case, with specific information about the
Small Claims Mediation Service. The Directions Questionnaire (Fast Track and
Multi-track) makes it clear that the court will want to know what steps have been
taken in relation to settling the case, with a legal representative asked to confirm
that ADR options and the possibility of costs sanctions have been explained to
the client.[18]

---

[17] *P4 Ltd v Unite Solutions plc* [2007] BLR 1; *Jarrom v Sellers* [2007] EWHC 1366 (Ch).
[18] CPR r 26.3.

3.11 On the basis of the statements of case, and the answers to any questionnaires, a judge can assess the appropriateness of the use of ADR at this stage, and the possibility that the case could be settled before further costs accrue. The judge may ask for further information. On allocation to the multi-track, the court will give case management directions, based on relevant model and standard directions[19] which include directions relating to the use of ADR.[20] Wherever appropriate it is desirable that proposed directions submitted in advance by the parties should include directions to enable mediation, for example requiring the disclosure of key documents (but probably not formal witness statements at an early stage as these may hinder rather than facilitate mediation). The judge can then give such directions and allow time for mediation, with further directions to come into force should mediation not result in a settlement.

3.12 The importance of case management in supporting the use of ADR is clear,[21] with robustness enhanced with the implementation of recommendations in Lord Justice Jackson's Review of Costs. Modern case management[22] includes an emphasis on parties agreeing directions if possible,[23] so the parties and the judge can seek to ensure that ADR as well as litigation are supported by directions. More coherent oversight of the use of ADR should be assisted by the use of docketing, making settlement more likely.[24]

3.13 Overall, case management directions, obligations, powers, and orders can be used by lawyers and judges to provide strategic support for the use of ADR options alongside preparation for litigation, managing each in a coherent way. A case management timetable should include appropriate provision for ADR.[25]

The use of ADR at an interim stage

3.14 The majority of cases in which proceedings are issued settle before trial. In addition to overall case and costs management, processes such as disclosure and the use of expert evidence can take into account what might facilitate an ADR process, not least in compliance with ongoing obligations under the overriding objective in relation to matters such as narrowing issues.

---

[19] CPR r 29.2, and see <http://www.justice.gov.uk/courts/procedure-rules/civil>.

[20] CPR PD 29 r 4.10(9), and see <www.justice.gov.uk/courts/procedure-rules/civil/> standard directions, A03 and B05.

[21] *Swain-Mason v Mills & Reeve LLP* [2011] EWCA Civ 14.

[22] 'Review of Civil Litigation Costs: Final Report' Chapter 39 and Recommendations 81 and 88, and see also Fifth Implementation Lecture 'Achieving a Culture Change in Case Management'.

[23] CPR r 29.4.

[24] Ninth Implementation Lecture 'Docketing: Completing Case Management's Unfinished Revolution'.

[25] *CIP Properties (AIPT) Ltd v Galliford Try Infrastructure Ltd* [2014] EWHC 3546 (TCC).

There are various ways in which interim orders can be used to support the use of **3.15** ADR, on the application of a party or on the initiative of the judge. For full coverage of the approach of the courts see Chapter 9.

- The court may order that a party or a party's legal representative attend court, and this may be used to support the use of ADR.[26]
- On an application for an interim order the court may give directions to support the use of ADR.[27]
- The court can order trial of a preliminary issue if the rest of a case might then settle.
- A court can give specific guidance on the progress of a case, with specific warnings that costs penalties may follow if the guidance is not followed.[28]
- An order may support the use of ADR for some issues in a complex case.[29]
- Several models for interim orders to support the use of ADR have been developed, providing, for example, for a party to provide a witness statement saying why ADR is not considered to be appropriate, and these can be adapted for other courts and circumstances.[30]

It may be reasonable for a party to refuse to agree to use ADR until after a key court **3.16** decision, for example the consideration of an application to strike out the other side's case.[31] It may be reasonable for a party to refuse to use ADR before issues are clarified in the statements of case, or before witness statements are available.[32] However it is not inherently reasonable to refuse to use ADR until after all the stages of litigation up to and including the exchange of witness statements are completed if steps could have been taken to facilitate the earlier use of ADR.

In many cases there may be a question as to the potential cost benefit of full **3.17** disclosure. Since 1 April 2013 a menu of options has been available for disclosure, and the parties should agree disclosure if possible. If not appropriate orders will be made at the first case management conference, with the costs budget in

---

[26] CPR r 3.1(2).

[27] *Honda Giken Kogyo Kabushiki Kaisha (a firm) v Neesam* [2009] EWHC 1213.

[28] *Brookfield Construction (UK) Ltd v Mott MacDonald Ltd* [2010] EWHC 659 (TCC) (per Coulson J).

[29] *Mouchel Ltd v Van Oord (UK) Ltd* [2011] WL 579031; *Supershield Ltd v Siemens Building Technologies FE Ltd* [2010] EWCA Civ 7.

[30] Practice Direction (The Multi-Track) PD 29 r 4.10(9) (an Ungley order), the *Admiralty and Commercial Courts Guide* Appendix 7 and the *Technology and Construction Court Guide* Appendix E and Section 7.

[31] *S v Chapman* [2008] EWCA Civ 800; *Mobiqa Ltd v Trinity Mobile Ltd* [2010] EWHC 253 (Pat).

[32] *Wethered Estates Ltd v Davis* [2006] BLR 86.

mind.[33] A court may make an order providing for disclosure appropriate to support the use of ADR.[34]

3.18 Several cases have illustrated problems with a high cost for expert evidence.[35] One alternative is for the parties to appoint an appropriate expert to carry out an early neutral evaluation. Focused directions in relation to expert evidence may support the use of shorter reports and controlled costs,[36] with parties furnishing estimates of costs for proposed expert evidence, and the issues to be covered as a basis for getting permission to use it. There is also provision for experts to give evidence concurrently, with experts addressing issues on an agreed agenda.[37] In making decisions about the use of expert evidence the courts and the parties can consider facilitating ADR as well as litigation.

The use of ADR before and during trial

3.19 Many cases settle at the door of the court or during trial as some of the costs of trial may still be avoided, and it is the last stage at which the outcome of the case is within the control of the parties rather than the judge. However earlier settlement can achieve greater saving of time and costs. A costs sanction might be appropriate where one party has made reasonable attempts to settle earlier and the other party had frustrated settlement attempts until close to trial.

3.20 A court may consider ADR options when giving directions preparatory for trial, such as ordering a split trial.[38] Offers made shortly before trial are best made coherently to avoid a confused picture emerging when costs are later considered.[39] Although settlement at the door of the court is quite common, a court will be slow to adjourn a trial for the use of ADR.[40]

---

[33] CPR r 31.5, as amended by the Civil Procedure (Amendment) Rules 2013. 'Review of Civil Litigation Costs: Final Report' Chapter 37 and Recommendations 77 and 78, and the Seventh Implementation Lecture 'Controlling the Costs of Disclosure', <http://www.judiciary.gov.uk/publications-and-reports/review-of-civil-litigation-costs/lectures>.

[34] *Arrow Trading and Investments Est 1920 v Edwardian Group Ltd* [2004] EWHC 1319 (Ch).

[35] *Trebor Bassett Holdings Ltd v ADT Fire & Security plc* [2011] EWHC 1936 (TCC); *Dyson Ltd v Vax Ltd* [2011] EWCA Civ 1206.

[36] CPR r 35.4, as amended by the Civil Procedure (Amendment) Rules 2013.

[37] Practice Direction 35 11.1–11.4; 'Review of Civil Litigation Costs: Final Report' Chapter 38 and Recommendations 79 and 80 and the Fourth Implementation Lecture 'Focusing Expert Evidence and Controlling Costs', <http://www.judiciary.gov.uk/publications-and-reports/review-of-civil-litigation-costs/lectures>.

[38] *Electrical Waste Recycling Group Ltd v Philips Electronics UK Ltd* [2012] EWHC 38 (Ch).

[39] *ADS Aerospace Ltd v EMS Global Tracking Ltd* [2012] EWHC 2904 (TCC).

[40] *Elliott Group Limited, Algeco Sas, Algeco Sa Belgique, Algeco GmbH, Algeco Holdings BV v Gecc UK (formerly known as Ge Capital Corporation), Ge Equipment Services Holding BV, Euro-TREC (France) Sas, GE Rail Services GmbH (formerly known as Ge Modular Space GmbH)* [2010] EWHC 409 (TCC).

The use of ADR in relation to appeals

ADR may be used after a judgment, to avoid an appeal, following permission to **3.21** appeal, or to assist with enforcement of an order made. The importance of the use of ADR at or before appeal has been emphasized in recent cases.[41] The level of costs may well be a concern at this stage, but it is not reasonable to refuse to mediate simply because costs already exceed the amount in issue. If permission to appeal is given the judge(s) giving permission will consider whether the case is suitable for mediation. Permission to appeal implies that the appeal has a reasonable prospect of success, and about 40 per cent of those granted permission to appeal succeed, so both sides are likely to have something to gain from mediation.[42] The Court of Appeal ADR scheme is outlined at 16.11–16.13.

In several cases parties have been penalized in costs for rejecting the use of ADR **3.22** after judgment and prior to an appeal, especially where the court has recommended that mediation be attempted. A winning party may have the amount of recoverable costs reduced,[43] or costs may be awarded on an indemnity basis.[44] It makes no difference that a party is confident of success on appeal.[45] However a party will not necessarily be penalized for refusing a late offer to mediate in reasonable circumstances.[46] In a case where an appeal is allowed and remitted for rehearing the judge may direct that the parties attempt mediation before the rehearing.[47]

The use of ADR in relation to assessment of costs

The assessment of costs can be very expensive and time-consuming. It is possible to make **3.23** an offer in relation to costs, or to use a form of ADR including arbitration or early neutral evaluation. It can be unreasonable to refuse to use mediation in relation to costs.[48]

C Practical Factors Relevant to Timing

Several factors may need to be weighed up in taking a decision as to timing of the use **3.24** of ADR. Each factor may apply differently to each party. There is no presumption

---

[41] *Oliver v Symons* [2012] EWCA Civ 267 (per Elias LJ).

[42] *Ghaith v Indesit* [2012] EWCA Civ 642 (per LJ Ward); 'Review of Civil Litigation Costs: Final Report' Chapter 34.

[43] *Neal v Jones Motors* [2002] EWCA Civ 173.

[44] *Virani v Manual Revert Y CIA SA* [2004] 2 Lloyd's Rep 14.

[45] *Dunnett v Railtrack* [2002] 1 WLR 2434.

[46] *Reed Executive plc v Reed Business Information Ltd* [2004] 1 WLR 3026.

[47] *Uren Corporate Leisure (UK) Ltd* [2011] EWCA Civ 66.

[48] *Lakehouse Contracts Ltd v UPR Services Ltd* [2014] EWHC 1223 (Ch); *Reid v Buckinghamshire Healthcare NHS Trust* [2015] EWHC B21 (Costs).

that litigation should continue unless ADR is shown to be preferable. The decision whether ADR is appropriate at a particular time is an objective and strategic one as regards how the case should most appropriately be pursued.

The overriding objective

3.25 The overriding objective is relevant to any consideration of the timing of the use of ADR, see 9.17–9.19.[49] Deciding how a case can be dealt with justly and proportionately, how expense can be saved, and how the case can be dealt with expeditiously and fairly all relate to the potential use of ADR as well as to the progress of litigation. Allotting an appropriate share of the court's resources will often raise the consideration of ADR, as will encouraging the parties to cooperate. The overriding objective will often support the use of ADR as early as is reasonably possible in a case.

The position as regards costs

3.26 Concern about the potential escalation of costs in litigation is a major driver for the use of ADR. Costs budgets, estimates of costs to date, the likely costs of going to trial, and the potential cost of an appropriate ADR process with reasonable prospects of success are usefully compared at key points in resolving a dispute.

The timeframe for reaching resolution

3.27 Reasonably swift resolution is another major driver for the use of ADR. The judge, lawyers, and parties may usefully engage in a comparative study of the specific steps needed, and the likely timeframe, for reaching resolution through litigation, or through ADR. The implications of any significant delay in achieving resolution may also be considered.

The issues in the case

3.28 Issues need to be reasonably clear before a dispute can be properly resolved. Pre-action exchanges should normally be sufficient to define the issues, though there may be reasons for waiting for the precision of statements of case. Once statements of case are in place the issues should be sufficiently clear for ADR to be used, and if not steps can be taken to clarify the issues sufficiently for ADR, unless there is good reason why issues need to proceed to trial.

---

[49] CPR r 1.1.

The availability of information

Sufficient information will need to be available for a case to be sufficiently evalu-   **3.29**
ated before a dispute can be properly resolved. This includes information as to the
strength of the case, and as regards remedies. However as long as it is reasonably
reliable, such information does not need to be in the form of formal evidence for
the purposes of ADR.

The availability and importance of evidence

Reasonably reliable information should be distinguished from formal evidence. In   **3.30**
non-adjudicative ADR it is not essential to prove a case, and this is a way in which
expense can be saved. Where issues are strongly contested and/or there are low levels
of trust between the parties, it may be necessary to wait until exchange of evidence
is completed to attempt ADR, but disclosure may be tailored to meet the needs of
the case. It is not essential for a lawyer to wait until full disclosure is complete to
evaluate a case, so long as the client is properly advised about what information is
available, and on the relative merits of litigation and ADR, so that the client makes
an informed choice and gives informed instructions.

The position as regards evidence in an adjudicative ADR process will be different   **3.31**
in that appropriate evidence may need to be made available to the decision-taker.
However the evidence that is required and provided will be a matter for the process
chosen and agreed.

The importance of interim applications

Proceeding with litigation may be justified where applications for interim orders   **3.32**
may be of importance in the case, where for example an interim injunction might
best protect a party's position. ADR may be undertaken once an interim order has
been sought. In adjudicative ADR an arbitrator may have interim powers, but
interim orders could not be made by a mediator, though parties may make pre-
conditions to agreeing to mediate.

The strength of a case

A party may form the view that a case is strong, and perceive that it is best pursued   **3.33**
to trial through litigation. A court will take an independent view of whether a case
is objectively strong, and will not necessarily see the strength of a case as justifying
a refusal to use ADR, see 11.11–11.14. Judges are increasingly prepared to take a
robust view where for example parties become entrenched and costs disproportionate, and an effective mediator could have assisted in resolving matters.

Antagonism between the parties

3.34 A high level of antagonism between the parties might suggest a case needs to proceed to decision at trial. This may be so if the antagonism manifests itself in difficulties relating to evidence and interim applications so the case is difficult to assess. However antagonism does not necessarily rule out ADR if other factors indicate it might be appropriate. An experienced mediator may be able to take a robust approach that produces some progress on issues, and/or re-evaluation.

Specific types of case

3.35 Some types of case present specific issues in relation to the timing of ADR. Concern has been expressed about late settlement in clinical negligence cases, where there has been a tendency for meritorious claims not to be settled until after the issue of proceedings, with calls for increased use of mediation. While there are concerns about stopping false or weak claims, an appropriately rigorous mediation process may be used. There are special considerations as the cost of the expert reports needed to evaluate a claim can make pre-action costs high. The Pre-Action Protocol for the Resolution of Clinical Disputes has been revised to support earlier resolution of claims.[50]

3.36 The review carried out by Lord Justice Jackson found that ADR, and in particular mediation, is particularly valuable in relation to low value construction disputes, and small business disputes, recommending that a streamlined procedure should be introduced for this type of case.[51]

---

[50] 'Review of Civil Litigation Costs: Final Report' Chapter 23 and Recommendations 26 and 33, and the Twelfth Implementation Lecture 'The Reform of Clinical Negligence Litigation', see <http://www.judiciary.gov.uk/publications-and-reports/review-of-civil-litigation-costs/lectures>.

[51] 'Review of Civil Litigation Costs: Final Report' Recommendations 42 and 43.

4

ROLES AND RESPONSIBILITIES
OF LAWYERS AND PARTIES IN ADR

A Overview

It is no longer realistic to regard alternative dispute resolution processes as being **4.01** optional. The roles and responsibilities of lawyers and parties are increasingly defined, and have developed quite rapidly in recent years through rules and case law. It is now important for a lawyer to advise on and for a client to consider ADR alongside litigation before issue of proceedings, in relation to case management and costs budgeting, as part of ensuring costs are proportionate. Potential penalties for not doing this include negative case management orders, possible sanctions, and adverse costs orders. If ADR is not properly handled there is a risk of an action for professional negligence against a lawyer.[1] There are potential complications where a litigant in person is involved. The professional duties of lawyers are considered in Chapter 6. This chapter provides a more general overview.

B Duties Under the Civil Procedure Rules

Lawyers and parties are required to assist the court in furthering the overriding objec- **4.02** tive,[2] which includes several provisions relevant to the appropriate use of ADR. There is a positive duty to assist the court in saving expense, in ensuring that a case is dealt with expeditiously and fairly and in a way that is proportionate to the issues, the importance of the case, the amount of money involved and the financial position of each party.[3] This applies not only to interactions with the court, but between the lawyer and his or her own client, and between the parties and their lawyers.[4] Duties

---

[1] *Michael v Middleton* [2013] EWHC 2881 (Ch).
[2] CPR r 1.3.
[3] CPR r 1.1.
[4] CPR r 1.4.

with regard to ADR are reinforced by the key court guides.[5] The point is not only to comply with obligations, but also to take appropriate action if an opponent does not.

C The Role of a Lawyer in Advising on ADR

4.03 The main elements of the role of a lawyer are potentially:

- as part of giving advice at key stages as litigation progresses, ensuring that the client is sufficiently aware of ADR alternatives to litigation;
- providing objective information on relevant ADR options, including potential benefits and drawbacks, or giving a client sufficient guidance on where/how to get information;
- advising the client on pre-action obligations relating to consideration of ADR;
- advising the client on obligations under the overriding objective in relation to ADR;
- ensuring that the client is aware of penalties that may result from an unreasonable refusal to use ADR;
- giving appropriate advice on funding and costs in relation to ADR;
- if ADR is selected, getting clear instructions on the form of ADR to be used, objectives to be achieved etc;
- if ADR is not selected, ensuring that objective reasons are identified and sufficient evidence of those reasons retained;
- if appropriate, assisting in the selection of an independent third party to conduct an ADR process;
- advising on strengths and weaknesses of a case as part of assessing a case for the use of non-adjudicative ADR, if necessary giving robust advice;[6]
- considering and advising on offers in relation to non-adjudicative ADR;
- advising on and drafting terms of settlement.

4.04 There has been judicial comment on the role and responsibilities of lawyers in relation to the use of ADR, and sometimes expressed in quite strong terms where there is concern as to the way a case has progressed. For example: 'It depresses me that solicitors cannot at the very first interview persuade their clients to put their faith in the hands of an experienced mediator ... to guide them to a fair and sensible compromise of an unseemly battle which will otherwise blight their lives for months.'[7]

---

[5] The *Chancery Guide* 2016 Chapter 18; the *Admiralty and Commercial Court Guide* Part G; and the *Technology and Construction Court Guide* Section 7.

[6] *Chinnock v Veale Wasbrough* [2015] EWCA Civ 441.

[7] *Faidi v Elliot Corporation* [2012] EWCA Civ 287 (per Elias LJ).

There is not a positive duty on lawyers to persuade a client to use ADR, but a lawyer who does not advise on ADR obligations and options, and potential penalties in relation to ADR, may be at risk of a professional negligence claim.

The role of a lawyer in an adjudicative process like arbitration will be in some ways **4.05** similar to the role in litigation, but particular attention may need to be paid to agreeing procedural detail. In a process like expert determination it will involve matters such as advising on the terms on which the expert will be appointed, the definition of issues to be decided, and the material to be provided. In adjudicative ADR these steps will be very important because of the limited options for appeal following a decision reached by an agreed process.

The role of a lawyer in non-adjudicative ADR processes is less formal, with the focus **4.06** falling most strongly on case analysis, identifying and formulating offers, evaluating proposals from the other side, and ensuring terms are clear and comprehensive. Engagement with the mediator may also be important. The Guidance Notes on Precedent H make it clear that estimated costs for ADR should cover settlement negotiations, including Part 36 and other offers, and advising the client, as well as drafting a settlement agreement or Tomlin order. For the role of the lawyer as an advocate see 15.48–15.53.

D Authority to Settle

Acting within authority to settle on the basis of sufficiently clear client instructions **4.07** is very important in using ADR, especially where a lawyer acts on behalf of a client in a non-adjudicative process. Any agreement reached should be within parameters set by client instructions, see 6.09–6.10.

A lawyer negotiating on a client's behalf should only reach a final agreement if so **4.08** authorized by the client. In negotiating as an agent, a lawyer will normally have apparent authority to settle on behalf of the client, so any agreement reached may be treated by the other side as binding. Any limit on authority to settle should not be exceeded. If a lawyer negotiates a settlement to a claim without the consent of the client, the client will still be bound due to the actual or ostensible authority to act on behalf of a client.[8] A lawyer who reaches an agreement but who did not in fact have authority to settle could be in a very difficult position as the agreement could be enforced against the client, who could bring a claim against the lawyer for acting without authority. It has been held that if a lawyer misrepresents the terms to a client the settlement may be

---

[8] *Waugh v MB Clifford & Sons* [1982] Ch 374.

set aside, but it is doubtful that this is still good law.[9] To protect both lawyer and client it is common to specify at the start of a negotiation at which the client is not present that any agreement should be expressly subject to client approval. If in any doubt it may be appropriate to check that an opponent has authority to settle.

E The Role of a Lawyer in Advising on Terms of Settlement

4.09 Save for in an adjudicative process which results in an award, one of the most important roles of a lawyer in relation to ADR is advising on terms of settlement. The main elements to cover are as follows, for detail see Chapters 18–20:

- a full list of issues to be settled, including matters such as interest and costs;
- what terms might be acceptable on each issue, in the light of legal and factual strengths and weaknesses (taking into account matters such as tax consequences);[10]
- the reasonableness and comprehensiveness of the overall settlement;
- the precise wording of terms, which may for example affect sums payable;[11]
- the detail of terms, eg interest, costs, dates of payment;
- in what form the settlement is best recorded;
- any matters relating to enforcement.

4.10 A range of problems relating to the finality of terms of settlement have arisen in recent cases, showing how important it is to tie down detail and contemplate potential problems. If the terms include an undertaking, a party may be released from the undertaking if circumstances change,[12] or if the action has been stayed the stay may be lifted.[13] A settlement cannot be challenged later on the basis of something of which the challenging party was already aware.[14]

F The Role and Responsibilities of a Client in Relation to ADR

4.11 As parties are required to help the court to further the overriding objective;[15] even if a party has strong or entrenched views, he or she has a duty to assist the court in

---

[9] *Re Roberts* [1905] 1 Ch 704.
[10] *Freedman v Freedman* [2015] EWHC 1457 (Ch).
[11] *Barden v Commodities Research Unit International (Holdings) Limited* [2013] EWHC 1633 (Ch).
[12] *Al Nahyan v Elite Performance Cars Ltd* [2015] EWHC 950 (QB).
[13] *Flax v Papaloizou* [2015] EWHC 1055 (QB).
[14] *Hayward v Zurich Insurance Company* [2015] EWCA Civ 327.
[15] CPR r 1.3.

dealing with a case in a proportionate way, saving expense, and ensuring that a case is dealt with expeditiously. The role of a party in an ADR process is in some ways different to the role in litigation. The use of an ADR process is based on a contractual agreement between the parties, and is thus within the control of the parties in a way that litigation is not. Parties need to understand and engage with the terms of an agreement to use of ADR, and the implications of that agreement, and may need advice. The distinctions between the role of a client in litigation, and in agreeing to an outcome of ADR, may need to be clearly explained, for example as regards the very limited possibilities for appeal, or the success of an application to set an agreement aside, where a party agrees to an outcome. In mediation a client will play a more significant role than at a trial, possibly making an opening statement, and discussing issues and offers with the lawyer and mediator.

G Addressing Concerns About ADR

A lawyer who takes the view that a case is appropriate for ADR may find it necessary to address concerns from the client, or from the lawyer or party on the other side. The following points may also be relevant to discussion in court as regards the potential use of ADR. **4.12**

Appropriateness of the litigation process

The litigation process in England and Wales is highly respected. However there are circumstances in which litigation may not be the most appropriate or effective process to address a particular dispute, and reasonable use of ADR is now an expectation such that reasons not to use ADR may need to be identified and articulated. **4.13**

Robustness of process

The litigation process is highly structured, and the approach of judges robust. Although ADR processes are less structured, they can still be robust. A robust approach can be a criterion in selecting a process, and any third party to be used in the process. **4.14**

Proposing ADR may indicate weakness

An adversarial system can foster competition, against which proposing ADR might be seen as indicating weakness. Judicial statements and court rules have made it clear that use of ADR and concessions are important elements in modern dispute resolution, and proposals relating to ADR can be worded strongly. ADR should be characterized positively as being about best process and risk management, achieving good outcomes more efficiently. **4.15**

ADR might undermine litigation

4.16 Litigation is normally conducted in a structured way with a timetable, and ADR might be seen to undermine that. In reality, relatively little in terms of information or strategy is really preserved until trial in a civil case. Increasingly ADR runs alongside litigation and can offer benefits in terms of narrowing and testing issues, and finding out at least as much as one reveals.

ADR can undermine control of a case

4.17 The Civil Procedure Rules provide a reasonably clear structure and roles. A more flexible ADR process may appear to offer less control and predictability, but in fact control of an ADR process lies primarily with the parties.

ADR might provide pressure to settle

4.18 Agreeing to use an ADR process might be seen to imply willingness to compromise. In practice ADR can be conducted on the basis that no concession will be made without clear justification, or without something equally significant being obtained in return. This is not to suggest that ADR is necessarily appropriate where it is proposed for tactical reasons that might include inappropriate pressure to settle.

ADR may be used as a delaying tactic

4.19 An ADR process could potentially be used as a delaying tactic, though this is less likely with robust case management. Any concern about delay should be articulated and more time-efficient ADR proposed.

Limited knowledge of ADR process may be a concern

4.20 Some parties and lawyers may be slow to accept ADR, feeling insufficiently familiar with or experienced in the use of it. Substantial information is available on the websites of the larger ADR providers, and many providers will be happy to provide further information and advice. Legal skills relevant to litigation can be adapted for the relative flexibility of an ADR process. Lack of sufficient knowledge will not be regarded as a good reason for resisting an ADR process that would otherwise be appropriate.

ADR may incur extra expense

4.21 There may be a concern that an unsuccessful ADR process might increase expense to no purpose. This should be rare if decisions as to the form and timing of ADR are taken with care. The success rate of ADR is relatively high, so wasted expense should only be a concern where there are clear reasons why ADR is likely not to succeed and those points cannot be addressed.

ADR may be abused where a claim lacks merit

An ADR process might be abused by a party with an unmeritorious claim who **4.22** would lose if the case went to court, and proposes the use of ADR to get an offer. This is a scenario in which the stronger party might reasonably refuse ADR, provided the belief in the strength of the case is well founded. Alternatively a face-to-face mediation process might be effective in making it clear to a potential litigant how weak his or her case is (subject to keeping the cost of the mediation itself low).

H Persuading Another Party to Use ADR

An ADR process is based on agreement. Once one side has decided that ADR is **4.23** appropriate it may be necessary to persuade the other side to agree to the process to be used, and the timing. It will also be necessary to agree the detail of the agreement to use ADR, and possibly to agree on an appropriate third party to conduct the ADR process. This may be challenging where the other party has different views on any of these matters.

It will be tactically important not only to secure an acceptable agreement as to pro- **4.24** cess, but also to ensure as far as possible that the other party views the ADR process positively. A proposal to use ADR may need to be framed carefully to secure agreement, but also to meet other criteria such as giving robust messages, and ensuring that the proposal can be referred to in relation to costs should the need arise.

Should agreement not be forthcoming it may be important to identify and con- **4.25** structively address problems. Any of the possible concerns about ADR noted in 4.13–4.22 may be answered with the points made there. Other possible techniques for securing agreement are as follows, and might be used by a party, a lawyer, or a judge engaged in case management. An ADR provider may be of assistance in securing agreement.

Identify and address concerns

Reasons for refusing to use ADR should be identified and addressed at the time.[16] **4.26** A refusal without reasons carries a risk of a costs penalty, so it is quite justifiable to

---

[16] *PGF II SA v OMFS Company* [2012] EWHC 83 (TCC).

ask for reasons, and a court can require a party refusing to use ADR to set out their reasons in a witness statement. Once reasons are given it will normally be possible to address them, or to respond if appropriate that the reasons given do not appear adequate and may be referred to in a later costs application.

Propose specific benefits that ADR might offer

4.27 It is often helpful to identify specific benefits that ADR might offer the other side. Constructive suggestions or a possible way ahead on an issue of importance to the other side might assist in getting agreement.

Offer information about ADR options

4.28 If a party might be resisting ADR through lack of sufficient knowledge, providing directions to an independent source of advice such as a website, or encouraging another party to speak directly to an ADR service provider may assist.

Propose a limited or simple ADR option

4.29 A limited or simple proposal may open a constructive dialogue. A suggestion of a negotiation limited to specific issues may open up options. A general proposal for mediation may be more tempting than a detailed one that the other side may view with suspicion, or a specific proposal to look at concerns of both sides may succeed.

Offer carrots

4.30 It may be appropriate to offer something to tempt the other party to engage in ADR. This does not need to be a potential concession, but perhaps an expression of willingness to consider a particular concern that a party has, provided ADR is attempted. It may be possible to offer flexibility, such as proposing three ADR providers and leaving the final choice to the other party.

Offer to pay reasonable ADR fees

4.31 Where one party considers a process such as mediation to be appropriate because, for example, it could offer significant savings in costs, it may be cost effective to offer, for example, to bear the fee of a mediator.

Engage the assistance of the judge

4.32 Once proceedings have been issued, a judge may support a reasonable proposal that ADR be undertaken. The case and costs management powers of the judge can be called upon to assist objectively in supporting the use of ADR, and ascertaining reasons for any objection. The judge may make a variety of orders to support the use of ADR. If a court has positively supported the use of ADR, a refusal to use it will more readily be seen as being unreasonable.

I Potential Liability of a Lawyer in Relation to ADR

The reasonable standard to be met by a lawyer in relation to provision of advice **4.33** relating to ADR is not yet fully developed, but the various responsibilities and duties which apply suggest that a lawyer could be open to complaint or potentially legally liable for:

- failing to give a client sufficient advice on ADR options in a case where the use of ADR would be in the client's interests, or failure to use ADR causes loss to the client in terms of a significantly poorer outcome or irrecoverable costs;
- failing to give a client sufficient advice about the merits of a case so that a client accepts an outcome to an ADR process that is clearly less favourable than the client should reasonably have achieved;
- failing to get sufficiently clear instructions, or acting beyond authority, in an ADR process, where this results in the client getting a clearly less favourable outcome;
- failing to advise a client about the risks of unreasonably refusing to use ADR, with the result that the client suffers an adverse costs order;
- giving clearly inadequate advice on the appropriateness of proposed settlement terms or enforcement issues.

The steps that a dissatisfied client might take are summarized below. It is relevant **4.34** to note that if a party voluntarily agrees to use an ADR process, and/or voluntarily agrees the outcome of a non-adjudicative process on the basis of adequate advice, it may be difficult for that client to raise any complaint, or to show causation of any loss. The lawyer will be best protected by keeping evidence that clear advice has been given on ADR options and costs, and the instructions given by the client. It is not necessary for a lawyer to wait until all information and evidence is available to be able to evaluate a case, so long as the advice given to the client makes clear what the lawyer has and has not been able to take into account. Client confidentiality may be waived by a client raising a concern, though communications in an ADR process would require waiver of without prejudice protection by both parties.

Any third party involved in an ADR process might separately be liable for breach of **4.35** contract or negligence, though the contract with the third party will usually seek to limit or exclude liability.

Complaints

4.36   A client who is dissatisfied with information or advice given in respect of an ADR process, or with the result of an ADR process may of course use the complaints process available within the firm or chambers, provided by the relevant professional body, or by the Legal Ombudsman.

Wasted costs

4.37   If proceedings are issued a lawyer could be personally liable for a wasted costs order, if an improper, unreasonable, or negligent act or omission on the part of the lawyer leads to a failure to achieve a reasonable outcome using an appropriate ADR process, as a result of which litigation costs were unnecessarily incurred or were not recoverable.[17] There must be a causal link between the poor conduct and the costs wasted.[18] The order may be that costs be disallowed, or that the lawyer pay the costs personally.[19] An unreasonable failure to engage in ADR may attract an adverse costs order, but a wasted costs order may be more appropriate where the client would have been likely to agree to ADR if properly advised. If a lawyer acts unreasonably in refusing to agree the terms of an order being drawn up following directions from a judge, the lawyer may be liable for costs incurred.[20]

Professional negligence

4.38   A lawyer has no immunity from an action for professional negligence in relation to a case.[21] A lawyer may be liable for negligence in relation to ADR if he or she:

- advises a client to accept too low a sum;[22]
- fails to investigate facts properly, so that the client recovers less that should have been recovered;[23]
- fails to pass important information to a client;[24]
- fails to make the client aware of the implications of unusual terms in an agreement;[25]

---

[17]   Senior Courts Act 1981 s 51(6); CPR r 46.8; Practice Direction 44—General Rules about Costs subsection 11—Court's Powers in Relation to Misconduct; Practice Direction 46—Costs Special Cases, sections 5.1–5.9.

[18]   *Ridehalgh v Horsefield* [1994] Ch 205.

[19]   *Tolstoy-Miloslavsky v Aldington* [1996] 1 WLR 736.

[20]   *Webb Resolutions Ltd v JV Ltd (t/a Shepherd Chartered Surveyors)* [2013] EWHC 509.

[21]   *Arthur JS Hall & Co (a firm) v Simons* [2000] 3 WLR 543.

[22]   *McNamara v Martin Motors & Co* (1983) 127 SJ 69.

[23]   *Dickinson v Jones Alexander & Co* [1990] Fam Law 137.

[24]   *Strover v Harrington* [1988] 1 All ER 769.

[25]   *County Personnel v Alan R Pulver* [1987] 1 All ER 289.

- undertakes responsibilities in relation to an agreement, but is responsible for a breach of what was undertaken.[26]

A lawyer will not be liable in negligence purely because advice given is not ultimately successful.[27] Nor will a lawyer be liable for failing to give advice on the commercial risks of an agreement or transaction of which the client should have been aware.[28] A lawyer will not necessarily be negligent in pursuing a weak case.[29] A lawyer does not have to give advice on aspects of a case such as potential tax consequences which are tangential.[30] Where reasonable advice from an appropriate barrister as to settling is given and a consent order is made, a client is unlikely to succeed in a claim for professional negligence where the client on reflection feels a better outcome might have been achieved.[31]

4.39

---

[26] *Al-Kandari v JR Brown & Co* [1987] 2 All ER 302.

[27] *Buckland v Farrar & Moody* [1978] 3 All ER 229.

[28] *Pickersgill v Riley, The Times* 2 March 2004.

[29] *Harley v McDonald Harley (a firm), The Times* 15 May 2001.

[30] *Swain Mason v Mills & Reeve* [2012] EWCA Civ 498, but see also *Freedman v Freedman* [2015] EWHC 1457 (Ch).

[31] *Dunhill v W Brook & Co* [2016] EWHC 165 (QB).

5

PRIVACY, PRIVILEGE,
AND CONFIDENTIALITY CLAUSES

A Importance of Privacy and Confidentiality in ADR

5.01 Privacy can be a particular attraction of an ADR process. Whereas litigation normally takes place in open court, ADR processes are normally private, which may be particularly relevant where there is commercial or personal sensitivity as regards the subject matter of a case. An ADR process, and the outcome of it, are normally protected from publicity by a confidentiality clause, save to the extent that it may be agreed something be made public.

5.02 Separately from the attractions of privacy for parties, it is important for public policy reasons that attempts to resolve a dispute take place in confidence. Parties must be able to communicate and feel free to make potential concessions with a view to settlement without fear that if the process does not succeed the potential concession might prejudice their position in any litigation. This has led to the development by the courts of the 'without prejudice' principle, which means that a communication made in a genuine attempt to settle an existing dispute cannot normally be referred to in court in proceedings.

5.03 As a third separate concept, there are legal professional duties between a lawyer and client in relation to client confidentiality, supplemented by the protection for communications between a lawyer and client provided by the principle of legal professional privilege.

5.04 The contents of this range of important protections relating to information and communication in ADR processes have overlapping purposes, but differences in objectives and coverage mean that it is important to distinguish between them. While all ADR processes are broadly private, there is no general absolute right of privacy.[1]

---

[1] *Farm Assist Limited (in liquidation) v The Secretary of State for the Environment, Food and Rural Affairs (No 2)* [2009] EWHC 1102 (TCC).

The separate protections of communications in ADR processes are as follows: **5.05**

(i) Professional duties of confidentiality. Professional codes of conduct include duties in relation to client confidentiality. See 6.11–6.13.

(ii) Legal professional privilege. This protects a communication made between a lawyer and client for the purposes of giving or receiving legal advice, including advice relating to ADR options. See 5.15–5.16.

(iii) The principle protecting 'without prejudice' communications made by one party to another with a view to settlement. See 5.17–5.26.

(iv) A contractual confidentiality clause. Confidentiality is normally protected by an express term in an agreement to carry out an ADR process, which will bind the parties and any third party who signs the agreement. A separate confidentiality clause may be included in any settlement which results from the ADR. See 5.27–5.35.

(v) Standards of ADR providers. A person trained as an arbitrator or mediator and holding him or herself out as such would be expected to comply with reasonable standards within that role. For example mediators will normally follow a mediation code of conduct that is likely to include a duty of confidentiality. See 13.29–13.43.

(vi) Regulatory standards. National and international regulation draws attention to the importance of confidentiality in ADR, see, for example, paragraph 4 of the EU Code of Conduct for Mediators. See 17.34.

The importance of protecting communications in ADR processes has been strongly   **5.06**
supported in recent cases. It has been held that communications in without prejudice negotiations should remain protected in later proceedings if the issue remained unresolved,[2] the House of Lords adding that further exceptions to the without prejudice principle should not be made, and that the court should be slow to lift without prejudice protection unless the reason for doing so is plain. It was said that: 'Communications made with a view to an amicable settlement ought to be held very sacred; for if parties were to be afterwards prejudiced by their efforts to compromise, it would be impossible to attempt an amicable arrangement of differences.'[3]

While confidentiality is of such importance, there may be good reasons for wishing   **5.07**
to make use of information derived from an ADR process. The main difficulties that may arise are:

• there may be a dispute about the precise terms of a settlement which cannot be resolved without reference to the ADR process;

---

[2] *Ofulue v Bossert* [2009] UKHL 16.
[3] *Ofulue v Bossert* [2009] UKHL 16 (per Lord Scott).

- a settlement might be challenged on the basis it was reached improperly, for example through fraud or misrepresentation during the ADR process;
- if an ADR process is not successful, a party may wish to use a communication made during the process as evidence relevant to an issue in the course of litigation;
- an allegation of potential negligence or breach of professional conduct on the part of a lawyer or third party involved in an ADR process may be difficult to pursue if it is not possible to use information from the ADR process itself.

5.08 In such cases it may be argued that a court should look at some material from the ADR process in the interests of justice. However, in most cases the decisions of the court have shown that the importance of maintaining confidentiality for settlement attempts will prevail. The following sections only outline relevant principles. The growing use of ADR is likely to lead to developing case law. Where a case has international elements it is important to note that professional conduct rules and the application of without prejudice and confidentiality principles can vary in different jurisdictions.

B Control of Information in ADR

5.09 In ADR processes there is no general duty of disclosure, save for what is agreed between the parties, or what is required to be disclosed under a litigation process relating to the dispute. Save for the extent to which information should be disclosed under a Pre-action Protocol, disclosure, or a court order, each party can choose what information is kept private, what is shared, and with whom it should be shared. This includes what is shared with another party, and what is shared with a third party such as a mediator, arbitrator, or expert.

5.10 Nonetheless, sufficient sharing of information will be necessary. Another party or a third party will usually ask for sufficient information and documentation to be convinced of the strength of a case, and may demand sufficient proof as a basis for making a concession or offer. The sharing of information may be by agreement, on a voluntary basis, or as a reaction to developments in the process.

5.11 In mediation the position will be governed by the mediation agreement, and any published rules of the mediation provider selected. It is common to agree what information the parties provide to each other and to the mediator. It is normally possible for a party to provide information to a mediator alone, on the basis the mediator should bear it in mind in progressing the case, but should not reveal it to the other side.

For arbitration and other adjudicative processes, the parties will normally agree on **5.12** the extent of mutual disclosure. If there is no agreement, the tribunal will determine the scope of disclosure. It is not acceptable for one party to provide information to the arbitrator alone.

For other kinds of evaluation or determination it is normal for the parties to agree **5.13** what material is given to the third party. This can include a possibility that each party can give the third party information that is not revealed to the other party to the dispute, if so agreed, though this may undermine trust in the process.

Inevitably the control of information and documents in an ADR process will be **5.14** strategic and tactical. A careful balance is needed between providing enough information to show the strength of a case, while not showing anything that is particularly sensitive or private. Requests should be made for the other side to provide necessary information and documents. A realistic attempt to settle may require a reasonably robust exchange of information.

C Legal Professional Privilege and ADR

The professional duty of confidentiality protects information provided to a lawyer **5.15** by a client, see 6.11–6.13. The principle of legal professional privilege is wider in protecting from disclosure all communications between a lawyer and client, where the purpose of the communication is giving or receiving legal advice.[4] Legal advice privilege only extends to communications between lawyers and their clients, and not communications with other professional people, even if they give legal advice.[5] This principle will cover legal advice relating to the use of ADR options. Legal professional privilege is the privilege of the client, and can be waived by the client. A lawyer should get permission from a client in advance for revealing anything protected by legal professional privilege in an ADR process. The court will not normally override this privilege, though the privilege may be lost where information is otherwise disclosed.[6] Information cannot be made privileged simply by being raised with a lawyer if it is otherwise disclosable. It may be difficult to show privilege where reports are prepared for more than one purpose.[7] An email that relates to the possibility of obtaining legal advice will not attract legal advice privilege, though the court has a residual discretion to protect confidential material.[8]

---

[4] *Three Rivers District Council v Bank of England (No 5)* [2003] EWCA Civ 474.
[5] *R (Prudential plc) v Special Commissioner of Income Tax* [2013] UKSC 1.
[6] *Guinness Peat Properties Ltd v Fitzroy Robinson Partnership* [1987] 1 WLR 1027.
[7] *Transport for Greater Manchester v Thales Transport & Security Ltd* [2013] EWHC 149 (TCC).
[8] *G v G* [2015] EWHC 1512 (Fam).

5.16 As regards communications with third parties, the test for privilege is slightly different. Where information or advice is sought from a third party, such as an expert, privilege may be claimed for a communication between a client or lawyer and the third party where the sole or dominant purpose of the communication is to assist in the conduct of litigation that has commenced or is reasonably in prospect. This should be distinguished from a communication with an independent third party in an ADR process, which is unlikely to attract legal professional privilege, though it would normally be protected by a duty of confidentiality. The privilege will also not apply to a meeting between lawyers and clients on opposing sides of a case, even where the purpose is to discuss tactics in potential litigation.[9]

D The 'Without Prejudice' Principle

5.17 The concept of 'without prejudice' has been developed by the courts as a matter of public policy. The intention is to protect from disclosure any communication made between parties with a view to settling an existing dispute. Parties should be free to be open as regards the use of information, argument, and possible proposals for settlement to enable ADR to be conducted rigorously. If such communications were not protected then ADR processes would be significantly, and often fatally, undermined. If anything said in an ADR process could be used in litigation parties would be unlikely to engage in meaningful discussion or make concessions.

5.18 The principle was initially developed to protect attempts to negotiate settlement. Any oral or written communication passing between parties made in an attempt to settle a dispute will be protected from disclosure in the current and any subsequent proceedings between the same parties and concerned with the same subject matter.[10] This is a matter of principle, and it is not necessary for the communication to be marked 'without prejudice'. The principle applies whether or not settlement is reached, and applies whether or not proceedings have been issued, so long as the main purpose of the communication is the settlement of a dispute.[11] The communication must be part of a genuine ADR process aimed at settlement.[12] The principle is applied broadly, and a court will not dissect an ADR process to identify specific material that might be admissible, as this would in itself undermine the principle of protecting without

---

[9] *Stax Claimants v Bank of Nova Scotia Channel Islands Ltd* [2007] EWHC 1153 (Ch).

[10] *Cutts v Head* [1984] Ch 290 and *Ofulue v Bossert* [2009] UKHL 16.

[11] *Barnetson v Framlington Group Ltd* [2007] EWCA Civ 502.

[12] *Rush & Tompkins Ltd v Greater London Council* [1989] AC 1280 and *South Shropshire District Council v Amos* [1986] 1 WLR 1271.

prejudice communications from disclosure.[13] The concept has been extended to other forms of ADR such as mediation.[14] See 13.59–13.63 for the specific application of the principle to mediation. The words 'without prejudice' may reserve a right to raise a point rather than seeking to protect a document from use in court.[15] Communications that are part of settlement discussions with a regulatory body might be protected by analogy to the without prejudice rule.[16]

In principle, if no agreement is reached a communication made in an attempt to **5.19** settle cannot be used in court, either in evidence or in a reference by a lawyer. The principle does not mean that anything said during an ADR process can never be used in other circumstances. For example, separate admissible evidence on the point may be used. It is quite acceptable that if there is a counsel-to-counsel negotiation each counsel can report back to his or her client on what was said as the lawyer is agent for the client.

The protection against disclosure is for the benefit of the parties seeking to settle. **5.20** It may be waived by the parties,[17] but the privilege is essentially joint and cannot normally be waived by one party alone.[18] The protection is for the parties, and if they agree to waive it so that information can be put before a court, the protection cannot be claimed by a third party such as a mediator or evaluator, though such a person may be separately protected by a confidentiality clause. No negative inference should be drawn from a refusal by a party to waive privilege.[19]

It is possible to exclude protection for specific purposes, though this should be done **5.21** expressly. It is, for example, common to make an offer 'without prejudice save as to costs', meaning that the normal principle applies, save that the communication may be referred to on the issue of costs. In order to be able to refer to a without prejudice letter when costs come to be considered the letter must expressly be made without prejudice save as to costs.[20] A court does not generally have power to look at without prejudice communications in relation to applications as to costs unless a

---

[13] *Unilever plc v Procter & Gamble Co* [2000] 1 WLR 2436 and *Williams v Hull* [2009] EWHC 2844 (Ch).

[14] *Mason v Walton on Thames Charity* [2010] EWHC 1688 (Ch).

[15] *Avonwick Holdings Ltd v Webinvest Ltd* [2014] EWCA Civ 1436.

[16] *Property Alliance Group Ltd v Royal Bank of Scotland Plc* [2015] EWHC 1557 (Ch).

[17] *Chantery Vellacott v Convergence Group* [2007] EWHC 1774 (Ch).

[18] *Somatra Ltd v Sinclair Roche & Temperley* [2000] 1 WLR 2453 and *Cumbria Waste Management Ltd v Baines Wilson* [2008] EWHC 786 (QB), but see also *Earl of Malmesbury v Strutt & Parker* [2008] EWHC 424 (QB).

[19] *Sayers v Clarke Walker* [2002] EWCA Civ 910 and *Reed Executive plc v Reed Business Information Ltd* [2004] EWCA Civ 887.

[20] *Reed Executive plc v Reed Business Information Ltd* [2004] EWCA Civ 887.

settlement process has been conducted on a basis that is without prejudice save as to costs, or the parties agree to waive the privilege.[21] 'Without prejudice' protection is not automatically waived by making a claim for indemnity costs which raises issues of conduct.[22]

5.22 There are particular approaches to disclosure in some specific types of case. In private law family cases concerning children, information revealed at an in court conciliation led by a judge in collaboration with the Cafcass officer and any mediator may not be seen as privileged.[23] However settlement discussions that are explored with a judge in financial remedies cases are seen as without prejudice, and as the judge may take an evaluative role, the judge will not take a further part in the case if it is not settled. Communications between the parties and a conciliation officer in employment cases are protected from disclosure.[24]

5.23 Without prejudice provides protection from disclosure where a communication is made with a view to settlement. While public interest requires that this be widely interpreted, the principle will not apply outside those circumstances. For example:

- the principle will not protect information that is disclosable for some other reason;
- the principle will not apply to peripheral matters such as terms of payment where settlement of a dispute is not in issue;[25]
- a communication will not be protected if it is made at a discussion before there is clearly a dispute between the parties;[26]
- a meeting is not without prejudice if negotiations are carried out to prevent a dispute arising rather than to resolve a dispute;[27]
- privilege does not apply to matters of detail once liability is admitted;[28]
- if an open offer is made, rather than one provisional on settlement being reached;
- possibly if a full admission on an issue is made, rather than a potential concession;[29]
- material prepared for a discussion between experts directed by a court is not protected by without prejudice privilege, even if it is envisaged it might be used in mediation;[30]

---

[21] *Reed Executive plc v Reed Business Information Ltd* [2004] EWCA Civ 887.
[22] *Vestergaard Frandsen v Bestnet Europe* [2014] EWHC 4047 (Ch).
[23] *Re T (a child)* [2015] EWCA Civ 719 and FPR 2010 PD 12B.
[24] Employment Tribunals Act 1996 s 18(7).
[25] *Bradford & Bingley plc v Rashid* [2006] UKHL 37.
[26] *BE v DE (Evidence: Without Prejudice Privilege)* [2014] EWHC 2318 (Fam).
[27] *Framlington Group Ltd v Barnetson* [2007] EWCA Civ 502.
[28] *Bradford & Bingley plc v Rashid* [2006] 1 WLR 2066.
[29] *The Dorchester Group Ltd v Keir Construction Ltd* [2015] EWHC 3051 (TCC).
[30] *Aird v Prime Meridian Ltd* [2006] EWCA Civ 1866.

- the words 'without prejudice' cannot be used to hide something that should be conveyed in an open communication.[31]

As the principle is a matter of public policy, it may not apply where justice demands **5.24** otherwise, for example because the principle is being abused.[32] However to protect the principle, exceptions must be consistent with the policy that parties should not be discouraged from settling their disputes.[33] The public interest in supporting parties in settling disputes is growing, so exceptions may become increasingly difficult to establish.[34]

Despite the concern to limit exceptions, the court may look at relevant communica- **5.25** tions made with a view to settlement:

- where the issue before a court is whether a settlement was reached, or what the terms of the settlement were;[35]
- where the issue before a court is the proper interpretation or construction of the terms of a settlement;[36]
- where the court is asked to consider if anything was agreed as to costs,[37] or as to contribution to damages;[38]
- where the issue before a court is whether a settlement should be set aside on the grounds of misrepresentation, fraud, or undue influence;[39]
- where the issue before the court is whether an estoppel has arisen as a result of a communication made with a view to settlement being relied on;[40]
- material may be disclosable in a separate later case,[41] but only such material as is directly relevant to the later case,[42] and relates to different issues;[43]
- material may be disclosable where there is a subsequent professional negligence claim against a lawyer involved in the ADR process;[44]

---

[31] *Buckinghamshire County Council v Moran* [1990] Ch 623.
[32] *Unilever plc v Procter & Gamble Co* [2000] 1 WLR 2436 (per Walker LJ).
[33] *Woodward v Santander UK plc (formerly Abbey National plc)* [2010] IRLR 834.
[34] *Ofulue v Bossert* [2009] UKHL 16.
[35] *Walker v Wilsher* [1889] 23 QBD 335; *Tomlin v Standard Telephones and Cables Ltd* [1969] 1 WLR 1378; *Brown v Rice* [2007] EWHC 625 (Ch).
[36] *Oceanbulk Shipping and Trading SA v TMT Asia Ltd* [2010] UKSC 44.
[37] *Tomlin v Standard Telephones and Cables Ltd* [1969] 1 WLR 1378.
[38] *Gnitrow Ltd v Cape plc* [2000] 1 WLR 2327.
[39] *Unilever plc v Procter & Gamble Co* [2000] 1 WLR 2436.
[40] *Hodgkinson & Corby Ltd v Wards Mobility Services Ltd* [1997] FSR 178 and *Unilever plc v Procter & Gamble Co* [2000] 1 WLR 2436.
[41] *Bradford and Bingley plc v Rashid* [2006] 1 WLR 2066.
[42] *Cattley v Pollard* [2007] EWHC 16 (Ch).
[43] *Cumbria Waste Management Ltd and Lakeland Waste Management Ltd v Baines Wilson* [2008] EWHC 786 (QB).
[44] *Youlton v Charles Russell* [2010] WL 1649039 and *Curtis v Pulbrook* [2011] WL 291736.

- a limited exception may allow information about settlement attempts to be put before a court to explain delay, or to obtain relief from a sanction;[45]
- a limited exception may also apply where there is a risk of serious harm, for example to a child.[46]

5.26   More difficult are the cases where there is an allegation of improper conduct during a settlement process. In such cases a court will normally uphold the principle that communications within a settlement process should not be disclosed. Not only is this necessary to support the principle, but any other approach could too easily lead to attempts to have tactics within an ADR process reviewed by a court, which would be highly undesirable. With this in mind, the improper conduct will need to be of a very serious nature. A court may be prepared to look at communications related to settlement where the principle might otherwise be used as a cloak for perjury, blackmail, or other 'unambiguous impropriety',[47] or where the principle is being abused, for example through dishonest or oppressive conduct.[48] However the importance of protecting communications made in an attempt to settle is such that only an unambiguous and serious case will lead a court to go behind the principle.[49]

E   Confidentiality Clauses

5.27   The above principles make confidentiality the norm in an ADR process. However each principle operates independently, so attention may need to be paid to the position in an individual ADR process, especially where sensitive information and/or a third party is involved. An agreement to use arbitration or mediation will normally include a confidentiality clause, and such a clause will often be included in an agreement for early neutral evaluation or expert determination. A settlement agreement will also quite often include a confidentiality clause.

5.28   A confidentiality clause will commonly bind the parties to a dispute, and any third party facilitator or decision-taker who signs an agreement. Many agreements used by ADR providers include a pro-forma term, but the precise wording should be checked, as it may fall to be construed by a court. A duty of confidentiality may be implied even if it is not express. A confidentiality clause could be enforced through

---

[45]   *Berg v IML London Ltd* [2002] 1 WLR 3271.
[46]   *Re D (Minors)* [1993] 2 All ER 693.
[47]   *Unilever plc v Procter & Gamble Co* [2000] 1 WLR 2436.
[48]   *Kitcat v Sharp* [1882] 48 LT 64 and *Best Buy Co Inc v Worldwide Sales Corpn Espana SL* [2011] EWCA Civ 618.
[49]   *Savings and Investment Bank Ltd v Fincken* [2003] EWCA Civ 1630; *Berry Trade Ltd v Moussavi (No 3)* [2003] EWCA Civ 71; *Aird & Aird v Prime Meridian* [2006] EWHC 2338 (TCC); *AAG Investments Ltd v BAA Airports Ltd* [2010] EWHC 2844 (Comm).

a contractual claim. A potential risk that a confidentiality clause may be breached can be restrained by injunction.[50]

It should be noted that while a third party such as a mediator or arbitrator will   **5.29**
normally be bound by a contractual confidentiality clause, others who attend an ADR process may not be bound by that contract, or by a professional code of conduct. While the 'without prejudice' principle will protect communications in the ADR process from being revealed in court, there is no principle that will necessarily protect privacy if someone else at the ADR process were to make something public. If relevant, a confidentiality agreement should be made with all those who attend.

Negotiation

Information disclosed during a negotiation between lawyers may be protected by   **5.30**
professional conduct responsibilities, see 6.11–6.13. Information will be normally protected from disclosure to a court in any subsequent litigation under the without prejudice principle. If other people take part in a negotiation, information will not necessarily be protected unless those involved are bound by contractual confidentiality.

Mediation

A confidentiality term in a mediation agreement will normally protect any commu-   **5.31**
nication between the parties, and between each party and the mediator from being revealed. In addition, where a communication takes place between a party and the mediator in a private meeting, that communication should only be revealed to the other side with the agreement of the party making the communication. If this is not a term of the mediation agreement, it may be an element of the code of conduct followed by the mediator. A court will not look at the content of a mediation process to decide whether a later refusal to mediate is reasonable.[51]

Any lawyers involved will have professional conduct responsibilities, and anything   **5.32**
said during the mediation will be protected by the without prejudice principle. It has been mooted that a distinct type of privilege may attach to the mediation process to cover all communications, whether they are covered by other principles or not, but there is no clear authority for such a principle.[52]

---

[50] *Venture Investment Placement Ltd v Hall* [2005] EWHC 1227 (Ch).
[51] *PGF II SA v OMFS Company* [2012] EWHC 83 (TCC).
[52] See for example the comments by Ramsey J in *Farm Assist Ltd v Secretary of State for Environment, Food and Rural Affairs (No 2)* [2009] EWHC 1102 (TCC) and 'Mediation Privilege?' (2009) 159 NLJ 506 and 550 by Mr Justice Briggs.

Experts, early neutral evaluation, or expert determination

5.33 Information may be provided to a third party in various circumstances in relation to an ADR process. The confidentiality of this information is best protected through a term in the agreement with that individual. One party may provide information that the party wishes to be kept confidential in relation to another party, but this should only be done if it has been agreed that this can be done as part of the process because of the risk that concerns will arise as to the basis upon which any conclusion or decision has been reached.[53]

Arbitration

5.34 It is a long-established principle of arbitration law that arbitral proceedings are private[54] and confidential.[55] Interestingly, there are no express provisions enshrining these principles in the Arbitration Act 1996. This is because both principles have a large number of exceptions and were too unsettled to formulate suitable provisions for the Act.[56]

5.35 Adjudicative processes such as arbitration are normally based on a written agreement, which will include terms as regards confidentiality. The courts have shown clear support for the confidentiality of documents prepared for an arbitration process as well as the process itself,[57] but deployment by a party of its own documents in an arbitration does not clothe those documents with any confidentiality that they did not already possess.[58] The limits of the duty of confidentiality in arbitration proceedings are still being developed. As the law now stands the principal cases where disclosure may be permitted are[59] where there is consent, where a court grants permission, where disclosure is reasonably necessary for the protection of the legitimate interests of an arbitrating party, or where the interests of justice require disclosure. In an adjudicative process it is not normally possible for one party to provide confidential information to the tribunal which is not disclosed to the other side.

F Potential Loss of Confidentiality

5.36 The main ways in which an issue relating to the confidentiality of ADR may come before a court are:

- if a party makes an application for the disclosure of oral or written communication in litigation after an ADR process fails;

---

[53] *Halifax Life Ltd v Equitable Life Assurance Society* [2007] 1 Lloyd's Rep 528.
[54] *Oxford Shipping Co Ltd v Nippon Yusen Kaisha* [1984] 3 All ER 835.
[55] *Ali Shipping Corp v Shipyard Trogir* [1999] 1 WLR 314.
[56] Departmental Advisory Committee on Arbitration Report paras 11–17.
[57] *Dolling-Baker v Merret* [1990] 1 WLR 1205.
[58] *Milsom v Ablyazov* [2011] EWHC 955 (Ch).
[59] *Emmott v Michael Wilson & Partners Ltd* [2008] EWCA Civ 184.

- if a party seeks to call as a witness someone who took part in an ADR process, which a court will not normally allow;[60]
- if an application is made for a costs sanction on the basis that another party caused an ADR process to fail,[61] though the court will rarely entertain such an application, and it may be difficult for the court to decide whether a party has acted unreasonably in refusing an offer to settle.[62] In relation to an application for a costs sanction, the court will normally limit itself to material that is without prejudice save as to costs, or where the parties waive privilege.[63]

The court will normally only consider information given during an ADR process, look at a document used in an ADR process, or hear evidence from a person involved in an ADR process where there are clear reasons why this would be in the interests of justice. The key considerations are normally as follows: **5.37**

- Precisely what sort of information is in issue? In what form was the information provided, to whom, and when?
- Which of the above bases for confidentiality might apply? Often more than one basis for confidentiality will be relevant and may need to be addressed.
- Is the information available in a form that is not protected by confidentiality?
- Are relevant people prepared to waive confidentiality? Note that all relevant persons must be prepared to waive confidentiality, if, for example, an ADR agreement applies to the parties and to a third party.[64]

If relevant and potentially identifiable information was exchanged in an ADR process, is protected by confidentiality, and is not available from an alternative admissible source, a court will probably only be prepared to look at the information if the interests of justice outweigh the importance of confidentiality for ADR. The relevant principles have been largely developed in relation to the development of the without prejudice principle, see 5.17–5.26, and strong judicial statements show how slow the courts should be to look at confidential information, see 5.06. It is likely that similar principles will be followed in relation to all attempts to look at communications that form part of an ADR process. **5.38**

---

[60] *Farm Assist Ltd (in liquidation) v Secretary of State for Environment, Food and Rural Affairs (No 2)* [2009] EWHC 1102 (TCC).

[61] *Halsey v Milton Keynes General NHS Trust* [2004] EWCA Civ 576.

[62] *Reed Executive plc v Reed Business Information Ltd* [2004] 1 WLR 3026.

[63] *Société Internationale de Télécommunications Aéronautiques SC (SITA) v The Wyatt Company (UK) Limited* [2002] EWHC 2401 (Ch).

[64] *Farm Assist Ltd (in liquidation) v Secretary of State for the Environment, Food and Rural Affairs (No 2)* [2009] EWHC 1102 (TCC).

5.39 Areas where a court might be prepared to look at relevant communications in an ADR process in the interests of justice or public policy probably include:

- where it is alleged that a settlement agreement was reached as a result of fraud, misrepresentation, or economic duress;[65]
- where there is an allegation of potential negligence or a breach of contract;
- to protect the well-being of a child, or prevent a criminal act;
- where there may be a statutory duty to disclose information, for example under the Proceeds of Crime Act 2002.

---

[65] *Farm Assist Ltd (in liquidation) v Secretary of State for the Environment, Food and Rural Affairs (No 2)* [2009] EWHC 1102 (TCC).

6

ETHICS

A Professional Responsibilities in ADR

This chapter briefly summarizes principles from legal professional codes of conduct **6.01** and legal professional ethics that relate particularly to the use of alternative dispute resolution. While legal professional duties are well articulated in relation to litigation, the position is less clear in relation to ADR, where general duties may need to be interpreted in a range of circumstances; for example there may be ethical issues arising from how a case is funded when a case is settled. For those regulated by the Solicitors Regulation Authority (SRA) the relevant source is the SRA Code of Conduct 2011, the 16th version being in effect from 1 April 2016.[1] For those regulated by the Bar Standards Board the relevant source is the 9th Edition of the Code of Conduct, which is included in the Bar Standards Board Handbook Second Edition which came into force in April 2015.[2]

The approach of these Codes is outcomes based, being founded on core principles/ **6.02** duties which are mandatory, supported by other mandatory provisions and guidance relating to how the principles/duties may be met. The duties in the Codes are relatively general, and there is limited specific guidance on the responsibilities of a lawyer in relation to ADR. Practitioners will appreciate the importance of a professional and ethical approach in processes that are largely confidential and where there may be limited court oversight.

B Solicitors

For those regulated by the Solicitors Regulation Authority, the SRA Code of **6.03** Conduct 2011 Version 16 sets out ten core Principles which regulate all aspects of practice, to support the achievement of mandatory Outcomes. The SRA recognizes

---

[1] See <http://www.sra.org.uk/solicitors/handbook/code/content.page>
[2] See <https://www.barstandardsboard.org.uk/regulatory-requirements/bsb-handbook/>

that the 'Outcomes' (O) can be satisfied in a number of ways, so they are supplemented by 'Indicative Behaviours' (IB) which give guidance on what behaviour is likely to be compliant, with further guidance. The following Principles are particularly relevant to the use of ADR:

- a duty to uphold the rule of law and proper administration of justice (Principle 1);
- a duty to act with integrity (Principle 2);
- a duty not to allow personal independence to be compromised (Principle 3);
- a duty to act in the best interests of each client (Principle 4);
- a duty to provide a proper standard of service for clients (Principle 5);
- a duty to behave in a way that maintains the trust the public places in the lawyer and in the provision of legal services (Principle 6).

6.04 A solicitor should meet the following Outcomes of particular relevance to ADR:

- treat clients fairly (O 1.1) and provide services to the client in a manner which protects their interests in the dispute or matter, subject to the proper administration of justice (O 1.2). This would include considering whether a conflict of interest has arisen (IB 1.12);
- have the resources, skills and procedures to carry out the client's instructions (O 1.4);
- provide a competent service to the client, delivered in a timely manner which takes account of the client's needs and circumstances (O 1.5);
- ensure clients are in a position to make informed decisions about the services they need, how their matter will be handled, and the options available to them (O 1.12);
- ensure clients receive the best possible information, both at the time of engagement and when appropriate as the matter progresses, about the overall cost of the matter (O 1.13). This Outcome can be achieved by discussing whether the potential outcomes of a client's matter are likely to justify the expense or risk involved, including any risk of having to pay someone else's legal fees (IB 1.13), and clearly explaining the likely fees and warning about other payments for which the client may be responsible (IB 1.14 to 1.19);
- not attempt to deceive or knowingly or recklessly mislead the court, or be complicit in another person doing so (O 5.1 and 5.2 and IB 5.4 and 5.5), or construct facts supporting a client's case or draft any documents relating to any proceedings containing any contention which the solicitor does not consider to be properly arguable (IB 5.7);
- not take unfair advantage of a third party (O 11.1), nor take unfair advantage of an opposing party's lack of legal knowledge where they have not instructed a lawyer (IB 11.7), or demand anything that is not legally recoverable (IB 11.8).

C Barristers

For those regulated by the Bar Standards Board, in the Code of Conduct which **6.05** came into effect from 30 April 2015 as part of the Bar Standards Board Handbook there are ten 'Core Duties' (CD) which regulate all aspects of practice, supplemented by mandatory 'Outcomes' (O) to be met and 'Rules' (R) to be followed, with Guidance notes. Many of the Duties, Rules, and Outcomes are broadly relevant to the appropriate use of ADR to resolve a dispute, and only the most directly relevant points are covered here. A barrister must meet the following Core Duties with relevance to ADR:

- act in the best interests of each client (CD 2);
- act with integrity and honesty (CD 3);
- maintain his or her independence (CD 4) and standards of integrity and honesty, and be seen to be doing so (OC6, RC8, and RC9);
- not behave in a way likely to diminish the trust and confidence which the public place in the barrister or in the legal profession (CD 5);
- provide a competent standard of work and service for each client (CD 7); with an expectation that clients receive a competent standard of work and service (OC10).

The following rules and outcomes may also be of particular relevance to ADR. **6.06**

- A barrister should ensure that a client knows what to expect and understands the advice given to them (OC13). A client should be able to have confidence in those instructed to act for him (OC15). A barrister should take reasonable steps to avoid incurring unnecessary expense (GC38), and should not mislead a client (RC19).
- A barrister is personally responsible for her or his work (RC20), and should use personal professional judgment, being able to justify decisions and actions regardless of the views of a client, solicitor, or other person (RC20). A barrister should not accept work she or he is not competent to handle (RC21).
- Subject to client confidentiality, a barrister must report to the BSB reasonable grounds to believe that there has been serious misconduct by a barrister (RC66).
- A barrister should not knowingly or recklessly mislead or attempt to mislead anyone (RC9), and should not draft any document containing any statement or contention which is not supported by the client or by instructions, or which the barrister does not consider to be properly arguable (RC9).
- The duty to act ethically and in the interests of justice is stressed (OC6–OC9).

• A barrister should not engage in seriously offensive or discreditable conduct towards a third party (GC25).

D Acting in the Client's Best Interests

6.07 Both barristers and solicitors are required to act in the best interests of a lay client without regard to their own interests (SRA Principle 4, BSB Core Duty 2, and OC11). For a solicitor this includes ensuring that a client is in a position to make informed decisions about the services they need (O 1.12), how their matter will be handled, and the options available to them. For a barrister this includes promoting fearlessly and by all proper and lawful means the client's best interests, without regard to his own interests or to any consequences to himself or to any other person (RC15), but it should be noted that the duty to the client is subject to the duty to the court (RC4). Acting in the client's best interests is likely to include an obligation to provide advice about options for resolving a dispute using an appropriate form of ADR as well as through litigation, especially where ADR might save costs, result in a quicker settlement, or better meet the client's objectives. It is likely also that a client should be made aware of potential costs penalties if the use of ADR is unreasonably refused, and how such penalties may be avoided.

6.08 This approach is supported by judicial statements including:

• 'All members of the legal profession who conduct litigation should now routinely consider with their clients whether their disputes are suitable for ADR';[3]
• 'The court has given its stamp of approval to mediation and it is now the legal profession which must become fully aware of and acknowledge its value'.[4]

E Acting within Instructions

6.09 A lawyer has a duty to act within client instructions at all times. This duty is not covered in detail within the Codes of Conduct, but is part of various professional duties, and a matter on contract and agency law. This can be of particular importance in relation to ADR, where a lawyer may play a substantial role in relation to the outcome of the dispute in a non-adjudicative process, especially in negotiation. It is advisable for a lawyer to get clear instructions on whether ADR be used, if so what kind of ADR, and what the client's objectives are. If there is any possibility

---

[3] *Halsey v Milton Keynes NHS Trust* [2004] EWCA Civ 576 (per Dyson LJ).
[4] *Burchell v Bullard* [2005] EWCA Civ 358 (per Ward LJ).

for misunderstanding or disagreement it may be appropriate to record the client's instructions in writing. It may be appropriate for a lawyer to check instructions before a final settlement is reached, or to negotiate subject to client approval. A client who initially instructs solicitors to reach a quick financial settlement may later feel that more might have been obtained on a fuller investigation, and consider suing lawyers for negligence.[5] It is important to act within instructions to help to ensure that the client properly understands the terms of settlement.[6] If a lawyer proceeds with a case in the hope of securing some outcome despite client instructions, the lawyer may be liable to pay costs.[7] On the importance of authority to settle see 4.07–4.08.

6.10 The only exception to acting within instructions would be where this duty conflicts with a professional duty to the court, to uphold the law, or to serve the public interest in the proper administration of justice. A lawyer also has a duty to act with integrity, and not to permit his or her professional independence to be compromised. This is likely to mean that a lawyer should not accept or act on instructions to behave improperly in an ADR process. These duties may in particular be relevant to what can properly be said in a non-adjudicative process, and what strategies and tactics may properly be used, see 6.14–6.15.

F Duties in Relation to Client Confidentiality

6.11 The SRA Code of Conduct expressly provides that protection of confidential information is a fundamental feature of the relationship with a client, as a matter of law and conduct, and that this is a continuing duty (O 4.1–O 4.5 and IB 4.1–IB 4.7). The affairs of a client should be kept confidential unless disclosure is required or permitted by law or the client consents, and the duty of confidentiality to one client takes precedence over a duty to another client. Effective systems and controls must be in place to enable the solicitor to identify risks to client confidentiality and to mitigate those risks.[8]

6.12 A barrister has a core duty to keep the affairs of each client confidential (CD 6), and this is supported by guidance which provides that the duty of confidentiality is central to the administration of justice, such that clients who put their confidence in their legal advisers must be able to do so in the knowledge that the information they

---

[5] *Dutfield v Gilbert H Stephens & Sons* (1988) 18 Fam Law 473.
[6] *Marsden v Marsden* [1972] Fam 280.
[7] *Flatman v Germany* [2013] EWCA Civ 278.
[8] SRA Handbook Chapter 4 and Outcomes 4.1, 4.3, and 4.5.

give, or which is given on their behalf, will remain confidential. A barrister must protect the confidentiality of a client's affairs, save for where disclosure is required by law, or the client gives informed consent (RC15, GC42–GC45).

6.13 The strength of these professional duties of confidentiality make it clear that a lawyer should not disclose information from a client in an ADR process without the clear permission or instructions of the client. This applies to disclosure to anyone, including an independent third party. Despite the strength of the duty of confidentiality, it may conflict with the duties to act honesty, and not to mislead, see 6.14–6.15. The lawyer may need to discuss this position with the client if he or she might otherwise be professionally embarrassed. The confidentiality of the process is not absolute and there are some exceptions.[9] On the use of confidentiality clauses see 5.27–5.35.

G Duties in Relation to an Opponent

6.14 Duties in relation to an opponent are of particular importance in non-adjudicative ADR. Such a process may be conducted orally, with or without an independent third party, and without strict requirements as to proof. Strategies and tactics may be used in negotiation, and professional standards and ethics may be of importance. Although the wording of the Codes of Conduct are slightly different, and distinctions can be made, any lawyer is required to act in the interests of justice, with integrity and honesty, and should not mislead an opponent, or take unfair advantage of a third party. A lawyer should not construct facts, and should not put forward a contention which is not supported by instructions, or is not properly arguable. A lawyer should not behave in a way which is likely to diminish the trust and confidence the public place in the profession, or bring the justice system into disrepute. A lawyer would be unlikely to be acting with integrity if he or she knows that the lay client is engaging in a non-adjudicative ADR process with an improper motive (such as to delay the resolution of the matter by litigation rather than attempt to reach settlement).

6.15 The meaning of these provisions is not fully developed, but some tactical moves might breach these principles. A lawyer should not say anything to anyone else involved in an ADR process which he or she knows or suspects is not true, whatever a client may propose to obtain a more favorable bargaining position. There is no positive duty to reveal information or evidence beyond what is required in a litigation process, or what has been specified in an agreement to use ADR.

---

[9] *Emmott v Michael Wilson & Partners Ltd* [2008] EWCA Civ 184; *Westwood Shipping Lines Inc v Universal Schiffartsgesellschaft MBH* [2012] EWCA 3837 (Comm).

However a lawyer can probably not withhold information if the failure to disclose it causes other information to be significantly misleading, even if the information may be detrimental to a client's case. If false or misleading information has been given, it may be challenged during an ADR process, and may result in the process breaking down. If the problem emerges later, any settlement reached as a result of fraud or misrepresentation might be challenged. If a mediator or other neutral in an ADR process believes that a position is being misrepresented or that information given is not accurate, those concerns may be expressed to the party, and in a serious case the third party may not be prepared to continue with the process.

H Duties in Relation to a Funder

Where funding arrangements involve an external body, whether through legal aid or **6.16** third party funding, there will normally be a regulatory or contractual requirement to inform that body if a settlement offer is made, and perhaps to get the approval of that body before finalizing settlement terms. The lawyer needs to act in the best interests of the client and not of the funder.

A lawyer acting under conditional fee agreement (CFA) or a damages-based agree- **6.17** ment (DBA) will be paid at least partly from costs or damages recovered in the case. This inevitably gives rise to some interest in how quickly a case is resolved and on what terms, so an appropriate professional and ethical approach will be required. The lawyer's interest is subject to the normal duties to the client in relation to instructions and acting in the client's best interests. It is very important that a lawyer gives objective and transparent advice.

I Duties in Relation to a Court

Both barristers (OC1–OC5 and RC3–RC6) and solicitors (O 5.1–O 5.8 and IB **6.18** 5.1–IB 5.13) (though in slightly different terms) have a primary duty to the court. This may sometimes create a tension in relation to ADR which may be different to the position as regards litigation:

- the duty of confidentiality owed to a client may limit matters relating to ADR that can properly be raised in court;
- concerns about the conduct of an ADR process are not normally open to the review of the court due to the 'without prejudice' principle, see 5.17–5.26;
- assisting the court in dealing with ADR issues may create tensions with client instructions.

J Lawyers who Provide ADR

6.19 Many lawyers are also qualified to act as mediators, adjudicators, or arbitrators, or may be asked to provide an early neutral evaluation of a case. The lawyer will still be bound by the appropriate rules of legal professional conduct, and those rules may have special application to the additional role. For example, a lawyer providing ADR services must avoid any potential conflict of interest. If the solicitor, or any member of the firm, has acted or had any connection with any of the parties to a dispute, this must be disclosed to all parties, and the lawyer should not proceed unless all parties consent in writing to the provision of the agreed ADR service.[10] Although barristers are generally not permitted to make any payment for the purposes of procuring professional instructions, they are permitted to pay a reasonable fee required by an ADR provider that appoints or recommends them to conduct mediation, arbitration, or adjudication services.[11] They are also permitted to enter into a reasonable fee-sharing arrangement with such an organization on comparable terms to other mediators. If the individual holds a further qualification as a mediator or adjudicator, an additional code of conduct relevant to that role may apply, see 13.29–13.43.

---

[10] SRA Handbook Chapter 3, Principle 4, Outcome 3.1, Outcome 3.5.
[11] The continuing legality of referral fees in this situation may need to be considered in the light of LASPO 2012 ss 56–60.

7

FUNDING ADR PROCEDURES

A Expense and Funding

The potential expense of litigation, and difficulties in procuring funding, provide **7.01** major drivers for the use of ADR. The position as regards litigation has led Lord Neuberger to talk of a continuing costs crisis, saying: 'Excessive litigation cost has for too long blighted our civil justice system. It is a blight which undermines our ability to provide effective access to justice.'[1] In his Review of Costs, Lord Justice Jackson expressed the view that it should be possible for a lawyer to offer a client a budget estimate for pursuing a case through litigation, and an alternative budget estimate for an appropriate form of ADR. Making such as comparison may appropriately assist parties, lawyers, and judges in a realistic cost-benefit analysis when taking decisions in relation to dispute resolution options. The substantial rise in the fees for issuing civil proceedings and civil hearings makes ADR options potentially even more attractive in costs terms, especially prior to the issue of proceedings.[2]

Lawyers have professional conduct duties in relation to explaining the potential **7.02** expense of dispute resolution to a client, and this is likely to include the cost of appropriate ADR options as well as litigation, see 6.04. The duty applies throughout a case, so adequate advice on the comparative expense of different relevant processes should be updated as the case progresses.

This chapter outlines how the potential expense of an ADR process may be deter- **7.03** mined, and how that expense may be funded. An ADR process is normally paid for equally by the parties agreeing to use the process (though it may actually be paid by a funder such as an insurer), but this is subject to agreement and one party may agree

---

[1] Ninth Implementation Lecture, 'The Role of Alternative Dispute Resolution in Furthering the Aims of the Civil Litigation Costs Review', <https://www.judiciary.gov.uk/publications/review-of-civil-litigation-costs-lectures/>.

[2] Court fees for the High Court, county court, and family court, see <https://www.gov.uk/government/publications/fees-for-civil-and-family-courts/court-fees-for-the-high-court-county-court-and-family-court>.

to fund the process to support the use of ADR. The potential cost of mediation may be added to a form H budget in relation to costs management.

7.04 The options for funding dispute resolution are developing significantly with the growth of third party funding, and the potential use of damages-based agreements with implications for how and when ADR is used, with possible incentives for early resolution. The removal of Legal Aid funding from most types of civil dispute has made the speed and lower cost of ADR options potentially more attractive. The growing use of alternative business structures (ABSs) may lead to business models which incorporate ADR in the handling of civil claims being seen as more attractive in terms of lower and more predictable expense.

7.05 A separate consideration is who may ultimately bear the expense of the dispute resolution process. While the general rule in litigation is that the unsuccessful party will normally be ordered to pay the costs of the successful party,[3] this does not normally apply in relation to an ADR process, save where a third party such as an arbitrator is given power to make an award of costs. There may in some cases be a change as regards who pays by later agreement between the parties, by a court order as to costs, or by another cost-shifting process, see Chapter 10.

B The Potential for ADR to Save Costs

7.06 The main reasons why an ADR may be cost effective are:

- an ADR process can often be completed for a fixed agreed fee;
- the parties can to a significant extent control related expenses through the agreement they make as to the ADR process to be used;
- the parties can avoid or control the expense of processes such as disclosure, or the preparation and exchange of witness statements;
- it may be easier for lawyers to estimate the cost of time needed to prepare for an agreed ADR process than for litigation;
- the use of ADR can assist in avoiding the kind of escalation of costs that can occur in adversarial litigation in which the parties become entrenched.

7.07 An ADR process will clearly be most cost effective where the main elements of expense are most tightly controlled. Decisions about the type of process used, whether there is a hearing, who attends, where the process is held, and what information and evidence is provided can make a significant difference. A large arbitration

---

[3] CPR r 44.2(2).

can be as expensive as a trial whereas a reference to a court's small claims mediation service may be free. Most ADR processes can be carried out at various levels of expense—while mediation can be free, a mediation commonly lasts for a day, and the fee for an experienced mediator can be significant.

C The Potential Cost of an ADR Process

The range of ADR options is such that this Handbook can only provide general guidance on elements of expense, and potential fees for common options. The main elements of expense for an ADR process may be: **7.08**

- the fee for the ADR process (see 7.11–7.21);
- the lawyers' fees to cover preparatory work and advice;
- a brief fee, if counsel is instructed in connection with the ADR process;
- any other disbursements;
- the expenses of the parties attending the ADR process;
- the expenses of lawyers attending the ADR process (if they attend);
- the expenses of anyone else asked to attend the ADR process;
- the sum due for the location of the place where the process is held (if any, and if not part of the fee for the process).

An estimate for the expense of an ADR process can be prepared from these elements. The different levels of fee for a process can often be found on the websites of ADR providers, or a quotation can be sought. Inevitably some expenses are the same as, or may overlap with, the expense of litigation. Providing a comparative budget for an ADR process may be more difficult at a later stage in a case, particularly after proceedings have been issued. A contingency that may need to be considered is the position if the ADR process fails or is only partly successful, so that the cost of the ADR process might be wholly or partly thrown away. **7.09**

Most ADR processes can be provided by an ADR service provider. This can offer benefits in terms of administration of documents and process, and identifying an appropriate third party. Some of the larger providers offer a full process for a set fee, which can offer convenience. On the other hand the use of smaller providers or individuals can be more cost effective, especially if the parties are prepared to carry out some administration themselves. Fees are often payable in advance. **7.10**

Negotiation

Readers are likely to be familiar with the normal expenses of a negotiation. Negotiation will be most cost effective if carried out through the use of written **7.11** offers or by telephone, where the direct cost of the process will normally be limited to the cost of the lawyer's time to frame offers, conduct the negotiation, and draw up appropriate terms for settlement. A joint settlement meeting at a neutral location will have significant additional expenses, see 12.16–12.17.

7.12   Each party will be liable for their own expenses for a negotiation, though payment of the costs of the negotiation may be negotiated as an issue. Costs incurred in the dispute to date may also be negotiated as part of a negotiated settlement, particularly if one party effectively 'wins' on the main issues, so that the party would have been likely to have secured an order for costs had the matter gone to court. Alternatively, as a tactic, one party may offer to pay the reasonable costs of the other for the negotiation in order to secure a concession. The agreement may be for payment of an agreed sum in respect of costs, or for one party to pay the other party's costs on the standard basis, subject to detailed assessment if not agreed. If the negotiation does not result in settlement, expenses related to negotiation may form part of the costs of the proceedings, see 10.18–10.21.

Mediation

7.13   The expense of a mediation will depend on the service provider or individual mediator used. The mediator's fee will depend primarily on the qualifications and experience of the mediator, the time that the process is likely to take, and the value of the claim. A mediator may charge a set fee or an hourly or daily rate, and may expect additional payment for preparation and for travel expenses. The level of contact with the mediator and the degree of preparation by the mediator before the mediation should be agreed as part of the fee. The training and experience of an individual should be checked, although mediation provider organizations which are accredited provider members of the Civil Mediation Council, and individual members should all meet set quality standards.[4] In a challenging case a more experienced and specialist mediator might be more likely to achieve success and therefore ultimately save cost, despite charging a higher fee.

7.14   What is included in the fee should be clarified before finalizing an agreement to mediate, and whether the fee is for the process or is charged to each party. The fee may cover only the cost of the time of the mediator, or a package may include a location for the mediation and other support services. The cost of a location may be significant if it is not included as it will often be necessary to have a room big enough for everyone to meet in, and separate rooms for each party to use.

---

[4]   See <http://www.civilmediation.org>.

As a broad guideline, for lower value disputes, the government provides a website   **7.15**
with a search facility for finding local mediators who will provide mediation for a
set fee.[5] At the time of writing this offered one hour of mediation for £50 plus VAT
per party to deal with a dispute valued at up to £5,000, or four hours of mediation
for £425 plus VAT for a dispute valued at up to £50,000. Low cost or free mediation is provided by some community, charitable, and not-for-profit organizations.[6]
A commercial provider might charge £1,000 plus VAT for a claim up to £75,000, or
£2,000 plus VAT for a dispute up to £125,000. Fees will be substantially higher for
an experienced mediator dealing with a complex dispute of high value. An hourly
rate may range from £200 to £500 plus VAT, and a daily rate from £800 to £3,500
plus VAT per party.

Liability for the fee of the mediator or the mediation service provider will normally   **7.16**
be covered by the written mediation agreement. A mediation agreement is a contract,
and a court will not have power to vary its terms,[7] other than on grounds applicable
to all contracts, though in appropriate circumstances costs related to mediation may
be considered when making a detailed assessment of costs.[8] Normally the mediation
fee will be shared equally, but it may be agreed that the fee will count as costs in the
case if the dispute is not settled and goes to trial. One party might agree to pay the
whole fee if that party has greater resources, or offers to do so to persuade the other
party to mediate. The parties can agree to vary the original agreement as to fees, if
for example one party was prepared to pay the whole fee in return for a concession
by the other side, though this is not often done.

Lawyers commonly attend a mediation in a higher value case, so expenses will   **7.17**
include payment for the time of the solicitors, and the brief fee for a barrister if a
barrister is briefed to attend. In addition to attendance, the lawyer's fees will need
to cover the costs of preparing written case summaries, liaising with the mediator in
advance, and potentially of drawing up terms of settlement. The parties must attend
a mediation and this will also be an expense. Witnesses or experts may also attend
by agreement.

Arbitration

Arbitration will generally be significantly more expensive than other ADR options,   **7.18**
especially if a relatively formal procedure similar to trial is used. An arbitration

---

[5] See <http://www.civilmediation.justice.gov.uk>.
[6] See <http://www.lawworks.org.uk>.
[7] *National Westminster Bank v Feeney* [2006] EWHC 90066 (Costs).
[8] *North Oxford Golf Club v A2 Dominion Homes Ltd* [2013] EWHC 852 (QB).

conducted by a single arbitrator on the basis of paperwork without a hearing will be significantly cheaper. It will be necessary to pay the fee of the arbitrator or the arbitration service provider, which is likely to depend on the complexity and value of the case.

7.19   As a broad guideline, the fee for an arbitration may be several thousand pounds for a hearing that lasts just a day, and tens of thousands for an arbitration lasting a week or more. The Chartered Institute of Arbitrators provides Cost Controlled Arbitration Rules for disputes where no more than £50,000 is at stake.[9] A paper-based or IT-based arbitration might be charged on an hourly fee for the arbitrator and could cost only a few hundred pounds. The payment of the arbitration fee will normally be covered by the arbitration agreement, which commonly provides for the fee to be shared equally by the parties.

7.20   Other expenses, depending on whether there is a hearing, may include the fees of the lawyers, the expenses of the parties (who often attend as witnesses), and of any other attendees. The expense of the location where the arbitration takes place may be substantial, especially in an international arbitration. The expenses incurred by each party before and at the arbitration will be borne by the party, although often the arbitrator is given discretion to make orders about the tribunal's fees and the parties' costs. It should be noted that costs management and the principle of proportionality will not apply in arbitration unless the parties so agree.

Early neutral evaluation, expert determination, and adjudication

7.21   The cost of an early neutral evaluation, an expert determination, or adjudication will depend on whether the process agreed is paper based or includes oral evidence and representations. The fee charged by the neutral third party or expert is likely to depend on the complexity of the case, the issues on which advice or decision is sought, and therefore the time the case is likely to take. The cost might typically be from £250 to £600 an hour. The other main element of expense will be the fees charged by the lawyers in preparing the papers for consideration and briefing the expert. Assistance with arranging independent expert determination or adjudication, or identifying an appropriate expert is offered by many ADR providers and professional organizations. A fee is likely to be charged for finding a suitable third party, which will be additional to the fee charged by the third party.[10]

---

[9] See for example <http://www.ciarb.org>.
[10] See for example <http://www.arbitrators.org>, <http://www.cedr.com>.

D Funding Bases for an ADR Process

The way in which a case is funded should have no direct impact on the way in **7.22** which it is conducted, or any dispute resolution process chosen. However funding may be relevant to the attractiveness of using an ADR process, to who needs to agree directly or indirectly to the use of ADR process, to who will pay for the ADR process, to the relative attractiveness of potential terms of settlement, and to who has to agree to final settlement terms. Insurers and third party funders may have financial objectives that are not identical to the objectives of a client. Expansion of the use of DBAs and fixed costs may increase the attraction of settlement, but may also raise issues.

The details and potential complexities of different funding options are beyond the **7.23** scope of this Handbook. In terms of principles:

- however a case is funded, it should be conducted in the best interests of the party;
- any funding agreement should envisage the possibility of settlement, and provide as clearly as possible for the proper management of an ADR process.

Self-funding

The self-funding client is likely to be closely concerned with the likely cost **7.24** effectiveness of ADR options. More transparency about costs through costs budgets and costs management, and greater client awareness of ADR, may support this.

Insurance

An insurer may take a relatively standardized approach to the use of ADR. There **7.25** may be complexities relating to the terms of the insurance policy, if, for example, legal costs are only covered up to a set amount (and especially if that amount potentially covers any cost liability to the other side as well as the party's own costs). Such a term might make the early use of cost-effective ADR important.

The active after the event (ATE) insurance market may protect a party against the **7.26** risk of having to pay the costs of the other side, but premiums can be substantial, and have ceased to be recoverable in respect of funding arrangements entered into on or after 1 April 2013. However ATE insurance continues to be used to manage risk, and this may be a factor in an ADR process. It may be a term of such insurance that a reasonable offer to settle should be accepted. An unrecoverable premium will affect the figure that the client is left with, though it may be possible to negotiate an overall figure that lessens the effect of this. It is a practical issue that ATE insurance is not necessary if a case is settled before issue, but the premium is lower if cover is secured early.

Third party or litigation funding

7.27   It is increasingly common for cases to be funded by third parties, who will bear the expense of dispute resolution in return for a share of damages recovered. Such arrangements have been held not to breach principles of maintenance and champerty.[11] A voluntary 'Code of Conduct for Litigation Funders' and a set of Rules have been drawn up by the Association of Litigation Funders of England and Wales.[12] The Code includes provision for a written Litigation Funding Agreement (LFA), which should state whether and if so how the funder may have any input into decisions relating to settlement, but this is a general provision and issues may emerge as the third party funder may have different views from the party on the relative merits of litigation and ADR. The lawyer should of course act in the best interests of the client.

Conditional fee agreement (CFA)

7.28   If a client enters a conditional fee agreement (CFA) there is a shift in some of the dynamics and arithmetic relevant to ADR options. The client will not pay legal fees if the claim is lost, may pay up to 100 per cent success fee if the case is won, and is likely to be left liable to pay disbursements. A solicitor funding disbursements may be subject to a costs order if the case is lost.[13] These points may have implications for how a client views ADR options, budgets, and potential terms of settlement. A CFA should provide as clearly as possible for the potential use of an ADR process, including what should happen if the case is settled. Settlement of the case will normally mean that the fee and success fee are payable to the lawyer, depending on the outcome reached. A claimant may be motivated to settle to keep disbursements down.

7.29   The overall figure that the client will be left with needs to be considered in relation to the terms of settlement. An unrecoverable success fee (and any ATE premium) will come from the claimant's damages, meaning that they will in effect be met from the sum the party receives,[14] though a lawyer may sometimes reduce a success fee

---

[11]   *Arkin v Borchard Lines* [2005] EWCA Civ 655.
[12]   Rules of the Association of Litigation Funders of England and Wales, <http://associationoflitigationfunders.com>.
[13]   *Cill Germany v Gavin Flatman* [2011] EWHC 2945 (QB).
[14]   'Review of Civil Litigation Costs: Final Report', Chapters 9 and 10 and Recommendations 7, 8, and 9.

to help to ensure agreement. Competition may drive down the level of success fees to attract clients, but client expectations may need to be managed carefully so that realistic offers are not turned down because the client is concerned about how little will be left in his or her pocket in a low value case. A negotiation or mediation may provide that the costs and success fee of a winning party are paid by the other side, but this can be a very contentious issue. Note that the success fee does not have to be revealed in advance as part of discussions as this would disclose the lawyer's view of the chance of success, but otherwise there are clear rules relating to notifying the other side where a party has CFA funding. For CFA agreements entered into before 1 April 2013, useful guidance for lawyers and mediators can be found in a paper published by the Civil Mediation Council.[15]

Damages-based agreements (DBA)

For funding arrangements entered into on or after 1 April 2013 it is possible for a **7.30** lawyer to take a case on the basis of being paid from any damages recovered.[16] The Damages-Based Agreements Regulations 2013[17] provide that a range of specified information must be given before a DBA is entered into, including a reasonable estimate of likely expenses. The circumstances in which the representative's payment, expenses, or costs, or part of them, are payable must be included in the terms and conditions of a DBA. This should cover not just the possibility that the case may settle, but define what will count as success, and perhaps also the mode of settlement, though it may be difficult to provide in advance for a range of potential ADR issues. There are caps of up to 50 per cent of recovered damages becoming payable as the lawyers' fee, but issues as to which damages will be taken into account may have significant implications for the terms of settlement.

In principle, DBAs should operate in many ways like CFAs. If clients see costs as **7.31** significantly reducing damages, then challenges to fees charged and demands for detailed assessments between lawyer and own client may well grow, though such disputes may be addressed through a process such as mediation. It is unlikely there will be an adverse costs order against a lawyer acting under a DBA.[18] In practical terms a good return may be achieved by a lawyer who works under a DBA and settles a case quickly, but there is a professional duty to ensure the form of funding is

---

[15] 'Mediation, CFCs and Conflicts of Interest', <http://www.civilmediation.org>.
[16] Legal Aid, Sentencing and Punishment of Offenders Act 2012 ss 44–45 which amends Courts and Legal Services Act 1990 s 58AA.
[17] The Damages-Based Agreements Regulations 2013.
[18] *Hodgson v Imperial Tobacco Ltd* [1998] 1 WLR 1056, but see also *Myatt v National Coal Board* [2007] 1 WLR 1559.

in the client's best interests. There has been limited use of DBAs to date, but it is possible the use will grow if there is a change in regulation following the recommendation of the Civil Justice Council,[19] and any revised rules on calculating what is paid under a DBA could have implications for settlement options.

Legal Aid Agency funding

7.32 If a party is publicly funded, lawyers have a range of duties in relation to funding and ADR. From 1 April 2013, with the removal of public funding from most types of civil dispute, these duties will have decreasing relevance as funded cases are concluded.[20] A party with Legal Aid Agency (LAA) (formerly Legal Services Commission) funding is in a relatively strong position in that the other side will face paying their own costs even if they win,[21] so are more likely to make an offer to settle.

- A party in receipt of public funding can be required by the LAA to attempt mediation before litigation, unless the dispute is not suitable.[22]
- LAA funding may cover the reasonable costs of negotiation or mediation if that is the most cost effective way of proceeding, but this should be checked in each case.[23]
- The LAA provides mediation through contracted providers for fixed fees.[24]
- The costs of processes such as early neutral evaluation or expert determination may be covered as a disbursement.
- Funding may not cover a trial unless reasonable attempts to settle have been made.
- A lawyer has an obligation to report a refusal of any reasonable offer to settle, and funding may be withdrawn.[25]
- The LAA must be told of a Part 36 offer, as the impact on success is relevant to funding. If an assisted party fails to beat a Part 36 offer they will have to pay the defendant's costs, and a case may need to be compromised to avoid such an effect.
- A client with LAA funding may be in a weaker position in that the LAA statutory charge may reduce the sum the client receives. This may be relevant to terms for settlement.

---

[19] The Damages-Based Agreements Reform Project, Civil Justice Council, August 2015.
[20] Legal Aid, Sentencing and Punishment of Offenders Act 2012 Part 1 and Sch 1.
[21] Administration of Justice Act 1920 s 11.
[22] *R (Cowl and other) v Plymouth City Council* [2002] 1 WLR 803.
[23] The Civil Legal Aid (Merits Criteria) Regulations 2013, and The Civil Legal Aid (Procedures) Regulations 2012.
[24] LSC Mediation Quality Mark Standard (MQMS) (3rd edn, 2012).
[25] The Civil Legal Aid (Merits Criteria) Regulations 2013, and The Civil Legal Aid (Procedures) Regulations 2012.

Other options

The opening up of funding possibilities raises some issues and questions in relation to   **7.33**
the use of ADR, but may also extend potential advantages in offering and using ADR.
A lawyer can offer for a fixed fee advice and analysis of a case, including advice on how
a client might pursue an ADR option such as mediation. A lawyer can represent a client on the basis the lawyer will not get a success fee under a CFA or a share of damages
under a DBA, but simply be paid through costs recovered if and when the case is won.
The lawyer could be at risk in relation to a possible adverse costs order, but it is acceptable for a solicitor to take on this risk,[26] and a solicitor indemnifying a client in respect
of disbursements will not normally be open to an adverse third party costs order.[27]

E Costs Management and Proportionality

The increased powers of the court to manage costs, and the new test for proportional-   **7.34**
ity in relation to costs, introduced from 1 April 2013, are making the potential cost of
litigation more transparent, and the relative cost effectiveness of ADR options clearer.

Costs management

Costs management applies to many multi-track cases commenced after 1 April 2013   **7.35**
unless the case is subject to fixed costs or it is otherwise ordered,[28] and to other cases
if the court so orders.[29] Costs management takes place alongside case management
to further the overriding objective and provide judges with a more proactive role,[30]
and Form H specifically provides for estimates of ADR costs to be given. The parties are encouraged to seek to agree costs budgets, but if they do not the court may
make a costs management order.[31] The budgets may be revised as the case progresses,
and reapproved if not agreed. It may be important to revise the budget with ADR
options and progress in mind, as on assessing costs on a standard basis the court
will have regard to the receiving party's last approved or agreed budget, and will not
depart from that unless there is good reason to do so.[32] The courts have endorsed the

---

[26] *Sibthorpe & Morris v London Borough of Southwark* [2011] EWCA Civ 25.
[27] *Flatman v Germany* [2013] EWCA Civ 278.
[28] CPR Part 3 Section II, inserted by the Civil Procedure (Amendment) Rules 2013.
[29] CPR rr 3.12–3.18 and Practice Direction 3E, Precedent H, Practice Direction 3E—Costs
Management, and CPR r 3.13.
[30] 'Review of Civil Litigation Costs, Final Report' Chapter 40 and Recommendations 89 and
92, and 'Costs Management: A Necessary Part of the Management of Litigation' Sixteenth Lecture,
<http://www.judiciary.gov.uk/publications-and-reports/review-of-civil-litigation-costs/lectures>.
[31] CPR r 3.15, 3.16, and 3.17.
[32] CPR r 3.18 and PD 43–48 Costs Section 6; *Henry v Mirror Group Newspapers* [2013] EWCA Civ 19.

benefits the budgeting can bring,[33] and once a budget is approved it is likely to be difficult to persuade a court to allow a revised budget simply because of inadequacies or mistakes.[34] In exceptional circumstances a costs capping order can limit the amount of future costs a party may recover pursuant to a later order for costs where there is a substantial risk that costs will be disproportionately incurred without such an order, but ADR options may be considered if such an order is sought.[35] In the context of ADR, the emphasis on the parties agreeing cost budgets if possible opens up possibilities for ADR options.[36] The Pilot found that costs management assisted parties in understanding their potential liability in relation to costs, and could assist with settlement, and this has also happened in practice.

7.36　Revised Guidance Notes on Precedent H were issued in June 2015. These notes indicate that estimated settlement costs should include negotiation, making Part 36 and other offers, advice to the client on ADR, and drafting a settlement agreement or order. The costs of mediation should be included as a contingency. The pre-action costs in the budget should include as relevant settlement discussion and advising on settlement and Part 36 offers. There remain some differences of opinion in practice as to how far potential settlement should be included in an initial budget, or whether an application should be made to vary the budget if a significant sum is required for ADR as the case develops.

Proportionality

7.37　The concept of proportionality was compromised by the decision that costs could be recovered if they were shown to be necessarily and reasonably incurred, even if the overall level of costs was not proportionate to the sum in dispute,[37] sometimes allowing recoverable costs to dwarf the sum in dispute.[38] There has been substantial judicial criticism in a range of cases where costs have grown out of proportion to the sum in dispute.[39] In an extreme case a claimant may technically win, but this may

---

[33] *Slick Seatings Systems v Adams* [2013] EWHC B8 (Mercantile).

[34] *Murray v Neil Dowlman Architecture Ltd* [2013] EWHC 872 (TCC).

[35] CPR r 3 Section III and Practice Direction 3F—Costs Capping, Practice Direction 44—General Rules about Costs sub-section 3—Costs Budgets as inserted by the Civil Procedure (Amendment) Rules 2013.

[36] CPR r 3.15(2) Practice Direction 3E—Costs Management paras 4 and 6.

[37] *Lownds v Home Office* [2002] EWCA Civ 365.

[38] 'Review of Civil Litigation Costs: Final Report' Chapters 3 and 4 and Recommendation 1 and 'Proportionate Costs', Lecture 15 of the Implementation Programme, <http://www.judiciary.gov.uk/publications-and-reports/review-of-civil-litigation-costs/lectures>.

[39] *Shovelar v Lane* [2011] EWCA Civ 802 (per Ward LJ); *Samuel Smith Old Brewery (Tadcaster) v Lee (t/a Cropton Brewery)* [2011] EWHC 1879 (Ch); *Egan v Motor Services (Bath) Ltd* [2007] EWCA Civ 1002 (CA); *Sutradhar v Natural Environment Research Council* [2006] 4 All ER 490; and *Finesse Group Ltd v Bryson Products* [2013] EWHC 3273 (TCC).

not be viewed by the court as success if costs are wholly disproportionate.[40] Such an approach to the recovery of costs in litigation tends not to encourage the use of ADR, and can create obstacles to settlement when costs are high.

The concept of proportionality has been more deeply embedded in the CPR by amendment to the overriding objective.[41] In addition for cases commenced after 1 April 2013 costs must be reasonably incurred and reasonable in amount, and proportionate to the sums in issue, the value of any non-monetary relief in issue, the complexity of the litigation, work generated by the paying party, and wider matters such as public importance to be recoverable.[42] This revised approach to case and cost management, and to the recoverability of costs, is likely to encourage the use of ADR if costs incurred in litigation may not be recoverable. A budget will not be approved where it is disproportionate or unreasonable in relation to the sum that may be recovered,[43] and costs will not necessarily be reasonable and proportionate just because they fall within an agreed budget.[44] If the costs of litigation are potentially disproportionate, ADR may be almost inevitable for a party who is not rich. There has been academic comment on the importance of implementing the test for proportionality effectively.[45] **7.38**

F Overall Financial Analysis and Risk

The range of potential methods for resolving a civil dispute, the increasing range of funding options, and the use of costs budgeting and the proportionality test in litigation show the importance of cost-benefit analysis, and consideration of risk management, of a kind that might be undertaken before entering a commercial transaction. This process is likely to need to take into account: **7.39**

- the damages realistically claimed in the case;
- the chances of success;
- the comparative cost of litigation and of an appropriate ADR process;
- the proportionate cost of each stage of litigation;
- the extent to which expense has already been incurred;
- the possibility that liability for costs may shift, see 10.08–10.24;
- the extent to which it may be possible to manage risk, for example through a Part 36 offer, see 10.25–10.31.

---

[40] *Marcus v Medway Primary Care Trust* [2011] EWCA Civ 750.
[41] CPR r 1.1, as amended by the Civil Procedure (Amendment) Rules 2013.
[42] CPR r 44.3 and CPR r 1.1(2).
[43] *Willis v MJR Rundell & Associates Ltd* [2013] EWHC 2923 (TCC).
[44] *Tray Foods v Manton* [2013] EWCA Civ 615.
[45] Sorabji J, 'Prospects for Proportionality: Jackson Implementation', (2013) 32 CJQ 213.

8

ADR PRIOR TO THE ISSUE
OF PROCEEDINGS

A The Context where No Proceedings have been Issued

8.01 The majority of civil disputes settle without the issue of proceedings. In these cases there are specific considerations as regards the use of ADR because, with the exception of a small number of cases where pre-issue applications are appropriate, a court will not be involved.

- A court may be prepared to make a pre-action order to facilitate ADR, see 8.06.
- Agreements to use ADR will need to be made without the support of a judge, so that it may be important to persuade another party to use ADR, see 4.23–4.32.
- There are limited circumstances in which a court can record the terms of a settlement reached without issue of proceedings in an order, see 8.08–8.09.
- There are limited circumstances in which an order as to costs can be made by the court where a case is settled prior to issue, see 8.10–8.13.

8.02 The consideration of ADR options as soon as possible in a civil dispute is key to securing greatest benefit from the use of ADR, and an approach that envisages settlement may prevent the escalation of the dispute. There is strong judicial support for the settlement of disputes wherever possible without resorting to the courts. Senior judges have said that 'insufficient attention is paid to the paramount importance of avoiding litigation whenever this is possible',[1] and that 'only those cases which truly call for, truly require, formal adjudication (should) utilise the limited resources available to the justice system'.[2] There have been a number of cases where

---

[1] *R (Cowl) v Plymouth City Council* [2002] 1 WLR 803 (per Lord Woolf); *MD v Secretary of State for the Home Department* [2011] EWCA Civ 453; *R (on the application of S) v Hampshire County Council* [2009] EWHC 2537 (Admin).

[2] Lord Neuberger, Master of the Rolls, The Fourth Keating Lecture 19 May 2010, 'Equity, ADR, Arbitration and the Law: Different Dimensions of Justice'.

a judge has expressed a clear view that a dispute should have been resolved without recourse to the courts.[3]

A revised version of the Practice Direction—Pre-action Conduct and Protocols **8.03** came into effect from 6 April 2015. The revised version increases the focus on ADR, aiming to enable the parties to understand each other's position, and to settle the issue between them without the need to start proceedings.[4] There should be a final review before proceedings are issued to see if proceedings can be avoided or issues narrowed.[5] Proceedings should only be issued as a last resort, and not normally while ADR is being actively explored, or as a purely mechanical step.[6] While ADR is not compulsory, specific options are set out with references to sources of further information.[7] The parties should continue to consider the possibility of reaching a settlement at all times, including after proceedings have been started.[8]

Pre-action consideration of ADR will inevitably be shaped by the possible impli- **8.04** cations if proceedings are issued, and the courts are taking an increasingly strict view of what is expected and evidence required, see 8.22:[9] if a party refuses to use ADR at a pre-action stage, but if it were used it had a reasonable chance of being successful, that party may be at risk of being ordered to pay subsequent costs of litigation.

An existing contractual agreement may provide for the immediate use of ADR, **8.05** specifying a particular ADR process to be used, or steps that need to be undertaken before litigation can be commenced, see 3.04–3.05. If necessary, such a clause will be enforced by a court, see 9.27–9.35.

B Powers of the Court Prior to Issue of Proceedings

A court will not have general powers to support the use of ADR at the pre-action **8.06** stage, but a judge may be prepared to use appropriate powers to make an order to support the use of ADR, for example ordering pre-action disclosure of a document relevant to the use of ADR.

---

[3] *Faidi v Elliot Corporation* [2012] EWCA Civ 287 (per Jackson LJ).
[4] Practice Direction—Pre-action Conduct and Protocols para 3.
[5] Practice Direction—Pre-action Conduct and Protocols para 6.
[6] *Bobby Prior v Silverline International* [2015] (unreported).
[7] Practice Direction—Pre-action Conduct and Protocols, para 10.
[8] Practice Direction—Pre-action Conduct and Protocols, para 9.
[9] *Fons HF v Corporal Ltd* [2013] EWHC 1278 (Ch).

C Part 36 Offers Prior to Issue

8.07   A Part 36 offer can be made before the issue of proceedings, see 10.25–10.31. In many cases, sufficient information should become available at the pre-action stage to enable a Part 36 offer to be formulated, and making such an offer may protect the position of a party. Making a Part 36 offer alone may not be considered a reasonable attempt to use ADR prior to the issue of proceedings as it does not provide for the exploration of issues or options.[10] However the fact that a Part 36 offer has been made might be part of a later argument in relation to a sanction.

D Settlements Reached with No Issue of Proceedings

8.08   If no proceedings have been issued the court cannot normally be involved in making a consent order. This has implications for enforcement as a separate action would need to be brought to enforce the settlement. Where a non-adjudicative ADR process such as negotiation or mediation has been used, a settlement reached before any proceedings have been issued will normally be recorded as a contract. The terms can then be enforced, if necessary, by bringing an action to enforce that contract, see Chapter 18. Where an adjudicative process has been used the resulting decision may equally be enforceable on the basis of contractual principles, as the parties will normally have agreed to the process in writing. For the enforcement of an arbitral award see Chapter 25.

8.09   There is an exception in the case of a cross-border mediation within the EU, see 17.35–17.36.[11]

E Pre-Action Costs

8.10   In a settlement reached without issue of proceedings the court will normally have no power to make any order as to costs.[12] The terms of the settlement should therefore incorporate any agreement as to costs. If there is no term, each party will bear their own costs. However if there is an agreement on all issues, including who should pay costs, and that is recorded in writing save that the amount has not been agreed,

---

[10]   *P4 Ltd v Unite Integrated Solutions plc* [2007] BLR 1.
[11]   Article 6 of the EU Directive on Mediation in Civil and Commercial Cases (Directive 2008/52/EC).
[12]   *President of India v La Pintada Cia Navegacion* [1984] 2 All ER 773; *BCT Software Solutions Ltd v C Brewer & Sons Ltd* [2003] EWCA Civ 939.

proceedings can be brought for the assessment of costs.[13] Costs only proceedings should only be issued once the parties have made a serious bona fide attempt to agree costs.[14]

If proceedings are later issued, the court's powers to make an order as to costs **8.11** include a power to make an order in relation to costs incurred before proceedings have begun.[15] The court can take into account offers to settle,[16] and an offer to settle made at a pre-action stage that ought reasonably to have been accepted but was not could lead to substantial unnecessary litigation costs. The court can also take into account the conduct of the parties at the pre-action stage.[17]

Although cost budgets are not required until proceedings are issued, when approv- **8.12** ing a cost budget a judge will not approve any costs already incurred, but may record comments on those costs, and take those costs into account when deciding if later costs are reasonable and proportionate.[18] The pre-action costs in the budget should include as relevant settlement discussion and advising on settlement and Part 36 offers.

In principle at the pre-action stage the parties should act in a proportion- **8.13** ate manner in all dealings with one another, and the proportionality of steps taken when compared to the size and importance of the matter is relevant to the assessment of compliance.[19] Parties should supply sufficient information to allow them to understand each other's position and make informed deci-sions about settlement, but the cost of identifying and exchanging information should not exceed what is reasonably required at a pre-action stage. It remains to be seen what impact the new test of proportionality will have on pre-action costs, see 7.37–7.38.

F Practice Direction Pre-Action Conduct and Protocols Requirements

The detail of these provisions is beyond the scope of this Handbook, but their focus **8.14** on settlement and the use of ADR at the pre-action stage has important implications. Key aims are to enable parties to settle the dispute between them without the need to

---

[13] CPR r 44.14.

[14] *Knowles v Goldborn (t/a Mercian Marble)* [2014] (Lawtel 29/1/14, Walsall CC, 6 January 2014).

[15] CPR r. 44.2, Senior Courts Act 1981, s 51.

[16] CPR r 44.2(4).

[17] CPR r 44.2(5)(a), Practice Direction—Pre-action Conduct and Protocols paras 13–16.

[18] Practice Direction 3E— para 2.4.

[19] Practice Direction—Pre-action Conduct and Protocols para 4.

start proceedings, and to support efficient management of proceedings that cannot be avoided.[20] This Practice Direction applies in all cases where no specific Pre-action Protocol applies, but the specific Protocols have similar terms. Sufficient fulfilment of the requirements is essentially a matter of what is appropriate for the dispute, and is accepted by the parties. It is specifically provided that only reasonable and proportionate steps need to be taken and the Practice Direction should not be used tactically to gain an unfair advantage. Disproportionate costs will not be recoverable.[21]

8.15 The core requirements are as follows, and a failure to comply can be met with a range of sanctions:[22]

- an exchange of letters with the claimant providing concise details of the claim, the basis on which it is made, a summary of the facts, what the claimant wants from the defendant and, if money, how the amount is calculated. In reply the defendant should confirm whether the claim is accepted and, if it is not accepted, the reasons why, together with an explanation as to which facts and parts of the claim are disputed and whether the defendant is making a counterclaim as well, providing details of any counterclaim;
- the disclosure of key documents relevant to the issues in dispute by the parties. A failure to provide information that could facilitate ADR may be penalized in costs.[23]

8.16 There are several provisions which specifically encourage the parties to consider using an appropriate form of ADR:

- before issuing proceedings the parties are expected to try to settle the issues without proceedings, and to consider a form of ADR to assist with settlement;[24]
- litigation should be a last resort, and the parties should consider whether negotiation or some other form of ADR might enable them to settle their dispute without commencing proceedings;[25]
- forms of ADR that may be appropriate are specifically named, including negotiation, mediation, arbitration, early neutral evaluation, Ombudsmen schemes, and Part 36 offers;[26]

---

[20] Practice Direction—Pre-action Conduct and Protocols para 3.
[21] Practice Direction—Pre-action Conduct and Protocols paras 4 and 5, 'Review of Civil Litigation Costs: Final Report' Chapter 35 and Recommendation 73.
[22] Practice Direction—Pre-action Conduct and Protocols, paras 6 and 13–16.
[23] *AP(UK) Ltd v West Midland Fire and Civil Defence Authority* [2013] EWHC 385 (QB); *Webb Resolutions Ltd v Waller Needham & Green (a firm)* [2012] EWHC 3529 (Ch).
[24] Practice Direction—Pre-action Conduct and Protocols para 3 (c) and (d).
[25] Practice Direction—Pre-action Conduct and Protocols para 8.
[26] Practice Direction—Pre-action Conduct and Protocols paras 9 and 10.

- the court may decide that there has been a failure of compliance when a party has unreasonably refused to use a form of ADR, or failed to respond at all to an invitation to do so;[27]
- where a dispute has not been resolved, the parties should review their respective positions, considering the papers and the evidence to see if proceedings can be avoided, or at least the issues narrowed, before the claimant issues proceedings.[28]

8.17 The court can monitor compliance with the pre-action requirements, making orders or imposing sanctions at a later stage:[29]

- The Directions Questionnaire (Fast Track and Multi-track) asks in Section C whether the pre-action protocol has been fully complied with, and for an explanation of any failure to comply or partial compliance. Any failure to comply may be relevant to directions given.[30]
- If proceedings are issued, the parties may be required by the court to provide evidence that ADR has been considered.[31] The parties should continue to consider the possibility of reaching a settlement at all times, including after proceedings have been started.[32]
- Compliance may be relevant to an order for costs, and the court may for example take a strict view of a failure to respond to a pre-action offer of ADR,[33] though if both sides act unreasonably the court may not impose a costs penalty on either side.[34]

8.18 The specific Pre-action Protocols set out the steps that the parties should follow as part of reasonable pre-action conduct in specific types of case. They have similar objectives to the Practice Direction Pre-action Conduct, and all specifically encourage the parties to consider whether some form of ADR would be more suitable than litigation.

G Making Reasonable Attempts to Settle where no Proceedings have been Issued

8.19 The Practice Direction Pre-action Conduct and Protocols requirements are relatively general. The majority of cases settle without issue of proceedings, so reasonable

---

27 Practice Direction—Pre-action Conduct and Protocols para 14.
28 Practice Direction—Pre-action Conduct and Protocols para 12.
29 Practice Direction—Pre-action Conduct and Protocols paras 13–16.
30 Practice Direction—Pre-action Conduct and Protocols para 13.
31 Practice Direction—Pre-action Conduct and Protocols para 11.
32 Practice Direction—Pre-action Conduct and Protocols para 9.
33 *Nelson's Yard Management Company v Eziefula* [2013] EWCA Civ 235.
34 Practice Direction—Pre-action Conduct and Protocols para 13; *Norbrook Laboratories Ltd v Carr* [2013] EWHC 476(QB).

compliance will be a matter for the parties to deal with as appropriate in inter-party communications. In addition to specific requirements, there may be a wider expectation of reasonable behaviour. A party who frustrates the potential use of ADR at an early stage by exaggerating a claim may be penalized in costs,[35] especially if this is accompanied by concealment of facts.[36] However an optimistic exaggeration that can be addressed by challenging a claim using available evidence will not be penalized.[37]

8.20 If there is a possibility that proceedings may be issued, it should be noted that a concern about the use of ADR should be raised at the time so that it can be addressed, and that sufficient contemporaneous evidence in relation to the use of ADR should be retained,[38] as such evidence might be needed to support or defend a later application to court.[39] Relevant evidence might include letters, emails and notes of meetings and telephone conversations between lawyer and client, and possibly a counsel's opinion, in addition to communications with the other side. It may be advisable to capture in writing matters noted in 8.21–8.22 that might not otherwise be recorded. Such material is likely to be covered by legal professional privilege, see 5.15–5.16, but this may need to be waived if an issue arises. Without prejudice protection is likely to apply, see 5.17–5.26 which can only be waived by a joint waiver by both sides. The use of open letters, or letters that are without prejudice save as to costs is to be preferred to avoid difficulties. Contemporaneous evidence of non-compliance by the other side should be retained for use in a possible application in litigation.

Proposing ADR

8.21 Reasonable consideration of the use of ADR before claim might include the following:

- advice from the lawyer to the client on the potential benefits of ADR, the types of ADR that might best suit the case, and the timing of the use of ADR;
- evidence of consideration of ADR options by the client, and the decision taken;
- if no form of ADR is thought appropriate, specific reasons why;
- a proposal to the other side as regards the reasonable use of ADR;
- a request to the other side in relation to any particular steps identified to facilitate the use of ADR;

---

[35] *Painting v Oxford University* [2005] PIQR Q5.
[36] *Widlake v BAA Ltd* [2010] PIQR P4.
[37] *Fox v Foundation Piling Ltd* [2011] 6 Costs LR 961.
[38] *PGF II SA v OMFS Company* [2012] EWHC 83 (TCC).
[39] *Halsey v Milton Keynes General NHS Trust* [2004] 1 WLR 3002.

- if the decision taken by a client might not be considered objectively reasonable, advice from the lawyer as regards the potential risks;
- the provision of sufficient information about the matters in dispute for the other party to make informed decisions about settlement, or reasons why it was inappropriate to provide such information;
- that proceedings were only started as a matter of last resort, because settlement could not be further explored at that time.

Responding to a proposal to use ADR

Responding to a proposal in relation to ADR made before claim might include the following: **8.22**

- if the proposal is accepted, any terms in relation to the acceptance;
- if a proposal is refused, sufficient reasons to show that the refusal is reasonable. A failure to reply might be seen as a refusal to engage in ADR.[40] A rejection of the use of ADR before issue of proceedings may be penalized,[41] though the failure may be balanced against other factors.[42] For case law on where a court may regard it as not unreasonable to refuse to use ADR,[43] see Chapter 11;
- if there is a concern about the use of ADR that might be addressed, that the concern is raised with the other party at the time;
- if there may be a request for further relevant information before a decision on ADR is taken;
- if one form of ADR is not thought suitable, a more appropriate form may be proposed,[44] and this is best done at the time and not in a later unrelated offer;[45]
- letters may usefully address the 'Halsey' factors relevant to the use of ADR (see 11.07–11.22), but should do so in ways which engage sufficiently with the details of the case in question.

The most significant risk of an insufficient response is that, if proceedings are issued, a sanction may be imposed, see 11.05–11.06, or an adverse order as to costs made. A court may ask the parties to explain what steps were taken to comply with the   **8.23**

---

[40] *PGF II SA v OMFS Company* [2012] EWHC 83 (TCC) (per Mr Recorder Furst QC), *PGF II SA v OMFS Co 1 Ltd* [2014] 1 WLR 1386 (CA) (Civ Div) (per Briggs LJ), Practice Direction—Pre-action Conduct and Protocols paras 11 and 14.

[41] *Jarrom v Sellers* [2007] EWHC 1366 (Ch); *Kupeli v Sirketi (t/a Cyprus Turkish Airlines)* [2016] EWHC 1478 (QB).

[42] *Seeff v Ho* [2011] EWCA Civ 186.

[43] *Euroption Strategic Fund Ltd v Scandinaviska Enskilda Banken AB* [2012] EWHC 749 (Comm).

[44] Practice Direction—Pre-action Conduct Annex A, para 4.2(4); *Corenso (UK) Ltd v Burnden Group plc* [2003] EWHC 1805 (QB).

[45] *Rolf v De Guerin* [2011] EWCA Civ 78.

Practice Direction Pre-action Conduct and Protocols, and may ask a party to explain any failure to comply,[46] requiring evidence.

H Potential Justifications for Non-Compliance

8.24 There are some circumstances in which non-compliance with pre-action requirements may be justified, though a court may be slow to accept non-compliance that is not clearly justified, especially if it frustrates settlement or increases costs unnecessarily.

- If the relevant limitation period is about to expire it may be necessary to issue proceedings to ensure that they are issued in time. Pre-action requirements should be satisfied so far as is reasonably possible in the time available. If proceedings are started to comply with the statutory time limit before the parties have followed the procedures in the Practice Direction or a relevant pre-action protocol, the parties should apply to the court for a stay of the proceedings while they comply.[47]
- A need to take action urgently may justify a failure to comply with pre-action requirements where, for example, telling another potential party in advance would defeat the purpose of an application, as would be likely to be the case in an application for a freezing injunction. However even in a case of urgency, the parties should still comply with the pre- action process to the extent it is reasonable to do so.

8.25 Non-compliance by another party will not in itself provide an excuse for failing to comply with pre-action requirements. The appropriate course of action is to raise the non-compliance specifically so it can be addressed if possible, and keep evidence of the non-compliance by the other side, rather than being lured into mirroring non-compliance.

---

[46] Practice Direction—Pre-action Conduct and Protocols paras 13–16; *R (Cowl) v Plymouth City Council* [2002] 1 WLR 803.

[47] Practice Direction—Pre-action Conduct and Protocols para 17.

PART 2

INTERPLAY BETWEEN ADR, CPR, AND LITIGATION

9

THE APPROACH OF THE COURTS TO ADR

A Introduction

Lord Justice Jackson in the 'Review of Civil Litigation Costs: Final Report' reported **9.01** that ADR, particularly mediation, has a vital role to play in reducing the costs of civil disputes, by encouraging the early settlement of cases. Parties should be encouraged to settle their dispute before resorting to the courts wherever possible. Where litigation cannot be avoided, then the parties should be encouraged to attempt settlement at the earliest possible stage in the litigation.

With the implementation of the Jackson Reforms on 1 April 2013, judges have taken **9.02** a more proactive role in the management of cases and costs, and this has included encouraging parties to use ADR where appropriate.[1] A judge's case management powers now specifically include carrying out an Early Neutral Evaluation with the aim of helping the parties settle the case.[2] Parties who fail to comply with rules, orders, or practice directions will find it more difficult to obtain relief from the court, including

---

[1] See CPR rr 1.1, 1.2, 1.4, and 3.1. See also Chapter 11.
[2] CPR r 3.1(2)(m) (as amended from 1 October 2015).

relief from any sanctions that are imposed in relation to the default.[3] If parties fail to act reasonably and proportionately in actively seeking to settle their dispute, they may find that the court will be increasingly willing to penalize their conduct by making an adverse costs order.[4] In an appropriate case, the court may be prepared to strike out a case. In *Binns v Firstplus Financial Group Ltd*,[5] the court struck out the proceedings where the claimant was able to obtain redress through an ADR process, and the only advantage of continuing proceedings was to try to secure a costs advantage.

9.03   From 1 April 2013, the new concept of judicial costs management has applied (with some exceptions) to many multi-track cases (and any other proceedings, including applications, where the court so orders).[6] The costs management provisions have resulted in the court managing both the steps to be taken and the costs to be incurred by the parties to any proceedings so as to further the overriding objective. Parties and their lawyers can no longer conduct litigation in a manner which does not keep the proportionality of costs being incurred at the forefront of their mind at all times.[7] These changes, including the recent increase in court and tribunal fees in 2014, and proposed further increases, make it increasingly important to use ADR to resolve a dispute. It may not be reasonable or proportionate to litigate the claim to trial when the costs of doing so exceed the sums in dispute. The filing and exchanging of costs budgets in multi-track cases also means that each party's costs are transparent to the other party and that may also be a factor which motivates the parties to use ADR, and to do so at an earlier stage of the case. Although the court encourages the parties to use ADR, the parties will need to be circumspect when budgeting for ADR. If the amount budgeted for ADR is unreasonably high, the court will reduce the amount set aside for ADR in the costs budget.[8]

9.04   The encouragement to parties to use ADR to resolve their dispute comes from a variety of means set out below:

- judicial encouragement for ADR as developed in case law;
- pre-action protocols;[9]
- court guides;
- the court's inquiry at the first case management conference whether ADR could be employed;

---

[3] See CPR rr 3.8 and 3.9.
[4] See Chapter 11.
[5] [2013] EWHC 2436 (QB).
[6] CPR Part 3, Section II (Costs Management) and PD 3E.
[7] *Gotch & Another v Enelco Ltd* [2015] EWHC 1802. See also *GSK Project Management Ltd v QPR Holdings Ltd* [2015] EWHC 2274 (TCC).
[8] *CRM Trading Ltd v Chubb Electronic Security Ltd* [2013] EWHC 3482 (QB); *CIP Properties (AIPT) Ltd v Galliford Try Infrastucture Ltd* [2015] EWHC 481 (TCC).
[9] See Chapter 8.

- the court's willingness to grant a stay for ADR to be considered and used;
- other case management ADR orders;
- the willingness of the courts to uphold and enforce ADR clauses in a contract;
- the court's willingness to make adverse costs orders or other sanctions against a party who unreasonably refuses to consider ADR;[10]
- the establishment and promotion of court mediation schemes,[11] judicial mediation schemes,[12] evaluation schemes,[13] and the development of the Civil Mediation Online Directory.[14]

B Judicial Encouragement of ADR

The courts have repeatedly encouraged the parties to use ADR in general,[15] and mediation in particular[16] in accordance with the overriding objective, proportionality, and the court's duty of active case management. Judges are prepared to question parties as to the steps taken to avoid litigation, and will robustly encourage them to cooperate in the use of ADR.[17] There is a duty on the parties to engage in ADR whenever that offers a reasonable prospect of producing a just settlement at a proportionate cost, and they should do this without the need for the court's intervention because it is a waste of the court's resources to have to manage the parties towards ADR by robust encouragement.[18] There is a continuing duty on the parties to consider ADR throughout the litigation.[19]   **9.05**

C Can the Court Compel the Parties to Use ADR?

Although the court can encourage the parties to use ADR and make orders facilitating the use of ADR, it cannot compel them to use ADR if they do not wish to do so and, if the parties do use an ADR process, it cannot make them reach a   **9.06**

---

[10] Considered in detail in Chapter 11.
[11] Considered in Chapter 16 at 16.05–16.13.
[12] See Chapter 16 at 16.17–16.23.
[13] See Chapter 22.
[14] See Chapter 16 at 16.14–16.16.
[15] See Chapter 1 at 1.04–1.10.
[16] See Chapter 13 at 13.07.
[17] *Dyson v Leeds City Council* [2000] CP Rep 42 (per Lord Woolf at [16]); *R (Cowl) v Plymouth City Council* [2001] EWCA Civ 1935 (per Lord Woolf at [1] and [25]); *MD v Secretary of State for the Home Department* [2011] EWCA Civ 453; *R (on the application of S) v Hampshire County Council* [2009] EWHC 2537; *Brookfield Construction (UK) Limited v Mott Macdonald Limited* [2010] EWHC 659 (TCC) (per Coulson J at [52]–[55]). Also, see CPR r 3.1(8).
[18] *PGF II SA v OMFS Company 1 Limited* [2013] EWCA Civ 1288 [at para 27].
[19] *Garritt-Critchley v Ronnan* [2014] EWHC 1774 [at paras 25–28].

settlement in that process. This was recognized in *Halsey v Milton Keynes General NHS Trust*,[20] where Dyson LJ stated that compulsion of ADR would be regarded as an unacceptable constraint on the right of access to the court and, therefore, a violation of Article 6 of the European Convention on Human Rights.

9.07 The Jackson Review of Costs has endorsed the view that 'mediation should never be compulsory, although courts should in appropriate cases encourage mediation by pointing out its benefits, by directing parties to meet and discuss mediation and by using the Ungley order (named after Queen's Bench Master Ungley, who first used it in the field of clinical negligence).[21] In *Mann v Mann*,[22] the court refused to give effect to an agreement so as to prevent a party from applying to the court for enforcement unless and until mediation had taken place, as this would amount to a restriction on the right of access to the court and the court could not compel the parties to engage in mediation. Instead the court robustly encouraged the parties to engage in ADR by making an Ungley Order.

9.08 There are many commentators who consider that in *Halsey*, Dyson LJ was wrong in holding that the court could not compel the parties to engage with an ADR process on the basis that it would infringe their Article 6 rights.[23] Support for the view that compulsory ADR orders would not infringe the Article 6 rights of the parties can also be derived from the EU Directive on Mediation in Civil and Commercial Matters ('Mediation Directive').[24]

9.09 Other European jurisdictions, for example Italy, compulsorily require the parties to engage in mediation as a precondition to issuing proceedings. The European Court, on a preliminary reference from Italy, ruled that even if domestic law made commencement of legal proceedings conditional on attempting settlement at a mediation, this would not infringe Article 6.[25]

---

[20] [2004] EWCA Civ 576 (per Dyson LJ at [9] and [10]).

[21] The Ungley Order can be found on the Online Resource Centre.

[22] [2014] EWHC 537 (Fam).

[23] For example, Mr Justice Lightman, in a speech entitled 'Mediation: Approximation to Justice' (28 June 2007) criticized the decision on the ground that the court failed to differentiate between different ADR processes such as arbitration (which does impose a permanent stay on proceedings) and mediation or negotiation (which does not prevent the parties resolving their dispute by trial). See also *Sir Anthony Clarke, The Future of Civil Mediations (2008) 74 Arbitration 4.*

[24] Directive 2008/52/EC. See Chapter 17, and also Article 5(1) and (2) of the EU Mediation Directive (reproduced in the Online Resource Centre).

[25] *Alassini v Telecom Italia SpA* (Joined Cases C-317–320/08) [2010] 3 CMLR 17 ECJ. Lord Dyson has since acknowledged, in light of the *Alassini* case and Article 5 of the Mediation Directive, that a form of compulsory mediation, which requires parties to mediate, but does not penalize them if they fail to do so (so that at most trial is delayed) involves no breach of Article 6, although compelling unwilling parties to mediate or use ADR is likely to achieve little (see *Arbitration* 2011, 77(3), 375–381).

In light of these recent developments, a mandatory order directing the parties to **9.10** take part in a non-adjudicative ADR process, such as mediation, is unlikely to be a breach of Article 6 provided the parties can continue with court proceedings if they failed to reach a settlement. Despite this, it is clear that the government does not intend to introduce any form of compulsory ADR.

The present position is that the court will, if appropriate, encourage a party to **9.11** attempt to resolve their dispute by ADR, and the strongest form of encouragement lies in the form of order made by the Commercial Court.[26] The courts are not pre-pared to compel parties to engage in an ADR process if they are unwilling to do so. However, that may change in the future. In *Wright v Michael Wright (Supplies) Ltd,*[27] despite strong encouragement from the courts, it proved impossible 'to shift intran-sigent parties off the trial track and onto the parallel track of mediation'. The court noted that it might be time to review the rule in *Halsey* where Dyson LJ commented that to oblige unwilling parties to use ADR would be to impose an unacceptable obstruction on their right of access to the court.

Even if the court is unwilling, at present, to compel reluctant parties to use ADR, it **9.12** can penalize a party in costs if they unreasonably refuse to attempt ADR, particu-larly if they are ordered by the court to do so.[28]

In some cases there is a requirement of mandatory *consideration* of mediation (eg, **9.13** automatic referral to mediation in small claims and under the Court of Appeal Mediation Pilot Scheme[29]). However, this is not the same as compulsory mediation. Automatic referral for consideration of mediation is simply a mandatory require-ment to engage with a mediator with a view to obtaining information on mediation and undertaking mediation if appropriate. It is not proposed that the parties should be coerced into mediation in the sense that mediation is made compulsory.[30]

It should also be noted that Article 6 is not, in principle, infringed if a party **9.14** waives their right to a trial process, for example by contractually agreeing to resolve a dispute by an adjudicative ADR process such as expert determination or arbitration.[31]

---

[26] See the Online Resource Centre for the Commercial Court ADR order.
[27] [2013] EWCA Civ 234, per Sir Alan Ward at [3].
[28] See Chapter 11.
[29] See Chapter 16 at 16.07–16.10 and 16.11–16.13.
[30] See Consultation Paper, CP6/2011 entitled 'Solving Disputes in the County Courts: Creating a Simpler, Quicker and More Proportionate System'. This can be viewed at <http://webarchive. nationalarchives. gov.uk/20111013033132/http://www.justice.gov.uk/consultations/consultation-cp6-2011.htm>.
[31] *Deweer v Belgium A/35* [1980] ECC 169.

D The Court Guides

9.15 There are a number of specialist court guides, each of which contains guidance relating to the use of ADR. The provisions of the main guides which deal with ADR are as follows:

- *Admiralty and Commercial Courts Guide* (9th edn, updated January 2016):[32] Section G and also para D8.3 (e) and Appendix 7 for the draft ADR order;
- *Chancery Guide* 2016, Chapter 18;[33]
- *Queen's Bench Division Guide* (updated December 2015): para 6.6;[34]
- *Technology and Construction Court Guide* (2nd edn, revised March 2014)[35]: para 7 and Appendices E and G. This Guide also sets out two ADR processes that can be carried out by the court if the parties agree, namely the Court Settlement Process (a form of judicial mediation)[36] and Judicial Early Neutral Evaluation.[37]
- *Mercantile Court Guide,* Chapter 7 and Appendix C, para 27 for the standard form of ADR order.[38]

E Pre-Action Protocols

9.16 Under the CPR, protocols were introduced to set out the steps that the parties should follow before issuing proceedings, as part of reasonable pre-action conduct.[39]

F The Overriding Objective and ADR

9.17 The CPR have at their heart the overriding objective of enabling a court to deal with a case justly and at proportionate cost. The CPR, rules 1.1 to 1.4 set out factors that are relevant to dealing with a case justly and at proportionate cost and what is required of the court and the parties.

9.18 The court is required to further the overriding objective by actively managing cases, and this includes encouraging the parties to cooperate with each other in the conduct

---

[32] See <https://www.justice.gov.uk/courts/rcj-rolls-building/admiralty-commercial-mercentile-courts>.

[33] See <https://www.justice.gov.uk/rcj-rolls-building/chancery-division>

[34] <https://www.justice.gov.uk/rcj-rolls-building/queens-bench/guidance>

[35] See <https://www.justice.gov.uk/downloads/courts/tech-court/tec-con-court-guide.pdf>.

[36] See para 7.6 of the Guide and also Chapter 16 at 16.21–16.22.

[37] See para 7.5 of the Guide and also Chapter 22 at 22.17–22.18.

[38] See <https://www.justice.gov.uk/downloads/courts/mercantile-court/mercantile-court-guide.pdf>.

[39] See Chapter 8.

of the proceedings, identifying the issues at an early stage, encouraging parties to use an ADR procedure if the court considers that appropriate, and facilitating the use of such procedure and helping the parties to settle the whole or part of a case.[40]

The parties and their lawyers are also under a duty to assist the court to further the overriding objective.[41]   **9.19**

G Case Management Powers and ADR

The court can also direct the parties to consider ADR at a case management confer-   **9.20**
ence or pre-trial review. Such an order can also be made at any case management conference attended by the parties. The Court of Appeal approved the use of such an order in *Halsey*[42] describing the Commercial Court order[43] as the strongest form of encouragement, but falling short of compulsion. An order referred to as the Ungley Order, or the Jordan ADR order may also be made.[44] A court which frequently encourages the parties to settle and grants numerous adjournments of the trial to enable settlement negotiations to take place is not likely to breach common law notions of fairness or Article 6 of the European Convention on Human Rights.[45]

Since 1 April 2013, as part of the Jackson Reforms, standard directions and model   **9.21**
directions have been used in all multi-track cases. These and other sample orders that can be made by the court to encourage the parties to use ADR and to facilitate its use can be found on the Online Resource Centre. In multi-track cases, when drafting case management directions, both the parties and the court should take as their starting point any relevant model directions and adapt them as appropriate to the circumstances of their case.[46] Parties can expect to face more robust judicial case management, and tougher enforcement of court orders, and these will include orders encouraging the parties to use ADR. Where a party, without good reason, fails to comply with a rule, Practice Direction, or relevant Pre-Action Protocol, under CPR r 3.1(5) the court can order that party to pay a sum of money into court, and may do so to concentrate a party's mind on ADR.[47] The court can make

---

[40] CPR r 1.4.
[41] CPR r 1.3.
[42] [2004] EWCA Civ 576 at [32].
[43] See the Online Resource Centre for the Commercial Court Order.
[44] See the Online Resource Centre for the Ungley and Jordan ADR Orders. See also CPR, PD 29 para 4.10(9).
[45] *Watson v Sadiq* [2013] EWCA Civ 822.
[46] See CPR r 29.1(2) and CPR r 29.4. Specimen Directions can be found on the Justice website at <http://www.justice.gov.uk/courts/procedure-rules/civil>.
[47] See *Lazari v London and Newcastle (Camden) Ltd* [2013] EWHC 97 (TCC).

an order for early or limited disclosure of documents to facilitate ADR.[48] The court will monitor compliance with any orders and directions,[49] and judicial continuity (ie ensuring the same judge handles the case throughout) will make it easier for the court to do this.

H Directions Questionnaires and ADR

9.22 Before the case is finally allocated to a track, the court will require the parties to file and serve a directions questionnaire in Form N181 (fast track and multi-track) or N180 (small claims track cases).[50] The directions questionnaire requires each party to inform the court whether they would like a stay for one month to try to settle the claim, or why it is not possible to reach a settlement at this stage. Parties are also asked to confirm whether they have complied with the relevant pre-action protocol and if not, to explain why there has been non-compliance.

9.23 The court does not have to accept the reasons put forward by any of the parties for refusing to try to settle the action or consider ADR at this stage. If the court considers those reasons to be weak or inadequate, it will direct the parties to attend a case management conference, to consider whether ADR should be attempted. The court can direct the parties to attempt ADR even if one party objects to this.[51]

I Granting Stays for ADR

9.24 The court's general powers of management include the power to make orders staying the whole or part of any proceedings until a specified date or event.[52] A stay suspends proceedings and so avoids the need for a party to prepare for the ADR process and the various stages of the litigation process at the same time, thus saving time and expense. When the stay no longer applies, the proceedings resume automatically from the stage reached when the stay was imposed.[53] The stay will be for a period of one month, although the court has power to extend this period, and will often do so.[54] The court

---

[48] *Mann v Mann* [2014] EWHC 537.

[49] See Lord Justice Jackson's Fifth and the Thirteenth Implementation Lecture in the implementation programme and CPR r 3.1(8) and CPR r 3.9 (as amended).

[50] CPR r 26.3, PD 4, and PD 26.

[51] *Shirayama Shokusan Co Ltd v Danovo Ltd (No 1)* [2003] EWHC 3306 (Ch) (where the order was made in the form of the Commercial Court order, available on the Online Resource Centre). See also *Guinle v Kirreh* [2000] CP Rep 62 and *Muman v Nagasena* [2000] 1 WLR 299.

[52] CPR r 3.1(2)(f) and r 26.4.

[53] *UK Highways A55 Ltd v Hyder Consulting (UK) Ltd* [2012] EWHC 3505 (TCC).

[54] CPR r 26.4(3) and PD 26 para 3.1.

can grant a stay of its own motion or at the request of one or more of the parties at the track allocation stage (or at any other time), for ADR to be considered.[55] If the court has stayed proceedings at track allocation stage, then the case will not be allocated to the appropriate track until the end of that period.[56] In multi-track cases, instead of granting a stay, the court may set a sensible timetable to allow the parties to take part in ADR as the case progresses. In such cases, a stay or a fixed window for ADR may lead to delay, extra cost and uncertainty.[57]

If a stay is granted for ADR to be attempted, the parties must keep the court **9.25** informed about the outcome of the ADR process. If it results in settlement, the parties will need to formally dispose of the court proceedings, perhaps by way of a Consent Order or a Tomlin Order. An application for a consent order to give effect to any settlement reached is treated as an application for the stay to be lifted.[58] If no settlement is reached during the ADR process, then the parties will need to apply to the court to get the stay lifted (if it has not expired) and for any further relevant directions so that the litigation can proceed.

The Online Resource Centre contains sample orders granting a stay to facilitate ADR. **9.26**

J Contractual ADR Clauses

The court may give effect to ADR by upholding and enforcing a contractual ADR **9.27** clause, which is a clause in a contract by which the parties agree to resolve their dispute primarily by ADR. It may define a particular ADR method which should be used, such as mediation, or it may specify a number of methods that need to be exhausted in turn before litigation can be commenced or continued. If an adjudicative form of ADR procedure is specified by the clause (such as expert determination, adjudication, or arbitration), it may also specify that the parties are to be bound by the decision. Such clauses are becoming increasingly common, particularly in contracts for services, insurance contracts, and construction contracts.

If the parties have agreed on a particular method by which their disputes are to be **9.28** resolved, then the court has an inherent discretionary power to stay proceedings brought in breach of that agreement and to require the parties to pursue the agreed dispute resolution process. The court will give effect to ADR clauses regardless of the type of ADR process that the parties have agreed to use.

---

[55] See CPR rr 3.1(2)(f), 26.4(2), and 24.4(2A).
[56] CPR r 26.5.
[57] *CIP Properties (AIPT) Ltd v Galliford Try Infrastructure Ltd* [2014] EWHC 3546 (TCC).
[58] CPR, PD 26, para 3.4.

9.29 ADR clauses must be drafted carefully. The contractual procedure must be clear and unambiguous to be enforceable. If it is not, the court will decline to enforce the clause.[59] In the past, the courts have not enforced a mere agreement to negotiate in good faith on the grounds that it was not sufficiently certain.[60] However, in recent years, the courts have more readily upheld or implied contractual obligations of good faith.[61] The court has upheld an ADR clause in a contract which required the parties to seek to resolve a dispute by friendly discussion in good faith and within a limited period before referring the dispute to arbitration.[62]

9.30 Provided the procedure envisaged by the contract is sufficiently certain to be enforceable, the court will uphold the clause and grant a stay of proceedings commenced in breach of the clause. The court has upheld an ADR clause that provided that if the dispute was not resolved by negotiation between the parties, they should attempt to resolve it in good faith through an ADR procedure recommended by the Centre for Dispute Resolution.[63]

9.31 On the other hand in *Sulamerica CIA Nacional de Seguros SA v Enesa Engenharia SA—Enesa,*[64] the Court refused to uphold an ADR clause which provided no unequivocal commitment to engage in mediation, there was no agreement to enter into any clear mediation process whether based on a model provided by a particular ADR provider or otherwise, and no provision was made for the selection of a mediator. There were therefore stages in the process where the parties would need to agree on a course of action before a mediation could proceed. In those circumstances, the clause did not give rise to a binding obligation to mediate which the court could enforce.

9.32 Recent cases have established that the courts will endeavour to find an interpretation to give effect to an ADR clause which is contained in a legally enforceable contract between the parties. In *Wah v Grant Thornton International Ltd,*[65] the court considered that there needs to be:

(a) a sufficiently certain and unequivocal commitment to commence a process;

(b) a means of discerning the steps each party was required to take to put the process in place;

---

[59] *Cott UK Ltd v FE Barber Ltd* [1997] 3 All ER 540.

[60] *Walford v Miles* [1992] 2 AC 128 HL and *National Transport Co-operative Society Ltd v Attorney General of Jamaica* [2009] UKPC 48.

[61] For example, see *Yam Seng Pte Limited v International Trade Corporation* [2013] EWHC 111 (QB); *Bristol Groundschool Ltd v Intelligent Data Capture Ltd* [2014] EWHC 2145 (Ch); *D&G Cars Ltd v Essex Police Authority* [2015] EWHC 226 (QB).

[62] *Emirates Trading Agency LLC v Prime Mineral Exports Private Ltd* [2014] EWHC 2104 (Comm).

[63] *Cable and Wireless plc v IBM United Kingdom Ltd* [2002] EWHC 2059 (Comm).

[64] [2012] EWHC 42 (Comm).

[65] [2012] EWHC 3198 (Ch).

(c) a process which was sufficiently clearly defined to enable the court to make an objective determination of the minimum each party must do to participate in it and an indication of how the process would be exhausted or properly terminable without breach.

In order to give effect to a clause, the court may imply criteria to enable it to determine what process was to be followed, and when and how that process might be considered successful or at an end.[66]

Provided the clause is sufficiently clear, in exercising its discretion to enforce such clauses by staying proceedings commenced in breach of the clause, the court may consider the following factors:[67] **9.33**

- the extent to which the parties had complied with the requirements in any pre-action protocol;
- whether the dispute is suitable for determination by the agreed ADR process;
- the costs of that ADR process compared to the costs of litigation;
- whether a stay would accord with the overriding objective.

The courts have enforced ADR clauses and stayed litigation commenced before the agreed ADR process in numerous cases.[68] **9.34**

The courts may also be willing to award damages for breach of an ADR clause. Those damages could consist of the costs reasonably incurred by a party in relation to proceedings brought in breach of an ADR clause which could not be recovered in those proceedings.[69] However, it is important to note that costs cannot be recovered as damages if the party seeking to recover those costs could have sought an order for their payment in the proceedings brought in breach of the contract between the parties.[70] Damages for breach of an ADR clause could also be assessed on the basis of the amount that a party could have obtained had the contractually agreed dispute resolution procedure been followed.[71] **9.35**

---

[66] See *Wah v Grant Thornton International Ltd* [2012] EWHC 3198 (Ch); *M v M* [2014] EWHC 537 (Fam).

[67] *DGT Steel & Cladding Ltd v Cubitt Building & Interiors Ltd* [2007] EWHC 1584 (TCC).

[68] See for example *Channel Tunnel Group Ltd v Balfour Beatty Construction Ltd* [1993] AC 334; *Cape Durasteel Ltd v Rosser & Russell Building Services Ltd* [1995] 46 Con LR 75; *Herschel Engineering Ltd v Breen Property Ltd* [2000] 70 Con LR 1; *DGT Steel & Cladding Ltd v Cubitt Building & Interiors Ltd* [2007] EWHC 1584 (TCC); *Turville Heath Inc v Chartis Insurance UK Ltd (formerly AIG UK Ltd)* [2012] EWHC 3019 (TCC).

[69] *Union Discount v Zoller* [2001] EWCA Civ 1755.

[70] *Carroll v Kynaston* [2010] EWCA Civ 1404.

[71] *Sunrock Aircraft Corp Ltd v Scandinavian Airlines System Denmark-Norway-Sweden* [2007] EWCA Civ 882.

K Costs Alternative Dispute Resolution

9.36 ADR can be used not only for resolving the substantive dispute between the parties, but also for disputes that arise during the assessment of costs following the conclusion of the proceedings. Recently, a Costs Alternative Dispute Resolution Panel (CADR) has been set up which comprises members of the costs judiciary, costs lawyers, and other costs experts. CADR uses all of the available ADR processes to resolve disputes about costs, including a non-binding or binding paper assessment of costs by a specialist assessor.[72]

---

[72] See <www.costs-adr.com> for the processes CADR offer in relation to assessment of costs, and the fees payable for these processes.

10

COSTS AND COST SHIFTING IN ADR

A Liability to Pay for an ADR Process

Each party will be liable to pay their own costs and expenses in relation to an ADR **10.01** process, unless some other agreement is reached. While in litigation it is the norm that costs will follow the event,[1] so that the loser will pay the costs of the winner, there is no such general rule in ADR, not least because in non-adjudicative ADR the outcome is by agreement with no 'loser'.

Given that high expenditure in dispute resolution is a major driver for the use of **10.02** ADR, options for getting costs orders or otherwise shifting costs are a significant consideration in making comparisons and taking strategic and cost effective decisions relating to the use of litigation and ADR. Costs may become a significant consideration for parties and lawyers as the case progresses and the level of costs grows, so that the possibility of shifting costs may itself become a potential issue in resolving the dispute. In litigation cost shifting is normal due to the principle that the loser will pay the costs of the winner to ensure that a successful claimant is fully compensated, but a party may incur expense in the expectation that it will ultimately be shifted to another party if the case succeeds, and this may divert attention from dispute resolution. Cost shifting is less common in other jurisdictions, and this may be a consideration in a case with international dimensions.[2] The revised test of proportionality and costs budgets and management may over time reduce possible issues in relation to costs shifting, with a stronger focus on the potential cost of litigation at an early stage and on the relative expense of litigation and ADR.

While cost recoverability is not the norm for ADR, there are ways in which costs can **10.03** be shifted in and in relation to the use of ADR. This can be done:

- as part of a settlement reached in negotiation or mediation, see 10.05–10.06;

---

[1] CPR r 44.2.
[2] For example, in the USA it is normal for a party to litigation to bear their own costs even if they win.

- through the use of a Part 36 offer, see 10.25–10.31;
- in an adjudicative ADR process as part of an award made by a third party, if the third party has been given power to award costs by agreement, see 10.07;
- if a case is litigated, through the general powers of the court in relation to costs where there has been a failure to make reasonable use of ADR (but note that the costs of an ADR process will not necessarily be incidental to litigation and thus subject to court order);
- if proceedings have been issued and the action is discontinued the claimant will be liable for the defendant's costs: CPR, r 38.6 (1). Unless this outcome is intended, if a case is settled after issue it is important that the claimant should not agree to discontinue the action. The court power to order some other outcome has been interpreted restrictively,[3] though a failure to reply to pre-action correspondence may justify a departure from the normal rule.[4]

10.04 Arguments in relation to the use of ADR and costs should meet the following criteria:[5]

- concerns about ADR and costs are best considered prospectively or at the time rather than retrospectively;
- any argument should be based on contemporaneous evidence captured when a decision relevant to costs is taken rather than constructed to try to justify earlier behaviour;
- difficulties in relation to the use of ADR should be raised and addressed at the time and not just saved for a later argument as to costs.

B Recovery of Costs within an ADR Process

Advance agreement on costs

10.05 It is normal for parties to agree that the fee for an ADR process be shared equally, with each party bearing their own additional ADR expenses, though one party may agree to pay the fee for an ADR process as part of persuading the other party to agree to use ADR. Such a term would be part of the agreement to use ADR, and will stand even if the process is unsuccessful, a court having no power to make a different award of costs as regards the ADR process.[6] However the parties can explicitly agree

---

[3] *Brookes v HSBC Bank* [2011] EWCA Civ 354.
[4] *Nelson's Yard Management Company v Eziefula* [2013] EWCA Civ 235.
[5] *PGF II SA v OMFS Company* [2012] EWHC 83 (TCC) (per Mr Recorder Furst QC).
[6] *Lobster Group Limited v Heidelberg Graphic Equipment Limited* [2008] 2 All ER 1173.

in advance that if the ADR process fails the court will have a discretion as regards costs if they so wish.

Subsequent agreement on costs

In non-adjudicative ADR, whatever is agreed as regards expenses can be varied by agreement. For example one party might offer to pay the whole cost of the ADR process in return for a specified concession by the other side. Agreement can relate solely to the expense of the ADR process, and/or to other costs in relation to the dispute such as the costs of litigation to date. The wording of any agreement should be clear as to what is covered. A set figure can be agreed in relation to costs, or a simple process for determining what should be paid, to avoid further costs in relation to assessment.

10.06

Award of costs in adjudicative ADR

In adjudicative ADR, the parties can agree to give the arbitrator or adjudicator the power to award costs. In arbitration the tribunal may make an award allocating costs between the parties, subject to any agreement between the parties.[7] Other than in arbitration, the third party will only have such power in relation to costs as the parties agree, so it should be clearly agreed what costs may be the subject of an award, and in the award what costs are covered. A court may assess the costs of proceedings before an arbitrator, umpire, or tribunal.[8]

10.07

C Recovery of ADR Costs within a Court Process

General principles

If the dispute is not fully resolved through ADR and litigation continues, the general discretion of the court in relation to costs under CPR Part 44 will apply.[9] The court has discretion whether costs are payable by one party to the other, the amount of those costs, and when they are to be paid.[10] The usual order is that costs will follow the event, but the court can make a different order.[11] The costs of the ADR process will normally still lie as outlined above, but this depends on the term agreed,

10.08

---

[7] Arbitration Act 1996 s 61(1), and see ss 59–65.
[8] CPR r 44.1 (2).
[9] Senior Courts Act 1981 s 51, and CPR Part 44, as substituted by the Civil Procedure (Amendment) Rules 2013.
[10] CPR r 44.2(1).
[11] CPR r 44.2(2).

see 10.12. The payment of costs may be covered by a contractual agreement which the court may not have power to vary.[12]

10.09   The matters to which the court should have regard when making a costs order can take into account the use of ADR options as well as litigation.[13] The judge will have regard to all the circumstances, including:

- the conduct of all the parties;
- whether a party has succeeded in part of his or her case, even if that party has not been wholly successful;
- any admissible offer to settle made by a party that is drawn to the court's attention, and which is not an offer to which the costs consequences in Part 36 apply.

10.10   In looking at the conduct of the parties, the factors the court will look at relate to the potential use of ADR as well as litigation:[14]

- conduct before, as well as during, the proceedings, and in particular the extent to which the parties followed Practice Direction Pre-action Conduct and any relevant pre-action protocol;
- whether it was reasonable for a party to raise, pursue, or contest a particular allegation or issue;
- the manner in which a party has pursued or defended the case or a particular allegation or issue;
- whether a claimant who has succeeded in the claim, in whole or in part, exaggerated his or her claim.

10.11   The power of the court to make orders in relation to a stated amount in respect of another party's costs, costs from or until a certain date, costs incurred before proceedings have begun, and costs relating to a particular step in or part of the proceedings[15] gives quite wide scope to take into account reasonable attempts to settle and the timing of those attempts. Where a case is settled prior to the issue of proceedings the powers of the court are limited, see 8.10–8.13.

10.12   If an ADR process fails, the court is likely to regard itself as bound by any contractual agreement that has been made by the parties as regards the expenses of ADR. The wording of the agreement between the parties needs to be considered as it may for example provide that the expense of ADR process be shared equally, but that the

---

[12]   *Chaplair Ltd v Kumari* [2015] EWCA Civ 798.
[13]   CPR r 44.2(4).
[14]   CPR r 44.2(5).
[15]   CPR r 44.2(6).

party's legal costs and expenses incurred in preparing for and attending the ADR process may be treated as costs in the case in any litigation where the court has power to order or assess costs.

If the parties settle a dispute without any agreement as to costs, one party cannot later argue that costs should be awarded on the basis that party had effectively won.[16] It may be reasonable to refuse an offer to settle if it is made on the basis that each side bear their own costs and this could have an unfair effect on the party refusing the offer.[17] **10.13**

If a settlement is reached

Where settlement has been reached after the issue of proceedings, the court should be informed.[18] The resulting settlement may go to court, for example to be recorded as a consent order, in which case the court will have a discretion as to costs (though it would normally accept what the parties have agreed if there has been agreement). Alternatively the settlement may take a form that leads to automatic entitlement to costs, if for example a Part 36 offer is accepted or an action is formally discontinued following agreement. **10.14**

A decision on costs alone

It is possible for a court to make a decision on costs alone where the parties have reached agreement on all other matters, either by agreement, or for example if an expert determination has been made by a person who was not given authority to make a decision as to costs. The principles to be applied are:[19] **10.15**

- the court has power to make a costs order when the substantive proceedings have been resolved without a trial but the parties have not agreed costs;
- the overriding objective is to do justice between the parties without incurring unnecessary court time and consequently additional cost;
- at each end of the spectrum there will be cases where it is obvious which side would have won had the substantive issues been fought to a conclusion. In between, the position will be less clear. How far the court will be prepared to look into the previously unresolved substantive issues will depend on the circumstances of the particular case;

---

[16] *R (on the application of Crookenden) v Institute of Chartered Accountants in England and Wales* [2013] All ER (D) 352 (May).
[17] *Newman v Framewood Manor Management Co Ltd* [2012] EWCA Civ 1727.
[18] CPR PD 39A, para 4.1; *Tasyurdu v Immigration Appeal Tribunal* [2003] EWCA Civ 447.
[19] *Brawley v Marczynski (Nos 1 and 2)* [2003] 1 WLR 813.

- in the absence of a good reason to make any other order, the fall-back position is to make no order for costs.[20]

At an interim stage

10.16 An interim application or hearing may take place in relation to an ADR process, such as an application for a stay to enable ADR to be attempted, or a case management hearing to determine whether the parties should attempt ADR. The costs of interim applications made in connection with the use of ADR are subject to the normal court discretion. If the hearing has taken place due to one party's unreasonable refusal to engage with an ADR process the court may order the party acting unreasonably to pay the other side's costs of and occasioned by the application or hearing.[21] One option is that the costs be 'costs in the case', so that the party awarded costs at the end of the case gets the costs, and this is supported by the *Admiralty and Commercial Court Guide*.[22] A sanction may be imposed at the interim stage for failure to make reasonable use of ADR, see Chapter 11.

As part of damages

10.17 A party's expenses in relation to an ADR process such as mediation can, in certain circumstances, be recovered as damages in subsequent litigation against a third party.[23]

At trial

10.18 At trial a judge will have the normal discretion as regards costs recoverable in court proceedings, though there is not complete clarity as to what may comprise potentially recoverable costs in relation to ADR. The distinction appears to be that the expenses of a separate ADR process will remain a matter of any agreement made by the parties, but that the judge will have a discretion as regards costs of ADR which may be regarded as 'incidental' to the proceedings.[24] The definition of 'costs' includes fees, charges,

---

[20] *Dearling v Foregate Developments (Chester) Limited* [2003] EWCA Civ 913.

[21] *Roundstone Nurseries Ltd v Stephenson Holdings Ltd* [2009] EWHC 1431 (TCC).

[22] *Admiralty and Commercial Court Guide* para G1.10: 'At a case management conference or at any other hearing in the course of which the judge makes an order providing for ADR he may make such order as to the costs that the parties may incur by reason of their using or attempting to use ADR as may in all the circumstances be appropriate. The orders for costs are normally costs in the case, meaning that if the claim is not settled, the costs of the ADR procedures will follow the ultimate event [so the unsuccessful party will be ordered to pay the successful party's costs incurred in connection with the ADR process], or that each side will bear their own costs of those procedures if the case is not settled.'

[23] *Youlton v Charles Russell (a firm)* [2010] EWHC 1032 (Ch).

[24] Senior Courts Act 1981, s 51.

disbursements expenses, and remuneration,[25] unless the context otherwise requires, and the context of carrying out a separate ADR process arguably creates a relevant distinction. Work done in relation to most ADR processes are not specifically mentioned in CPR, Parts 44 to 48 or PD 43 to 48. The only exception is that a bill of costs can include work done in connection with negotiations with a view to settlement.[26]

As well as questions relating to the definition of costs, there may be practical matters **10.19** as regards how far money spent can be divided into money spent in relation to litigation and to ADR. Authority in case law does not draw very clear lines, and the point does not always appear to have been fully argued.[27] There is authority for the court to make orders where ADR costs are incidental to litigation,[28] and this is generally taken to include the costs of negotiation as it is not common to make a separate agreement for the costs of this process. It is likely that a court has no discretion in relation to the costs of a stand-alone ADR process,[29] and it has been said that a clear distinction should be drawn between the costs of the ADR process (which will fall as agreed in the ADR agreement) and the other costs of the case.[30]

An unreasonable failure to use ADR may result in a sanction as part of a final deci- **10.20** sion as to costs at trial, with liability for part of the costs being shifted, even if a party has taken some steps in relation to ADR,[31] see Chapter 11. A sanction may result in a higher rate of interest being paid on specified damages, or the assessment of costs on an indemnity basis from the date on which a reasonable offer which ought to have been accepted,[32] or where a party has resisted a sensible approach to finding a solution to the proceedings.[33]

The overall decision on costs at trial can be very complex if there are several issues **10.21** in relation to the use of ADR to be considered, such as a mix of offers to mediate

---

[25] CPR r 44.1, as provided by the Civil Procedure (Amendment) Rules 2013.

[26] Practice Direction 47—Procedure for Detailed Assessment of Costs and Default Provisions para 5.12.

[27] *Chantrey Vellacott v The Convergence Group plc* [2007] EWHC 1774 (Ch); *Société Internationale de Télécommunications Aéronautiques SC (SITA) v The Wyatt Company (UK) Limited* [2002] EWHC 2401 (Ch).

[28] *McGlinn v Waltham Contractors Ltd* [2005] EWHC 1419 (TCC); *Halsey v Milton Keynes General NHS Trust* [2004] EWCA Civ 576.

[29] *Roundstone Nurseries Ltd v Stephenson Holdings Ltd* [2009] EWHC 1431 (TCC).

[30] *National Westminster Bank plc v Feeney and Feeney* [2006] EWHC 90066 (Costs); *Lobster Group Ltd v Heidelberg Graphic Equipment Ltd* [2008] EWHC 413 (TCC).

[31] *Laporte v Commissioner of Police of the Metropolis* [2015] EWHC 371 (QB).

[32] *Southwark LBC v IBM UK Ltd (Costs)* [2011] EWHC 653 (TCC); *Barr v Biffa Waste Services Ltd (Costs)* [2011] EWHC 1107 (TCC).

[33] *Epsom College v Pierse Constructing Southern Ltd (in Liquidation) (Costs)* [2011] EWCA Civ 1449 (per Lord Justice Rix).

and Part 36 offers made over a period of time. The position may be even more difficult where parties have failed to respond to each other's offers, or offers are made late.[34] Such cases may need very careful analysis, and may involve issues raised by both sides that the court feels it has no option but to make no order as to costs. It is to be hoped that the use of costs budgets and costs management will limit complex arguments arising at a late stage.

The amount of costs

10.22   The amount to be paid may be agreed between the parties, if appropriate using ADR. The growing use of fixed costs limits disputes about the amount to be paid in respect of costs in low value cases.[35] The fixed fee relates to what is recoverable through a court order and the parties could agree a different amount in respect of costs should they wish to.

10.23   If the amount of costs payable is not agreed or specified it will need to be assessed. The assessment of costs is beyond the scope of this Handbook, save for some points of particular relevance to ADR. When assessing costs on a standard basis, the courts will only allow costs which are proportionate to the matters in issue. The revised test for proportionality providing that costs which are disproportionate in amount may be disallowed or reduced even if they were reasonably or necessarily incurred,[36] may support the use of ADR earlier in a case.

10.24   Concerns about the time and expense spent on the assessment of costs, provide scope for the use of ADR, and options such as mediation, arbitration, and neutral evaluation are available.[37] The possibility of an agreed settlement forms part of the assessment of costs,[38] as a party must make an open offer to settle the costs on a detailed assessment, and a party may also make a Part 36 type offer in relation to costs.[39] There is also a procedure for provisional assessment of costs in respect of bills up to £25,000, which provides for a provisional assessment made on paper by the district judge. Either party may then ask for an oral hearing, but the party making

---

[34] *Shovelar v Lane* [2011] EWCA Civ 802; *Multiplex Construction (UK) Ltd v Cleveland Bridge (UK) Ltd* [2008] EWHC 2280 (TCC); *Brookfield Construction (UK) Limited v Mott MacDonald Limited* [2010] EWHC 659 (TCC); *Kayll v Rawlinson* [2010] EWHC 1789 (Ch); *Oliver v Symons* [2011] EWHC 1250 (Ch); *Camertown Timber Merchants Ltd v Sidhu* [2011] EWCA Civ 1041; *ADS Aerospace Ltd v EMS Global Tracking Ltd* [2012] EWHC 2904 (TCC).

[35] CPR rr 45 and 46.

[36] CPR r 44.3(2).

[37] 'Review of Civil Litigation Costs: Final Report' Chapters 44–45 and Recommendations 104 and 109, and the Eighth Implementation Lecture 'Assessment of Costs in the Brave New World', <http://www.judiciary.gov.uk/publications-and-reports/review-of-civil-litigation-costs/lectures>.

[38] CPR r 47.19.

[39] CPR r 47.20, PD 47 para 8.3.

the request is at risk of paying for that hearing unless they achieve a favourable variation of 20 per cent or more.[40]

D Part 36 Offers

Although based in the Civil Procedure Rules rather than being strictly speaking a **10.25** form of ADR, the potential use of a Part 36 offer is key to strategy and cost management in considering the range of options available to settle a case. A Part 36 offer lies on the interface between litigation and ADR, and consideration and review by a party of the potential appropriate level for a Part 36 offer at suitable intervals from the pre-action stage right through to appeal can form a sound part of taking litigation and ADR decisions. The details of the operation of Part 36 are beyond the scope of this Handbook and should be researched separately. The following paragraphs are limited to points of particular relevance to the use of ADR.

A Part 36 offer can be used strategically as part of an overall ADR strategy by a **10.26** claimant or defendant.[41] One option is to make a Part 36 offer instead of proposing negotiation or mediation. This may be useful in focusing the mind of the other side on a particular figure while avoiding any significant discussion of issues. Alternatively, a Part 36 offer may be used to initiate or provide an advance baseline for an ADR process such as negotiation. A third option is to use a Part 36 offer to protect a party's position after an unsuccessful ADR process which has helped to clarify some facts and issues. It should be noted that while the making of a Part 36 offer can be relevant to whether reasonable use has been made of ADR, simply making a Part 36 offer will not exempt a party from making reasonable use of other forms of ADR such as mediation.[42]

It is crucial to appreciate that to have full effect a Part 36 offer must meet all the **10.27** CPR requirements in terms of being made in writing, stating that it is intended to have effect as a Part 36 offer, stating whether it applies to the whole claim, or if not which issues, and so on. Any acceptance of the offer must also be in writing. Revisions to Part 36 came into effect for offers made on or after 6 April 2015,[43] for example allowing an offer to be automatically withdrawn after the expiry of the relevant period, with a new Part 36 Offer to Settle form (N242A). Part 36 forms a

---

[40] CPR PD 47 paras 14.1–14.6.
[41] *Bellway Homes Ltd v Seymour (Civil Engineering Contractors) Ltd* [2013] EWHC 1890 (TCC).
[42] *PGF II SA v OMFS Company 1 Limited* [2013] EWCA Civ 1288.
[43] Civil Procedure (Amendment No 8) Rules 2014 (SI 2014/3299).

self-contained code into which it has been said more general principles should not be imported.[44] Recent cases emphasize the importance of accuracy of drafting to meet all Part 36 requirements. An offer that does not meet all Part 36 requirements will stand as an offer without Part 36 consequences,[45] though a minor defect may be corrected.[46] While a Part 36 offer usually states a sum of money for settlement, non-financial terms can be included if they are stated clearly enough to become binding terms.[47] The offer does not have to be in terms that a court could order.[48] While there is no obligation to provide reasons for a Part 36 offer, the other side should be in a position to assess the offer.[49] The wording is interpreted as it would be understood by a reasonable solicitor.[50] To avoid a claimant getting a cost benefit by making a high offer and then succeeding in full, for an offer made on or after 6 April 2015 it will be relevant whether the offer was made as a genuine attempt to settle the proceedings.[51]

10.28   It is very important to keep the position as regards Part 36 offers under review throughout the case. As further information emerges a figure offered may be appropriate and may need to be withdrawn or replaced with a new offer. A change in circumstances may be relevant to when a Part 36 offer should be accepted.[52] A Part 36 offer stays in effect and can be accepted after the relevant period, even if the offer is rejected, a counter offer is made, or the offeror makes a further offer.[53] From 6 April 2015 a time limited offer can be made,[54] but unless this is done the offer will only cease to be current if it is formally withdrawn.

10.29   It is vital to be clear about the cost consequences of a Part 36 offer may be, as opposed to those for an open or a without prejudice save as to costs offer. While costs consequences are automatic if a Part 36 offer is accepted within the relevant period, after that time the court has a discretion. It may be relevant that although a Part 36 offer was accepted, an offer to mediate had been unreasonably refused.[55] It seems that a party who beats a Part 36 offer may still have some discount on costs

---

[44] *Gibbon v Manchester City Council* [2010] 1 WLR 2081.
[45] *C v D* [2011] EWCA Civ 646; *Thewlis v Groupama Insurance Company Ltd* [2012] EWHC 3 (TCC); *PHI Group Ltd v Robert West Consulting Ltd* [2012] EWCA Civ 588.
[46] *Hertsmere Primary Care Trust v Administrators of Balasubramanium's Estate* [2005] 3 All ER 274.
[47] *Jolly v Harsco Infrastructure Services Ltd* [2012] EWHC 3086 (QB).
[48] *Jockey Club Racecourse v Willmott Dixon Construction* [2016] EWHC 167 (TCC).
[49] *Uwug Ltd (in liquidation) v Ball* [2015] EWHC 74 (IPEC).
[50] *Onay v Brown* [2010] Costs LR 29.
[51] CPR r 36.17(5) (e).
[52] *Yentob v MGN* [2015] EWCA Civ 1292.
[53] *C v D* [2012] 1 All ER 302.
[54] CPR rr 36.9 and 36.10.
[55] *PGF II SA v OMFS Company* [2012] EWHC 83 (TCC).

awarded if there has been a failure to engage in ADR or comply fully with pre-action requirements.[56] Conduct after a Part 36 offer has been made may be relevant, for example as to whether costs be paid on an indemnity basis.[57] It may be unjust to disapply the normal costs consequences where there has been a later acceptance of a Part 36 offer, but the burden of showing that normal consequences are unjust is a formidable obstacle.[58] A Part 36 offer that has been made and withdrawn may still be relevant to costs consequences.[59] A court can make an issue based or proportionate costs order, even where a claimant made a Part 36 offer that was not exceeded at trial.[60] A claimant's failure to accept an offer which the claimant fails to better at trial may be cancelled out in costs terms by a defendant's unreasonable failure to mediate.[61] An unsuccessful Part 36 offer cannot be treated as if it were successful just because it is very close to the final outcome of the case,[62] or vice versa.[63]

The purpose of Part 36 is to encourage the making and acceptance of realistic **10.30** offers. The challenge is in carefully assessing the figure to offer that is on the edge of what is reasonable to provide protection. Each party should consider making, reviewing, or withdrawing a Part 36 offer at a realistic level to control risk in relation to costs, and potentially to impose pressure to settle. A Part 36 offer may be made in respect of a counterclaim or other additional claim, or by an appellant or respondent on appeal.[64] Making a more advantageous offer is treated as a new offer rather than a withdrawal of the original offer.[65] It may be difficult to frame a Part 36 offer where a case is complex, where it includes significant non-financial issues, or where face to face engagement with the other side to examine issues is important.[66] If a party is not realistically able to make a Part 36 offer (because of the exposure to liability for costs if the offer is accepted), that party should still make an offer that is expressed to be without prejudice save as to costs.[67] The

---

[56]   *Straker v Tudor Rose* [2007] EWCA Civ 368.

[57]   *Ontulmus v Collett* [2014] EWHC 4117.

[58]   *Purser v Hibbs* [2015] EWHC 1792 (QB).

[59]   *Uwug Ltd (in liquidation) v Ball* [2015] EWHC 74 (IPEC); *Gulati v MGN Ltd* [2015] EWHC 1805 (Ch).

[60]   *Webb v Liverpool Women's NHS Foundation Trust* [2015] EWHC 449 (QB).

[61]   *Northrop Grumman Mission Systems Europe Ltd v BAE Systems (Al Diriyah C41 Ltd (No 2)* [2014] EWHC 3148 (TCC).

[62]   *Hammersmith Properties (Welwyn) Ltd v Saint-Gobain Ceramics and Plastics Ltd* [2013] EWHC 2227 (TCC).

[63]   *Sugar Hut Group v AJ Insurance Service* [2016] EWCA Civ 46.

[64]   CPR f 36.2(3), CPR r 36.4.

[65]   CPR r 36.9(5).

[66]   *Raggett v Governors of Preston Catholic College* [2012] EWHC 3641 (QB); *Mehjoo v Harben Baker* [2013] EWHC 1669 (QB).

[67]   *Magical Marking Ltd v Ware and Kay LLP* [2013] EWHC 636 (Ch).

offer should be a genuine offer to settle the case, and not just to attract Part 36 consequences.[68]

10.31 To encourage the use of Part 36 by both parties in a dispute, from 1 April 2013 if a defendant fails to beat a claimant's Part 36 offer, the claimant's damages can be increased by 10 per cent, or by 5 per cent if the value of the damages is above £75,000, subject to an overall cap of £500,000.[69] There have been some concerns about the practical effect of this provision.[70]

Qualified one-way cost shifting

10.32 Qualified one-way cost shifting (QOCS) was introduced from 1 April 2013 in personal injury cases, including clinical negligence.[71] The effect is that a claimant can still recover costs if successful, but will generally not be at risk of having to pay the defendant's costs if the claim fails. The interrelation with Part 36 is defined in that if a claimant is awarded a lower amount of damages than the offer made, the normal Part 36 principles will apply, but only up to the level of the damages recovered. Although introduced to balance the non-recovery of a success fee and ATE insurance premium, QOCS may in due course be extended to other types of case, as a part of the context within which risk is managed and ADR options considered. The protection will not be available if a claim has been struck out for lack of reasonable grounds, as being an abuse of the court's process or the conduct of the claimant is likely to obstruct the just disposal of the proceedings, or where the claim is on the balance of probabilities fundamentally dishonest.[72]

---

[68] CPR r 36.17(5)(e).

[69] Legal Aid, Sentencing and Punishment of Offenders Act 2012 s 55; Offers to Settle in Civil Proceedings Order 2013, SI 2013/93.

[70] *Thai Airways International Public Co Ltd v KL Holdings Co Ltd* [2015] EWHC 1476 (Comm), *Cashman v Mid Essex Hospital Services NHS Trust* [2015] EWHC 1312 (QB).

[71] CPR rr 44.13–44.17, Practice Direction 44—General Rules about Costs section 2—Qualified One-way Costs Shifting.

[72] CPR r 44.15 and 44.16, see also *Shah v Ul Haq* [2009] EWCA Civ 542; *Brighton & Hove Bus v Brooks* [2011] EWHC 2504 (Admin); *Fairclough Homes Ltd v Summers* [2012] UKSC 26.

11

SANCTIONS FOR REFUSING TO ENGAGE IN ADR PROCESSES

A Introduction

The court can penalize a party who unreasonably refuses to: **11.01**

- comply with an order made by the court directing the parties to attempt to resolve the dispute by ADR;
- accept an offer made by the other side to attempt to settle the dispute using an ADR process before the issue of proceedings; or
- accept an invitation by the other side to use an ADR process during the course of litigation, or even after judgment and prior to the hearing of an appeal.

The orders that the court can make include: **11.02**

- depriving the party of costs even if they are successful in the litigation;
- ordering them to pay some or all of the other side's costs even if they are successful in the litigation;
- ordering them to pay costs on an indemnity basis ('an indemnity costs order');
- ordering a higher rate of interest to be paid on damages awarded; or
- depriving a party of interest on damages awarded by the court.

The most common sanction that is imposed for unreasonably failing to consider **11.03** or use an ADR process to resolve the dispute is to make an adverse order for costs. Since the Jackson Reforms were implemented in April 2013, the courts have been more robust in penalizing parties who fail to take reasonable and proportionate steps to settle their dispute using ADR processes where it is appropriate to do so, particularly if a case management order directed the parties to use ADR. It can be expected that any case management orders made by the court, including those encouraging the use of ADR, in particular mediation, will be enforced more rigorously than has previously been the case.[1] The court also has power to strike out a case

---

[1] See Lord Justice Jackson's Fifth and Thirteenth Implementation Lectures, <http://www.judiciary. gov.uk/publications-and-reports/review-of-civil-litigation-costs/lectures>, CPR r 3.1(8), and CPR r 3.9.

if the claimant has the opportunity to obtain full redress through an ADR process, and continuing litigation in the hope of obtaining a costs advantage is not a reasonable or proportionate use of the court's resources.[2]

B The Court's General Powers to Make Costs Orders

11.04 The court's general discretion in relation to costs is set out in CPR r 44.2, which is explained in Chapter 10, at 10.08–10.10. The orders that a court may make in relation to costs can be wide-ranging and varied and include those set out in CPR r 44.2(6).

C Failure to Comply with Pre-Action Protocols

11.05 The court can take into account the extent of the parties' compliance with the Pre-Action Protocols and Practice Direction Pre-Action Conduct and Protocols when making case management and costs orders.[3] Non-compliance can include an unreasonable refusal to use a form of ADR or failing to respond at all to an invitation to do so.[4] The court can ask the parties to provide evidence that ADR has been considered. A party's silence in response to an invitation to participate in ADR might be considered unreasonable by the court and could lead to the court ordering that party to pay additional court costs.[5] The sanctions that a court can impose for non-compliance with the protocols include:[6]

- staying the proceedings;[7]
- ordering that the party at fault pays the costs, or part of the costs, of one or more of the other parties;
- an order that the party at fault pays those costs on an indemnity basis;[8]

---

[2] *Binns v Firstplus Financial Group Plc* [2013] EWHC 2436 (QB). See also *Andrew v Barclays Bank Plc* [2012] CTLC 115, where the court stayed litigation as a remedy could be obtained under a scheme established by the Financial Services Authority.
[3] Practice Direction Pre-Action Conduct and Protocols, para 13.
[4] Practice Direction Pre-Action Conduct and Protocols, para 14 (c). Also, see Chapter 8 for relevant details about how the Pre-Action Protocols and Practice Direction Pre-Action Conduct and Protocols encourage the use of ADR and the steps that the parties should take in relation to the consideration of ADR pre-issue.
[5] Practice Direction Pre-Action Conduct and Protocols, para 11.
[6] Practice Direction Pre-Action Conduct and Protocols, para 16.
[7] Practice Direction Pre-Action Conduct and Protocols, para 15(b). See Chapter 9 at 9.22–9.24 in relation to stays and the Online Resource Centre for examples of orders granting stays.
[8] See CPR rr 44.3 and 44.4.

- if the party at fault is the claimant who has been awarded a sum of money, an order depriving that party of interest on that sum for a specified period, and/or awarding interest at a lower rate than would otherwise have been awarded;
- if the party at fault is the defendant, and the claimant has been awarded a sum of money, an order awarding interest on that sum for a specified period at a higher rate (not exceeding 10 per cent above the base rate) than the rate which would otherwise have been awarded.

Adverse costs orders have been made in a number of cases for failing to follow **11.06** reasonable pre-action conduct in accordance with the provisions and spirit of the Protocols and Practice Direction Pre-action Conduct and Protocols.[9] However the court has refused to strike out a claim for non-compliance with the relevant provisions of Practice Direction Pre-Action Conduct then in force.[10] Non-compliance may result in an indemnity costs order, however.[11] The court may also penalize a party for failing to consider ADR pre-issue.[12]

D Unreasonable Refusal to Consider ADR

The court has power to deprive a winning party of some or all of their costs if they have **11.07** acted unreasonably in refusing to agree to ADR. The court should not discriminate against successful public bodies by being particularly disposed to make an adverse costs order against them for refusing to agree to ADR.[13] Even in judicial review cases,

---

[9] See for example *Thornhill v Nationwide Metal Recycling Ltd* [2011] EWCA Civ 919 (claimant ordered to pay 80 per cent of the defendants' costs of an interim application for non-compliance with the provisions of Practice Direction Pre-action Conduct then in force). Further recent cases where the court, in making a costs order, took into account a party's failure to act reasonably in exchanging information about the case, narrow the issues, or discuss ADR options include *Nelson's Yard Management Co v Eziefula* [2013] EWCA Civ 235; *AP (UK) Ltd v West Midland Fire and Civil Defence Authority* [2013] EWHC 385(QB); *Forstater v Python (Monty) Pictures Ltd* [2013] EWHC 3759 (Ch), and *Barker v Barnett* [2015] EWHC 1375 (QB). See also *Webb Resolutions Ltd v Waller Needham & Green (A Firm)* [2012] EWHC 3529 (Ch), where costs sanctions were imposed on a claimant for failing to disclose relevant documents sought by the defendant before proceedings were commenced pursuant to the Professional Negligence Pre-Action Protocol.

[10] *Pell Frischmann Consultants Ltd v Prabhu* [2013] EWHC 2203 (Ch).

[11] *Chemistree Homecare Ltd v Abbvie Ltd* [2013] EWHC 264 (Ch); *Forstater v Python (Monty) Pictures Ltd* [2013] EWHC 3759 (Ch). *Consortium Commercial Developments Limited v Prestigic Holdings Ltd & Another* [2014] WL 2807781.

[12] *Burchell v Bollard* [2005] EWCA Civ 358; *Jarrom v Sellers* [2007] EWHC 1366 (Ch). Also, see *P4 Ltd v Unite Integrated Solutions plc* [2006] EWHC 2924 (TCC), where the court was prepared to penalize a successful defendant in costs for failing to accept the claimant's offers to mediate before proceedings were commenced.

[13] See *Halsey v Milton Keynes General NHS Trust* [2004] EWCA Civ 576 at paras 9, 13, 16, 28, 34–35, 50, 54, and 81–82.

the courts have made it clear that, except for good reason, such proceedings should not be permitted to continue if a significant number of the issues between the parties could be resolved outside the litigation process.[14] A judge may require a party to justify a decision not to embark on ADR, and, in 2002, Lord Woolf commented that: 'Today, sufficient should be known about alternative dispute resolution to make the failure to adopt it, in particular when public money is involved, indefensible.'[15]

11.08 The leading case is *Halsey v Milton Keynes General NHS Trust*.[16] In *Halsey*, the Court of Appeal held that the general rule[17] that costs follow the event should not be departed from unless it is shown that the successful party acted unreasonably in refusing to agree to ADR. The unsuccessful party bears the burden of proving this. In considering whether the winning party acted unreasonably in failing to agree to use ADR, the court will consider all of the circumstances of the case, including but not limited to the following matters:

  (i) the nature of the dispute;

 (ii) the merits of the case;

(iii) the extent to which other settlement methods have been attempted;

(iv) whether the costs of the ADR process would be disproportionately high;

 (v) whether any delay in setting up and attending ADR would have been prejudicial;

(vi) whether the ADR process had a reasonable prospect of success.

11.09 The *Halsey* factors have generated a great deal of case law, and a more detailed discussion of each of the factors is set out below. The *Halsey* factors also apply where a claimant pursues proceedings rather than consider ADR through a compulsory scheme established by the Financial Services Authority.[18] The courts will refuse to allow a claim to proceed if the action is brought only to recover costs in circumstances where full compensation, but not costs, could be obtained under an ADR scheme, and such a claim could be struck out under CPR r 3.4.[19] The court has also applied the *Halsey* factors and penalized a party who unreasonably refused to

---

[14] See, for example, *MD v Secretary of State for the Home Department* [2011] EWCA Civ 453, where the court refused to allow a claim for declaratory relief to succeed where an apology and a complaints procedure had been set up to assess compensation by the Secretary of State. See also *R (on the application of S) v Hampshire County Council* [2009] EWHC 2537 (Admin).

[15] *R (Cowl) v Plymouth City Council* [2002] EWCA Civ 1935 (per Lord Woolf).

[16] [2004] EWCA Civ 576. See also *Laporte v Commissioner of Police of the Metropolis* [2015] EWHC 371 (QB).

[17] See CPR r 44.2(2).

[18] *Andrew v Barclays Bank plc*, [2012] CTLC 115.

[19] *Binns v Firstplus Financial Group Plc* [2013] EWHC 2436 (QB).

use ADR after judgment in order to settle costs which were the subject of detailed assessment proceedings.[20]

The nature of the dispute

Most cases are not, by their very nature, unsuitable for ADR. However there may **11.10** be some cases in which ADR may not be suitable because the court is required to determine issues of law or construction, a legal precedent is necessary, issues involving allegations of fraud or other commercially disreputable conduct may be raised that require resolution at trial, urgent injunctive relief, a search order or a freezing order may be required, a point of law may need to be resolved, or the case may be a test case. In such cases, it is unlikely that a party will be found to have acted unreasonably in refusing to use an ADR process.

The merits of the case

The fact that a party reasonably believes their case to be strong is relevant to the **11.11** question of whether a refusal of ADR is reasonable, otherwise one party could use the threat of a costs sanction to obtain a nuisance-value offer and force a settlement in respect of a case lacking merit. The key consideration is whether the party's assessment of the merits of the case is reasonable.

If a party reasonably believes he or she has a very strong case, that may well be a suf- **11.12** ficient reason for refusing to mediate (or negotiate), particularly if this is borne out at trial. A party may reasonably believe that they have a strong case even if they did not succeed in some issues at trial.[21] However, if the case is a borderline one, then it is likely to be suitable for ADR, and a party's belief that the case was strong is not likely to be a sufficient justification for refusing ADR, unless there are factors that tip the scales the other way.[22]

If defendants, who face what they consider to be unfounded claims, wish to **11.13** take a stand and contest them rather than make payments (even nuisance-value

---

[20] *Morris v Htay* [2015] WL 1839014 (2 February 2015).

[21] *Swain Mason v Mills & Reeve* [2012] EWCA Civ 498.

[22] Dyson LJ in *Halsey v Milton Keynes General NHS Trust* [2004] EWCA Civ 576 at [19] rejected the view to the contrary expressed by Lightman J in *Hurst v Leeming* [2002] EWHC 1051 (Ch). Also, see *Hickman v Blake Lapthorn* [2006] EWHC 12 (QB) where it was held that the second defendant was not unreasonable for refusing to mediate on the grounds that he believed that he had a strong case. The court judged his estimation of the strength of the case to be optimistic but not unreasonable. Also *Société Internationale de Télécommunications Aéronautiques SC (SITA) v The Wyatt Co (UK) Ltd* [2002] EWHC 2401 (Ch), where a third party was not unreasonable in refusing mediation where it had a strong case (a belief which was borne out by the trial).

payments) to buy them off, the courts are slow to characterize such conduct as unreasonable so as to deprive defendants of their costs, if they are ultimately successful.[23] A successful party will not be deprived of some or all of their costs for rejecting mediation if the claim did not warrant any issues of sufficient substance to justify mediation.[24] However, this position seems to ignore the positive effect that mediation can have in resolving disputes even if claims have no merit. The mediator can bring a new independent perspective to the parties if using evaluative techniques, and not every mediation has to end with a payment to the claimant. In *Northrop Grumman Mission Systems Europe Ltd v BAE Systems (Al Diriyah C41) Ltd*,[25] it was held that the fact that a party believed that they had a watertight case might well be sufficient justification for a refusal to use ADR, although that ignored the fact that mediation could have a positive effect, even if the claim has no merit. The judge considered a mediator could have brought the parties together without requiring a payment from one party to the other. That being so, a party's reasonably held view that it had a strong case provides only limited justification for refusing ADR.

11.14 A defendant who rejected mediation where there was no merit in the claim, but who indicated on a 'without prejudice save as to costs' basis that it was prepared to forgo its costs if the claim was dismissed, is unlikely to be found to be acting unreasonably.[26]

Extent to which other settlement methods have been attempted

11.15 The court will take into account the fact that settlement offers have been made, but been rejected by the successful party.[27] On the other hand, if reasonable offers have been made by the successful party and rejected by the unsuccessful party, then this may show that the unsuccessful party had an unreasonable view of the merits of their case and that mediation may serve no purpose and therefore the successful party may not have been unreasonable in refusing to agree to it.[28] The court will

---

[23] *Daniels v Commissioner of Police for the Metropolis* [2005] EWCA Civ 1312.

[24] *Morris v Davis* [2012] EWHC 1981 (Ch) (per Robert Ham QC at [11]–[17] and [21]). Also, see *ADS Aerospace Ltd v EMS Global Tracking Ltd* [2012] EWHC 2904 (TCC) and *Newman v Framewood Manor Management Co Ltd* [2012] EWCA Civ 1727.

[25] [2014] EWHC 3148.

[26] *Euroption Strategic Fund Ltd v Skandinaviska Enskilda Banken AB* [2012] EWHC 749 (Comm); *Swain Mason & Others v Mills & Reeve (A firm)* [2012] EWCA Civ 498 at [62] to [78].

[27] See *Vernacare Ltd v Environmental Pulp Products Ltd* [2012] EWPCC 49, where the successful party's costs were reduced by 5 per cent for its failure to engage more constructively with the defendant's attempts to negotiate.

[28] *ADS Aerospace Ltd v EMS Global Tracking Ltd* [2012] EWHC 2904 (TCC).

also bear in mind that ADR processes such as mediation may succeed where direct settlement discussions between the parties have failed.[29]

Where the parties have shown a genuine and constructive willingness to resolve **11.16** the issues between them, the successful party may not be automatically penalized for not agreeing to a form of ADR proposed by the other side, particularly where negotiations were taking place between the parties which eventually resulted in a Part 36 offer from the defendant that was accepted by the claimant. The court could only speculate on whether or not a mediator would have achieved any better or quicker result or could have persuaded the defendant to make the eventual offer at an earlier stage.[30] Similarly, it may not be unreasonable for a successful party with a strong case to refuse to engage in mediation where they had indicated at all times that they were prepared to engage in without prejudice discussions and there was no good reason why that approach should not be tried, particularly where those negotiations would be quicker and would cost substantially less than mediation.[31] Where a party commenced judicial review proceedings whilst simultaneously pursuing a complaint to the Independent Adjudicator, the defendant had not been unreasonable in refusing an offer to use mediation, because adjudication was a form of ADR and the parties were fully engaged in that process.[32]

A successful party may be penalized in costs for rejecting mediation, even if they **11.17** have made an effective Part 36 offer or unreasonably refused an offer to settle made outside the regime in CPR Part 36.[33]

Whether the costs of ADR would be disproportionately high

This is a factor that may be of particular importance if the sums at stake are rela **11.18** tively small. In such cases, ADR processes such as mediation might cost as much as a day in court. However, this is unlikely to be a significant factor in the vast majority of cases and certainly not in low value cases in the small claims track where the court operates a free mediation scheme, or in many fast track cases where low-cost, fixed-fee mediations can be arranged through the Civil Mediation Online Directory.[34]

---

[29] *Halsey v Milton Keynes General NHS Trust* [2004] EWCA Civ 576 (per Dyson LJ at [20]).
[30] *Corenso (UK) Ltd v Burnden Group plc* [2003] EWHC 1805 (QB).
[31] *ADS Aerospace Ltd v EMS Global Tracking Ltd* [2012] EWHC 2904 (TCC).
[32] *R (on the application of Crawford) v Newcastle upon Tyne University* [2014] EWHC 1197 (Admin).
[33] See Chapter 11 at 11.30–11.32.
[34] See <http://www.civilmediation.justice.gov.uk>, Chapter 16 at 16.14–16.16.

Whether delay in setting up and attending ADR would be prejudicial

11.19   If an ADR process is proposed at a late stage of the litigation and is likely to result in the trial being delayed, this may be a reason for refusing to agree to it. Successful parties have been judged not to have been unreasonable in refusing mediation which was proposed only two months before trial,[35] three weeks before trial,[36] 20 days before trial,[37] or 13 days before the trial.[38]

Whether ADR had a reasonable prospect of success

11.20   The burden is on the unsuccessful party to show that an ADR process such as mediation would have had a reasonable prospect of success. However, as Dyson LJ remarked in *Halsey*, this should not be an unduly onerous burden to discharge because the unsuccessful party does not have to show that ADR or mediation would have succeeded, but rather that there was a reasonable prospect that it would have succeeded.[39]

11.21   The courts have refused to penalize a party for refusing to agree to mediation in the following circumstances:

- where the relationship between the parties was so bad that mediation did not have a realistic prospect of success;[40]
- where there was 'insufficient room for manoeuvre to make mediation a venture which might have real prospects of success in achieving compromise';[41]
- where one party had a strong case and the conduct of the other party indicated that they were not willing to accept a nuisance payment and there was no evidence that they would have settled the claim at that level, even through the good offices of a mediator;[42]

---

[35] *Palfrey v Wilson* [2007] EWCA Civ 94.

[36] *Société Internationale de Télécommunications Aéronautiques SC (SITA) v The Wyatt Co (UK) Ltd* [2002] EWHC 2401 (Ch). It was also held that a third party was not unreasonable in refusing two other earlier offers to mediate in circumstances where the mediation concerned the claim between the claimant and the defendant, the third party had insufficient time to prepare for the mediation, the defendant's reasons for suggesting mediation was not to settle the third party claim but rather to persuade the third party to contribute something to the settlement of the claimant's case, and its offers to mediate were disagreeable in tone and designed to bully and browbeat the third party into mediation.

[37] *ADS Aerospace Ltd v EMS Global Tracking Ltd* [2012] EWHC 2904 (TCC).

[38] *Park Promotion Ltd (t/a Pontypool Rugby Football Club) v Welsh Rugby Union Ltd* [2012] EWHC 2406 (QB).

[39] See *Halsey v Milton Keynes NHS Trust* [2004] EWCA Civ 576 (per Dyson LJ at [28]).

[40] *Re Midland Linen Services Ltd* [2005] EWHC 3380 (Ch).

[41] *McCook v Lobo* [2002] EWCA Civ 1760.

[42] *ADS Aerospace Ltd v EMS Global Tracking Ltd* [2012] EWHC 2904 (TCC).

- where a party's attitude and character was such that he or she was incapable of a balanced evaluation of the facts so that mediation had no real prospect of success.[43]

On the other hand, where there was no objective reason to conclude that ADR had no reasonable prospect of success, this burden will not be discharged.[44] **11.22**

E Other Factors

The court in *Halsey* made it clear that the factors discussed above were not exhaustive. In deciding whether a party was unreasonable in refusing ADR all the facts and circumstances of the case must be considered. These include whether an ADR order had been made by the court, whether further information or expert evidence needed to be obtained and/or disclosed before ADR was undertaken, and the impact that Part 36 offers have on a refusal to engage in ADR. **11.23**

Whether an ADR order was made by the court

Where a successful party refuses to agree to ADR despite the court's encouragement that is a factor which the court will take into account when deciding whether the refusal was unreasonable. The court's encouragement may take different forms. The stronger the form of encouragement, the easier it will be for the unsuccessful party to discharge the burden of showing that the successful party's refusal was unreasonable.[45] **11.24**

If a party refused to engage in ADR, despite the fact that an order was made in the form in Appendix 7 of the *Admiralty and Commercial Court Guide*,[46] then 'he runs the risk that for that reason alone his refusal to agree to ADR would be held to have been unreasonable, and that he should therefore be penalised in costs'.[47] In *Wilson v Haden (t/a Clyne Farm Centre)*,[48] a defendant suffered a costs sanction because it did not attempt ADR despite being ordered by the court to do so, it ignored correspondence from the claimant suggesting the use of ADR, and it did not file a witness **11.25**

---

[43] *Hurst v Leeming* [2002] EWHC 1051 (Ch); also, see *Nigel Witham Ltd v Smith* [2008] EWHC 12 (TCC).

[44] *Gaston, Boughton v Courtney* [2004] EWHC 600 (Ch). Also, see *PGF II SA v OMFS Company* [2013] EWCA Civ 1288.

[45] *Halsey v Milton Keynes General NHS Trust* [2004] EWCA Civ 576 (per Dyson LJ at [29]).

[46] The Commercial Court ADR order can be also be found on the Online Resource Centre.

[47] *Halsey v Milton Keynes General NHS Trust* [2004] EWCA Civ 576 (per Dyson LJ at [31]).

[48] [2013] EWHC 1211 (QB).

statement indicating why it considered ADR to be inappropriate in accordance with the ADR order made by the court.

11.26 A successful party was also penalized in costs for ignoring two ADR orders made by the court in *Gaston, Boughton v Courtney*,[49] and at the appeal stage, for ignoring the recommendations of the Court of Appeal that the parties should try to mediate the dispute using the Court of Appeal Mediation Scheme.[50]

Obtaining further evidence or information before using ADR

11.27 It may not be unreasonable to refuse to take part in ADR until the issues in the case have been clarified by each party's case being set out in statements of case or until evidence has been exchanged, if the true nature of the dispute could not be ascertained until then.[51] If the claim is particularly complex, it might not be unreasonable to refuse to attempt mediation until the claim is properly pleaded in a statement of case.[52]

11.28 A defendant was held not to have acted unreasonably in refusing to mediate in group litigation brought by the claimants until expert evidence had been obtained so that it could be seen whether the claimant had a case.[53]

11.29 However, it may not be reasonable to reject ADR for these reasons if the parties could have obtained the information required during the proposed ADR process. In such cases, the court may deprive the successful party of their costs.[54] A robust approach was taken by the court in *PGF II SA v OMFS Co*[55] where the court at first instance rejected the defendant's argument that a successful mediation could only take place later in the year when expert reports on diminution in value were available. The defendant did not raise this point at the time the request to mediate was made by the other party. The court observed that it was open to the defendant to ask for the claimant's report and to obtain their own report in reply prior to a mediation taking place. Any such inhibitions to mediation could have been overcome had they been raised by the defendant at the time. The first instance decision was upheld by

---

[49] [2004] EWHC 600 (Ch).

[50] See *Dunnett v Railtrack Plc* [2002] EWCA Civ 303. See also *Ali Ghaith v Indesit Company UK Limited* [2012] EWCA Civ 642 where the Court of Appeal criticized the parties for failing to use mediation when the Court granting permission to appeal had recommended they should do so.

[51] See *Wethered Estates Ltd v Davis* [2005] EWHC 1903; *Nigel Witham Ltd v Smith* [2008] EWHC 12 (TCC).

[52] *Williams v Seals* [2014] EWHC 3708 (Ch) at [48].

[53] See *Corby Group Litigation v Corby DC* [2009] EWHC 2109 (TCC). A similar result was reached in *Mobiqa Ltd v Trinity Mobile Ltd* [2010] EWHC 253 (Pat).

[54] *Jarrom v Sellars* [2007] EWHC 1366 (Ch).

[55] [2013] EWCA Civ 1288.

the Court of Appeal. The court is likely to disregard an offer to mediate which is made subject to an unreasonable condition.[56]

The impact of Part 36 offers on a refusal to use ADR

The court may penalize a successful party for refusing to use mediation, even if they had made other reasonable attempts to settle the matter such as making a Part 36 offer which the other party does not beat at trial.[57] This is particularly so where the circumstances showed that the unsuccessful party had taken an unrealistic view of the merits of the case (and therefore failed to accept reasonable offers made by the other party), and these issues could have been explored fully in mediation. Offers for settlement in such cases are unlikely to be a proper substitute for the process of ADR which involves parties engaging with each other and a third party, such as a mediator, to resolve a dispute. In such circumstances, the aspirations of each party are soon brought within realistic bounds.[58] It is not appropriate to penalize a party who beat a Part 36 offer simply on the basis that the offer was almost appropriate and the successful party should have negotiated, particularly where the court did not have full information about negotiations which may have taken place.[59] However, the court may be prepared to penalize a claimant who, at trial, beat a Part 36 made by the defendant where it was not reasonable for the claimant to continue part of its claim, particularly if the court has full information about the negotiations which took place.[60]

11.30

Pursuing litigation in a 'no holds barred' manner, and failing to make reasonable early concessions so as to reduce the scope and costs of the trial, is something that the court can take into account as part of 'all of the circumstances of the case' under

11.31

---

[56] R (Royal Free London NHS Foundation Trust v Secretary of State for the Home Department [2013] EWHC 4101 (Admin).

[57] See Dunnett v Railtrack Plc [2002] EWCA Civ 303, where the successful defendant was not awarded the costs of the appeal for refusing mediation when it had been recommended by the court, despite the fact that the defendant had made a modest Part 36 offer instead. Also, see P4 Ltd v Unite Integrated Solutions plc [2006] EWHC 2924 (TCC), where the defendant made an effective Part 36 offer of £6,000 which the claimant rejected but where the claimant only recovered £387 at trial. Ordinarily, the defendant would have been awarded the costs of the claim, but instead the court ordered the defendant to pay the claimant's costs up to the latest date for acceptance of the Part 36 offer and the claimant to pay the defendant's costs after that point because the defendant's conduct in failing to mediate and provide information prevented the parties resolving the case at minimal cost. See also Wilson v Haden (t/a Clyne Farm Centre) [2013] EWHC 1211 (QB) where, in assessing costs, the court took account of a party's failure to engage in ADR.

[58] P4 Ltd v Unite Integrated Solutions plc [2006] EWHC 2924 (TCC).

[59] Hammersmatch Properties (Welwyn) Ltd v Saint-Gobain Ceramics & Plastics Ltd [2013] EWHC 2227 (TCC).

[60] Sugar Hut Group Ltd v AJ Insurance [2014] EWHC 3775 (Comm). Reversed on appeal – see [2016] EWCA Civ 46.

CPR r 36.17(5) in deciding whether it would be unjust to order that a defendant, who had made an effective Part 36 offer, which the claimant failed to beat at trial, should recover some or all of its costs from the claimant from the expiry of the relevant period for accepting the Part 36 offer.[61] In *Vernacare Ltd v Environmental Pulp Products Ltd*,[62] 5 per cent was deducted from the claimant's costs and in *Lilleyman v Lilleyman (No 2)*,[63] the judge disallowed 20 per cent of the defendant's costs for the no holds barred approach to the litigation.

11.32   An even more robust approach was taken by the Court of Appeal in *PGF II SA v OMFS*,[64] where a defendant made a successful Part 36 offer which the claimant did not accept until the day before trial. The usual costs order under CPR r 36.10(5) which was then in force (now CPR r 36.13(5)) would have provided for the claimant to recover its costs up to the expiry of the relevant period for accepting the offer and the claimant to pay the defendant's costs from that date to the date of acceptance. However, the court deprived the defendant of its costs because the defendant was unreasonable in refusing to respond to the claimant's offers to use mediation, which the court found would have had a reasonable prospect of success. However, it may be unjust to require a claimant to pay the defendant's costs following the rejection of a Part 36 offer, which the claimant did not beat at trial, where settlement would not have resolved the real issues in dispute between the parties.[65]

Unreasonable refusal of other offers

11.33   Both parties should proactively look for ways to settle a case sooner rather than later and appropriate costs orders can be made to reflect the pointlessness of the litigation proceeding.[66] A successful party may also be deprived of some or all of their costs if they act unreasonably in failing to accept an offer made by a defendant to settle the case which is not made pursuant to Part 36, and they fail to recover more than

---

[61] *Lilleyman v Lilleyman & Another (No 2)* [2012] EWHC 1056 (Ch), where Briggs J ordered that a defendant, who made an effective Part 36 offer which the claimant failed to beat at trial, should nevertheless, only recover 80 per cent of its costs incurred after the time for acceptance of the offer, the 20 per cent disallowance being an appropriate reflection of the defendant's unreasonable conduct in failing to make sensible early concessions. See also *Sycamore Bridco Ltd v Breslin* [2013] EWHC 583 (Ch), where a claimant recovered only 60 per cent of its costs, despite beating a Part 36 order made by the defendant, to reflect the fact it had fought and lost some issues at trial.

[62] [2012] EWPCC 49.

[63] [2012] EWHC 1056 (Ch).

[64] [2013] EWCA Civ 1288.

[65] *Smith v Trafford Housing Trust* (Costs) [2012] EWHC 3320 (Ch).

[66] *Bellway Homes Ltd v Seymour (Civil Engineering Contractors) Ltd* [2013] EWHC 1890 (TCC) at [32].

that offer at trial.[67] However, an offer which is not made under Part 36 should not be treated as directly analogous to a Part 36 offer when considering what costs order should be made under CPR Part 44.[68]

F The Claimant's Failure to Initiate ADR Processes

The court makes a distinction between cases where the successful party *rejects* an **11.34** offer of ADR made by the other side and those cases where there has been a failure by the successful party to *initiate* ADR proceedings.

In *Vale of Glamorgan Council v Roberts*,[69] the court distinguished *Halsey* on the basis **11.35** that those guidelines did not apply to a case where the successful party did not initiate ADR (as opposed to refusing an offer of ADR made by the other party), and held that it would be going too far to disallow costs incurred by a successful party simply because that party did not initiate suggestions for mediation (or, by analogy, any ADR process).

A different order is likely to be made if the successful party deliberately exaggerated **11.36** the amount of the claim and failed to initiate ADR.[70] However, the court refused to make an adverse costs order against a successful claimant who had exaggerated his claim (but where there had been no finding of dishonesty or misrepresentation against him) where the claimant did negotiate and realistically and promptly accepted the defendant's offer to settle.[71]

In *Vale of Glamorgan v Roberts*, there was no suggestion that the claimant failed to **11.37** comply with the terms of the relevant Pre-action Protocol or Practice Direction Pre-Action Conduct and Protocols. It is clear that a party who fails to comply with the requirements of the Pre-action Protocols and Practice Direction Pre-Action Conduct and Protocols to a significant extent is likely to find that their failure to do so is penalized in costs.[72]

---

[67] *Brit Inns Ltd (in Liquidation) v BDW Trading Ltd* (Costs) [2012] EWHC 2489 (TCC). See also *Walker Construction (UK) Ltd v Quayside Homes Ltd* [2014] EWCA Civ 93, where the successful defendant (who only recovered only a small proportion of their counterclaim) was found to be unreasonable in refusing to accept a Calderbank offer made by the claimant and was therefore ordered to pay the claimant's costs from the date of the Calderbank offer to the date of judgment.

[68] *F & C Alternative Investments (Holdings) Ltd v Barthelemy (Costs)* [2012] EWCA Civ 843.

[69] [2008] EWHC 2911 (Ch).

[70] *Painting v Oxford University* [2005] EWCA Civ 161; *Widlake v BAA Ltd* [2009] EWCA Civ 1256.

[71] *Fox v Foundation Piling Ltd* [2011] EWCA Civ 790.

[72] See 11.05–11.06 above.

G Failing to Make an Offer to Settle a Claim

11.38 Recent cases have demonstrated that the courts will not only take into account an unreasonable refusal to consider ADR in making adverse costs orders, but may penalize a party in costs if they failed to make any offer or a reasonable offer to settle the claim. It is clear that both parties should be proactively looking for ways to settle the dispute, particularly where the costs of the claim and any counterclaim exceed, or are likely to exceed, the value of the claim.[73]

11.39 In *Fitzroy Robinson Ltd v Mentmore Towers Ltd*,[74] in considering the appropriate costs order, the court took into account the defendant's unreasonable refusal of offers to mediate and failure to make a timely offer to settle the case after the conclusion of the trial of liability. The court therefore ordered the defendant to pay the claimant's costs on an indemnity basis from the date of the pre-trial review.

11.40 The Court of Appeal also took into account the fact that the defendant failed to make a realistic offer to settle the case until late in the day in deciding the issue of costs in *Fox v Foundation Piling Ltd*[75] and in *Medway Primary Care Trust v Marcus*.[76] Defendants faced with a dishonest or exaggerated claim may not wish to make a Part 36 offer because of the automatic costs consequences which flow on acceptance pursuant to CPR r 36.13. However, approving *Fox v Foundation Piling Ltd*,[77] the Supreme Court noted that such defendants could make a Calderbank offer to settle the genuine parts of the claim, and the costs of that part, but on the basis that the claimant would pay the defendant's costs in respect of the fraudulent parts of the claim.[78]

---

[73] See *Bellway Homes Ltd v Seymour (Civil Engineering Contractors Ltd)* [2013] EWHC 1890 (TCC).

[74] [2010] EWHC 98.

[75] [2011] EWCA Civ 790.

[76] [2011] EWCA Civ 750.

[77] [2011] EWCA Civ 790.

[78] See *Summers v Fairclough Homes* [2012] 1 WLR 2004. In *Magical Marking Ltd v Ware & Kay LLP* [2013] EWHC 636 (Ch) the court penalized the defendants, who were in substance the successful party, by ordering a 15 per cent reduction in the costs payable to them because they had failed to concede the limited negligence the court found proved, and failed to make a Calderbank offer. See also *Walker Construction (UK) Ltd v Quayside Homes Ltd* [2014] EWCA Civ 93, where the Court of Appeal, applying *Medway Primary Care Trust v Marcus* [2011] EWCA Civ 750 and *Fairclough Homes v Summers* [2012] 1 WLR 2004, found that the judge at first instance had failed to give appropriate weight to the fact that the claimant could not make a Part 36 offer in respect of an exaggerated counterclaim because acceptance of that would have entitled the defendant to recover all of their costs, but as the claimant had made a reasonable Calderbank offer instead, the trial judge erred in failing to order the defendant to pay the claimant's costs from the date of the Calderbank offer to the date of judgment.

H Delay in Consenting to ADR

In *Nigel Witham Ltd v Smith*[79] the court considered whether a party could be **11.41** penalized for agreeing to mediation late in the day when the majority of costs had been incurred, although they did in fact mediate the dispute. The court held that where the successful party has unreasonably delayed in consenting to mediation, this may lead to an adverse costs order, but no order was made on the facts.

A party did not act unreasonably in refusing to consider mediation until its applica- **11.42** tion to strike out the other side's case had been disposed of by the court.[80]

I Both Parties at Fault

Where both parties are at fault, the court may penalize both of them by refusing **11.43** to make any costs order at all, whatever the outcome of the case.[81] A court may be unwilling to penalize the successful party for refusing to use ADR, if the other party also acted unreasonably.[82] In *Rolf v De Guerin*,[83] the Court of Appeal after reviewing the key authorities, including *Halsey*, made no order for costs where the claimant was the winner, but only just (she had failed in most of her claim) and the defendant had unreasonably rejected the claimant's offers to attempt to settle by negotiation or mediation, particularly as a trial should be regarded as the last resort in a small building case and mediation was particularly appropriate for cases of this type. The defendant put forward three reasons for refusing to agree to mediation or a settlement meeting until the eve of the trial, all of which were rejected by the Court of Appeal:

- the behaviour of the claimant's husband and the fact that, at mediation, the defendant would have been unable to persuade the mediator what he was like;
- he would have had to accept 'his guilt' at mediation; and
- he wanted his day in court and he was proved correct.

---

[79] [2008] EWHC 12 (TCC).
[80] *S v Chapman* [2008] EWCA Civ 800.
[81] *Longstaff International Ltd v Evans* [2005] EWHC 4 (Ch); *Rolf v De Guerin* [2011] EWCA Civ 78.
[82] See *Courtwell Properties Ltd v Glencore PF (UK) Ltd* [2014] EWHC 184 (TCC); *Northrop Grumman Mission Systems Europe Ltd v BAE Systems (Al Diriyah C4I) Ltd* [2014] EWHC 3148 (TCC) and *Lakehouse Contracts Ltd v UPR Services Ltd* [2014] EWHC 1223 (Ch).
[83] [2011] EWCA Civ 78.

11.44 The court has made no order for costs in a number of other cases where the claimant did not succeed in a substantial part of the claim, but the defendant failed to take part in mediation when suggested by the claimant,[84] or the defendant made no offer to settle the claim.[85]

J Rejecting ADR Before the Hearing of an Appeal

11.45 The court may penalize a successful party by depriving them of the costs of the appeal for refusing ADR after trial and pending an appeal, and this is particularly so if the successful party ignores a recommendation of the Court of Appeal that the parties should try to mediate the dispute using the Court of Appeal Mediation Scheme.[86]

11.46 Other adverse costs orders that have been made for refusing ADR at the appeal stage are as follows:

- the winning party to an appeal had its costs reduced by £5,000 because it failed to heed advice given by the court to attempt mediation;[87]
- the successful respondent was awarded its costs to be assessed on the indemnity basis because of the appellant's refusal to mediate, despite encouragement by the court to use the Court of Appeal mediation service.[88]

11.47 However, a different view was taken by the court in *Reed Executive plc v Reed Business Information Ltd*,[89] where the Court of Appeal refused to penalize the successful appellant/defendant for refusing an offer by the claimant to mediate when the defendant had a reasonable and justifiable belief in its prospects of success in the appeal.

K Backing out of ADR

11.48 The court may penalize a successful party for agreeing to explore settlement in an ADR process, and then backing out of it at the last moment, particularly where there is at least a prospect that the ADR process would have succeeded if it had been allowed to proceed.

---

[84] See *Seeff v Ho* [2011] EWCA Civ 186.

[85] *Abbott v Long* [2011] EWCA Civ 874.

[86] *Dunnett v Railtrack plc* [2002] EWCA Civ 303 (per Brooke LJ at [15]). Also, see *Ali Ghaith v Indesit Company UK Limited* [2012] EWCA Civ 642 where the Court of Appeal criticized the parties for failing to use mediation when the court granting permission to appeal had recommended they should do so (per Longmore LJ at [26] and Ward LJ at [29]).

[87] *Neal v Jones Motors* [2002] EWCA Civ 1731.

[88] *Virani v Manuel Revert Y CIA SA* [2004] 2 Lloyd's Rep 14.

[89] [2004] EWCA Civ 887.

Adverse costs orders have been made in these circumstances in the following cases: **11.49**

- The successful defendants were penalized in costs for withdrawing from a mediation the day before it was due to take place on instructions from their insurers. Having agreed to mediation, it will be difficult for those resiling from it to show that it had no realistic prospect of success.[90]
- The successful appellant was not awarded their costs of the appeal for pulling out of the mediation two days before the date fixed for the meeting.[91]
- The defendant withdrew from a mediation meeting days before it was due to take place and was therefore ordered to pay the claimant's costs thrown away by the late cancellation of the mediation process.[92]

L Unreasonable Conduct in Mediation

The principles in *Halsey* were extended in *Carleton (Earl of Malmesbury) v Strutt and*   **11.50**
Parker[93] to unreasonable conduct in the mediation. However, this was only possible because the parties agreed that privilege should be waived in all 'without prejudice' matters. As a result, the court was able to find that the claimant's position at the mediation was plainly unreasonable and unrealistic and that, if they had made an offer that reflected their true position, the mediation might have succeeded or the defendants could have protected themselves by making a Part 36 offer. In the circumstances, justice was done by awarding the claimant only a portion of their costs to reflect the unreasonable stance they took in the mediation.

The court will usually only enquire into conduct that took place in the mediation if   **11.51**
all parties to the mediation consent to waive privilege and confidentiality. As this is not likely to happen often, an order of this type is likely to be very rare.

M Indemnity Costs Orders for Failing to Consider ADR

The court can make an indemnity costs order where there has been unreason-   **11.52**
able conduct to a high degree.[94] The courts have power to take a strong view about the rejection of ADR, if necessary by imposing indemnity costs orders, or

---

[90] *Leicester Circuits Ltd v Coates Brothers plc* [2003] EWCA Civ 333.
[91] *McMillan Williams v Range* [2004] EWCA Civ 294.
[92] *Roundstone Nurseries Ltd v Stephenson Holdings Ltd* [2009] EWHC 1431 (TCC).
[93] [2008] EWHC 424 (QB).
[94] See *Reid Minty (a Firm) v Taylor* [2001] EWCA Civ 1723. Also, see *Excelsior Commercial & Industrial Holdings Ltd v Salisbury Hamer Aspden & Johnson (Costs)* [2002] EWCA Civ 879; *Balmoral Group Ltd v Borealis (UK) Ltd (Indemnity Costs)* [2006] EWHC 2531 (Comm).

ordering that a higher rate of interest should be paid on any damages that might be recoverable.[95]

11.53　Such an order was made in *Rowallan Group Ltd v Edgehill Portfolio No 1*,[96] where the claimant issued proceedings during the course of a mediation hearing, with no prior letter before claim. Where a claim was speculative, risky, and was conducted in a manner which displayed little regard to proportionality or reasonableness, an indemnity costs order could be made.[97]

11.54　In *Southwark LBC v IBM UK Ltd (Costs)*[98] and *Barr v Biffa Waste Services Ltd (Costs)*[99] indemnity costs were awarded from a certain date in circumstances where there was a failure to accept a reasonable offer which ought to have been accepted. These cases were considered in *Epsom College v Pierse Constructing Southern Ltd (in Liquidation) (Costs)*[100] where the court upheld the indemnity costs order made by the judge at first instance but on different grounds. Lord Justice Rix (at para 71) stated that the requirements for making an indemnity costs order could be met where there has been an unreasonable failure to accept offers of settlement, or a party has resisted a sensible approach to finding a solution to the proceedings.

11.55　A defendant was awarded indemnity costs where court time, costs, and resources were wasted as a result of the claimant's unwillingness to accept an offer of settlement from the defendant that they had indicated they were prepared to accept only a few days earlier and there was no justification for their change of position.[101] An indemnity costs order has also been made because of unreasonable conduct on the part of the claimant in failing to accept an early 'drop hands' offer from the defendant,[102] and also where there was a continuing failure by the defendants to engage in ADR from the start without good reason.[103]

---

[95]　*Dyson v Leeds City Council* [2000] CP Rep 42 (per Ward LJ at [18]).

[96]　[2007] EWHC 32 (Ch). See also *Phoenix Finance Ltd v The Federation Internationale De L'Automobile & Ors* [2002] EWHC 1242 (Ch), where indemnity costs were ordered for failing to engage in any pre-action conduct.

[97]　*Euroption Strategic Fund Ltd v Skandinaviska Enskilda Banken AB* [2012] EWHC 749 (Comm). See also *Excalibur Ventures LLC v Texas Keystone Inc (Costs)* [2013] EWHC 4278 (Comm) and *Intercity Telecom Ltd v Solanki* [2015] 2 Costs LR 315.

[98]　[2011] EWHC 653 (TCC).

[99]　[2011] EWHC 1107 (TCC).

[100]　[2011] EWCA Civ 1449.

[101]　*Igloo Regeneration (General Partner) Ltd v Powell Williams Partnership (Costs)* [2013] EWHC 1859 (TCC).

[102]　*A & E Television Networks LLC v Discovery Communications Europe Ltd* [2013] EWHC 276 (Pat).

[103]　*Garritt-Critchley v Ronnan* [2014] EWHC 1774 (Ch).

By contrast, the court refused to award costs on an indemnity basis: **11.56**

- against a party who unreasonably withdrew from mediation;[104]
- where the claim raised arguable issues, was not pursued in a disproportionate or unreasonable way, but was dismissed at trial, and where the claimant refused a low offer of settlement from the defendant even though it would have better off accepting the offer than pursuing the case to trial.[105]

The court has sounded a warning note to parties who seek indemnity costs after set- **11.57** tlement. Such parties must behave in a proportionate way, and where an application for indemnity costs is likely to involve a conflict of evidence, the applicant needed 'to think long and hard about whether it was appropriate to pursue the application, because there could be few, if any, cases in which there should, in effect, be a trial of issues settled by acceptance of an offer or by settlement reached in some other ADR process'. [106] The policy of encouraging the abandonment of unsustainable claims should not be undermined by awarding indemnity costs, unless there was a really strong case for doing so.[107]

A party cannot usually rely on without prejudice correspondence in support of an **11.58** application for indemnity costs on the basis that the other party was unreasonable in not discussing settlement, and a party making such an application is not impliedly waiving privilege in without prejudice correspondence.[108]

N Silence in the Face of an Invitation to Use ADR

In *PGF II SA v OMFS Co 1 Ltd*,[109] the court extended the *Halsey* principles and held **11.59** that, as a general rule, silence in the face of an invitation to participate in ADR was itself unreasonable, regardless of whether there was a good reason for the refusal to engage in ADR. The court noted that there might be rare cases where ADR was so obviously inappropriate that to characterize silence as unreasonable would be pure formalism, or where the failure to respond was the result of a mistake, in which the onus would be on the respondent to prove that explanation. The court held that there were sound practical and policy reasons for such a modest extension to the

---

[104] *Roundstone Nurseries Ltd v Stephenson Holdings Ltd* [2009] EWHC 1431 (TCC).
[105] *Elvanite Full Circle Limited v AMEC Earth & Environmental (UK) Limited* [2013] EWHC 1643 (TCC).
[106] *Courtwell Properties Ltd v Greencore PF (UK) Ltd* [2014] EWHC 184 (TCC).
[107] *Forstater v Python (Monty) Pictures Ltd* [2013] EWHC 3579 (Ch).
[108] *Vestergaard Fransden A/S v Bestnet Europe Ltd* [2014] EWHC 4047 (Ch).
[109] [2013] EWCA Civ 1288.

Halsey principles, firstly because an investigation of the reasons for refusing to use ADR, advanced for the first time at a costs hearing perhaps months or years later, posed forensic difficulties for the court in deciding whether those reasons were genuine. Secondly, a failure to provide reasons was contrary to the objective of requiring parties to consider and discuss ADR. Any difficulties or reasonable objections to a particular ADR proposal should be discussed, so that the parties narrowed their differences. This approach would also serve the policy of proportionality.

11.60   Practice Direction Pre-Action Conduct and Protocols and the Pre-Action Protocols (which were revised and reissued with effect from 6 April 2015) also provide that a party's silence in response to an invitation to participate or a refusal to participate in ADR might be considered unreasonable by the court and could lead to the court ordering that party to pay additional costs.[110]

11.61   However, silence in the face of an offer to mediate did not attract a costs sanction in *R (Crawford) v Newcastle upon Tyne University*,[111] where the defendant did not respond to the claimant's offer to mediate, but it could not be said that they refused to engage with ADR because at the time the parties were fully engaged with another ADR process, namely adjudication before the Independent Adjudicator.

O What Practical Steps should be Taken by a Party to Avoid Sanctions?

11.62   Recent cases[112] have demonstrated that the court is more likely to be sceptical about arguments raised retrospectively to justify a refusal to engage in ADR and that silence in the face of an invitation to participate in ADR is, as a general rule, of itself unreasonable, regardless of whether an outright refusal, or a refusal to engage in the type of ADR suggested, or to do so at the time suggested, might have been justified by the identification of reasonable grounds.

11.63   A party who is faced with a request to engage in ADR, but who believes that they have reasonable grounds for refusing to participate in an ADR process at that stage of the proceedings should consider the following practical steps to avoid a sanction:

- do not ignore an offer to engage in ADR. Failure to respond is likely to be treated as an outright refusal;[113]

---

[110] Para 11, Practice Direction Pre-Action Conduct and Protocols.
[111] [2014] EWHC 1197 (Admin).
[112] See, in particular, *PGF II SA v OMFS Co I Ltd* [2013] EWCA Civ 1288.
[113] See *PGF II SA v OMFS Co I Ltd* [2013] EWCA Civ 1288.

- respond promptly, in writing, giving clear and full reasons why ADR is not appropriate at this stage of the dispute or proceedings. The reasons given, where possible, should be justified in light of the relevant principles derived from *Halsey* and subsequent cases which are explained in this chapter. The response should be contained in an open letter or in a letter marked 'without prejudice except as to costs';
- if lack of evidence or information is an obstacle to a successful ADR process being undertaken at that time, this must be canvassed with the other party to the dispute in the correspondence, and consideration should be given to whether that evidence or information can be obtained during the ADR process or in advance of the process. If court proceedings have already commenced, a judge may be prepared to make an order against a recalcitrant party directing further information or evidence to be disclosed prior to using ADR;
- letters replying to requests to engage in ADR should be written with care. A party may have good reason to refuse ADR at that point in time, but the correspondence should not be written in such a way that closes off exploration of ADR processes at a later date. An outright refusal to use ADR at any time is more likely to be construed as unreasonable.

P Privileged Material and Sanctions

Any communications passing between the parties that are aimed at settlement are **11.64** privileged from disclosure by operation of the without prejudice rule.[114] In *Halsey*,[115] the court accepted that if the integrity and confidentiality of the mediation process is to be preserved, the court should not know, and therefore should not investigate, why the process failed to result in an agreement. This is likely to be equally true of all other non-adjudicative ADR processes.

In *Reed Executive plc v Reed Business Information Ltd*,[116] the Court of Appeal applied **11.65** *Walker v Wilsher*[117] and held that the court has no jurisdiction to order disclosure of oral or written communications that were expressed to be 'without prejudice' (whether in party-to-party negotiations or third-party assisted negotiations) for the purpose of deciding the question of costs and whether a party acted unreasonably in refusing ADR. It found that *Halsey* did not change that general rule. Even if there were such a jurisdiction, disclosure should be refused as a matter of discretion. It is

---

[114] See Chapter 5 at 5.17–5.26.
[115] [2004] EWCA Civ 576.
[116] [2004] EWCA Civ 887.
[117] 1889 LR 23 QBD 335.

open to a party to avoid the rule by providing that the communications are taking place expressly on the basis that they are 'without prejudice save as to costs'. The court can then look at those communications after issues of liability and remedies have been determined, in order to decide the question of costs. The court recognized that the fact that it cannot look at 'without prejudice' material means that in many situations it may not be able to determine whether the winning party has acted unreasonably in refusing an offer to attempt to resolve the matter by an ADR method. This was the case in *Wethered Estate Ltd v Davis*[118] where the court was not prepared to enquire into the reasons why the mediation failed as it was important that the without prejudice nature of the mediation process was maintained unless the parties themselves waived it by clear and unequivocal consent. The court will also not usually be able to look at without prejudice material on an application for indemnity costs.[119]

11.66 There clearly have been cases where the court has been referred to without prejudice material in order to decide the question of costs, and in particular whether an adverse costs order should be made against a party for refusing to participate in ADR. This was the case, for example, in *Société Internationale de Télécommunications Aéronautiques SC (SITA) v The Wyatt Company (UK) Limited.*[120] Here it was apparent that without prejudice material was shown to the judge after judgment on liability had been delivered and before argument took place about costs. The material provided to the judge included letters written in an attempt to persuade the third party to take part in mediation, including attendance notes of without prejudice meetings of the lawyers, which also recorded events that took place at the mediation meeting and remarks alleged to have been made by the mediator. It is not clear whether all of the communications that were referred to the judge were marked 'without prejudice save as to costs'. To the extent that they were not, the parties waived privilege. Such cases are likely to be rare.

11.67 It is clear from these cases that if a party makes an offer to explore settlement using some form of ADR process, they should make sure that correspondence is marked 'without prejudice except as to costs' if they want to refer it to the court on the question of costs if the other side unreasonably refuses to consider the ADR process. Otherwise a party will not be able to refer to the without prejudice material in making submissions about costs and sanctions unless all parties to the dispute waive privilege.

---

[118] [2005] EWHC 1903 (Ch).
[119] See *Vestergaard Fransden A/S v Bestnet Europe Ltd* [2014] EWHC 4047 (Ch).
[120] [2002] EWHC 2401 (Ch).

PART 3

NEGOTIATION

12

NEGOTIATION AND JOINT
SETTLEMENT MEETINGS

A Negotiation as a form of ADR

Negotiation is the most commonly used form of ADR, but it is not dealt with in **12.01** detail as most readers will be familiar with negotiating. It is a very flexible process involving written and/or oral communication between parties and/or their lawyers with a view to reaching a settlement. Although written or telephone negotiations are likely to be most cost effective, a meeting may be appropriate where there is a range of issues and options which can be more effectively discussed face to face.

A negotiation process of some kind may take place at many stages as a dispute is **12.02** settled, and such an approach is supported by the principles in the overriding objective. However if the approach taken is not kept reasonably clear and controlled, offers to mediate, Part 36 offers, and other proposals relevant to settlement may overlap in a way that can lead to confusion as to potential settlement terms, and unnecessary complexity in relation to later arguments as to costs.[1]

---

[1] See for example *Shovelar v Lane* [2011] EWCA Civ 802; *Brookfield Construction (UK) Limited v Mott MacDonald Limited* [2010] EWHC 659 (TCC); *Kayll v Rawlinson* [2010] EWHC 1789

B The Negotiation Process

12.03 The negotiation process is subject to contractual principles. For there to be a binding agreement, there must be an offer which has been accepted, and the terms of the agreement must be sufficiently clear to be enforceable.[2] Once offer and acceptance are in place, even if oral or by exchange of emails, provided the terms are sufficiently clear to meet normal contractual principles the agreement is binding, even if the precise wording of a consent order has yet to be agreed.[3] Some terms may be agreed before an overall agreement is finalized, and care may be needed to ensure that points made orally in the early stages of discussions are not seen as potentially binding representations.[4] There will need to be consideration for the agreement to be binding, but this will normally be provided by both sides making some compromise. It will be a matter of fact when terms are sufficiently clear and have been accepted so that a binding agreement has been reached, see 18.01–18.03.

12.04 A binding agreement can only be reached by the parties, or individuals properly acting on behalf of each party with authority to settle. Where a lawyer negotiates on behalf of a client the lawyer will normally act as an agent. Any agreement reached by the lawyer will therefore bind the client (even if it is not within the instructions given by the client) unless it has been agreed in advance by the lawyers that any terms agreed will be subject to client approval. It is relatively common to agree that terms will be subject to client approval as this provides some security for a lawyer where, for example, instructions include some flexibility. The lawyer has a professional duty to ensure terms are complete and clear, see 4.09. A term that for example a party will use reasonable endeavours to achieve a particular end may give rise to practical difficulties.[5]

Professional conduct and ethics

12.05 Key professional conduct and ethical principles are covered in Chapter 6. It is of particular importance in negotiation that a lawyer should have authority from the client to settle (see 4.07–4.08), and should act within instructions (see 6.09–6.10). Any limit on authority should be made clear in the negotiation if relevant.

(Ch); *Oliver v Symons* [2011] EWHC 1250 (Ch); *Camertown Timber Merchants Ltd v Sidhu* [2011] EWCA Civ 1041.

   [2] *Siebe Gorman and Co Ltd v Pneupac Ltd* [1982] 1 All ER 377.

   [3] *Bieber v Teathers Ltd (in Liquidation)* [2014] EWHC 4205 (Ch); *Newbury v Sun Microsystems Ltd* [2013] EWHC 2180 (QB).

   [4] *Palmer v University of Surrey* Lawtel 10.4.2014.

   [5] *Cany Lions Ltd v Bristol Cars Ltd* [2014] EWHC 928 (QB).

Within a negotiation, the professional conduct obligation not to mislead an oppo- **12.06** nent is important, see 6.14–6.15. This has implications for what is said, what is not said, and how documents and evidence are used.

A lawyer should respect client confidentiality when negotiating, see 6.11–6.13. **12.07** Although communications are without prejudice, the lawyer should not reveal information that the client has provided without the consent to the client. Where a case involves sensitive information there may need to be an advance discussion as to what may be revealed in a negotiation.

The principle of 'without prejudice' will apply to all communications made as **12.08** part of an attempt to settle a case, whether they are oral or written, see 5.17–5.26. However a court may need to separate out which elements are without prejudice in a very wide-ranging meeting.[6] A meeting to discuss 'battle tactics' rather than negotiate is not privileged.[7] It is important to keep negotiation sufficiently distinct from litigation as 'without prejudice' confidentiality only protects communications made with a view to settlement.

Procedure and evidence

There are no specific requirements for the exchange of evidence in relation to nego- **12.09** tiation. Evidence will only be available to the extent that it has been gathered by the party, or exchanged under a pre-action or disclosure process that has taken place. If any evidence is required from the other side it should be sought by request, perhaps making the provision of the information a precondition to negotiating, or using an appropriate formal process before the negotiation takes place. It is a matter of strategy and tactics whether any further evidential material is used or sought during a negotiation. Any document used in a negotiation which is not otherwise disclosable will be protected by the principle of without prejudice.

Careful decisions may need to be taken as to who should attend a negotiation. **12.10** A lower number of participants will make the process more cost effective and easier to control. A client may wish to be present, and this can make it easier for the lawyers to take instructions and review the acceptability of options. However, a client can complicate strategic or tactical options, and it may be better for clients to be available in separate rooms nearby or available for consultation by telephone. In a complex case an expert such as an accountant might attend, or be available for consultation.

---

[6] *Unilever plc v Procter & Gamble Co* [1999] 1 WLR 1630.
[7] *Stax Claimants v Bank of Nova Scotia Channel Islands Ltd* [2007] EWHC 1153 (Ch).

12.11 There are no formal rules for procedure in a negotiation. The elements can be controlled by the agreement of an agenda before or at the start of a negotiation. Most face-to-face negotiations include similar identifiable stages, which normally occur in the following order. The stages may not be followed very clearly for strategic or tactical reasons, but insistence on a relatively structured process can be useful:

- agenda setting and/or opening by each side;
- seeking and exchanging information on issues—questioning and listening are important at this stage;
- discussion of the merits on each issue, using arguments on law and evidence to provide a sound basis for potential demands, offers, and concessions;
- offers and concessions are traded and explored;
- agreement in principle, for which clarity and completeness are vital;
- detailed agreement of terms/preparation of draft settlement;
- as an alternative, deadlock, or failure to agree. Some terms may still be agreed, or issues narrowed.

12.12 The framing of offers and the seeking of potential concessions can be challenging. Potential demands, offers, and concessions are best planned in advance, with a realistic comparison of what might be available were the case to go to trial. Offers and concessions should be clearly stated whether in writing or orally to avoid any confusion. Full control of figures is of great importance. For example an offer should specify whether it is intended to include the costs, and where relevant whether it includes the costs of preparation of the bill of costs, interest, and VAT, and will be treated as including these if it does not say otherwise.[8]

12.13 Once agreed, the settlement binds the parties immediately, unless it has been agreed that the terms will only become binding in certain circumstances, see 18.14. Any risk in relation to an oral agreement may be addressed by agreeing at the start of a negotiation that any agreement reached will only be enforceable when it has been reduced to a final form in writing and signed.[9] It should be clear whether the parties intend to settle all or only some of the issues between them, see 18.08–18.09.[10]

12.14 The enforcement of a negotiated agreement will depend partly on when the terms become finally agreed and binding, and partly on the form in which the terms are recorded, see Chapters 18, 19, and 20. A court will only enforce an agreement if the terms are clear.[11] If agreed terms are not all incorporated into a later order they can

---

[8] Practice Direction 46—Costs Special Cases 19.

[9] *Smallman v Smallman* [1971] 3 All ER 717.

[10] *Kensington International Ltd v Republic of Congo* [2008] 1 All ER 1144; *Brown v Rice* [2007] EWHC 625 (Ch); *Khanty-Mansiysk Recoveries v Forsters* [2016] EWHC 522 (Comm).

[11] *Wilson & Whitworth Ltd v Express Newspapers Ltd* [1969] 1 WLR 197.

still be enforced if there has not been an agreement that only a final agreement in writing will be binding.[12] Contractual principles will apply to determine whether an agreement reached as a result of negotiation may be challenged, see 20.08.

C Negotiation as a Context for Mediation

Mediation is effectively a facilitated and more structured form of negotiation. The **12.15** key difference is the addition of an independent third party as mediator. While the addition of a third party might suggest a shift of control, the dynamic is still very much one of negotiation between the lawyers and the parties. Lord Justice Jackson concluded that: 'Mediation can ... identify common ground which conventional negotiation does not reach.'[13] An effective mediator can facilitate negotiation in many ways, for example maintaining structure, leaving the parties and lawyers free to focus on issues, assisting in the framing of offers, and providing an independent view.

D Joint Settlement Meetings

Over recent years the practice of holding a joint settlement meeting (JSM) has **12.16** evolved, largely in relation to personal injury claims. This involves a particular format that mixes aspects of negotiation and mediation, and which could easily be adapted for other types of case where appropriate. The parties may agree to use a JSM, or a judge may make an order for a JSM in an appropriate case.[14] A JSM will be covered by the principles outlined above so that, for example, it is protected by the without prejudice principle.[15]

The meeting is normally attended by the parties, their legal representatives, and a **12.17** representative of the insurer. Each party is in a separate room with their lawyers, and the barristers from each side meet in a third room to hold a without prejudice discussion, and to exchange and discuss potential offers. The barristers can get additional instructions and discuss options by visiting the parties and other lawyers in their separate rooms. This format can be successful because all the relevant people are together in one building though not in the same room. It may be cost effective as it is not necessary to have a neutral third party to reach agreement.

---

[12] *Horizon Technologies International Ltd v Lucky Wealth Consultants Ltd* [1992] 1 All ER 469.
[13] 'Review of Civil Litigation Costs: Final Report' Chapter 4 para 3.32.
[14] Useful Guidelines for a JSM have been issued by the Manchester District Registry and County Court, see <http://www.northerncircuit.org.uk/wp-content/uploads/2010/01/JSM-Code.pdf>.
[15] *Jackson v Ministry of Defence* [2006] EWCA Civ 46.

PART 4

MEDIATION

13

MEDIATION: GENERAL PRINCIPLES

A What is Mediation?

13.01 Mediation is a flexible, cost-effective, confidential process which can be arranged relatively speedily, in which a neutral third party (the mediator) facilitates discussions and negotiations between the parties in dispute within a relatively structured but flexible process, in a formal setting, during a defined period of time, all of which helps to create an impetus for settlement. Mediation has been described as a form of neutrally assisted negotiation.[1] The parties themselves remain in control of the issues they would like to discuss and the outcome, including the terms of any settlement, which need not necessarily be based on the underlying legal rights or obligations of the parties. Instead, the parties, with the assistance of the mediator, can reach a solution which is tailored to their real needs and interests. There are different styles of mediation and these are discussed in Chapter 14 at 14.03–14.18.

---

[1] *Aird v Prime Meridian Ltd* [2006] EWCA Civ 1866 (per May LJ at [5]).

B Does Mediation Work?

Research carried out into court-mediation schemes and statistics released by ADR **13.02** providers indicate that mediation is an effective ADR process for timely resolution of many different kinds of dispute. Research has also demonstrated that mediation tends to have a higher success rate in achieving settlement where the parties voluntarily agree to the process, rather than being forced to mediate by the court under a court scheme which referred cases to mediation.[2]

Evidence from ADR providers also shows that increasing use is being made of medi- **13.03** ation year on year, and that around 70 per cent to 80 per cent of cases settle at the mediation. For the minority of cases that do not settle at the mediation, they often settle shortly thereafter.[3]

C Why does Mediation Work?

Mediation is an effective process because the presence of a mediator can assist the **13.04** negotiation process between the parties in the following ways:

- the mediator adds a new dynamic to and creates a balance between the different negotiating styles and personalities of the parties and their lawyers;
- by following the rules of principled negotiation the mediator can help the parties to work through the deadlock that can be created by purely positional or competitive negotiation, not least by reframing and managing the timing of offers and concessions;
- the mediator can be skilled at managing and diffusing strong feelings that may be the key barrier to reaching settlement;
- mediators will bring their own personal attributes to the table, such as patience, empathy, ability to listen, good judgment, good communication skills, creativity, the ability to think 'outside the box', impartiality, authority, and the ability to

---

[2] See for example Professor Hazel Genn's report into mediation schemes at Central London County Court between 1996 and 1998 'The Central London County Court Pilot Mediation Scheme: Evaluation Report' (DCA Research Paper 5/98), the report by Professor Hazel Genn and others, 'Twisting Arms: Court Referred and Court Linked Mediation Under Judicial Pressure' (Ministry of Justice Research Series 1/07). Also, see Professor Genn's report 'Court-Based ADR Initiatives for Non-family Civil Disputes: The Commercial Court and the Court of Appeal' (2002).

[3] By way of example, see the Mediation Audits conducted by CEDR, <http://www.cedr.com>. Also, see the annual ADR Pledge Reports for 2001 to 2009 published by the Ministry of Justice to monitor the effectiveness of the government's pledge to use ADR to resolve any suitable dispute involving government departments and agencies if the other party agreed, <http://www.justice. gov.uk>.

command respect, all of which can help the parties to review and re-evaluate their case and their needs and interests.

13.05   Mediation may also be effective for other reasons:

- mediation is a flexible process and can be tailored to meet the needs of the case;
- it results in a speedier resolution of the dispute than litigation. Mediation can be arranged relatively quickly, often within a matter of days;
- it is cost effective, particularly if the parties select a low-cost, time-limited, fixed-fee mediation through the Civil Mediation Online Directory, or use one of the court or judicial mediation schemes;[4]
- it is a confidential and private process. This is particularly useful if the publicity generated by a trial would be damaging to the commercial or personal interests of one or more of the parties;
- it avoids an adverse precedent being set by the court;
- it avoids the emotional stress that some individuals may feel about giving evidence in court;
- a settlement that is reached by mutual agreement is more likely to preserve relationships than a court-imposed solution. This can be particularly important in family, neighbour, and employment disputes, in some commercial matters, and in public sector disputes involving health or local authorities;
- mediation enables the parties to be more creative when reaching a settlement. The terms of settlement may provide for matters that could not be achieved within the constraints of the litigation process and include matters which the court would have no power to order, such as an apology, a good reference, or the continuation of a business relationship on different terms;
- even if settlement is not reached at the mediation, going through the mediation process may help the parties to understand each other's case, narrow the issues, and, in some cases, settlement may be more easily achieved after the mediation;
- the court may direct the parties to consider mediation, thus imposing a requirement on the parties to engage with the process seriously and with the intention of settling the case;
- the parties are likely to be paying for the mediation, both in relation to their own legal costs and their contribution towards the expenses of the mediation (such as the venue) and the mediator's fee, as well as any indirect costs such as their time, lost wages, or holiday entitlement caused by their attendance at the mediation. This generates an impetus to settle, so that the costs and time spent in relation to the mediation should not be in vain;

---

[4] See Chapter 16 for the court and judicial mediation schemes and information about referrals to mediation using the Civil Mediation Online Directory.

- mediation puts control into the hands of the parties themselves. It gives them a forum where they can air their grievances in a confidential process, without the risks inherent in litigation.

D Comparison Between Negotiation and Mediation

Before the parties embark on mediation they should first attempt to settle the dispute **13.06** by direct negotiation between them as this will normally be less expensive and may narrow issues.[5] However, mediation is a more formal and structured process than negotiation, the parties will be active participants in the process even if lawyers are instructed to attend the mediation, and the negotiations will be facilitated by the mediator. These may also be contributing factors to the success of mediation in assisting the parties to reach a settlement, even if direct negotiations between the parties have failed.

E Judicial Endorsement of Mediation

The courts have readily endorsed and encouraged the use of ADR in general.[6] **13.07** However, in many cases, the courts have stressed the importance of mediation in particular, the flexibility this process provides for resolving disputes, with minimal expense, and the skill that mediators employ to achieve results satisfactory to the parties, which in many cases are beyond the powers of the courts or lawyers to achieve. Useful guidance about the benefits of mediation can be obtained, in particular, from the following cases:

- *Dunnett v Railtrack plc* [2002] 1 WLR 2434 (per Brooke LJ at [14]);
- *Halsey v Milton Keynes General NHS Trust* [2004] EWCA Civ 576 (per Dyson LJ at [15]);
- *Burchell v Bullard* [2005] EWCA Civ 358 (per Ward LJ at [43]);
- *Egan v Motor Services (Bath) Ltd* [2007] EWCA Civ 1002 (per Ward LJ at [53]);
- *Faidi v Elliot Corporation* [2012] EWCA Civ 287 (per Jackson LJ at [35] and [36]);
- *Oliver v Symons* [2012] EWCA Civ 267 (per Ward LJ at [53]);
- *Wright v Michael Wright Supplies Ltd* [2013] EWCA Civ 234 (per Ward LJ at [2] and [3]);
- *Bradley v Heslin* [2014] EWHC 3267 (Ch) at [24];
- *Northrop Grumman Mission Systems Europe Ltd v BAE Systems (Al Diriyah C41) Ltd* [2014] EWHC 3148 (TCC) (per Ramsey J at [57–75]);
- *Garritt-Critchley v Ronnan* [2014] EWHC 1774 (Ch).

---

[5] See Chapter 12.
[6] See Chapter 1 at 1.04–1.10.

F Disputes Suitable for Mediation

13.08 Mediation is suitable for all disputes which raise issues capable of being resolved by negotiation, whatever the subject matter of the underlying cause of action. It is used in all kinds of contract, tortious and consumer claims, neighbourhood, housing and family disputes, and regulatory and public sector disputes.

13.09 Indicators for using mediation are described in Chapter 2, particularly at 2.31–2.40 and 2.42–2.48. The parties may also have contractually bound themselves by a dispute resolution clause to attempt to resolve a dispute by mediation before embarking on litigation (or arbitration).[7] Mediation can also be useful for resolving multi-party disputes involving multiple issues,[8] including those which raise conflict of law and jurisdictional issues.[9] Mediation should be considered if the court has encouraged or directed the parties to attempt settlement by mediation, or where the parties may face adverse costs orders or other sanctions if they unreasonably refuse to mediate.[10]

13.10 Mediation may not be appropriate in the circumstances described in Chapter 2 at 2.49–2.61. Mediation may also not be appropriate in debt claims where there is no sustainable defence as it may be more advantageous in such cases to issue proceedings and apply for summary judgment.

G The Timing of Mediation

13.11 If the dispute is suitable for mediation, consideration needs to be given to the timing of it. Mediation can theoretically take place at any stage up to trial and even pending an appeal as is aptly demonstrated by the Court of Appeal Mediation Scheme.[11] General points about the timing of ADR are discussed in Chapter 3. The emphasis should be on the parties consensually agreeing on the best time to mediate. The court should try to set a timetable for trial that allows the parties to take part in ADR along the way.[12]

---

[7] See for example *Cable & Wireless plc v IBM United Kingdom Ltd* [2002] EWHC 2059 (Comm). Also see Chapter 9 at 9.27–9.35 for the court's approach to ADR clauses.

[8] See Chapter 16, at 16.30–16.35.

[9] See *A Practical Approach to Alternative Dispute Resolution* by Susan Blake, Julie Browne, and Stuart Sime (OUP, 4th edn), Chapter 19 at 19.03–19.05.

[10] See Chapters 9 and 11.

[11] See Chapter 16 at 16.11–16.13.

[12] *CIP Properties (AIPT) Ltd v Galliford Try Infrastructure Ltd* [2014] EWHC 3546 (TCC).

If the parties have fully defined the issues, disclosed key information and quanti-   **13.12**
fied the claim and any counterclaim, then the most advantageous time to embark
on mediation will be before proceedings are issued. The advantages of doing so are
described in Chapter 3 at 3.06.[13]

If further information or documentation needs to be obtained to enable an evalu-   **13.13**
ation of the strengths and weaknesses of each party's position to be assessed, there
is no reason why the parties could not agree that this should be done in advance of
mediation, or as part of the agreed mediation procedure.[14]

If mediation cannot reasonably be undertaken before issue of proceedings, the best   **13.14**
time to attempt it may be shortly after exchange of statements of case or after disclosure of documents.[15] The later the mediation takes place in the litigation, the
greater the decrease in the costs savings that can result from a mediated settlement.
Parties who wish to attempt mediation after issue should consider applying for a
stay of the proceedings and a suspension of the timetable set by the court in order
to save costs.[16]

Any decision to refuse mediation at any point in time should be objectively reason-   **13.15**
able on the facts of the particular case and the party refusing it must be prepared
to explain and justify this to the court. If a refusal is judged to be unreasonable, an
adverse costs order may be made against that party.[17]

H Persuading a Reluctant Party to Consider Mediation?

General factors relating to addressing concerns about ADR and persuading a party   **13.16**
to use ADR are discussed in Chapter 4 at 4.12–4.32. Assuming the case is suitable
for mediation, and the time is right for mediation to be attempted, if one party

---

[13] Also, see for example, *Egan v Motor Services (Bath) Ltd* [2007] EWCA Civ 1002 (per Ward LJ
at [53]); *Bradford v James* [2008] EWCA Civ 837 (per Mummery LJ at [1]).

[14] The decision in *PGF II SA v IMFS Company* [2013] EWCA Civ 1288 demonstrates that the
court may not accept that it was reasonable to refuse to mediate on the basis that further information
or evidence needed to be obtained first, unless this was canvassed with the other party and an attempt
made to overcome any such inhibitions at that time.

[15] Research carried out by Nicholas Gould, Claire King, and Philip Britton 'Mediating
Construction Disputes: An Evaluation of Existing Practice, 2010' (see <http://www.fenwickelli-
ott.com/mediating-construction-disputes-download>) found that the largest number of successful
mediations took place in the early stages of litigation (specifically during exchange of statements of
case or during or as a result of disclosure). A smaller cluster of cases undertook successful mediations
shortly before trial after exchange of witness statements and (if applicable) expert's reports.

[16] See CPR r 26.4 and Chapter 9 at 9.24–9.26.

[17] See Chapter 11.

wishes to try mediation and the other party does not, consideration should also be given to approaching an ADR provider[18] to give neutral and independent advice about the benefits of mediation, assess whether it would be appropriate given the facts and circumstances of the particular dispute, and, if so, advise how the process could be tailored to meet the needs of the parties. If only one party approaches the ADR provider, that party will be solely responsible for any fees charged for acting as broker. The person acting as broker will not usually conduct the mediation. If an individual mediator (as opposed to an ADR provider organization) is approached by one party to act as a broker, he or she may decline to do so on the grounds that the other party may not perceive the broker to be neutral. The person acting as broker will want (usually) to disclose dealings and communications with all parties. For that reason, the parties should be careful about revealing confidential information to the broker at this stage. If the dispute is suitable for mediation, the broker will liaise with the reluctant party and will seek to persuade that party to engage in the process.

I What can be Done by the Court to Make a Reluctant Party Consider Mediation?

13.17 The court can do a number of things to make a reluctant party consider mediation. In particular:

(i) the court can offer strong judicial encouragement to the parties to mediate their dispute. However, the court will not compel parties to mediate if they are unwilling to do so;[19]

(ii) the court can make an ADR order directing the parties to consider ADR, in particular mediation. This is rapidly becoming part of the standard pre-trial case management directions.[20] Sample orders can be found on the Online Resource Centre accompanying this book;

(iii) although the courts will not mandate parties to use mediation against their will, in some cases, the courts can direct the parties to make contact with a mediator to consider mediation. This should be regarded as mandatory *consideration* of mediation, rather than mandatory mediation. Where such an order is made, the parties will have to do more than merely consider mediation; instead they will be required

---

[18] For a list of accredited providers see for example the Civil Mediation Online Directory, <http://www.civilmediation.justice.gov.uk>, or the Civil Mediation Council's website, <http://www. civil-mediation.org>. Also, see the Online Resource Centre.

[19] See Chapter 1 at 1.06–1.15, Chapter 9 at 9.05–9.14 and Chapter 13 at 13.07.

[20] See Chapter 9.

to meet or have telephone contact with a mediator who will provide the parties with information about mediation, assess whether it would be an appropriate process to use to settle the dispute, and attempt to persuade the parties to use mediation. This compulsory *consideration* of mediation, by attending what is becoming known as a Mediation Information Assessment Meeting (MIAM), should not be confused with compulsory mediation. Although the court may compel the parties to consider mediation, it will not compel them to mediate if they do not wish to do so. Compulsory consideration of mediation currently takes place in most family disputes,[21] in some small claims cases since 1 April 2013,[22] and in some cases in the Court of Appeal.[23] At present, it is not proposed to introduce referral for mandatory consideration of mediation in fast track or multi-track cases, although this may be implemented for fast track cases at some future date;

(iv) the court can stay proceedings (assuming that proceedings have been issued) and direct the parties to attempt to resolve the dispute by ADR.[24] Sample orders granting a stay for mediation to be attempted can be found from the Online Resource Centre accompanying this book;

(v) the court may be able to assist the parties to resolve their dispute by mediation by making appropriate orders for advance disclosure of information or documents relating to one or more issues in the case on the application of one or both parties;

(vi) if both parties consent, judicial mediation can be undertaken. At present judicial mediation is confined to cases in the Construction and Technology Court under the Court Settlement Process,[25] some family cases, and in employment cases in the Employment Tribunal;[26]

(vii) if one or both parties have acted unreasonably in refusing to use mediation to resolve the dispute, the court may mark its disapproval in the form of adverse costs orders.[27]

J The Costs of Mediation

The general aspects of the costs of ADR processes are dealt with in Chapter 7, with **13.18** the costs of mediation being explained in 7.13–7.17. Mediators' fees may be less

---

[21] See FPR Parts 3, 9, 12 and PD 3A, 9A, and 12B.
[22] See Chapter 16 at 16.07–16.12.
[23] See Chapter 16 at 16.13–16.15.
[24] See Chapter 9 at 9.24–9.26.
[25] See Chapter 16, at 16.21–16.22.
[26] See Chapter 16 at 16.23.
[27] See Chapter 11.

if a court or fixed-fee mediation scheme is used.[28] If the parties use an ADR provider, the fee charged may be higher than the fees that would be payable should a mediator be appointed directly by the parties because the ADR provider has to cover their administrative costs in selecting and referring the case to a mediator on their panel and administering the process. A discount on the usual fee may be offered if the ADR provider operates, and the parties select, an express mediation service by which the parties use the ADR provider to select the mediator, but carry out most of the other administrative work themselves, such as booking the venue and agreeing the date.

13.19   Fees payable to a mediator or an ADR provider are usually payable in advance of the mediation, and if they are not paid the mediation may be cancelled and the parties are likely to have to pay some or all of the cancellation charges. Any additional charges (caused by the mediation taking longer than expected for example) will be billed after the mediation.

13.20   In some circumstances, a party may be able to recover their own mediation costs and their share of the mediation fees and expenses from the other party in the course of the litigation.[29] Alternatively a party may be able to recover some or all of their mediation party costs and their share of the fees and expenses of mediation by the settlement agreement that is reached in the mediation.

K The Funding of Mediation Costs, Fees, and Expenses

13.21   The different ways of funding ADR costs, fees, and expenses are discussed in Chapter 7. Where a party is funded under a CFA agreement entered into before 1 April 2013, useful guidance for lawyers and mediators can be found in a paper published by the Civil Mediation Council entitled 'Mediation, CFAs and Conflicts of Interest'.[30]

L The Mediator's Role

13.22   A mediator must have the trust and confidence of the parties throughout the mediation. Building up that trust and rapport starts from the first contact with the parties

---

[28] See the low-cost, fixed-fee, time-limited mediations that take place through the Civil Mediation Online Directory (Chapter 16 at 16.14–16.16), and the Mayor's and City of London County Court, Small Claims and Court of Appeal Mediation Schemes discussed in Chapter 16 at 16.05–16.15.
[29] See Chapter 10.
[30] This paper can be downloaded from the CMC's website, <http://www.civilmediation.org>.

and continues until the end of the mediation or any post-mediation discussion. The mediator's role can be said to fall into three discrete areas:

- organizing the mediation process;
- acting as facilitator during the process;
- acting as intermediary between the parties.

Organizing the mediation process

Before the mediation

When appointed, the mediator will usually contact the parties (or their lawyers) **13.23** and explain, in a pre-mediation meeting or by telephone, the nature and, if necessary, the costs of the mediation process, how they should prepare for it, and the role that the mediator and the parties will play in the mediation. He or she will discuss with each party who should attend the mediation, and will check that the attendees for each party have authority to settle the case, and whether there are any limits on their authority. If there are likely to be limits on a party's authority to settle, the mediator will advise on what needs to be done to ensure that settlement is not thwarted because one party lacks authority at the mediation. The mediator will also check whether there are any time constraints affecting the mediation and will set the timetable for events that need to happen prior to the mediation such as the date by which the mediation agreement should be signed and returned and the date by which position statements and other documents, which may include costs schedules, should be provided and exchanged. If the parties have used an ADR service provider to provide a mediator, then it is likely that the service provider rather than the mediator will make the practical arrangements for the mediation. These matters are discussed in detail in Chapter 14.

At the mediation

The mediator will also perform an organizational role at the mediation. In particu- **13.24** lar, the mediator will:

- chair the meetings and manage the process;
- set the agenda for the mediation by suggesting the order in which issues should be negotiated, and amend it if necessary as the mediation progresses;
- control the form that the mediation follows on the day (and discuss with the parties and/or decide whether any modifications should be made to the process to meet the needs of the case or the parties);
- decide when discussions should take place in joint or private meetings;
- impose or suggest a time limit for delivery of opening statements in the initial joint meeting;

- decide whether further joint meetings should take place during the negotiation phase in addition to the opening joint meeting;
- prevent interventions by the other side during the opening statement of the opposing party;
- control the form of questions that one party may put to the opposing party in the opening joint session.

All of these matters are dealt with in detail in Chapter 15.

Acting as a facilitator

13.25   The mediator will assist the parties to negotiate with one another in a more effective manner than they would be able to achieve on their own. The mediator will do this in the following ways:

- gather information from the parties both at the pre-mediation stage[31] and during the mediation[32] about the issues in dispute and their needs and interests;
- help the parties to identify the legal and factual issues, and their underlying needs and objectives;
- encourage the parties to treat the mediation as their 'day in court' and to air their feelings and emotions, particularly in private meetings, so that the matter can move forward;
- help the parties to listen to each other and communicate more effectively with each other;
- discourage or defuse confrontational or aggressive communications between the parties that will hinder negotiations, and reframe them if necessary;
- encourage the parties to analyse the strength and weakness of their own case and the case presented by the other side;
- perform the role of 'reality-checker', perhaps by assuming the role of devil's advocate, if the parties are unrealistic in their assessment;
- encourage the parties to think about the BATNA (best alternative to a negotiated agreement) and the WATNA (worse alternative to a negotiated agreement), and ensure that they have carried out a full risk assessment, including the costs (and irrecoverable costs) of proceeding to trial;
- review the negotiations that have already taken place between the parties, and encourage each party to reflect on why they failed and how they can change their position to move the matter forward;

---

[31] See Chapter 14 at 14.47–14.48.
[32] See Chapter 15.

- encourage brainstorming and the generation of options for settlement, including the identification of common ground between the parties;
- create and use strategies and options to end deadlock between the parties.

Acting as intermediary

The mediator will act as the 'go-between' or 'shuttle-diplomat' during private meetings of the parties. The mediator will convey offers, concessions, and information, rejections, concessions, and counter-offers from one party to another. The parties will negotiate through the mediator as intermediary, rather than with each other face to face. This can be very effective in achieving progress to an overall settlement. The mediator will keep a record of any agreement reached on individual issues as the negotiation progresses, as this will help with drawing up any final overall settlement agreement. **13.26**

In order for the mediator to carry out these functions, it is vital that each party trusts and has confidence in him or her. To build up that trust, the mediator must ensure that he or she is even-handed in his or her dealings with the parties. The mediator may be rigorous and testing as 'devil's advocate', but should not do or say anything that gives the impression he or she is not impartial, and should not force a solution on the parties. All of these matters are discussed in detail in Chapter 15. **13.27**

Post-mediation role

Even if the mediation does not result in settlement, it is not uncommon for the parties to engage the mediator to broker settlement negotiations at a future date particularly if the trust and respect of both parties has been gained and retained.[33] **13.28**

M Ethical Conduct Required of the Mediator

Mediators are in a position of considerable responsibility. They have the ability to influence whether or not a settlement takes place between disputing parties and the terms of that settlement. Mediation is conducted on the basis that the parties are encouraged to speak freely and confidentially to the mediator in private meetings about their interests and concerns and their assessment of the merits of their case and the extent of offers or concessions they are prepared to make or accept. It follows from this that mediators are likely to be the recipients of highly confidential **13.29**

---

[33] See Chapter 15 at 15.31–15.35.

and sensitive information from each party to the dispute. It is therefore of crucial importance that mediators act in a professional and ethical way.

13.30   Most mediators operate under a code of conduct. This may be the code of conduct used by the ADR provider of whom the mediator is a member and by whom the mediator is accredited, or mediators in private practice may devise and operate under their own code of conduct. Members of the Civil Mediation Council (CMC), whether registered provider members or individual members,[34] are expected to comply with the European Code of Conduct for Mediators.[35] This Code is entirely voluntary and mediators or ADR organizations do not have to adopt it or operate under it, but most mediators and ADR organizations offering a mediation service do operate under a code which contains the same or similar provisions to the EU Code.

13.31   Mediators who are professionally qualified in another field of expertise will also be expected to comply with the code of conduct prescribed by their governing or regulatory body.[36]

13.32   Any mediator who accepts instructions to mediate in a dispute between two or more parties should comply with the ethical standards discussed below.

Competence

13.33   Mediators must be competent and knowledgeable in the process of mediation. This should include proper training in mediation skills and the process of mediation, and a system for Continuing Professional Development (CPD) to refresh and update their skills. The mediator should be competent to conduct the mediation bearing in mind the nature and complexity of the dispute and the needs and objectives of the parties. Mediators should also provide information to interested parties relating to their background and experience so that they can make an informed choice.[37]

Independence and neutrality

13.34   A mediator must ensure there is no conflict of interest with any of the parties directly or indirectly affected by the dispute. If circumstances exist which do or may give rise to a conflict of interest or affect his or her neutrality (such as previously acting for or advising one of the parties in an unrelated matter or having a personal or social relationship with one party), these should be disclosed immediately to the parties. The

---

[34]   Accreditation is considered at 13.44 and the role of the Civil Mediation Council at 13.45–13.48.

[35]   The EU Code of Conduct for Mediators can be downloaded from the Online Resource Centre supporting this book.

[36]   See Chapter 6 for the ethical obligations of solicitors and barristers.

[37]   European Code of Conduct for Mediators paras 1.1 and 1.2.

mediator should only consent to act in such circumstances if the parties expressly authorize this (in writing).[38] There may be some situations in which a mediator should refuse to act even if there has been full disclosure to and consent from the parties, such as circumstances in which the mediator might benefit financially or personally from the outcome of the mediation, or the mediator has had a prior personal or professional relationship with one of the parties to the dispute.

Impartiality

The mediator should at all times act, and endeavour to be seen to act, with impartiality towards the parties.[39] **13.35**

The mediation procedure

The mediator should ensure the parties understand the nature and purpose of the mediation process, the terms of the mediation agreement, the fees payable, and the obligations of confidentiality imposed on the parties and the mediator. The mediator should also explain the procedure to be followed in the mediation, which can be modified or agreed following discussions between the mediator and the parties.[40] **13.36**

Fairness

The mediator should act fairly between the parties, ensuring that all parties have adequate opportunities to be involved in the process and that the process is conducted in a manner which is fair to both parties. The concept of fairness also means that mediators must take care to avoid any party being forced into mediation or a mediation settlement agreement as a result of abuse or threats or other unconscionable conduct. However, because the essence of mediation is that the parties make their own decisions about how to resolve their dispute, the notion of fairness would not extend to the mediator ensuring that the terms of any proposed settlement are fair to each of the parties, although this is subject to the need to have overall fairness in the process so that each party is in a position to freely make their own decisions about the dispute. **13.37**

The mediator should also be careful not to put undue pressure on a party to settle the dispute. If this happened, the agreement could be set aside for undue influence or duress. The mediator must not press a party into settlement in order to maintain a high personal settlement rate. **13.38**

---

[38] European Code of Conduct for Mediators para 2.
[39] European Code of Conduct for Mediators para 2.2.
[40] European Code of Conduct for Mediators para 3.1.

Confidentiality

13.39 The mediator must keep confidential all information arising out of or in connection with the mediation, including the fact that the mediation is to take place or has taken place, unless compelled to give full disclosure by law or on public policy grounds. Any information disclosed in confidence to mediators by one of the parties must not be disclosed to the other parties without permission or unless compelled by law.[41]

Termination of the mediation

13.40 The mediator should terminate the mediation, and inform the parties (if appropriate) if they believe a settlement to be unenforceable or illegal, or that continuing the mediation is unlikely to result in settlement.[42]

13.41 The mediator should also explain that the parties have the right to withdraw from the mediation at any time, and without giving any reason for doing so.[43]

13.42 If agreement is reached at the mediation, the mediator should ensure that all parties understand the terms of the agreement, and that they consent to it. The mediator may, if requested by the parties and competent to do so, give advice on how the agreement can be formalized and made enforceable.[44] The mediator should also ensure that any files or documents, including personal notes that are retained following the mediation, should be securely and confidentially stored. Many mediators adopt the practice of destroying any notes they made in front of the parties at the end of the mediation and returning any case papers supplied to the parties.

Practice administration

13.43 The Civil Mediation Council Code of Good Practice for Mediators[45] also requires mediators to:

- have an efficient system of personal practice administration (para 11);
- have access to a complaints resolution system (para 12);
- make effective arrangements for obtaining peer review and feedback and an effective system for obtaining and reviewing feedback (para 13);

---

[41] European Code of Conduct for Mediators para 4. Also, see paras 13.49–13.58 below on the nature of the obligation of confidentiality.

[42] European Code of Conduct for Mediators para 3.2.

[43] European Code of Conduct for Mediators para 3.3.

[44] European Code of Conduct for Mediators para 3.3.

[45] See <http://www.civilmediation.org>.

- be insured to cover errors, omissions, and negligence: the CMC recommends a minimum of £1 million of such insurance or a higher level if appropriate (para 14);
- be sensitive to diversity, equality, and anti-discrimination issues (para 15).

N Accreditation and Regulation of Mediation

Training and accreditation requirements

Accreditation of mediators takes place at present in the following ways: **13.44**

- many ADR organizations have their own systems in place for training and accrediting member mediators. In order to become accredited, a mediator must satisfy requirements for training and continuous professional development. Although these vary between providers and organizations, most training providers currently comply with the minimum requirements of training that are laid down by the CMC for the Registered Provider Scheme,[46] and in some cases will exceed those requirements. The training requirements differ depending on the date of the training, and are more onerous for those undertaking training from 1 April 2011. For those undertaking training up to 31 March 2011, the training had to include not less than 24 hours of tuition and role play, and this increased to 40 hours from 1 April 2011;
- family mediators are accredited by the Family Mediation Council (FMC);[47]
- the Law Society has prescribed training standards and has a system of accreditation for solicitor mediators on its Family and Civil and Commercial Panels.[48] The Law Society's Family Mediation Scheme meets the FMC's standards and the LSC's requirements for publicly funded MIAMs and mediation;
- the Bar Council also maintains a Mediation Directory and the barristers who appear in the Mediation Directory have all completed training with an approved training provider;
- the CMC registers ADR civil and commercial mediation organizations and individual mediators.[49]

---

[46] See <http://www.civilmediation.org>.

[47] See <http://www.familymediationcouncil.org.uk>. The FMC has recently approved a new 'Assessment of Professional Competence' Scheme which sets out steps that mediators must take to demonstrate their competence in order to apply for Assessed Professionally Competent Mediator (APCM) status.

[48] See <http://www.lawsociety.org.uk>. Law Society accredited practitioner panel civil and commercial members must also have some practical experience consisting of at least 90 hours of mediation experience over the preceding two years including at least four civil and commercial mediations comprising a minimum total of 30 hours.

[49] See <http://www.civilmediation.org> and paras 13.45–13.48 below.

O The Civil Mediation Council

13.45 The CMC was constituted in 2003 to represent the interests of mediation providers and mediators, inspire parties to use civil and commercial mediation and other dispute resolution options, and promote the highest standards of skill, conduct, and integrity in mediation. Family mediation is not currently regulated or represented by the CMC.[50] From 1 January 2015, the CMC became incorporated as a company (CMCL) and its aim is to develop the role of the CMC as the trusted authority for mediation in England and Wales. At the time of writing, the CMC had over 350 individual members and over 85 member organizations across the UK. The CMC currently operates three membership schemes: the Registered Mediation Provider Scheme; the Individual Registered Mediator Scheme; and the Workplace Mediation Provider Registration Scheme. Details of the eligibility requirements for each of these schemes can be found on the CMC's website.[51]

13.46 CMC registration is regarded as a kite mark of quality. In order to be a registered provider, the provider must meet minimum requirements in respect of the number, training and accreditation, and practical experience of mediators on its panel, adopt the obligations in the EU Model Code of Conduct for Mediations (or a similar code), operate a published complaints procedure, capture feedback about its mediators from the parties in mediation, operate a CPD policy for its mediators, and have adequate insurance in place (which must be not less than £1 million for each mediator). Individual mediators who are employed by or who have work referred to them by that provider are not individually accredited. It continues to be up to the providers to ensure that individual mediators are properly trained and accredited, insured and supervised, and that they fulfil their CPD and practice requirements.

13.47 Individual mediators who apply for registration under the Individual Registration Scheme have to comply with similar requirements. Registration is regarded as a kite mark of quality and individual mediators can advertise themselves as a CMC registered mediator.

13.48 The CMC also operates an internal Members' Complaints Resolution Service. This enables members (or clients of members) who have a complaint which has not been resolved through the member's own complaints scheme to refer the

---

[50] See <http://www.familymediationcouncil.org.uk> for the regulation of family mediation.
[51] See <http://www.civilmediation.org>.

complaint to the CMC for resolution (if possible) by a fixed-fee, time-limited mediation.

P Confidentiality in Mediation

The mediation agreement will usually contain a term that neither party can reveal **13.49**
any detail of the mediation process or any information obtained during the mediation without the express consent of the other party.[52] Even in the absence of an
express confidentially clause, one is likely to be implied, because it would destroy
the basis of mediation if either party could publicize the matters that took place
between them and the mediator.[53] The mediator also owes a duty of confidentiality
to the parties. A confidentiality clause adds weight to the without prejudice rule[54]
and it may be wider than it.

In *Aird v Prime Meridian*, the court accepted that a confidentiality clause reinforces **13.50**
the without prejudice rule. However May LJ went on to state:

> This cannot of course be taken literally, since it would obviously not apply
> to documents produced for other purposes which were needed for and pro-
> duced at the mediation, for example their building contract or the anteced-
> ent pleadings in the proceedings ... but the general intent of the provision is
> clear, and it accords with the generally understood 'without prejudice' nature
> of mediation.[55]

Unless the mediation agreement provides to the contrary, the mere fact that the **13.51**
parties have agreed to try and resolve the dispute by mediation or have had a mediation is not confidential; the confidentiality therefore attaches to the events during
the mediation process, rather than the bare fact that the parties are about to or have
embarked on mediation.

Information given to the mediator

Any information given to the mediator during the process and in particular anything **13.52**
revealed to him or her during the private meetings of the parties is also protected by
the confidentiality obligation. The mediator cannot reveal this information to the
other side or any other party unless the party providing the information expressly

---

[52] See Chapter 5 at 5.27–5.29.
[53] *Farm Assist Ltd (in liquidation) v The Secretary of State for the Environment, Food and Rural Affairs (No 2)* [2009] EWHC 1102 (TCC) (per Ramsey J at [29]).
[54] See Chapter 5 at 5.17–5.26.
[55] See *Aird v Prime Meridian* [2006] EWCA Civ 1866 at [5].

consents. The duty of confidentiality will apply even after the mediation process has been completed or terminated.

Can the mediator enforce the confidentiality clause?

13.53 Unlike the without prejudice rule which exists only for the benefit of the parties in mediation,[56] the express or implied term of confidentiality exists not just between the parties themselves, but also between the parties and the mediator. The parties cannot waive confidentiality so as to deprive the mediator of his or her right to have the confidentiality of the mediation preserved; confidentiality must be waived by all parties to the obligation.[57]

When will the court override the confidentiality provisions?

13.54 The obligation of confidentiality is not absolute, and the court has power to permit evidence of confidential communications in mediation to be given or produced if it is in the *interests of justice* to do so.[58] In *Farm Assist (No 2)*, the court did make an order overriding confidentiality because it was necessary for the court to ascertain what was said and done at the mediation in order to determine whether the settlement agreement reached at the mediation should be set aside for economic duress.

13.55 Other situations in which the court may override confidentiality and enquire into the events that occurred during the mediation, which may include an order requiring a mediator to disclose documents or be called as a witness to give evidence about the mediation, are as follows:

- the circumstances described in Chapter 5 at 5.39;
- an action by one or both parties against the mediator for breach of contract or negligence;[59]
- an action by a party against their solicitors for professional negligence arising out of their conduct of a claim which was settled at mediation or arising out of their conduct at the mediation.[60]

---

[56] See Chapter 13 at 13.63.
[57] See *Farm Assist Ltd (in liquidation) v The Secretary of State for the Environment, Food and Rural Affairs (No 2)* [2009] EWHC 1102 (TCC).
[58] See footnote 57.
[59] See 13.66–13.69 for more detail about the circumstances in which a claim could be brought against a mediator.
[60] See *Youlton v Charles Russell* [2010] EWHC 1032 (Ch).

To permit confidentiality to be overridden in anything other than in very excep-   **13.56**
tional and limited circumstances will seriously undermine the mediation process.
In view of the strong promotion of mediation by the judiciary, this is unlikely to
happen.[61]

It should be noted that different (and narrower) grounds for overriding confidenti-   **13.57**
ality exist in cross-border disputes.[62]

Other exceptions to confidentiality

Confidential information may have to be disclosed by the mediator (even in the   **13.58**
absence of a court order) in other circumstances. These exceptions may also be spelt
out in the mediation agreement:

- where disclosure is required by law, for example where disclosure is required
  under the Proceeds of Crime Act 2002, or HM Revenue and Customs exercises
  its statutory powers to compel disclosure;[63]
- disclosure is necessary to prevent risk of harm to the public at large;
- disclosure may be necessary if the mediator believes there is a risk of significant
  harm to the health, life, or well-being of a person or a threat to their safety if
  confidential information is not disclosed. This can arise particularly in a family
  mediation concerning children;
- disclosure is necessary to prevent criminal activity, or prevent the mediator being
  charged with colluding in the commission of an offence or if a failure to disclose
  the confidential information may amount in itself to a criminal offence on the
  part of the mediator.

Q The Without Prejudice Rule in Mediation

The without prejudice rule and exceptions to it[64] apply to communications pass-   **13.59**
ing between the parties made in the context of a mediation, so generally speaking,
communications that take place in relation to or during the mediation which are
made for the purposes of settling the dispute, cannot be relied on or referred to in

---

[61] Following *Farm Assist (No 2)*, the CMC issued Guidance Note No 1 'Mediation Confidentiality',
which can be downloaded from its website at <http://www.civilmediation.org>.

[62] See EU Mediation Directive in Civil and Commercial Cases (Directive 2008/52/EC), Article 7
and CPR r 78.26–78.28, discussed in Chapter 17 at 17.20–17.25.

[63] The CMC has prepared a guidance note on the obligations of mediators under the Proceeds of
Crime Act 2002, which can be downloaded from <http://www.civilmediation.org>.

[64] See Chapter 5 at 5.17–5.26.

subsequent court proceedings if the mediation is unsuccessful.[65] The court will generally respect the without prejudice, confidential nature of mediation, and will not usually investigate why mediation failed to result in a settlement[66] and, in normal circumstances, the court will refuse to order disclosure of documents and communications that took place within mediation, including any notes made or retained by a mediator.[67]

13.60 The court may grant an injunction to restrain a party from referring to any part of the discussions that took place during the mediation.[68]

13.61 The without prejudice rule will clearly apply to communications aimed at settlement that take place between the parties before the mediation agreement is signed, or before the mediation commences, as well as communications that take place during the course of the mediation. The following communications will be protected from disclosure by operation of the without prejudice rule:

- any oral or written communications between the parties or the parties and the mediator made specifically for the purposes of exploring settlement, such as position statements, correspondence about the mediation and offers or concessions whether made before, during, or after the mediation;[69]
- communications created for the purpose of trying to persuade the parties to mediate;[70]
- it may also operate to protect information obtained from investigations carried out as part of the mediation process.[71]

---

[65] *Brown v Rice* [2007] EWHC 625 (Ch).

[66] *Halsey v Milton Keynes General NHS Trust* [2004] EWCA Civ 576 (per Dyson LJ at [14]).

[67] *Cumbria Waste Management Ltd v Baines Wilson* [2008] EWHC 786 (QB).

[68] *Venture Investment Placement Ltd v Hall* [2005] EWHC 1227 (Ch). In *Mason v Walton-on-Thames Charity & others* [2010] EWHC 1688 (Ch), the claimant sought permission, in advance of the hearing of a preliminary issue, to rely on without prejudice communications that had been produced in the course of mediation in order to oppose the position one of the defendants adopted in the litigation. The court refused permission as no exceptions to the exclusionary without prejudice rule applied and secondly the claimant contractually agreed, by a clause in the mediation agreement which she had signed, to abide by the without prejudice confidential nature of the process.

[69] *Reed Executive plc v Reed Business Information Ltd* [2004] EWCA Civ 887; *Brown v Rice* [2007] EWHC 625 (Ch).

[70] *Instance v Denny Bros Printing Ltd* [2000] FSR 869.

[71] See *Smiths Group plc v George Weiss*, 22 March 2002 (unreported), where it was held that accounts of interviews conducted by each party's expert with employees and former employees with a view to establishing work done by them during a particular year, as part of the agreed mediation procedure and for use in the mediation, should be expunged from the report of the expert for the purposes of litigation (the mediation having failed to result in settlement).

Communications that are not protected by the without prejudice rule in mediation

At present, there is no special category of 'mediation privilege'.[72] In addition to the general exceptions mentioned in Chapter 5 at 5.23–5.26, it should also be noted that: **13.62**

- the rule will not protect documents that were not created for the purposes of exploring settlement, even if those documents were used in the mediation, if those documents ought to be disclosed as part of standard disclosure during the course of litigation. It will also not apply to a joint statement made following a meeting of the experts instructed by each party that was created for use in the mediation as such a statement is one that the experts must produce if the court directs it under CPR r 35.12;[73]
- the court can look at communications that took place in a mediation to decide if the mediation resulted in a concluded settlement and the existence of a clause in the agreement to mediate which provides that there is no agreement unless it was in writing and signed by the parties is not sufficient to oust this usual exception to the without prejudice rule;[74]
- the mediation agreement itself is not protected by the without prejudice rule and it can be produced to prove its terms;[75]

---

[72] Mr Justice Briggs has suggested that public policy may require a new 'mediation privilege' which is limited to confidential information given to a mediator by one party and which could operate in a similar way to Legal Professional Privilege (see 159 NLJ 506 and 159 NLJ 550). Other commentators go further and suggest that there should be a statutory privilege protecting the confidentiality of communications made by the mediator and the parties in the context of mediation. Such statutory protection exists in the United States and more recently, the Law Reform Commission of the Republic of Ireland in its *Report on Alternative Dispute Resolution: Mediation and Conciliation, 2010,* has recommended that communications made in the context of mediation and conciliation should be the subject of a distinct form of privilege which is protected by legislation.

[73] *Aird v Prime Meridian Ltd* [2006] EWCA Civ 1866.

[74] See *Brown v Rice* [2007] EWHC 625 (Ch). See also *AB v CD Ltd* [2013] EWHC 1376 (Ch), where the mediator was required to give evidence and to disclose notes he had made and communications received from the parties from the conclusion of the mediation meeting until settlement was reached by the parties some two weeks later, in order to assist the court to determine whether the dispute had settled by agreement following the conclusion of the mediation meeting. The court also admitted evidence of what took place at the mediation in order to determine whether a settlement agreement was binding on the parties in *Universal Satspace (North America) LLC v Kenya* (QB), 20 December 2013 (unrep). In *Barden v Commodities Research Unit (Holdings) Ltd* [2013] EWHC 1633 (Ch), the court ordered disclosure of the notes of the mediation and the parties and their lawyers also made witness statements describing the course of negotiations in the mediation in order to determine the factual matrix which the court should consider when construing the settlement agreement to determine if it was inclusive or exclusive of tax.

[75] *Brown v Rice* [2007] EWHC 625 (Ch).

- if *all* parties to the mediation waive privilege, the communications can be placed before the court.[76] However, there is no implied waiver of the without prejudice rule simply because a party makes an application for indemnity costs.[77]

Can the mediator rely on the without prejudice rule?

13.63 The without prejudice rule exists for the benefit of the parties and it can be waived by them. It is not a privilege of the mediator, so if the parties waive it, the mediator cannot rely on it to prevent non-disclosure of communications arising out of the mediation. This is so even if the mediation agreement contains an express provision as to the without prejudice nature of the mediation process.[78]

R Legal Advice Privilege in Mediation

13.64 Legal advice privilege[79] will also be upheld in mediation and the privilege will not be waived by one party subsequently bringing proceedings against the other party to the mediation to have the settlement agreement reached in mediation set aside on the grounds of economic duress.[80]

S The Mediator as Witness

13.65 The mediation agreement will usually contain a clause by which the parties agree not to call the mediator or any of his or her employees or agents as a witness or expert or consultant in any proceedings. The court will consider this

---

[76] *Cumbria Waste Management Ltd v Baines Wilson* [2008] EWHC 786 (QB), where the claimant sued its former solicitors following a settlement reached at mediation. The solicitors sought disclosure of the communications in the mediation. However, although the claimant expressly or impliedly waived privilege by bringing the action against the solicitors, the court held that the privilege also belonged to the other party to the dispute (DEFRA) and in the absence of waiver of the privilege by DEFRA, the court could not order disclosure of the communications within the mediation.

[77] *Vestergaard Fransden A/S v Bestnet Europe Ltd* [2014] EWHC 4047 (Ch).

[78] *Farm Assist Ltd (in liquidation) v The Secretary of State for the Environment, Food and Rural Affairs (No 2)* [2009] EWHC 1102 (TCC).

[79] See Chapter 5 at 5.15.

[80] *Farm Assist Ltd (in liquidation) v Secretary of State for Environment, Food and Rural Affairs* [2008] EWHC 3079, where the Secretary of State was refused disclosure of documents covered by legal advice privilege both before and during the mediation, consisting of advice given to the claimant about the merits of the claim, the offers to be made during the mediation, and the response to offers made by DEFRA.

clause, as part of all of the circumstances of the case, in deciding whether the mediator should be required to give evidence. Notwithstanding the existence of such a contractual provision, the court may require the mediator to be called as a witness to give evidence about events occurring during the mediation if it is in the interests of justice to do so.[81] In *AB v CD Ltd*,[82] the court ordered the mediator to give evidence as to the events that took place after the mediation in order to determine if a binding settlement had been reached between the parties.

T Can a Mediator be Sued?

Legal proceedings

A mediator acts under a contract made with the parties. It is likely that the contract contains an implied term that the mediator should act with reasonable care and skill. Theoretically, it is possible that a claim could be brought against a mediator for breach of contract, or in negligence if there was a failure to act with care and skill. This may be the case for example if the mediator gave the parties legal advice in the mediation that was incorrect, or negligently evaluated their claim, or brought undue pressure or made any misrepresentations, or acted negligently in relation to the drafting of a settlement agreement (if the mediator assumed responsibility for the drafting of this document) or failed to convey accurately offers or acceptance of offers from one party to another. Such claims are likely to be difficult to prove, and are likely to raise difficult issues of causation (particularly where the parties are independently advised by lawyers who are present at the mediation) and loss. **13.66**

If a settlement was reached as a result of undue pressure exerted on that party by a mediator, then this may provide grounds for overturning the settlement agreement.[83] The mediator may also be liable if he or she personally recommends a settlement at a certain level to the parties, if that settlement was unreasonable on the facts of the case.[84] **13.67**

Some mediation agreements will contain an exclusion clause that purports to exclude the mediator from liability for negligence or breach of contract. This may be unenforceable in law or unfair under the Unfair Contract Terms Act 1977. **13.68**

---

[81] *Farm Assist Ltd (in liquidation) v The Secretary of State for the Environment, Food and Rural Affairs (No 2)* [2009] EWHC 1102 (TCC).

[82] [2013] EWHC 1376.

[83] See *Tapoohi v Lewenberg* [2003] VSC 410.

[84] See *McCosh v Williams* [2003] NZCA 192.

Disciplinary proceedings

13.69 It is possible that disciplinary proceedings could be brought against a mediator who acts improperly or not in accordance with the code of conduct adopted by the ADR service provider by whom he was accredited and appointed or by his or her professional organization.

14

PREPARATION FOR THE MEDIATION

A Introduction

Once the parties have decided to use mediation to resolve the dispute, they need **14.01**
to plan for the process. The preparatory work required for a mediation includes
selecting and appointing a suitable mediator, agreeing the terms of the agreement
to mediate, locating and booking (if necessary) the venue for the mediation, collat-
ing the key documents, and drafting the position statement or case summary. All
of these matters are covered in this chapter, together with practical considerations
that lawyers should bear in mind in order to effectively advise and prepare a client
for the mediation process.

The lawyer who is instructed to attend the mediation will also need to consider the **14.02**
negotiating strategy and tactics to be employed during the mediation.[1]

B Styles of Mediation

Once the parties have decided to embark on mediation, they need to consider the **14.03**
form of mediation that they wish to use, as this may have a bearing on the type of
mediator they need to appoint, and the preparation that needs to be undertaken for
the mediation.

Mediation tends to follow two main forms: facilitative mediation and evalua- **14.04**
tive mediation (sometimes called directive mediation). Facilitative mediation is
the norm.

Facilitative mediation

The mediator, as a neutral or impartial third party, helps the parties to solve their own **14.05**
problems by facilitating negotiations between the parties. A facilitative mediator

---

[1] See Chapter 12.

will focus primarily on the real interests and concerns of the parties rather than the strict legal merits of their position.

14.06 Although the mediator is there as a facilitator, the mediator's role is not a passive one. The facilitative mediator will:

- ask questions that test the strengths and weaknesses of each side's case;
- explore each party's situation and help them to identify what they really need or want to achieve from the dispute;
- encourage the parties to think about the likely outcome of litigation and the costs of obtaining that outcome;
- focus each party's attention on their underlying objectives and needs (what is important and why this is so), rather than on a strict analysis and evaluation of the merits of their case;
- help the parties to work out a creative solution that is in their best interests;
- assist the parties to negotiate more effectively by formulating offers in a way that may be more attractive to the other side, and considering the timing and staging of offers and concessions.

14.07 A mediator using a purely facilitative mediation model will not express a personal opinion on the merits of each party's case or evaluate the likely outcome of a dispute or put forward his or her own proposals for settlement. A facilitative mediator is also likely to exert less control over the process than an evaluative mediator and will generally be less interventionist and challenging in the questions asked of the parties about the way in which they have assessed the merits of the case.

14.08 Facilitative mediation is the primary form of mediation. Whether any particular mediator favours a facilitative or an evaluative style is something that the parties should take into account when selecting a mediator, or agreeing the scope of the mediator's role in the mediation.

Evaluative mediation

14.09 The evaluative mediator will generally facilitate settlement by adopting a facilitative style. However, such a mediator will go beyond the role of facilitator and, if asked, will actually evaluate the issue or claim and the strengths and weaknesses of each party's case. An evaluative mediator may also be asked to recommend a form of settlement, or a range of options for settlement. The evaluation will usually be carried out in a legalistic way, with emphasis on the legal and factual issues and an evaluation of the evidence in relation to the issues. The evaluation is not binding on the parties, but it may assist the parties to negotiate a settlement. Lawyers or professionals who have expertise in the subject matter of the dispute sometimes have a natural tendency to be evaluative mediators.

The parties will determine whether the mediator's role moves from the normal facili- **14.10** tative role to an evaluative one. Both parties may jointly ask the mediator to evaluate the claim, or one or more discrete issues in the claim, or recommend a suitable range for settlement or one party may do so privately in relation to their own position. The mediator will not usually evaluate a claim or issue unless specifically invited to do so.

Evaluative mediation does have some perceived disadvantages: **14.11**

- an evaluation is likely to favour one side's case over another. This can lead to a perception that the mediator is not neutral and unbiased and this may destroy the effectiveness of the mediation process;
- there is also a perception that evaluative mediators can coerce the parties into settlement;
- in some cases, an evaluation can result in a hardening of position on the part of the party whose case is more likely to succeed, with the consequence that the parties are likely to become more entrenched in their positions;
- the mediator will also seldom be provided with all of the documentation in a case. Any evaluation that is provided may not be based on complete information and may therefore be misleading. Providing an evaluation may also expose the media-tor to a potential claim in negligence.[2]

For these reasons, evaluative mediation is more likely to be the exception rather than **14.12** the norm. Some ADR providers do not permit their mediators to express an opinion on the merits of the dispute or give an indication of the likely outcome and others may suggest that the non-binding evaluation should be delivered openly in a joint meeting of the parties, or at least the same advice should be given to both parties in identical terms. An opinion given jointly to the parties is less likely to give rise to undue pressure or coercion than an opinion given to one party alone.

However, evaluative mediation also has some advantages. It can speed up the settle- **14.13** ment negotiations and provide the reality check that is needed to enable the parties to move towards settlement. The mediator must take great care not to impose his or her evaluation or preferred outcome on the parties.

If evaluative mediation is sought, this should be specified in advance (as some **14.14** mediators may be unwilling to do this). Where the mediator agrees to provide an

---

[2] See Chapter 13 at 13.66–13.69.

evaluation, this will usually be recorded in the agreement to mediate, or added to it by way of addendum if the evaluation is sought during the course of the mediation.

14.15   If an evaluation is required, it may be advantageous for this to be provided early in the mediation. However, the mediator may leave the evaluation until near the end of the bargaining phase and then provide a non-binding opinion in a final last-minute effort to help the parties to resolve the differences between them.

14.16   Evaluative mediation is very similar to judicial conciliation and some commentators refer to it as conciliation. However, in this book, where the evaluation and/or recommendation as to the form of settlement takes place in the context of mediation, it is referred to as evaluative mediation rather than conciliation. It is also a form of early neutral evaluation[3] in that the outcome is similar, although the process is different because in early neutral evaluation, the neutral party evaluating the issue or dispute will not also facilitate negotiations between the parties. Where the evaluation takes place in the context of mediation, it is referred to in this book as evaluative mediation, rather than early neutral evaluation.

Transformative mediation

14.17   Some commentators also make reference to a third style of mediation, namely that of 'transformative mediation'.

14.18   Transformative mediation tends to focus on improving the relationship and communication between the parties rather than having the settlement of the dispute as its primary focus. Transformative mediators aim to help the parties to improve their communication so that they can resolve their own dispute. The parties themselves will control the nature of the discussions, with the mediator primarily providing a reflective role. Whilst some mediators will display some aspects of a transformative mediation style during the course of mediation, most will also use elements of a facilitative or an evaluative approach.[4]

C Selecting a Mediator

14.19   The parties may select a mediator through personal recommendation or prior experience. Alternatively, a mediator can be found using the online directories or search engines maintained by organizations such as the Civil Mediation

---

[3] See Chapter 22.

[4] For further information on transformative mediation see Robert A Baruch Bush and JP Folger, *The Promise of Mediation, The Transformative Approach to Conflict* (Jossey-Bass, 2005) and <http://www.transformativemediation.org>.

Council, the Family Mediation Council, or other professional bodies such as the Bar Council, the Law Society, the Academy of Experts, or the Royal Institute of Chartered Surveyors. A party may choose to engage the services of one of the ADR providers to provide a shortlist of mediators with the relevant expertise from its panel. If an ADR provider is used, it will usually also administer the mediation process, including:

- arranging the date of the mediation;
- booking the venue;
- providing the parties with the agreement to mediate;
- ensuring that the mediator has no conflict of interest;
- advising on the documents and statements that each party should provide for the mediation; and
- dealing with any concerns or queries that the parties may have about the process.

Some ADR providers may offer a fast track mediation service for parties who wish to arrange their own venue and only require a mediator; a discounted rate will usually operate for this more limited service. **14.20**

In large and complex disputes, the parties may need to appoint more than one mediator. If so, there may be scope for choosing mediators with complementary styles and areas of expertise. **14.21**

Factors influencing the selection of a mediator

A good mediator is also someone who will have some or all of the following qualities: good listening and communication skills, strong observation skills, persistence, determination, diplomacy, incisiveness, empathy and sensitivity, patience, firmness, good attention to detail, the ability to think creatively when resolving a dispute, flexibility, the ability to inspire trust and respect, good analytical skills, skilled questioning techniques, good judgment, relevant mediation experience, excellent negotiation skills and techniques, and a commitment to reaching settlement. Depending on the nature of the dispute and the needs of the parties, it may also be important for the mediator to have sound knowledge of the legal, technical, or factual issues in dispute. A mediator's charges and fees, and their availability, will also be relevant factors. **14.22**

Other factors that will determine the selection of the mediator include the following matters. **14.23**

Personal recommendation

Lawyers for the parties may be able to recommend a particular mediator based on personal experience or based on the recommendation of others in their firm or **14.24** chambers. ADR organizations may be able to make available feedback from clients on particular mediators that they recommend.

Personality

14.25 It is important that the parties have trust and confidence in the mediator and that they feel that they can have an open and effective working relationship. The mediator's personality should work with those of the parties. Parties with strong personality traits may require a mediator with a strong and authoritative personality for the mediation to work effectively.

Expertise in the subject matter of the dispute

14.26 The parties may want to select a mediator who is familiar with the subject matter of the dispute. This is also likely to be helpful if expert evidence is to be considered during the mediation. A mediator who has no underlying expertise at all in the subject matter of the dispute, whether as a lawyer or an expert in the relevant field, is less likely to focus on the relative merits of each case and the likely outcome if the matter went to trial, and will be more interested in devising a creative solution to the problem. Such a mediator is also more likely to adopt a purely facilitative rather than an evaluative approach to mediation[5] and may lack sufficient knowledge about the issues to act as an effective 'reality-tester'.

Expertise gained as a lawyer

14.27 In some cases, expertise acquired as a lawyer may well be desirable. Such a mediator will appreciate the procedural background and practicalities of litigation, the role the courts play in managing litigation costs and possible costs orders that may be made, the commercial realities of the matter, and the complexities of the legal or factual position of each party. Such expertise is also likely to be useful if robust legal, factual, or evidential reality-testing or evaluative mediation is required.

Expertise gained as a professional in other fields

14.28 A non-lawyer mediator who has expertise in the underlying nature of the dispute, such as an accountant or an engineer, may be desirable if the underlying issues are so technical that expertise is required to understand them in order to facilitate meaningful negotiations between the parties, or if evaluative mediation is sought. However the mediator's expertise in the subject matter of the dispute may make it more difficult for him or her to remain or appear neutral and to keep the parties

---

[5] See 14.05–14.16 above.

focused on reaching settlement rather than debating the merits of complex technical positions.

Preferred style of mediation

The choice of mediator may also depend on the style of mediation that the parties **14.29** prefer. If the parties wish to appoint an evaluative mediator to express a view on the merits of their respective cases, or the likely outcome or range for settlement, it may be desirable to select a mediator who has expertise in the subject matter of the dispute.[6]

Practical experience as a mediator

Care also needs to be taken to select a mediator with relevant practical experience. **14.30** The parties will want to ensure that the person selected has a proven track record in relation to the mediations undertaken. The parties can ask a mediator to provide a detailed curriculum vitae, information about the number and type of mediations he or she has undertaken as a lead mediator, the outcome of those mediations, and the names and addresses of referees.

Accreditation and professional indemnity insurance

The mediator selected should also be properly trained and accredited and operate **14.31** under an appropriate code of conduct.[7] It is also important to check whether a mediator has professional indemnity insurance.

Interview

Bearing in mind the points set out above, the parties may wish to draw up a shortlist **14.32** of suitable prospective mediators and question them before selecting and engaging the mediator of their choice. Such questioning will enable the parties to explore some of the points made above which are of particular importance to them.

Language and cultural considerations

The parties should consider whether it is necessary to have a mediator who can **14.33** mediate in the first language of the parties. This is particularly important in a cross-border or international dispute. The mediator should also share or be familiar with the cultural background of the parties, and should be sensitive to cultural diversity.[8]

---

[6] See 14.03–14.16 above for the difference between evaluative and facilitative mediation styles.

[7] See Chapter 13 at 13.44–13.48.

[8] See the guide to choosing the right mediator produced by the International Mediation Institute (IMI), <http://www.imimediation.org>, available as a web app. In cases with an international or European flavour, the IMI also maintains a directory of accredited mediators, which can be found on its website. Relevant details can also be found on the Online Resource Centre for this title.

A team of mediators

14.34 Complex or multi-party disputes or international disputes may require more than one mediator to be appointed. In such cases, care needs to be taken to ensure the team of mediators contains the right blend of expertise, age, gender, professional experience, and linguistic/cultural background as well as compatible personalities and mediation styles. The co-mediators need to ensure that they work as a team in all respects.

D The Duration of Mediation

14.35 A typical mediation will last up to a day, with negotiations usually commencing some way into the day. In time-limited, fixed-fee mediations, the mediation will usually last around three hours (and the free mediations undertaken under the Small Claims Court Mediation Scheme will last one hour or less).[9] In more complex, multi-party, or high value cases, it is not uncommon for mediations to last anything between two and five days. Some mediations can also take place on a number of separate occasions arranged over a number of months. This is particularly the case in complex or multi-party disputes or international disputes. A number of meetings also tend to be held in family disputes, particularly in cases involving children.

14.36 If there is doubt about how long the mediation is likely to last, it may be best to book the mediation for a fixed period, but with all parties prepared to extend the time or adjourn to another day if further time is needed.

E Selecting a Venue

14.37 If the parties are using an ADR provider, the provider may select and book the venue for the mediation. A mediator in private practice may also conduct the mediation in his or her own premises. Otherwise the parties themselves will have to choose the date and select an appropriate venue for the mediation. A number of practical factors will govern the choice of venue, and these include cost, the size of the premises required and the equipment and facilities needed.

14.38 If the parties undertake a time-limited, fixed-fee mediation under a court scheme[10] or agree to judicial mediation[11] the mediation may take place at the local court, sometimes outside normal court hours. If this happens, only one room may be

---

[9] See Chapter 16, particularly 16.07–16.12.
[10] See Chapter 16 at 16.05–16.15 for the main court mediation schemes.
[11] See Chapter 16 at 16.17–16.23.

available for the mediation and that will usually be occupied by the mediator, with each party being shuttled in and out of the room for private meetings with the mediator during the process. Where the parties arrange the mediation themselves, a neutral venue is likely to be best, such as a hotel, or a designated conference centre because it has no association with either party and all participants are away from their familiar environment and are less likely to get distracted from the issues. However, the mediation can be held at the offices or chambers of the lawyers for one of the parties or at the premises of one of the parties in order to save costs.

Ideally, at least three rooms will be required for the mediation, one for the joint **14.39** meeting, and two separate rooms, one for each of the parties. A fourth room for the private use of the mediator can be useful, but it is not essential. If there are more than two parties, sufficient rooms should be made available to ensure that each of the parties have their own room. In large multi-party disputes it may be possible for parties of a certain class or those united by a common issue to share a room. It is worthwhile checking that the rooms are sound-proofed if they are next door to one another; if they are not, the parties will not feel comfortable having a frank discussion in private meetings.

Unless the parties have elected to have a time-limited, fixed-fee mediation, the **14.40** mediation meeting may last all day, and can run into the evening, so this should be borne in mind when selecting a venue. It would be very inconvenient if the venue had to be vacated at a certain time, particularly if a crucial stage was reached in the negotiations. It is important that facilities for refreshments are readily available in or close to the venue. The venue also should be comfortable, conducive to settlement discussions, and equipped with all of the usual facilities such as flipcharts, telephone, facsimile machine, computer and internet points, and photocopying and printing facilities.

The layout of the main meeting room that will be used for the joint sessions is par- **14.41** ticularly important. It should not be laid out in an adversarial style resembling that of a courtroom. A room containing a single table which is large enough to accommodate all of the parties will be more conducive to a successful mediation.

F The Agreement to Mediate

In the United Kingdom, with the exception of mediations arranged in employment **14.42** cases through ACAS, mediation has no form of statutory framework. In most cases, the regulatory framework for mediation derives from the contract between the parties and the mediator, comprised in the agreement to mediate.

14.43 The parties to mediation will be required by the mediator (or the ADR service provider) to sign an agreement to mediate (usually in their standard form) before or at the mediation. These standard form agreements are amended from time to time.

14.44 The agreement to mediate represents the contract between the mediator and the parties. It sets out the terms on which the mediator is appointed, the scope of the mediation, and the obligations of the parties to each other and to the mediator in respect of the mediation.

14.45 Most agreements to mediate contain the following key clauses. The parties may wish to vary the standard form agreements so that they are more specifically tailored to the circumstances of the particular case.

- The scope of the mediation: reference should be made to the dispute that is being referred to mediation. This should be defined with care. If only some of the issues are being referred to mediation, the agreement should make this clear.
- Practicalities, such as the names of the parties and the mediator, the identity of those attending the mediation, the date, time and place of the mediation, the duration of the mediation, and confirmation that each party signing the agreement (or a representative attending the mediation) has authority to settle the case. If the mediator is a member of a firm, company, or other type of organization, the agreement to mediate will usually make it clear whether the mediator is an independent contractor or the agent of the firm, company, or organization. In relation to the duration of the mediation, it is becoming increasingly important to define this with care, not least so that parties know precisely when the obligations in the agreement to mediate, such as confidentiality, are legally binding on them, what is covered by the fee agreed, and when further mediation fees can be charged (eg, if the mediation extends beyond the scheduled time). It is also equally important for the duration to be specified so that the parties are clear about whether continuing negotiations after the conclusion of the mediation day are covered by the terms of the agreement to mediate. If so, then any settlement agreement reached subsequently must comply with the form required by the agreement to mediate in order to be legally binding.[12]
- The process is confidential and that the parties will keep confidential all information arising out of or incidental to the mediation.[13] If the parties are particularly concerned about confidentiality, they may want to tailor this clause to suit their own circumstances.

---

[12] See *Brown v Rice & Patel* [2007] EWHC 625; *AB v CD* [2013] EWCA Civ 1376. See also 15.01–15.03.

[13] See Chapter 5 at 5.27–5.29, 5.31–5.32 and Chapter 13 at 13.49–13.58 for a full discussion about confidentiality.

- Communications passing between the parties and/or the mediator during the mediation process will be protected from disclosure by the 'without prejudice' rule and should not be disclosed to any third party or used in litigation unless they are disclosable by law.[14]
- The mediator is neutral and impartial and will not reveal confidential information entrusted to him or her without the consent of the person who provided it, unless disclosure is required as a matter of law.
- The parties will not call the mediator as a witness in later legal proceedings in connection with the dispute or in relation to any matter arising out of the mediation, or require the mediator to disclose any notes made during or in relation to the mediation, and they will indemnify the mediator for the costs of resisting or responding to such an application.[15]
- The mediation will be conducted under the mediation model rules or procedure and Code of Conduct of the mediator/organization concerned, details of which can usually be found on the organization's or mediator's website.
- Any settlement reached at the mediation will not be binding on the parties until it is recorded in writing and signed by the parties. The court has considered the nature and effect of this clause in a number of cases. In *Brown v Rice*,[16] the court held that a clause in this form meant that any settlement agreement reached between the parties was not complete or legally binding until it was reduced into writing and signed by the parties, unless that clause was waived or varied by the parties, or the parties were not otherwise able to rely on it. More recently, the courts have upheld a settlement agreement which did not fully conform with this clause by finding that an oral agreement to sign a written settlement agreement reached at mediation was a collateral contract which the court could enforce, and the collateral contract was not covered by the ambit of the clause in the agreement to mediate.[17] In *AB v CD Ltd*,[18] the court held that the clause did not apply, because the mediation had ended on rejection of an offer which remained open for acceptance after the mediation, and the continued negotiations between the parties did not take place under the terms of the mediation agreement, and so a settlement agreement that was not in writing and signed by the parties was binding and enforceable.
- The agreement will also set out the costs and expenses of the mediation and who is responsible for paying them and the date(s) by which they must be paid. It will

---

[14] See Chapter 5 at 5.17–5.26 and Chapter 13 at 13.59–13.63 for a discussion of the without prejudice rule in the context of mediation.

[15] See Chapter 13 at 13.65 for detail about calling a mediator as a witness.

[16] [2007] EWHC 625 (Ch).

[17] *Universal Satspace (North America) LLC v Kenya* (QB) 20 December 2013 (unrep).

[18] [2013] EWHC 1376 (TCC).

also usually specify when additional fees will be payable (eg, additional fees payable to the mediator in the event that the mediation extends beyond a specified time and the rate at which these fees will be charged).

• Finally, the agreement may provide that the parties agree they will not bring a claim against the mediator, either at all, or except in limited specified circumstances (eg, gross or wilful misconduct and dishonesty).

14.46 The courts have recognized that agreements to mediate are valid and that they contain enforceable terms.[19] The court may also grant an injunction to restrain breach of a confidentiality clause in such an agreement.[20]

G Pre-Mediation Meeting/Contact

14.47 Once the parties commit to the process and a mediator has been appointed, it may be necessary to have some form of pre-mediation contact between the mediator and the lawyers for each party (or perhaps even with the parties) to enable the mediator to get a better understanding of the issues in dispute, and to determine whether the typical mediation process[21] needs to be personalized to meet the needs of the parties and the case. If the parties are referred to or seek the assistance of a mediator or broker to help them decide whether to use mediation, and they decide during that meeting to use mediation, all of these preliminary matters can usually be discussed then. However, the mediator will usually get the parties to sign the agreement to mediate before discussing the matters raised below.

14.48 If the mediator has had no prior contact with the parties to help them to decide whether to use mediation, then he or she will usually contact them (or, more usually, their lawyers) by telephone, video or telephoning conferencing technology, or by e mail before the mediation in order to:

• check that the parties understand the process;
• obtain information on any particular needs and objectives that each party may have;
• discuss practical matters such as the venue, the date and time of the mediation, the duration of the mediation, and any special arrangements that need to be made for any of the parties;
• identify the individuals who should attend the mediation, advise on the documents to be provided and the preparation that each of the parties should do for the mediation;

---

[19] See *Brown v Rice* [2007] EWHC 625 (Ch).
[20] *Venture Investment Placement v Hall* [2005] EWHC 1227 (Ch).
[21] See Chapter 15.

- set the timetable for the mediation and the dates by which steps should be taken by each party in order to prepare for the mediation. This is usually also set out in a letter to the parties;
- explore who is intending to take lead in the negotiations and in the opening plenary session, and the role that the lay clients will have;
- explore with the lawyers, particularly where the lay client is a public body, a company, partnership, or backed by an insurer, that the representative attending the mediation has full authority to settle the dispute, whatever emerges during the negotiation process, or at the very least robust arrangements are in place to seek additional authority where necessary. If he or she has not, the mediator will try to persuade the lawyer to ensure that someone more senior, who has the appropriate authority, attends the mediation;
- form a view of the personalities of the parties involved and the way they interact with the other parties and the strength of feeling they have in respect of the issues;
- discuss how to approach and structure the mediation.

H The Attendees

It is very important to identify all of the relevant individuals who should attend   **14.49**
the mediation. Factors influencing the selection of the participants include the following:

- Who has direct knowledge of the key issues in the case?
- Who is most closely and personally affected by the dispute or the resolution of it?
- If relevant, who has the necessary technical expertise?
- Does resolution of any particular issue require expert evidence and the attendance of an expert at the mediation?
- Who has authority to settle the dispute?
- What message will the identity and status of the participants send to the other side?

In low value claims, to maintain cost effectiveness, the mediation will involve usu-   **14.50**
ally only the parties themselves, but complex, high-value or multi-party disputes may involve more individuals and a higher degree of preparation (including the drafting of position statements and the compilation and exchange of key documents). The key attendees may include the following individuals.

Representatives of the parties

Each of the parties will have to determine who should attend the mediation. If the   **14.51**
parties are individuals, then it is likely that they themselves will almost invariably attend as they will have direct knowledge of the facts and issues in dispute. If the

parties are public bodies, companies, or unincorporated associations or a partnership, then the representative will most likely be the person who has the most direct personal knowledge of the issues in the case. The parties will also be permitted to bring a friend or relative with them for support, although these individuals may not be able to enter the mediation rooms due to shortage of space. If they are permitted to enter they may be asked to sign a confidentiality agreement.

Person with authority to settle

14.52   If one of the parties is a firm, company, public body, or an unincorporated body, it is important that someone attends who has authority to settle the action up to the maximum value of the claim. A failure to do so may render the mediation ineffective. It will usually be an express term of the agreement to mediate that each party will ensure that the mediation will be attended by someone who has authority to settle the dispute (in so far as this is possible). If it is genuinely impossible for the party who has authority to settle the dispute to attend the mediation, then robust arrangements should be made to ensure that they are available throughout the day to be contacted by email and/or by telephone. It is not uncommon to find that the person attending the mediation only has authority (eg, from their board, or claims manager) to settle the dispute up to a prescribed limit. If the proposed settlement exceeds that limit, authorization will have to be obtained from another person, and it may not even be possible to obtain it that day. In such cases, the parties may have to conclude the mediation by signing a 'Heads of Agreement' document that sets out the agreed terms, subject to formal authorization being obtained by one or both parties. This can be risky because there is no binding settlement until authorization is obtained and the settlement agreement is signed, so the parties can resile from their position. An alternative would be to adjourn the mediation until authority has been obtained, or so that the person who has the relevant authority up to the maximum value of the claim can attend the mediation.

Lawyers

14.53   If the parties have instructed lawyers in relation to the dispute, then the lawyers will usually attend the mediation (although this will rarely be the case, in the interests of saving costs, in mediations in small claims cases). Usually a representative of the solicitors acting for the parties will attend the mediation. Counsel may also be instructed to attend instead of or, more rarely, in addition to the instructing solicitor. It can be useful to have a lawyer present at the mediation to advise the client on offers, concessions, and any overall settlement proposals, particularly in complex or large value claims as the mediator is unlikely to advise any party on the merits of the proposed settlement or about their legal position. If a party is unrepresented, then a pro bono organization such as the Bar Pro Bono Unit, or Law Works, can be approached to see if free representation can be arranged.

Insurers

Thought needs to be given to the position of insurers. If any party is going to be **14.54** indemnified under a policy of insurance, then a representative of the insurer, who has the requisite authority to settle the claim, may need to attend the mediation, or at least be available on the day to approve any settlement.

Interest groups

Some mediations may involve other parties, such as representatives of the community. **14.55**

Experts

Sometimes (although this is relatively rare) an expert may need to be consulted **14.56** during the course of the mediation, by one or more of the parties, or by the mediator, in order to gain a better understanding of the issues in the case. The expert may be one who has already been instructed jointly, or by one of the parties, for the purposes of actual or proposed litigation. If each party has obtained their own expert evidence, it may be useful for the experts to meet in a 'without prejudice' meeting during the mediation to see if they can narrow the issues and identify areas of agreement or dispute between them, which may make it easier to resolve the dispute overall.

If the parties have not yet obtained expert evidence, an expert may be jointly **14.57** instructed for the purposes of the mediation if the parties and/or the mediator consider that this would be beneficial.

If the parties require an expert to be present at the mediation, this should be dis **14.58** cussed with the mediator in advance so that proper consideration can be given to the extent of the expert's involvement at the mediation and, in particular, whether the expert should give oral evidence at a joint meeting or simply be available to assist the mediator and/or the instructing party in private meetings if required.[22]

Witnesses of fact

It is very rare for witnesses of fact to attend a mediation. However, occasionally, **14.59** especially where the dispute revolves around the evidence of conflicting factual

---

[22] For the difference between joint and private meetings see 15.10–15.14.

witnesses, it may be useful, by prior arrangement with the mediator, for those witnesses to attend the mediation to give evidence at the opening joint session or to be present to assist the parties or the mediator if required.

14.60 Once each party has identified the individuals who will attend the mediation, the mediator and the other party should be informed of the names and position of each of the attendees. The identity and position held by the attendees may also send a clear message to the other side about the value that a party places on mediation and the commitment they are making to the process.

I The Position Statements

14.61 The mediator may ask each party to provide him or her with a statement setting out their case. This is sometimes referred to as a position statement (which is the term that is used in this text), a case summary, a statement of case, written submission, party statement, or even an issue statement. However, this is only likely to be required in more complex cases. The parties will rarely be asked to prepare a position statement for a case which is being mediated under the Small Claims Court Mediation Scheme.[23] A position statement is not always required for modest value fast track county court cases referred to a mediator for a time-limited, fixed-fee mediation through the Civil Mediation Online Directory.[24] It will usually always be prepared and provided in multi-track cases. However, lawyers acting for parties in mediation may consider that it is useful to prepare one even if it is not formally requested by the mediator.

14.62 Where a position statement is required by the mediator, he or she will usually stipulate the time limit within which the position statements (and supporting documents) should be provided. In more complex cases, this will usually be around 7 to 14 days in advance of the mediation.

14.63 On occasions, particularly if the mediation is taking place before proceedings have been issued, the lawyers should consider and canvass with the mediator whether there should be sequential or simultaneous exchange of position statements. If an ADR order is made by the court, then this may also direct the parties to exchange case summaries or position statements and supporting bundles of documents for use in the ADR process. If position statements are exchanged by the parties, there is no reason why an additional, confidential position statement should not be prepared for the mediator's eyes only.

---

[23] See Chapter 16 at 16.07–16.12 for the details of this Scheme.
[24] See Chapter 16 at 16.14–16.16 for more information about this Directory.

The position statement is not intended to be a formal document like a statement **14.64** of case used in litigation. The document is primarily intended to ensure that the mediator is fully briefed on each side's case. Where the statements are disclosed by the parties, they form an important tactical function of giving the opposing party an insight into the strengths of the other side's case, and what they hope to achieve from the mediation.

The aims in drafting the position statement

There are no set rules for drafting the position statement or case summary. However, **14.65** it should not read like a statement of case. It should be written in plain English and be capable of being understood by the parties as well as the lawyers and mediator.

The lawyer or party drafting the statement should bear in mind the following **14.66** matters:

- It should be clearly laid out, easy to navigate, with appropriate use being made of headings and subheadings where necessary.
- It should be logically ordered.
- It should be precise.
- It should be concise. Whilst there is no set page length (unless the mediator imposes one), position statements are usually no longer than five to ten pages.
- It needs to be persuasive. It should set out the key issues in a focused, concise way, rather than being a detailed discursive document that will lack impact due to over-lengthy explanation.

The content of the position statement

It is suggested that the position statement should set out the following requirements **14.67** as *essential* matters:

- *Heading*: it should be headed up with the names and description of the parties (as in a statement of case) and marked 'Confidential and Without Prejudice and for use in the Mediation only'. It should clearly identify the party on whose behalf the statement is made.
- *Formalities*: it should also include the date and time of the mediation, the name of the mediator, a list of the individuals attending the mediation on behalf of the party on whose behalf the statement is made, and their connection with the dispute.
- *Facts*: it should briefly outline the key facts of the case and the nature of the matters in complaint. It is also useful to indicate whether proceedings have been issued and, if so, what has happened in relation to the litigation.

- *Issues*: it should identify the issues in the case, both legal and factual. The state-ment should also identify the key issues that are of vital importance to the parties at the date of the mediation. This may be different from the list of factual and legal issues that arise in the case as it involves focusing on the matters that are of primary concern to the party. If these issues are resolved, all else tends to follow or fall away, so the mediation will primarily focus on these issues.
- *Outline of the party's case on the issues*: the statement needs to clearly set out the party's position in relation to each of the issues. The statement may make brief reference to statements of case, key documents or evidence, and matters of law that support the party's position, and indicate which documents the mediator should read before the mediation. It is important that this document informs the mediator and the other side of the merits of the case, and therefore the strength of the party's negotiating position in relation to the disputed issues of fact or law. However, it should be written in a non-confrontational style and care needs to be taken to ensure that nothing is expressed in such a way that it leads to further entrenchment of positions or discourages the other side from moving towards settlement.
- *The party's interests and objectives*: the key objectives that the party wants to achieve at the mediation should be identified. This section can draw attention to the costs of proceeding to trial, the element of irrecoverable costs, the desire to preserve relationships, the time it will take to resolve the depute if mediation is unsuccess-ful or any other factors that influenced the party to mediate rather than litigate the dispute. It should also make clear the party's commitment to resolving the dispute, if possible, at the mediation and it may emphasize the benefits that set-tlement could bring to both parties.
- *Further information required*: the statement may identify any further information that needs to be obtained from the other party before the matter can be resolved.
- *Negotiations*: any offers, including offers made under Part 36 of the CPR, or con-cessions that have already been made, should be explained. It may explain why offers have been rejected. If any issues in the case have already been resolved by negotiation, this should also be noted.

14.68 There should be no objection at all to a statement in this form being provided to the other party. However if the case summary is not disclosed to the other party and it is intended to be a confidential document for the mediator's eyes only, this should be clearly stated on the face of the document.

14.69 After careful consideration, the parties may also wish to set out an opening offer, or a road map for settlement (eg, if agreement can be reached in relation to issue X, the party will abandon the claim on issue Y). However, tactically, it may be best to do this, using the skills of the mediator as facilitator, during the mediation.

If proceedings have been issued and the parties have already prepared an agreed case **14.70** summary and a list of issues, for example for a case management conference in a multi-track case, then these matters do not need to be set out again in the position statement. Reference can simply be made to that document, and a copy can be annexed to the position statement. If the mediation is taking place before proceedings have been issued, it would be helpful if the position statements set out each party's case as fully and clearly as possible, to enable the mediator and the other side to understand the issues in the case and each side's position in respect of them.

The position statement may be accompanied by two separate documents, unless the **14.71** nature of the dispute renders these unnecessary. These two documents should be agreed with the other side and then all parties can refer to them at the mediation:

- *Chronology*: this should include the chronological dates relevant to the complaint, as well as the chronological negotiation history, and a chronological history of the proceedings (if proceedings have been issued).
- *Dramatis personae*: this document is really for the benefit of the mediator. It should identify the parties, their legal advisers, the experts, the witnesses for each side, the insurers (if relevant), and the name of the person for each party who has authority to settle the dispute.
- *Precedent H Schedule of Costs*. If a schedule of costs has been prepared for litigation (in the form of Precedent H or a modified version of it) it is important to have this at the mediation.

Joint position statement

The parties can also agree to prepare a joint statement that they can both use at the **14.72** mediation, although such a statement is likely to be limited to the facts, the issues, and an explanation of each party's case in relation to the issues.

J The Key Supporting Documents

Agreed bundle

The parties should cooperate with one another in relation to the documents that **14.73** are provided to the mediator and produce agreed bundles where possible. This will be particularly important if the mediator has imposed a maximum page number in relation to the supporting documents that should be provided. The documents should be sent to the mediator by the time specified, and if no time is specified, it would be desirable to let the mediator have these documents at least seven days before the mediation is due to take place.

14.74 The agreed bundle should consist of:

- statements of case if proceedings have been issued and detailed letters of claim if they have not;
- witness statements that have been disclosed by the parties;
- any expert reports disclosed by the parties;
- case management orders that have been made (so that the mediator understands the procedural timetable governing the dispute);
- Part 36 offers or other offers that have been made but not accepted;
- any relevant key documents that have been disclosed relating to the liability or quantum issues in dispute. Plans and photographs can be a useful visual aid to have available for some types of dispute. It is particularly important to ensure that up-to-date documents are prepared for the mediation in respect of quantum, together with supporting documents such as accounts and receipts;
- any other relevant correspondence between the parties.

Confidential bundles

14.75 If a joint bundle of core documents has been agreed, then each party may produce for the mediator, if required, a small bundle of additional documents that they do not wish him or her to reveal to the other side. The confidential documents could consist of documents that have not yet been disclosed to the other party, issues that they may be willing to compromise on, or even perhaps counsel's opinion on liability or quantum. Care should be taken to mark this bundle as 'strictly confidential' and to explicitly state that the mediator should not disclose these documents to the other side.

14.76 Some parties may wish to send almost all of the documents that they have to the mediator. In a complex commercial dispute, this can run to many boxes of material. If the mediator is charging an hourly rate for preparation and is required to read several boxes of documents, then the preparation fee alone is going to be substantial. It is usually not helpful to prepare voluminous bundles of documents for use in the mediation. Each party should endeavour to exercise restraint and select only the key documents in the case.

14.77 When compiling the key documents, the lawyers should bear in mind that the documents are necessary to:

- inform the mediator of the issues in the dispute, the strength of the party's case in relation to those issues or that undermine the position of the other side;
- enable the mediator to adequately test the other side's case;
- support the negotiating stance taken by the party and the objectives it wishes to achieve at the mediation.

Some mediators may stipulate the maximum length of the bundle of documents **14.78**
that should be provided by each party. This should be adhered to unless there are
exceptional reasons why a greater volume of documents should be provided.

Sometimes parties will not want to disclose documents in the mediation because **14.79**
they feel that it will adversely affect the chances of settlement being reached. This
may be so if proceedings have not yet been issued or disclosure has not yet taken
place. In mediation, there are no formal procedural rules which require disclosure
of relevant documents (unlike litigation). However, parties should bear in mind
the provisions of the CPR and the Pre-action Protocols that encourage a 'cards on
the table' approach to litigation. If the document would have to be disclosed in the
litigation, it may be best to disclose it in the mediation. Failure to disclose crucial
documents that have a major effect on the case may give rise to a risk of any settlement being overturned on the grounds of misrepresentation or (less likely, as the
parties are not in a fiduciary relationship to one another) material non-disclosure.

If documents are disclosed to the mediator in confidence he or she will not reveal **14.80**
the existence or content of these documents to the other side. However, from an
ethical point of view, the mediator is likely to refuse to communicate any offer or
other information to the other side which is directly contradicted by the existence
of a confidential document of which he or she is aware.

K Disclosure of Other Documents

Lawyers acting for the parties may need to explore with the mediator whether **14.81**
there should be simultaneous or sequential disclosure of other relevant supporting documents that are not in the agreed bundle and which have not yet been
disclosed. Any documents that are provided by one party to the mediator will
not be disclosed to the other party unless the party providing those documents
agrees that the mediator has authority to disclose them to the other party. If
there is no objection to disclosure, each party may wish to arrange for copies
of these documents to be sent directly to the other party or provide additional
copies to the mediator or ADR provider with a request that they be sent to the
other side.

L Complete Case Papers

Although the documents to be provided to the mediator are likely to be limited **14.82**
in scope, it is often useful to ensure that the complete set of papers relating to the

dispute is available at the mediation in case reference needs to be made to them to resolve a matter that arises during the process.

M Further Information the Mediator may Require

14.83 The mediator may contact one or more of the parties, by telephone or in writing, before the mediation to seek further information about any of the following matters:

- an issue in the case;
- offers or negotiations that have taken place between the parties and why these have been rejected;
- the key objectives of the party and an indication of concessions or offers that they would be willing to make;
- the method of funding for the case;
- if proceedings have been issued, the nature of any costs orders that may already have been made in the case. These may need to be considered as part of the overall settlement;
- the costs incurred by the parties to date, and the further costs that they are likely to incur if settlement cannot be agreed at the mediation.

N Risk Assessment

14.84 The lawyers acting for each party should ensure that a full risk assessment is carried out in relation to the client's case before the mediation. In particular, they should identify the client's objectives and plan a route map for how these can be achieved in the mediation.

14.85 As part of the preparation for mediation, the lawyer will need to carry out a thorough legal, evidential, and practical risk assessment of the client's and the other party's case. This will reveal the client's *position* in respect of the issues to be determined at trial, and enable an overall evaluation of the client's case to be reached.

14.86 Having a clear understanding of the lay client's position is essential in the following respects:

- The lawyer can work effectively with the mediator to ensure the mediator is presented with a clear view of the legal and evidential strengths of the client's position and any weaknesses in the other side's position. This will assist the mediator to embark on rigorous reality-testing when they meet with each party privately.

- The client's position can be explained to the other side using the mediator as a facilitator which, psychologically, can have the cathartic effect of enabling the client to express their concerns, and have them acknowledged in some form by the other party.
- The lawyer will be able to advise the client effectively throughout the process, particularly when making or accepting offers. The client needs to have a clear appreciation of what is likely to happen if settlement is not reached, so that proposals can be considered against that benchmark. The lawyer also needs to ensure that any agreement reached deals with all of the relevant issues.

Understanding the client's position (and that of the other party) is likely to involve **14.87** consideration of the following matters:

- the legal and factual merits of the client's case (and the opposing party's case);
- the evidence that is available to support the client's case (and the opposing party's case) and the further evidence that could be obtained. It is important to attend mediation with the most up-to-date information available in relation to the heads of loss that will be the subject of negotiation. If need be, ensure that recent expert's reports on quantum, schedules of loss, and supporting documents are obtained (and disclosed where appropriate) prior to the mediation;
- how the lay client's case on each issue could best be argued and what arguments can be put forward to refute the claims made by the opposing party;
- the chances of succeeding on each issue at trial (both liability and quantum) in respect of the client's case (and the opposing party's case);
- the overall prospects of success of the client's claim (and any opposing defence and counterclaim, if relevant);
- the costs to date;
- the likely future costs that would have to be incurred to take the case to trial;
- the likely element of irrecoverable costs;
- the likelihood of recovering the costs/damages from the other party;
- if the claim/defence fails, the extent to which the lay client will have to pay the costs of the other party, and the likely amount of those costs;
- how litigation will be funded;
- whether there is the likelihood of either party appealing, and if so, the length of time this could take and the amount such an appeal could cost;
- the other risks or disadvantages of proceeding to trial.

The key stages that need to be undertaken in preparation for mediation are shown **14.88** in Figure 14.1.

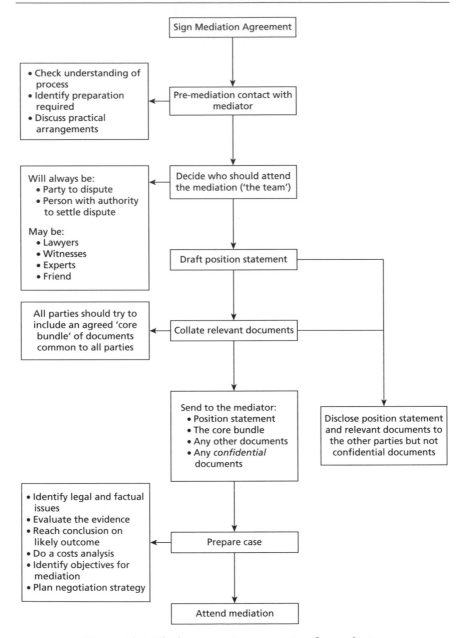

Figure 14.1 The key stages in preparation for mediation

O Options for Settlement

Once the lawyer has gained a thorough understanding of the client's legal position **14.89** and has evaluated the client's case, the lawyer then needs to consider the possible options for settlement. At this stage of the preparation, the focus will shift from consideration of the client's *position* to the client's personal and commercial *interests and needs*. The questions that the lawyer will need to consider with the client will include the following:

- What does the client really want? This will involve consideration of matters other than the client's legal position, including the client's personal and commercial situation and other practical, non-legal matters which may be a motivating factor in respect of settlement.
- How can the client's needs and interests be achieved?
- Could a potential settlement could cover wider considerations and concerns of the lay client, including matters that a court has no power to order?
- What is the other party likely to want? Can any of their interests or needs be met by the client? If so, how or by what means?
- What common ground exists between the parties?
- What are the obstacles to settlement? Can any of the obstacles be overcome? If so, how or by what means?
- What settlement proposals should be offered? How might they be structured or presented?
- What negotiation styles and strategies should be employed during the mediation?
- What costs and risks would the client incur if settlement is not achieved?
- What is the best alternative to a negotiated settlement (BATNA)?
- What is the worst alternative to a negotiated settlement (WATNA)?
- How will any settlement be funded? If the client is likely to be the paying party, it is important to ensure that the client attends mediation with accurate information about their current financial position. It may also be necessary to ensure that taxation advice can be obtained (if necessary) during the mediation on the implications of a proposed settlement.

P Specimen Settlement Clauses

As part of essential preparation for mediation, a lawyer should research specimen **14.90** clauses that may need to be included in the mediation agreement. Copies of the relevant precedents should be brought to the mediation. The lawyer may also need to spend some time in advance of the mediation drafting specimen clauses, which can then be revised, if need be, if settlement is reached so that they reflect the terms agreed. Recent cases demonstrate the degree of care that lawyers need to take when drafting settlement agreements reached at a mediation. Subsequent litigation may be brought to decide whether a settlement agreement was sufficiently certain enough to amount to a binding agreement,[25] or to construe its terms.[26] A lawyer could be sued for professional negligence if a settlement agreement is not drawn up with reasonable care and skill, or if it failed to properly reflect the terms orally agreed, or if was drafted with unnecessary ambiguity. A lawyer may also be negligent if he or she failed to recognize that an agreement reached and drawn up at mediation was too vague in some respects to give rise to a legally binding agreement and failed to advise the lay client in those terms, thus saving the client the costs of seeking to enforce the agreement.[27]

Q Conclusion

14.91 The value of effective preparation for the mediation cannot be underestimated. Effective drafting of position statements and careful compilation of documents will enable a party to influence the mediator so that he or she is able to be more effective in devising creative solutions and carrying out a 'reality check' with the other side. They will also show the other side the strength of the case. The mediation itself will proceed more effectively and efficiently if each party's position is made clear in advance. In high-value cases, the costs of preparation are likely to be very small compared to the sums at stake and the sums that would be spent in litigation or arbitration. However in low-value or medium-value cases (particularly small claims and fast track cases) the parties will need to take care to ensure that the costs of preparation remain proportionate to the sums sought to be recovered in the claim.

---

[25] *AB v CD Ltd* [2013] EWHC 1376 (TCC).
[26] *Barden v Commodities Research Unit International (Holdings) Ltd* [2013] EWHC 1633 (Ch).
[27] *Frost v Wake Smith & Tofields* [2013] EWCA Civ 772.

15

THE MEDIATION PROCESS

A When does the Mediation Start?

It can be important to know when a mediation starts and ends for a number of **15.01**
reasons:

- The confidentiality which attaches to mediation discussions will probably not apply before the mediation starts and after it ends.
- In mediations taking place in cross-border disputes, the statutory limitation period is suspended during mediation.[1]
- An ADR clause in a contract may require parties to commence or finish mediation by a particular time.
- It may be important to know whether an offer was made during or after the end of the mediation process. For example, where a mediation agreement contained a fairly typical term to the effect that a settlement reached in the mediation would not be binding until it was reduced to writing and signed by the parties, an issue may arise as to whether an oral offer and acceptance was made in the mediation or after the mediation had ended.[2]

In many cases, it is difficult to pinpoint the moment mediation begins with any **15.02**
accuracy. Does mediation begin when:

- the mediator is appointed;
- the pre-mediation meeting/contact takes place as described in Chapter 14;

---

[1] See Chapter 17 at 17.26–17.29.

[2] In *Brown v Rice & Patel* [2007] EWHC 625 (Ch), the court held that an offer that remained open for acceptance after the mediation was still an offer made in the mediation and therefore an oral acceptance of it did not give rise to a legally binding agreement because one party reneged before the agreement was reduced to writing and signed by the parties as required by the agreement to mediate. By contrast, in *AB v CD Ltd* [2013] EWHC 1376, an offer which remained open for acceptance after the conclusion of mediation did amount to a continuation of the mediation, but once that offer was rejected, any further negotiations between the parties did not take place under the terms of the agreement to mediate as the mediation terminated on rejection of that offer, so an acceptance of a fresh offer made after that time could give rise to a legally binding settlement agreement even if it was not in writing and signed by the parties.

- the mediation agreement is signed by each party, or where the parties sign the agreement on different days, at the time when the last party signed it;
- the substantive mediation meeting takes place?

15.03 When the mediation begins and ends can often only be ascertained by examining the intention of the parties from the facts and circumstances of the case. The outcome may not be easy to predict. It would be prudent to consider the events which will constitute the commencement and termination of the mediation in advance and to record these in the mediation agreement or in correspondence.

B The Stages in Mediation

15.04 Before the mediation formally begins, the mediator will usually go to each party's room for introductions to be effected, to ensure that all present have signed the agreement to mediate so that they are all bound by the confidentiality obligations which it will contain, and to address any concerns anyone may have about the process, or any new issues that may have arisen since the parties agreed to refer the dispute for mediation. The typical mediation will go through four key stages, which are discussed in detail in this chapter:

(1) *The opening stage.* This will consist of introductions and each party setting out their formal position in relation to the issues in the case. It will usually take place in the opening joint session (sometimes called a plenary session).

(2) *The exploration (or information) stage.* This can take place partly in open joint meetings and partly in closed private meetings, or exclusively in an open joint meeting or alternatively a closed private meeting, depending on the preferences of the parties, the issues in the case, and the view of the mediator.

(3) *The negotiation (or bargaining) stage.* This will almost invariably take place in closed private meetings (sometimes referred to as 'caucuses' or 'closed sessions') with the mediator acting as broker between the parties.

(4) *The settlement (or closing) stage.* This will usually take place in joint meetings between all of the parties and/or between the lawyers of the parties who will have the task of drawing up the agreement.

15.05 The key stages in the mediation process are shown in Figure 15.1.

15.06 Although most mediations will go through the stages outlined, mediation is a flexible process and it is possible to devise a bespoke process to meet the needs of a particular case. In complex cases, with multiple issues or parties, the mediation can take place over a number of sessions on different days, with each separate session perhaps focusing on a particular issue. In some cases involving the breakdown of

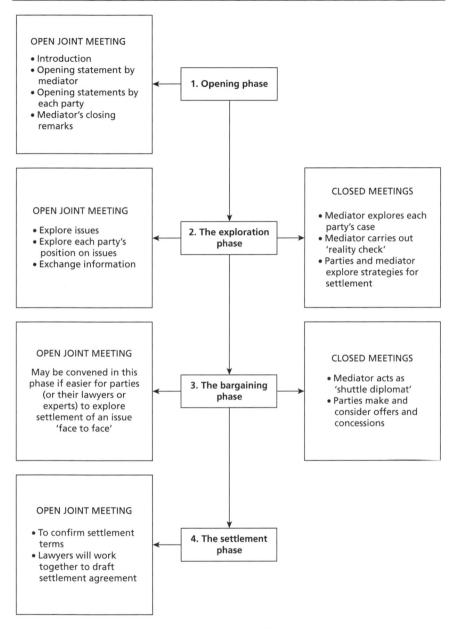

Figure 15.1 The typical mediation process

a personal or business relationship such as a partnership, where emotions may run high, it may be beneficial to dispense with all or some part of the opening joint session to lessen the amount of time that the parties spend together. Some mediations may work best if the parties meet and work together, with or without their lawyers. The mediation process is flexible enough for the parties to personalize it to best fit the facts of the case.

15.07 The stages of mediation may also not always take place in the strict sequential order described and not all of the stages will be present in every case. In some mediations, the stages can take place at the same time in relation to different issues. It is quite possible for the parties to be in the bargaining stage in relation to issue one, at the information stage in relation to issue two and even at the settlement phase in relation to issue three all at the same time.

C The Opening Stage

The opening joint meeting (plenary session)

15.08 The sequence of events at the opening joint meeting is likely to be as follows:

- *Introduction*: the mediator will seat the parties appropriately, effect introductions, and may ask the parties to sign a copy of the mediation agreement (even if they have each previously signed a copy in advance) as doing so can help to reinforce their commitment to the process.
- *The mediator's opening statement*: the mediator will then make a formal opening statement which will cover matters such as the effectiveness of mediation, an outline of the voluntary, non-binding nature of the process, the role of the mediator, and the parties in that process, the mediator's neutrality and impartiality, an explanation of the concepts of confidentiality and without prejudice, and, in the event that settlement is reached, the need to have a settlement agreement drawn up and signed by the parties before the close of the mediation. The mediator will also check at this stage that the parties present have authority to authorize settlement or, if not, that the person who has ultimate authority is easily contactable by telephone (or email) and will remain so throughout the mediation.
- *Opening statements by the parties*: the mediator will usually ask each of the parties to outline their case and what they hope to achieve at the conclusion of the dispute. They may do this by making brief reference to the position statement or case summary that they prepared. The opening statement should be concise (aim for no longer than twenty minutes in a mediation lasting a day). The mediator will usually ask the other side not to interrupt the party delivering the statement. It is common for the opening statement to be made by counsel or the solicitor instructed

by the party, but it can be delivered by the parties themselves. The mediator will fix the order in which the parties are asked to make these statements. Usually, the claimant in the dispute will be asked to begin. The statement should be addressed to the other side, as well as the mediator. It should be concise yet persuasive. It should cover the key issues and the strength of the lay client's case in relation to those issues and address the concerns of the other side where possible. It is not necessary in opening to go through all of the documents and statements of case. There is plenty of time to do this later in the process. The statement needs to be pitched at the right level so that it persuades the parties and sets the tone for the settlement discussions to follow. If the lawyer makes the opening statement on behalf of the client, he or she should emphasize the lay client's willingness to settle the dispute. Either the lawyer or the mediator can invite the party to speak at the end of it. This should be discussed and decided in advance so that the party has time to prepare what he or she wants to say. It can be effective to enable a client to speak directly to the other party, particularly if they are likely to come across as a measured, credible witness. It can also be useful to let the client explain the effect the dispute has had on him or her (or perhaps make an apology for what has happened, if that is appropriate). However, the client should be guided to explain matters in a factual measured way because the aim of the joint meeting is not to escalate or inflame the dispute, but rather to lay the groundwork to enable settlement to be achieved. At the conclusion of each party's opening statement, the mediator may ask questions to clarify anything which is unclear. The mediator may also give the other side the opportunity to ask questions to clarify any matter that they did not understand but will not permit the other side to conduct a cross-examination about the submissions made in the opening statements. The second party to deliver the opening statement does not have to respond to the first party's statement, but rather should concentrate on their own position. However if there are points that can be refuted clearly and succinctly, this can be done.

- *Witnesses and experts*: lay or expert witnesses may, in certain cases, attend a mediation.[3]
    - *Lay witnesses*: it is rarely necessary or desirable for live evidence to be given at the mediation. However, if an issue of fact divides the parties and depends on the evidence of a particular witness, it may be proposed that an assessment of the credibility of the witness should be made by all of the parties, and this will usually take place during the opening joint session. How this is done, whether by an oral statement or by questioning or both, needs careful consideration.
    - *Expert evidence*: where there is a dispute between the experts in relation to an important issue in the case, the parties may each want the other party to hear

---

[3] See Chapter 14 at 14.56–14.60.

from their expert so that the party can reach a view on which expert's opinion is more likely to be accepted by the court before an overall settlement can be reached. In such a case, the experts may give their evidence by a presentation at the opening joint session.

- *Closing the opening joint meeting*: the mediator will then draw the opening session to a close by explaining that the mediation will move into the next phase, and that this will take place primarily in private meetings of the parties. The mediator may set a timetable for these private sessions, and indicate which party he or she will see first and the initial time that is likely to be spent with each party. After the first private meeting with each party, it is likely that the pace of negotiations will increase and the mediator will be moving from one party to another with offers and counter-offers on a very frequent basis.

Extension of the plenary session

15.09 Where the parties are reasonably cooperative and civil towards one another, some mediators may extend the joint opening session to do some or all of the following:

- get the parties to agree the key issues that need to be discussed, and to agree the order in which they will deal with these issues. The mediator may record these matters on a flipchart;
- get the parties to work together to explain a particular issue for the benefit of the mediator;
- enable the parties to plug any relevant gaps in the information;
- brainstorm the figures that comprise the claim and the counterclaim (if any), the costs that each party has incurred to date, and the future costs that will be incurred by each party if the dispute is not settled at the mediation. This can be effective in focusing minds on overall figures and settlement, rather than on positional issue-driven bargaining;
- brainstorm ideas for settlement. These can be recorded (in any order) on a flip-chart.

The separate private meetings (or closed meetings)

15.10 Almost all mediations will involve the parties spending time in closed meetings. These meetings are sometimes called 'separate private meetings', 'caucuses', or 'closed meetings' to distinguish them from the open joint meetings of the parties. In these meetings the parties will meet privately, without the other side being present, to explore the issues and discuss settlement confidentially with the mediator. This tends to be the key stage in the mediation process.

The purpose of private meetings is to: **15.11**

- give the parties privacy to discuss the issues in the case and their own negotiating strategy and proposals for settlement;
- enable the mediator to meet with the parties privately to discuss the dispute and strategies for settlement and to test the reality of their assessment of the case;
- enable the parties to consider proposals from the other side and make a considered response to those proposals;
- enable the mediator to frame and communicate offers and counter-offers in a constructive way.

In the closed private meetings, two stages of the mediation usually take place: **15.12**

- the exploration/information stage (although in some cases, this can take place in a joint session as described above). Some commentators refer to this as the 'problem-solving' stage;
- the negotiating/bargaining stage.

Although these stages of the mediation usually take place in private meetings, there   **15.13**
is nothing to stop the parties and the mediator carrying out these stages in an open joint meeting if this would be useful. Mediation is a very flexible process and the mediator will make use of open and closed meetings in a way that best meets the needs of the parties.

It is impossible to state with any accuracy the percentage of time spent in the joint   **15.14**
or open meetings because the balance between the two will depend on the type of mediation, the subject matter of the dispute, and the relationship between the parties. To a very large extent, the mediator will go with his or her instinct on the day having observed the parties and the way they are reacting to one another.

D The Exploration/Information Stage

In the closed private meetings, in the presence of the mediator, the parties can embark   **15.15**
on a rigorous assessment of their case without the other side being present, and without losing face if they revise their positions several times on any issue or in relation to the overall settlement that they hope to achieve. The mediator performs a number of important roles during the closed private meetings and these roles are discussed below.

Carrying out a 'reality test'

The 'reality test' that the mediator can provide is an extremely valuable part of the   **15.16**
mediation process. The mediator will try to do this as neutrally as possible ('Why',

'What if … ?') so as to avoid the perception that he or she is expressing any personal views on the merits of the case. The mediator will carry out a reality check by:

- assisting the parties to review and accurately evaluate the strengths and weaknesses of their own case and that of the other side and challenging their factual and legal perceptions about the case;
- focusing each party's attention on gaps in the evidence, facts which they may have difficulty proving at trial and anything which may affect the court's assessment of the credibility of a particular witness or expert;
- helping the parties to work out what their best, worst, and most realistic case outcomes are if the matter proceeds to trial, together with the costs of legal proceedings, including the element of irrecoverable costs which would be payable even if one party succeeds and gets a judgment and costs order in their favour.

Probing the underlying issues

15.17 The mediator will try to work out what concerns and issues underlie the dispute. Mediators find that the formally presented factual and legal issues in the case are often only 'the tip of the iceberg'. There are many underlying matters which may underpin any dispute, such as anger, anxiety, lack of trust, resentment or competition, and economic factors. The mediator will often need to explore these with the parties to assist them to reach a settlement. The mediator may encourage the parties to give vent to their private feelings and concerns. This is cathartic, and some parties are only able to move forward to resolve the dispute once they have done this.

Helping the parties to devise options for settlement

15.18 The mediator may explore with the parties some or all of the following matters to try to help them to generate options for settlement:

- ask them to consider any wider factors that impact on settlement, such as adverse publicity, the need to maintain a relationship with the other party, damage to reputation, and the effect that a failure to achieve settlement may have on third parties;
- ask them to consider the consequences of a settlement not being reached;
- encourage them to focus on what they could achieve if they were not expending time, money, and energy on the dispute;
- suggest they might focus on their interests (that is commercial and personal needs) rather than their strict legal positions;
- encourage them to explore the likely outcome if the litigation proceeds to trial, including the element of irrecoverable costs;

- encourage them to be more creative in looking at options for settlement, particularly options that may not readily be available in court proceedings, but which may nevertheless be of real value to the parties. This can involve consideration of matters that are outside the scope of the dispute and which a court would have no power to order. For example:
  - in a boundary dispute, agreeing to 'sell' a piece of land to the other side for a sum above its true market value that reflects the importance of that small piece of land to the other side;
  - in a commercial case involving the supply of goods, agreeing to supply goods for a prescribed period of time to the other side for an agreed price that is perhaps lower than the usual market price for goods of that type;
  - in a libel case providing a public apology by an agreed method;
  - agreeing to accept damages by way of periodic payments;
  - devising new systems that will prevent a recurrence of the complaint in the future.

E The Negotiating/Bargaining Stage

At some point during the private meetings, the parties will start to think about **15.19** putting forward proposals for settlement. The mediator may draw on his or her own negotiating experience so as to assist the parties with their negotiations and the mediator may do this by helping the parties to move from a positional to a principled negotiating strategy so that a constructive dialogue can take place. In the later stages of the bargaining phase, small issues may divide the parties and prevent them from reaching overall settlement. Mediation can be more effective than direct negotiation at closing the final gap between the parties and the mediator will employ every skill and technique at his or her disposal to ensure that the parties make the final push towards settlement. The mediator will usually judge when the mediation should move from the exploration to the bargaining phase. To assist guiding the parties towards settlement, some mediators may, at the outset, try to ascertain the settlement range by asking parties to give him or her, on a strictly confidential basis, their best, middle, and bottom settlement offers, or figures that they would accept.

The bargaining phase of a mediation can be conducted on the basis of simultaneous **15.20** exchange of offers, or a sequential exchange. For a one day mediation, the mediator may try to get the parties to exchange their first round of offers just before or immediately after lunch. The remainder of the day will then be spent refining and revising these opening proposals.

15.21 In this stage, the mediator has two main roles and these are described below.

- *Acting as a shuttle-diplomat*: before the mediator leaves a private meeting with a party, he or she will sum up the discussions that have taken place and any offers, concessions, or information that he or she is authorized to communicate to the other side. The mediator will then 'shuttle' between the parties, putting forward offers, concessions, information, and responses to offers for their consideration and generally acting as the intermediary between the parties. Although this can be very effective, there are also disadvantages in that the parties are not working together to the same degree, the process takes longer, and there may be a perceived risk that confidential information may be inadvertently leaked by the mediator to the other side. For these reasons, rather than engage in 'shuttle mediation', sometimes the mediator will convene a joint meeting, so that the parties can negotiate directly between themselves.
- *Devising strategies to help the parties work through deadlock*: it is one of the most important parts of the mediator's role to help the parties to explore other remedies and solutions that will enable them to move the settlement discussions forward. The mediator may employ the following tactics and strategies to move through deadlock:[4]
  - A review can be undertaken of what has been already achieved at the mediation, to encourage the parties to stay engaged with the process.
  - The mediator may identify the cause of the impasse, without breaching confidentiality.
  - A rigorous reality-testing can be undertaken with the parties (or their lawyers) to get them to reassess their position on the merits and reassess their risk.
  - One issue can be divided into many, so as to create greater opportunities for settlement.
  - Proposals may be reframed to make them seem more attractive. Reframing is an important tool of the mediator. It involves re-phrasing concepts so that they appear to be less confrontational or aggressive, or presenting them in a way so that they appear more attractive to the other party.
  - Different members of each team may be asked to meet to brainstorm settlement options to overcome the impasse, thereby introducing new energy into the process.
  - If a deadlocked issue could be resolved by obtaining a determination from a third party such as an expert, the mediator may suggest that the mediation be

---

[4] Also, see Chapter 13 at 13.24–13.27.

adjourned for a short time to enable a determination or a non-binding evaluation to be obtained on that issue.[5]

– The mediator may suggest ways to bridge the gap between the parties for the consideration of the parties such as sealed offers.

– If the parties agree, the mediator may hold a joint meeting of the parties or the lawyers for the parties or both and suggest terms for settlement which may be mutually acceptable. This is not an evaluation of the merits and neither should it be regarded as the mediator offering his or her own opinion of the likely outcome. The terms are suggested as a practical solution to the dispute for the consideration of the parties. The parties will then give their response (which can include a revised offer or concession) to these proposals to the mediator in a private meeting.

– If requested to do so by the parties, the mediator may evaluate one or more of the issues and give them a non-binding opinion on the likely outcome.[6]

Joint meetings of the legal representatives of the parties

The mediator may call the legal representatives of the parties together for one or **15.22** more joint meetings in the bargaining phase of the mediation if this is likely to help the parties to reach agreement on one issue or an overall settlement. It can be useful for discussing issues of a legal nature or the merits of an issue.

Joint meetings between the lay clients

In some mediations, it may be beneficial for the parties to negotiate some or all of the **15.23** issues directly with one another. This will only be considered if the parties have a reasonable working relationship with one another. These meetings may not always include the lawyers acting for the parties. Even if the mediator conducts 'shuttle mediation' for most of the bargaining phase, when the negotiations are almost completed, the mediator may bring the lay clients together to agree the remaining outstanding issues, particularly if the overall settlement is likely to involve a future relationship between the parties.

Joint meetings of the experts

If experts are present for each party then joint meetings may be convened between **15.24** the experts during the bargaining phase, usually without the lawyers or the parties being present, to see if agreement can be reached or disputes narrowed on technical issues or on issues of quantum.

---

[5] See Chapter 22 for Early Neutral Evaluation and Chapter 24 for Expert Determination.
[6] See Chapter 14 at 14.09–14.16 for evaluative mediation.

F The Settlement/Closing Stage

If settlement is reached

15.25 If a settlement is reached, the mediator will confirm the terms agreed with each of the parties. The mediation agreement will usually include the necessary safeguard that no settlement is binding on the parties unless it is recorded in writing and signed by the parties. At this stage, important issues may arise as to the form of the agreement.[7] Whatever form the settlement agreement takes, the mediator will usually ensure that the parties do not leave the mediation until the agreement has been recorded in writing and signed by the parties and the mediator as their input is frequently required as the fine points of detail are hammered out between the lawyers. If a written signed agreement is not drawn up at the mediation, there is always the possibility that the parties may resile from the settlement before the binding agreement has been drawn up.

15.26 If the parties are represented by lawyers, they will have the task of drawing up the settlement agreement. It is useful to have a laptop computer together with some sample precedents at the mediation to assist with this task. A number of recent cases have demonstrated the care that lawyers need to take when drafting the agreement, and when advising the client on the effect of this. Although a lawyer will owe no duty to a client to ensure that mediation results in a legally enforceable agreement, a claim could lie in negligence if a settlement is not achieved because the settlement agreement was not drafted with reasonable care and skill, or if the client is not properly advised on the effect of any agreement reached at mediation.[8] The lawyer needs to take the utmost care to achieve precision in the drafting of clauses, otherwise subsequent litigation may be brought to construe the terms and effect of the settlement agreement.[9] The court is likely to be robust in upholding settlement agreements reached at mediation,[10] and may even uphold an oral agreement that a party would sign the written settlement agreement within a specified time limit after the mediation as a collateral contract that the court could enforce. The clause in the mediation agreement that provided that there was no binding settlement until it had been reduced to writing and signed by the parties did not operate to prevent

---

[7] See Chapter 18.

[8] See *Frost v Wake Smith & Tofields Solicitors* [2013] EWCA Civ 772.

[9] The court had to determine the meaning of a settlement agreement reached in mediation to determine if a payment was to be made net of tax in *Barden v Commodities Research Unit (Holdings) Ltd* [2013] EWHC 1633 (Ch). See also *AB v CD Ltd* [2013] EWHC 1376 (TCC), where the court had to imply a term into a settlement agreement in order to uphold it.

[10] See *Rothwell v Rothwell* [2008] EWCA Civ 1600.

the court from taking the oral agreement made between the parties at the mediation into account. This oral agreement gave rise to a collateral contract which did not come within the terms of the agreement to mediate.[11]

If the parties are acting in person, the mediator may suggest that the parties draw **15.27** up a heads of agreement, a memorandum of agreed terms, or a memorandum of understanding and sign it so that the legal representatives of each party can then draw up the formal settlement agreement after the mediation. Although the court will apply an objective test to determine whether the parties intended to create legal relations, usually a memorandum of understanding or a heads of agreement is not intended to be legally binding.[12] If issues do then arise on the form or content of the agreement the mediator may be involved in resolving them. Occasionally a settlement agreement may be reached which provides for a binding determination of an issue to be carried out by an agreed expert. Where an expert is instructed pursuant to a mediation settlement agreement, the appointment of the expert is under the agreement, rather than by court order, even where the court orders the expert to be appointed pursuant to the agreement, and accordingly CPR, Part 35 does not apply to the expert's determination.[13]

Once the final terms of the settlement agreement have been drafted, the mediator will **15.28** usually oversee the signing of the parties' agreement. Some mediators take the view that the content of any settlement agreement is a matter solely for the parties and their lawyers, on the basis that the mediator cannot owe a duty of care to both parties.

If no settlement is reached

If no settlement is reached, the mediator usually will record this. The mediator **15.29** is likely to summarize the closing positions of the parties, which may form the baseline for further settlement discussions outside the mediation. In suitable cases, the mediator may invite the parties simply to adjourn the mediation for further information to be obtained, or for the parties to consider their positions or some other ADR process. The mediator may invite the parties to let their closing offers remain open for acceptance for a limited period of time after

---

[11] *Universal Satspace (North America) LLC v Kenya* (QB), 20 December 2013 (unrep). See also *Bieber v Teathers Ltd (in Liquidation)* [2014] EWHC 4205 (Ch), where the court held that a concluded agreement had been reached between the parties' solicitors by email, even though the settlement agreement remained to be drawn up between the parties. The further agreement only related to the form of words needed to carry the agreement into effect, rather than matters of substance to be negotiated.

[12] See, for example, *Sax v Tchernoy* [2014] EWHC 795 (Comm).

[13] *Beauty Star Ltd v Janmohamed* [2014] EWCA Civ 451.

the mediation. It is important to discuss and agree whether the mediation is to be regarded as continuing during this period for the reasons outlined at 15.01 above. Many parties who do not reach settlement on the day of the mediation do so shortly afterwards.

G The Closing Joint Meeting

15.30 The mediator will convene the closing meeting if:

- a settlement has been reached on all of the issues or on some of the issues;
- settlement is not likely to be achieved;
- one of the parties wishes to terminate the mediation;
- the mediation needs to be adjourned, for example because no settlement has been reached but the parties believe that an agreement could be achieved by subsequent discussion at another time, or for another ADR process to be considered.

H The Mediator's Role Following the Conclusion of the Mediation

15.31 If mediation does not result in settlement, usually the mediator will have no further involvement with the case unless the parties seek further assistance from the mediator.

15.32 In cases where the parties are likely to continue to explore settlement themselves after the mediation, the mediator and the parties should agree whether the mediation has merely been adjourned (so that any further settlement discussions between the parties take place under the terms of the mediation agreement) or whether the mediation has ended, so that any further settlement discussions take place outside of it. This can be important in relation to costs, particularly if the mediation agreement sets out the manner in which the parties will bear the costs of the mediation. It can also be important for determining the form of settlement and for the other reasons mentioned at 15.01 above.

15.33 If the mediation does not result in settlement, the parties may ask the mediator if he or she is prepared to provide a written opinion or guidance on the likely outcome of the dispute or a written settlement recommendation (and thus become an evaluative mediator). A separate fee may be payable for this.

15.34 After the mediation, some mediators return the case papers to the parties but others destroy the mediation papers and their notes.

If settlement is reached at the mediation, the settlement agreement may provide that any dispute about implementation of the settlement shall be referred back to the mediator. **15.35**

I Main Variations in the Process

Mediation is a flexible process. The typical stages of the process as described in this chapter can be varied to suit the subject matter of the dispute and the needs of the parties. For example, in family proceedings, it is rare for the mediator to convene separate meetings with the parties to avoid any impression that he or she is not completely neutral. In cases that raise public policy or environmental issues the mediation may take place in public before interested parties rather than in private. If the relationship between the parties has broken down completely the mediation can take place in private closed meetings only. **15.36**

The key variants in the process are outlined below. Reference should also be made to the various mediation schemes described in Chapter 16. **15.37**

Evaluative mediation

The parties may, either in advance of the mediation or during the course of the mediation, ask the mediator to give one or both parties a non-binding neutral evaluation of the likely outcome should the case go to trial or an evaluation of the merits of one or more of the issues in the case or to suggest a reasonable basis for settlement of the dispute.[14] **15.38**

J Med-Arb

This is a hybrid process which provides that if no settlement can be agreed at the mediation, the parties may invite the mediator to act as arbitrator to determine the dispute and make an award that will be binding or non-binding as agreed by the parties. **15.39**

The main advantages of the process are that the parties save time and money because the same neutral acts as both mediator and arbitrator, and they have certainty that the dispute will be resolved by one method or the other. The main criticisms of the process revolve around the fact that the same neutral person is both mediator and arbitrator. He or she will therefore be in possession of confidential information provided by the **15.40**

---

[14] See Chapter 14 at 14.09–14.16.

parties, or the parties will be inhibited in providing confidential information for fear that it could prejudice them in any resulting arbitration. Such a challenge was successfully made on this basis in proceedings to enforce an adjudication award where the adjudicator had previously acted as mediator.[15] This problem can be minimized if the mediator conducts the mediation in joint sessions (a more common occurrence in family mediations).

15.41 If settlement is agreed at the mediation, the parties may appoint the mediator as arbitrator and ask him or her to draw up the settlement agreement as an arbitration consent award, which would then become enforceable at law. Parties wishing to do this should commence the process by an arbitration agreement.

K Arb-Med

15.42 This reverses the process. A simplified form of arbitration takes place first, followed by mediation. The arbitration award is sealed and not revealed to the parties unless they are unable to reach settlement at the mediation that will follow the arbitration. The same neutral person will change role from arbitrator to mediator. The uncertainty generated by the unknown award often forces the parties to reach a settlement at the mediation.

15.43 The main criticism of this process is that if mediation results in settlement, the time and money taken to arbitrate the dispute first will have been wasted.

Telephone mediations

15.44 In some situations, mediation may need to be conducted by telephone rather than in face-to-face meetings. This may happen:

- in the Small Claims Court Mediation Scheme;[16]
- if the parties have been restrained by a court order from meeting each other;
- if the parties live a long geographical distance from one another.

15.45 The stages in the telephone mediation process are as follows:

- the mediator will hold pre-mediation discussions by telephone with the parties;[17]
- the mediation can take place by a telephone conference, with all the parties being telephoned at the same time by the mediator, so that they can hear what is said, and participate, as if they were present at a joint meeting;

---

[15] See *Glencot Development and Design Co Ltd v Ben Barrett & Son (Contractors) Limited*, [2001] BLR 207.

[16] See Chapter 16 at 16.07–16.12.

[17] For the purpose and content of these pre-mediation discussions, see Chapter 14 at 14.47–14.48.

- if separate discussions are needed with the parties (to mimic a separate private meeting), then the telephone conference will be terminated and the mediator will then ring each party on their private telephone line;
- the negotiating phase can take place by the mediator acting as shuttle diplomat in separate telephone conversations with the parties, or by the parties making offers and concessions during a joint telephone conference, or a mixture of the two;
- in any event, the mediator should confirm the agreement reached and ensure each party assents by arranging a final joint telephone conference call;
- the parties will usually record and sign the terms of the draft agreement in writing, using email or fax, before the mediation ends.

There are a number of ADR providers who offer a telephone mediation service. **15.46** Sometimes face-to-face mediations which are adjourned resume in whole or part as telephone mediations.

Mediations conducted online

Mediation can also take place on the internet (also known as e-mediation or online **15.47** mediation). This can be useful if the parties reside in different countries. A number of internet organizations now offer online ADR services. It is likely that this will develop further in the future.

L Mediation Advocacy

The Standing Conference of Mediation Advocates (SCMA) has stated[18] that **15.48** 'Mediation Advocacy is the technique of presenting and arguing a client's position, needs and interests in a non-adversarial way'. To do this effectively, a lawyer needs to be thoroughly well prepared for the mediation.[19] The advocate will usually also deliver the opening statement on behalf of the client at the mediation and also act in the client's best interests in working with the mediator and negotiating with the other parties throughout the process.

There are a number of key differences between mediation and court proceedings, **15.49** which advocates should bear in mind.

- Mediation is an informal, non-adversarial process.
- There is rarely any opportunity for forensic witness handling skills.

---

[18] See <http://www.scmastandards.com>. The SCMA has also published Standards and Competencies in Mediation Advocacy (these can be accessed on the SCMA's website).
[19] See Chapter 14 for the preparation that a lawyer needs to undertake for mediation, including, in particular, the matters described at 14.84–14.90.

- The aim is not to win, but to ensure that an appropriate settlement is reached.
- The emphasis has to be on formulating solutions, and searching for the common ground between the parties.
- Clients should be encouraged and assisted to separate their positions from their interests and needs, and what lies behind individual positions should be explored.
- Problem-solving rather than confrontational negotiation techniques should be used.
- An ability to assist the client to stay engaged with the process is important.
- The client's needs and personal and commercial interests must be prioritized, as well as an ability to formulate offers and respond effectively to offers.
- It is important to identify matters where further information needs to be exchanged and ensure an effective exchange of information between the parties on those matters.
- An ability to negotiate effectively in respect of legal costs is needed.
- The focus is on the parties and not the lawyers. The mediator will speak directly to the parties as well as communicating with them through the lawyers. The lawyer is a valuable part of the team, but not necessarily the leading player in it.
- The mediator will not (usually) be making any determination on the issues of the case, so does not need to be 'won over' or persuaded of the strength of the case in the same way as a judge. Nevertheless, the advocate must ensure that the mediator has a clear appreciation of the merits of the case so that he or she can effectively counter arguments made by the other party during private meetings with them. In the private meetings, the lawyer will work collaboratively with the client and the mediator, to provide information, engage in reality-testing of the client and the other side's position and interests, and generate options for settlement. The advocate will also ensure the mediator respects client confidentiality and accurately conveys information and offers to the other party. The lawyer also needs to have a good understanding of the strategies that can be used to break deadlock and should work with the mediator to formulate proposals that may overcome deadlock.
- Where settlement is reached, the advocate needs to be able to draft a complete, unambiguous, effective, and enforceable agreement and do all that is possible to assist effective implementation of the agreement by keeping open channels of communication between the parties, including dealing with any legal or practical issues that arise after the settlement has been concluded at the mediation (eg, securing a court order if this is required).
- An ability to recognize when it would be in the client's best interests to end the mediation, or when settlement terms cannot result in a final and binding agreement at the mediation, and to give the client appropriate advice in these situations is important.

The lawyer needs to work with the mediator during the closed sessions and embrace **15.50** the skills that the mediator has by virtue of his or her role and expertise to help further the lay client's goals. This may appear counter-intuitive to a lawyer not experienced in mediation.

The advocate will usually need to discuss the strengths (and possible weaknesses) **15.51** of the client's case with the mediator, as well as the strengths and weaknesses in the other side's case. The advocate may provide the mediator with information which can be passed to the other party, and may enlist the assistance of the mediator in obtaining information from the other party.

The lawyer can derive assistance from the mediator when advising a client who has a **15.52** misguided or unreasonably optimistic assessment of their case or position. Both the lawyer and the mediator can work together to help the client come to a more realistic assessment of their position. The lawyer should also appreciate that the mediator may wish to talk directly to the lay client during private meetings and be sensitive to the need not to 'take over' the private meetings.

The International Mediation Institute (IMI) introduced a certification process for **15.53** mediation advocates in 2013, which includes a set of competency criteria for mediation advocates which include both general knowledge and practical skills requirements. The criteria cover a great deal of the matters covered in this handbook. A copy of the IMI's competency criteria for mediation advocacy can be found on the website supporting this book or can be downloaded from the IMI's website.[20]

---

[20] See <https://imimediation.org/mediation-advocacy-criteria>.

16

COURT MEDIATION SCHEMES
AND OTHER SCHEMES

A Introduction

16.01 A number of court and other mediation schemes have developed over recent years. Some of these provide low-cost, time-limited mediations such as the Court of Appeal Mediation Scheme, the Mayor's and City of London County Court Scheme, the Small Claims Court Scheme, and mediation referrals that take place through the Civil Mediation Online Directory which is maintained by the Ministry of Justice. Some courts also operate judicial mediation schemes (the Family Courts, the Technology and Construction Court, and the Employment Tribunal). More recently, following the introduction of mandatory mediation information assessment meetings (MIAMs) in family cases with the implementation of the Family Procedure Rules 2010, a number of pilot schemes have been set up in some county courts and in the Court of Appeal to see if mandatory referral for consideration of mediation has benefits in other areas.

16.02 There are a growing number of specialist mediation schemes such as the INTA scheme and the Intellectual Property Office Mediation Scheme for intellectual property disputes, healthcare sector schemes, tax schemes, and numerous trade association schemes. Other more specialist mediation processes are used in high value, high profile, highly complex claims and multi-party disputes, such as deal mediation, consensus building in cases involving public policy issues, project mediation, and the executive tribunal process.

16.03 Whilst community mediation has been used successfully for some time to resolve community disputes, the concept has recently been extended to achieve restorative justice in some criminal cases.[1] A detailed consideration of sector specific schemes and mediation in family and employment cases is outside the scope of this handbook.

---

[1] See <www.restorativejustice.org.uk>.

B Historic Schemes

A number of mediation pilot schemes took place in the county court that **16.04** paved the way for the creation of the National Mediation Helpline, which was disbanded with effect from 1 October 2011 and replaced with the Civil Mediation Online Directory.[2] These schemes were all the subject of research which did a great deal to influence the development of mediation in the United Kingdom.[3]

C Current Court Mediation Schemes

Some county courts have their own mediation scheme, as does the Court of Appeal. **16.05** Some schemes are linked to external ADR providers who supply the mediators, but some may have a mediator attached to the court.

Mayor's and City of London County Court Mediation Scheme

The Mayor's and City of London County Court Scheme was launched in May **16.06** 2006. It is a fixed-cost, time-limited scheme administered by the City Disputes Panel with the assistance of a number of ADR providers. Mediations take place at the International Dispute Resolution Centre in Fleet Street, London. The cost to each party (at the time of writing) is £275 plus VAT for three-hour mediation for claims up to £15,000 and £425 plus VAT for a four-hour mediation. For claims greater than £50,000 a four-hour mediation will cost £550 plus VAT per party. If the mediation extends beyond the fixed time limit any additional fees must be agreed with the mediation administrator.[4]

---

[2] See 16.14–16.16 below for detail about the Civil Mediation Online Directory.

[3] See (i) Central London County Court pilot scheme, which was reviewed in 1998 by Professor Hazel Genn (see DCA Research Paper 5/98); (ii) the Central London County Court Compulsory Mediation Pilot Scheme. Both schemes were reviewed by Professors Hazel Genn and Paul Fenn and others in the 2007 report 'Twisting Arms: Court Referred and Court Linked Mediation Under Judicial Pressure' (Ministry of Justice Research Series 1/07); and (iii) the National Mediation Helpline (NMH) which provided low-cost, fixed-fee, time-limited mediations for disputes in civil and commercial cases, with the majority of county court mediation referrals taking place through the NMH until it was disbanded.

[4] In February 2012, Professor Simon Roberts carried out a review into the operation of the first five years of the Scheme to 31 May 2011. During that period 106 cases were referred to mediation by the court where both parties agreed (usually this direction was made at the track allocation stage) and the settlement rate achieved over that period was 66 per cent. The report can be viewed at <http://www.citydisputespanel.org>.

The HMCTS Small Claims Mediation Scheme

16.07 The Small Claims Mediation Service was established by Her Majesty's Courts Service (now known as Her Majesty's Courts and Tribunals Service (HMCTS)) in 2007–08 following the success of the in-house small claims mediation pilot in Manchester County Court. It is a free service for defended small claims cases. From 1 April 2013, small claims cases will include personal injury claims where the value of the claim is not more than £10,000 overall and the value of the claim for personal injuries is not more than £1,000; any claim which includes a claim by a tenant of residential premises against a landlord where the tenant is seeking an order requiring the landlord to carry out repairs or other work to the premises where the cost is estimated to be not more than £1,000 and the value of any other claim for damages is not more than £1,000; or any claim for damages with a value of not more than £10,000.[5]

16.08 The small claims mediation service operates in all county court centres, with the mediators in the employ of HMCTS rather than being paid by the parties. It has proved to be highly successful and was used to resolve over 15,000 disputes in the two-year period prior to February 2012.[6]

16.09 The court will refer the parties to the scheme where the conditions in CPR r 26.4A are satisfied. From 1 April 2013, all small claims cases with the exception of road traffic accident, personal injury, or housing disrepair cases, or any claim in which a party does not agree to the referral, will be automatically referred to the Small Claims Mediation Service. There is nothing to stop the parties from agreeing that any case proceeding in the Small Claims Track from requesting mediation in their Directions Questionnaires, and if they do so, the case will be referred to the Mediation Service.[7] This should not be confused with compulsory mediation—it is rather a mandatory requirement to engage with a small claims mediator. The automatic referral for consideration of mediation will involve a court-appointed mediator contacting the parties (probably by telephone in most cases) to give them information about mediation and to attempt to persuade them of the benefits of mediation. This contact is likely to result in these cases actually being mediated under the small claims scheme.

16.10 If the parties agree to mediate their dispute (and as the service is free, there is little reason for them not to do so), then a court mediator (who is not a member of

---

[5] See CPR r 26.6(1)–(3).

[6] Information derived from the Government's Response to the Consultation paper 'Solving Disputes in the County Courts: Creating a Simpler, Quicker and More Proportionate System' published in February 2012 (see <http://www.justice.gov.uk/downloads/consultations/solving-disputes-county-courts.pdf>).

[7] CPR r 26.4A(4).

the judiciary) will contact them, and a mediation will be undertaken usually by telephone. If this is not possible, a meeting can be arranged. The telephone mediations are generally conducted by private discussions with each party rather than in a joint telephone conference call. The mediation, whether conducted by telephone or by a meeting, will typically last about one hour. If the mediation is unsuccessful, then the case will be determined by a district judge. If the court is not notified that a settlement has been agreed, then the claim will be allocated to a track no later than four weeks from the date of the last Directions Questionnaire.[8] If the claim is settled by mediation, then the proceedings will automatically be stayed, with permission to apply for judgment for the unpaid balance of the outstanding sum due under the settlement agreement or for the claim to be restored for hearing of the full amount claimed, unless the parties have agreed that the claim is to be discontinued or dismissed.[9]

Court of Appeal Mediation Scheme

The Court of Appeal Mediation Scheme was first set up on a voluntary basis in 1997, although it had a low take-up and a less than 50 per cent success rate. A revised scheme was launched in 2003. With the exception of family cases, the revised scheme is currently administered by CEDR. In family cases, the Court of Appeal will select the mediator from the Law Society's Family Mediation Panel, the UK College of Mediators, or the Solicitors' Family Law Association.   **16.11**

The key features of the scheme are as follows: **16.12**

- When considering an application for leave to appeal, the court will consider whether the matter is suitable for mediation.
- If a party has selected or the court has recommended that mediation be tried, the Court will pass details of the case to CEDR, who will then contact the parties.
- If all parties agree to mediation, they will be sent the names of three suitable mediators from a Panel which is approved by the Court, and they must select one from this list. The Panel includes mediators from a number of specialist areas, including Commercial, Personal Injury, Shipping, Employment, and Intellectual Property. In the event of disagreement, CEDR will make the selection.
- The parties will usually find and pay for the venue.
- The preparation for the mediation and the mediation meeting will follow the same steps as those described in Chapters 14 and 15, although no witness of fact

---

[8] CPR r 26.5(2A).
[9] CPR r 26.4A(5).

or expert witnesses usually give evidence in appeal mediations, although they can attend and give assistance if required.

- The scheme is entirely voluntary and the parties are free to terminate the mediation at any time and without giving a reason.
- The mediator's role is to facilitate a settlement of the matter.
- The parties can ask the mediator to offer his or her opinion on issues that arise in the case, although the mediator may not be willing to do so.
- As a condition of entering into the scheme, the parties have to agree not to make any claim in relation to the mediation against the mediator, the Court or its officials, or CEDR, the administrators of the scheme.
- All discussions in and documents created for the mediation are confidential and 'without prejudice' although, as an exception to this, the mediator will make a short report to the court setting out the date and outcome of the mediation; but the court will not have power to enquire into the events that took place during the mediation.
- The mediation is usually completed within three months of referral to CEDR, so there is usually no need to stay the appeal.
- If settlement is reached, the agreement would normally be placed on the court record, although the parties can keep the terms of settlement confidential if they wish.
- In non-family cases, the fixed fee for each party at the time of writing was set at £850 plus VAT, although in exceptionally complex cases or high value cases above £1 million, a higher fee may be proposed by CEDR, subject to the approval of the court. The fixed fee covers four hours preparation time by the mediator and a mediation meeting of five hours duration. Any extension of time for the mediation and any additional fees arising in connection with that have to be agreed between the mediator and the parties.
- In family cases, the parties can opt for a fixed fee of £850, or they can agree to pay the mediator an hourly rate of £170 per hour plus VAT, based on the mediator's actual preparation and mediation time; but the total fee will be capped at £850 plus VAT.
- In all cases, parties of limited means who cannot obtain public funding can apply for the fee to be waived.

Court of Appeal mediation pilot scheme

16.13 In March 2012, a new mediation pilot scheme was launched in the Court of Appeal that commenced on 2 April 2012 and ran for one year. It has since been extended and revised and was intended to run until 31 March 2015, although it may be extended further. It applied to all personal injury, clinical negligence, contract claims up to the value of £250,000, inheritance disputes where the value of the estate is £500,000 or less, and boundary disputes. Such cases were automatically recommended for mediation to CEDR unless, exceptionally, a judge directed otherwise. Arrangements were put in place to assist litigants in person who qualify for free help. Under the pilot, LawWorks Mediation provided a pro bono legal adviser to assist the parties in the mediation and if necessary, a pro bono mediation took place if there were two unrepresented parties. If the case fell within the pilot, the parties received a mediation information pack and CEDR Solve or LawWorks Mediation would contact them directly with a view to getting them to agree to mediate. The automatic referral to mediation in these cases meant that the parties were mandated to consider it. The pilot operated on the basis of mandatory consideration of mediation, not mandatory mediation.[10] A refusal to consider mediation was likely to be penalized in costs.[11]

D Civil Mediation Online Directory

This was set up on 1 October 2011 to replace the National Mediation Helpline. This Online Directory, which is maintained by the MOJ, can be used by parties to find an ADR provider organization who operates in their local area who will carry out a time-limited, low-cost, fixed-fee mediation. The parties must explicitly specify that they found the provider using the Directory when they initially contact the provider for the fixed fees to apply. Only ADR provider organizations who are accredited by the CMC under its Provider Accreditation Scheme[12] are eligible to be registered on the Directory (see <www.civilmediation.justice.gov.uk>). **16.14**

The amount of the fixed fee depends on the value of the claim (which is calculated by adding together the sums claimed in the claim and any counterclaim). At the time of writing: **16.15**

- cases with a value of £5,000 or less will cost each party £50 + VAT for a one-hour mediation and £100 + VAT for a two-hour mediation;
- cases between £5,001 and £15,000 cost £300 + VAT per party for a three-hour mediation appointment;
- cases between £15,001 and £50,000 cost £425 + VAT per party for a four-hour mediation.

---

[10] See Chapter 13 at 13.17(iii) for more detail about mandatory mediation information assessment meetings and the distinction that must be drawn between these meetings and mandatory mediation.

[11] See Chapter 11.

[12] See Chapter 13 at 13.45–13.47.

The fee will be individually negotiated between the parties and the selected provider where the case has a value over £50,000.

16.16   It is the parties who will take the initiative in making referrals to the provider of their choice using the Directory. The Online Directory therefore operates differently from the National Mediation Helpline (NMH) because a referral to the NMH could be made by the Court. Unlike the NMH, no systems appear to have been agreed between the MOJ (who operates the Directory) and the providers who are registered on the Directory in relation to response times and the standard procedure that should be applied by providers once a case is referred to them. The experience of users may therefore differ depending on which provider they select. However, the Directory does offer advantages over the NMH in that the parties are able to choose the provider from amongst those registered on the Directory who operate in their local area.

E Judicial Mediation Schemes

16.17   Apart from family cases, which are outside the scope of this handbook, judicial mediation (sometimes referred to as 'in-court mediation') is carried out in two main areas, each of which are considered in turn:

- the Technology and Construction Court (the court settlement process); and
- the Employment Tribunal.

16.18   Despite the existence of the judicial schemes in these courts, there is nothing to prevent the parties using a mediator of their own choice to help them resolve their dispute.

16.19   Mediation carried out by judges is not free from controversy. Some commentators believe that it is not appropriate for judges to assume the role of mediator as their primary function is to determine the rights and obligations of the parties according to the law based on a fair trial and the rules of natural justice. Judges are trained to be evaluative rather than facilitative and this may not necessarily be appropriate in the context of mediation. During mediation, a party will usually have private and confidential discussions with the judge as mediator, and whilst this may sit uncomfortably with the concepts of judicial impartiality and neutrality which are the cornerstones of the judicial system, this is unlikely to give rise to any real problems unless the judge undertaking mediation continues to exercise a judicial role in respect of the case.

16.20   On the other hand, the neutrality, impartiality, clear analytical skills, and familiarity with the underlying law which is relevant to the dispute could also be said to make judges excellent 'reality checkers' so as to facilitate effective negotiations between the parties. Judges are also likely to be highly effective evaluative mediators and any view they express as to the likely outcome of trial is likely to have a strong influence on the parties. There may also be a costs saving to the parties as they do not (usually) have to pay an additional court fee for judicial mediation and the mediation will also usually take place in the court premises.[13]

Court settlement process in the Technology and Construction Court

The court settlement process (CSP) is a form of mediation carried out in the **16.21** Technology and Construction Court (TCC) by the assigned or another TCC judge with the consent of the parties.[14] The process and the procedure will be regulated by the Court Settlement Order which will be made, with appropriate modifications, in the form set out in Appendix G of the Technology and Construction Court Guide.

The main features of the process are as follows: **16.22**

- It is a private and confidential, without prejudice, voluntary, non-binding process.
- The settlement judge (in effect, the mediator) can conduct the CSP in any manner as he or she considers appropriate, taking into account the wishes of the parties and the circumstances of the case and the overriding objective.
- A Preliminary Court Settlement Conference will take place to determine the procedure, the venue, duration, and disclosure to be made by the parties (and provided to the Judge) in advance of the CSP.
- Unless the parties otherwise agree, during the CSP, the settlement judge may communicate with the parties together or separately, including private meetings at which the settlement judge can express views on the dispute. A party can request a private meeting with the settlement judge during the process.
- The settlement judge will not disclose information given to him or her in confidence by one party to the other party or to any other person at any time.
- If the CSP does not lead to settlement, the parties can ask the settlement judge to provide them with a written assessment on some or all of the issues in the dispute, the likely outcome of the case, and what would be an appropriate settlement.
- Nothing said during the CSP prejudices the position of the parties in the litigation or subsequent arbitration or adjudication.
- Each party shall bear their own costs and share equally in the court costs of the CSP, unless otherwise agreed.

---

[13] See Henry Brown and Arthur Marriott, *ADR Principles and Practice* (3rd edn), paras 5.028–5.036.

[14] See the *Technology and Construction Court Guide* (2nd edn, 3rd rev, March 2014).

- The settlement judge will perform no further 'judging' role in the litigation and nor can he or she be called as a witness in any proceedings arising out of or connected with the CSP and also has the same immunity from suit as judges in court proceedings.[15]

Judicial mediation in Employment Tribunals

16.23 The Employment Tribunals Judicial Mediation Scheme operates throughout England and Wales. Suitable cases for judicial mediation are selected by the judge at a case management hearing. A key factor is whether there is an ongoing relationship between the parties, although it is unlikely that equal pay claims would be suitable for this process. If both parties agree, the regional employment judge will decide, bearing in mind the issues in the case and the Tribunal's resources, whether the case should be referred for judicial mediation. The judge will act as mediator and will assist the parties to resolve their dispute but will not make a decision or give an opinion about the merits of the case. The process is private and confidential, and nothing in the mediation can be used in subsequent court proceedings and the judge acting as mediator will have no further involvement with the case. It should be noted that judicial mediation is not an alternative to ACAS conciliation, and it is possible for both processes to take place in relation to the same case.

F Mediation in Specific Cases

Mediation in cases in the Commercial Court

16.24 The Commercial Court will usually make an ADR order, which strongly encourages the parties to attempt to resolve their dispute by ADR (usually mediation). The order usually requires the parties to cooperate with one another by exchanging lists each containing the names of three mediators who are able to conduct a mediation by the date fixed by the court. If the parties cannot agree, the court will usually select a mediator or provide that the mediator should be selected by an ADR organization. If the case does not settle, the parties are required to file a statement explaining what steps were taken to resolve the dispute by mediation, and why those steps failed.[16] A sample ADR order can be found on the Online Resource Centre.

---

[15] See Nicholas Gould, Claire King, and Phillip Britton 'Mediating Construction Disputes: An Evaluation of Existing Practice' (London, Kings College, Centre of Construction Law and Dispute Resolution, 2010) at <http://www.fenwickelliott.com/mediating-construction-disputes-download>.

[16] An evaluation of the Commercial Court's practice of using ADR orders was undertaken by Professor Hazel Genn in 2002 (see DCA Research Paper 'Court-based ADR Initiatives for Non-family Civil Disputes: The Commercial Court and the Court of Appeal').

Complex construction, engineering, and technology disputes

Construction, engineering, and technology disputes are particularly suitable for **16.25** mediation because huge costs and a vast amount of time can be spent litigating these cases. The parties can use the judicial mediation scheme[17] but they may prefer to have control over the selection of the mediator. When the parties choose to mediate outside the court settlement process then the mediation will typically follow the general process explained in Chapters 14 and 15 but with some differences:

- There may be more than one pre-mediation meeting to discuss and agree the procedure for the mediation.
- The mediation meeting may be more formal and may take place over a number of days with the parties having the ability to make revised proposals as each stage takes place.
- The mediation may involve the presentation of detailed expert or factual evidence.
- The mediator will usually be a lawyer, and may also be assisted in the resolution of the dispute by an expert in the relevant field.
- A formal evaluation of the party's case may form part of the mediation.[18]

Family cases

In family cases, the general approach is that the courts should be used as a mat- **16.26** ter of last resort and mediation has been established as an ADR method since the introduction of the Family Law Act 1996. In publicly funded cases, there is a presumption that mediation should usually be tried before litigation. A detailed consideration of family mediation is outside the scope of this Handbook.[19]

Workplace mediation

This is a growing area of business in the mediation field and it concerns conflict **16.27** avoidance and management in the workplace. The aim is to resolve internal complaints and disputes and grievances before they result in the commencement of formal disciplinary or internal complaints investigation procedures and a loss in time and productivity.[20] Mediation is particularly effective because of the need to maintain a continuing working relationship and the fact that the parties can, if

---

[17] See 16.21–16.22 above.
[18] Useful information can be found at <http://www.tecsa.org.uk>.
[19] Useful information about family mediation can be found on the Family Mediation Council's website at <http://www.familymediationcouncil.org.uk>.
[20] The Department for Business Innovation and Skills (BIS) has recently launched a regional mediation pilot scheme for small and medium-sized enterprises (SMEs) in Cambridge and Manchester. Under the pilot (which will run for 12 months), BIS will fund mediation training for employees

necessary, craft a complex negotiated settlement agreement (or memorandum of understanding) which court proceedings could not achieve.

16.28 The 2009 ACAS Statutory Code of Practice on Discipline and Grievance recommends that disciplinary and grievance procedures should be resolved within the workplace if possible, and, if necessary, independent third parties, such as an internal or external mediator, should be used to help resolve the problem. The government also intends to make mediation more accessible and less costly for small businesses and make it an accepted part of dispute resolution.[21] The Civil Mediation Council maintains a register of mediation providers who are accredited to provide workplace mediations.[22]

Mediation in employment disputes

16.29 Conciliation schemes for claims which have been brought or which are intended to be brought in the Employment Tribunal have been offered by ACAS since 1984. From 6 May 2014, in most cases, it has been mandatory for parties to attempt to resolve their dispute using the ACAS Early Conciliation Service before they commence proceedings in the Employment Tribunal. In addition, fees have recently been introduced for issuing proceedings in the Employment Tribunal and a hearing fee is also payable. It is likely that these measures will result in mediation and ADR being used more widely in employment cases. ACAS mediation and conciliation schemes are regulated by statute, unlike most other mediation processes in the UK, which are regulated by the contract made between the parties.[23]

G Mediating Multi-Party Disputes

16.30 Mediation has proved to be effective in multi-party disputes. Such disputes can take two forms:

- those involving large numbers of claimants or defendants; and
- those cases where there are only a limited number of parties to the main dispute, but a large number of parties have been added to the dispute as additional parties. This is commonly the case in construction claims.

---

from a group of 24 SMEs in each pilot area in 2012–13 in order to help to resolve workplace disputes before they reach the Employment Tribunal stage. If the pilots are successful, the government will consider introducing them into other areas of England, Scotland, and Wales.

[21] The government published a Consultation Paper on Resolving Workplace Disputes. The consultation closed on 20 April 2011. The government's response to the Consultation was published on 23 November 2011. Both the Consultation and the Response can be found at <http://www.bis.gov.uk/Consultations/resolving-workplace-disputes>.

[22] See <http://www.civilmediation.org>.

[23] See <http://www.acas.org.uk>.

A team of mediators may need to be appointed to mediate multi-party claims. **16.31** A number of things make them different from mediation of other claims, in particular, the need to:

- effectively manage a large number of parties;
- have efficient systems in place for information management;
- ensure that effective strategies are in place to assist the parties with time management while the mediator is occupied in private meetings with one or more of the other groups or parties.

In group litigation involving a very large number of claimants, it may be necessary **16.32** to divide them into a number of sub-groups, each of whose claims raise issues similar to others in terms of liability or quantum, and then appoint parties to represent the interests of each group. Consideration also needs to be given to the effective management of the large volume of documents that such cases can generate and the use that will be made of those documents in the mediation.

During the mediation, the lawyers and the mediator will have to draw up strategies **16.33** for managing the long periods of delay that will inevitably occur as the mediator sees the parties or representatives of each sub-group in private meetings. It is hard to keep the impetus and energy for settlement going within each of the teams where there are long periods of delay.

Mediating very complex claims involving multiple parties will often give rise to **16.34** issues about the funding of the mediation, and issues of confidentiality, publicity, and about the neutrality of the mediator.

Mediation is a very flexible process, so it can be tailored to meet the needs of a **16.35** multi-party dispute. The mediator will discuss with the lawyers the structure and form of the mediation, together with the order in which the issues will be discussed and the time that the mediation is likely to take. Planning effectively for substantive mediation is key, so a number of preliminary pre-mediation meetings are likely to be needed for this purpose to identify the interest groups, formulate and agree the issues, agree ground rules for the mediation process, determine how and by whom the mediation process should be funded, and resolve issues between different groups such as disclosure and information requests. Such disputes may need to involve a team of mediators. It is also useful to use the organizational and managerial skills that an ADR provider can provide. It is usually time-efficient to deal with as many issues as possible in joint sessions in multi-party disputes, so such mediations tend to have extended joint sessions with much of the exploration phase of the mediation taking place in those sessions. They may also involve post-mediation meetings to divide a global offer between a number of different parties. Mediating multi-party cases can take several months with various mediation meetings taking place during that time.[24]

H Other Mediation Processes

Project mediation

16.36 This is useful for resolving problems that may arise during the currency of long-term contracts, or contracts involving a lengthy chain of parties such as contractors and subcontractors on a large-scale building project. The aim of project mediation is to prevent problems escalating into entrenched disputes that may hinder or delay the project. The project mediator will usually be selected on the basis of his or her experience in the relevant industry. The mediator will be available to the appointing parties during the currency of the project and will have discussions with relevant parties involved in the project in relation to any matters of concern to prevent disputes arising that might impact on the performance of the contract. If need be, the project mediator will also carry out a formal mediation, although the aim of project mediation is to solve problems before that becomes necessary.[25]

Mini-trial or executive tribunal

16.37 This is a form of evaluative mediation. It is particularly useful in corporate disputes. Each party to the dispute will make formal legal submissions to a panel, which is comprised of senior executives from each company and chaired by a neutral adviser. The executives, their lawyers, and the neutral adviser will then adjourn to discuss settlement of the issues in the case. The neutral adviser may act as a mediator to facilitate negotiations. If asked, the neutral adviser may also agree to assume an evaluative role by providing an opinion on the merits of the case and the likely outcome if it went to trial.

16.38 This process is advantageous because:

- it can be arranged relatively speedily;
- it involves key executive officers of both companies at an early stage in the dispute, who have authority to settle the matter;

---

[24] Useful perspectives about mediating multi-party disputes and complex cases can be found in *Mediators on Mediation* (Tottel Publishing, 2005), ch 13 'Mediating Multi-party Disputes' by David Richbell and ch 14 'The Impossible Takes a Little Longer—Mediating Really Complex Cases' by Eileen Carroll and Dr Karl Mackie.

[25] For example, a project mediation model was devised to help the Olympic Delivery Authority to identify and resolve disputes that arose during the construction of the Olympic Park for the London Olympics 2012 by setting up an Independent Dispute Avoidance Panel (IDAP) consisting of ten construction professionals. All parties still had the right to refer any dispute or difference to adjudication or arbitration.

- it enables the parties themselves to have control over the outcome;
- it is cost-effective and will represent a significant saving in the costs of a trial, particularly if it is carried out at an early stage of the litigation process;
- it enables the parties to create a more flexible settlement outcome than that which could be ordered by the court in litigation or arbitration;
- the procedure is flexible and can be created by the parties, in conjunction with the neutral chairperson, to best suit the needs of the parties and the subject matter of the dispute.

However the process itself is more formal and structured than a typical mediation. **16.39** Each side will usually make detailed written submissions, supported with relevant documents. The parties control the information placed before the Tribunal and can also put confidential documents before the Tribunal, although these should be clearly marked as confidential. At the hearing, each party will make formal oral submissions to the Tribunal. The parties may also agree to call evidence from witnesses and experts at the hearing.

The process is useful for resolving disputes of a complex nature. Even if over- **16.40** all settlement is not reached at a mini-trial of this nature, often agreement can be reached on some issues, so narrowing the issues that need to be considered at trial.

The parties can select and appoint the neutral person privately, or they may **16.41** engage the services of an ADR provider to nominate a suitable person. If an ADR provider is used, they will probably also provide the venue and manage the process.

Consensus-building mediation

A variation in the mediation process can take place in cases involving environ- **16.42** mental and other public policy issues that affect a number of different interest groups. A neutral third party will be appointed to identify and consult all of the interest groups and will promote consultation and negotiations between them with the aim of achieving a consensual outcome that satisfies the parties and all of the various interest groups. This approach historically has been more commonly employed in the USA and Australia, but a number of organizations in the UK have developed schemes to mediate disputes in cases involving environmental or public policy issues.[26]

---

[26] See, for example, the Royal Institution of Chartered Surveyors (RICS) Planning and Environmental Mediation Service and the Environmental Council (see <http://www.the-environment-council.org.uk>).

Deal mediation

16.43   Mediation is not always about dispute resolution. Mediators can be used to broker deals between negotiating parties, particularly in relation to complex high-value, multinational contracts in the energy, telecommunications, or intellectual property sectors. Using mediators to broker complex deals can reduce the risk of stalemate in negotiations and can help to create sound long-lasting contractual relations.[27]

I Community Mediation

16.44   There are a large number of community mediation schemes in every area of the UK. They can be used to mediate a wide range of matters, including neighbour disputes, disputes about noise, litter, nuisance claims, parking, harassment, pets, some landlord and tenant disputes, and small debt claims.

16.45   Community mediators currently operate outside the terms of reference of the Civil Mediation Council. There is currently no umbrella group that draws together community mediation services (a company known as Mediation UK did fulfil that role, but it went into liquidation some years ago). It is relatively easy to find a number of community mediation groups local to any particular area by using the internet.[28] Local community mediation services are usually funded by community trusts or the local authority and many have charitable status and are usually run by volunteers, including volunteer mediators.

16.46   The key characteristics of community mediation schemes are as follows:

- they are usually free to the users;
- lawyers seldom are instructed to attend community mediations;
- referral is made by contacting the local service directly;
- an initial meeting (usually face-to-face, but contact may be made by telephone) will be made with the initiating party;
- if the dispute is suitable for mediation, the community service provider will usually contact the other party;
- if all parties agree, a mediation meeting is arranged to try to determine the dispute;

---

[27] See L Michael Hager and Robert Pritchard, 'Deal Mediation: How ADR Techniques Can Help Achieve Durable Agreements in the Global Markets' (1999) *ICSID Foreign Investment Law Journal,* reproduced at <http://www.dundee.ac.uk/cepmlp/journal/html/vol6/vol6-12.html>. The International Mediation Institute has also collated a number of articles and webcasts on deal mediation which can be accessed from its website at <http://imimediation.org/deal-mediation>.

[28] A fairly comprehensive (but by no means exhaustive) online directory of local community mediation providers can be found by searching the online Directory of UK Mediation at <http://www.intermedial.org.uk>.

- the mediators are volunteers, but they will usually have received mediation training, in many cases by attending training courses organized by the local community mediation provider;
- co-mediators are often assigned to a dispute;
- the mediation meeting can last from anything between one and three hours, depending on the type of dispute and the number of parties involved and the practice operated by local organization;
- each party will outline the nature of the dispute for the mediator and what they wish to achieve by the mediation. The parties will rarely provide position statements or a bundle of documents;
- the venue for the mediation will usually be a local community centre, or the offices of the community service provider;
- the dispute is usually resolved in a joint meeting, although separate meetings can take place if this is appropriate, with the mediator 'shuttling' between the two parties;
- if agreement is reached, it can be recorded in writing, or it may remain as a verbal agreement. In either case, it is unlikely to be legally binding on the parties.

The College of Mediators has recently set standards for community mediators. **16.47**

J Pro Bono Mediation and LawWorks

LawWorks is an independent charity that operates throughout England and Wales. **16.48** It has over 150 mediators who are willing to provide mediation services pro bono to those who cannot afford to pay the usual costs associated with mediation. It is free to both parties if one party qualifies. If a party is entitled to a fee remission in respect of the court fees, then they are also eligible for free mediation through LawWorks. In all other cases, LawWorks will assess whether a party qualifies by ascertaining if that party's gross annual income is below a prescribed amount or that person is in receipt of a means-tested benefit.[29]

---

[29] See <http://www.lawworks.org.uk>.

17

EU DIRECTIVE ON MEDIATION
IN CIVIL AND COMMERCIAL CASES

A Introduction

17.01 As mediation becomes more widely used in international disputes, attempts have been made to standardize the process.[1] The European Parliament and Council has also attempted to introduce standardization in EU cases with the EU Directive on Mediation in Civil and Commercial Cases (Directive 2008/52/EC) ('the EU Mediation Directive') and the EU Code of Conduct for Mediators. The text of the EU Directive can be found on the Online Resource Centre for this handbook.

B The EU Mediation Directive

17.02 The EU Mediation Directive was published in the *Official Journal of the European Union* on 24 May 2008 and came into force 20 days after that date.[2] Member states were required to implement the Directive into national law by 21 May 2011.

Objective of the Directive

17.03 The objective of the Directive is to facilitate access to ADR and to promote the amicable settlement of disputes by encouraging the use of mediation and by ensuring a balanced relationship between mediation and judicial proceedings.[3]

17.04 Mediation is comprehensively defined in Article 3. It is clear that it includes mediation initiated or ordered by the court, judicial mediation (except where the judge retains a judicial role in the case), and compulsory mediation.[4] The Directive makes it

---

[1] To this end the United Nations Commission on International Trade Law (UNCITRAL) developed a Model Law on International Commercial Conciliation (although it is called conciliation, the process is, in effect, mediation). See <http://www.uncitral.org>.

[2] See Article 13.

[3] See Article 1.

[4] See Article 5(1) and (2).

clear that court-ordered compulsory mediation (which exists in some member states) is still a voluntary process, despite the fact that parties are ordered to arrange and/or attend mediation, because the parties are not compelled to reach agreement in the process and they can litigate their dispute if mediation does not result in settlement.

Application of the Directive

The provisions of the Directive apply only in cross-border disputes, in civil and commercial matters.[5] However nothing prevents member states from applying any provisions of the Directive to their own internal processes.[6]   **17.05**

The Directive is not intended to apply to: **17.06**

- pre-contractual negotiations;
- processes of an adjudicatory nature such as judicial conciliation schemes, consumer complaint schemes, arbitration, and expert determination, or to processes by which a formal recommendation is issued, whether or not it is to be legally binding as to the resolution of the dispute. It therefore will not apply to early neutral evaluation;
- revenue, customs, or administrative matters or to the liability of the state for acts and omissions in the exercise of state authority.[7]

Implementation of the Directive by the UK

The EU Directive has been implemented in the UK by the Cross-Border Mediation (EU Directive) Regulations 2011[8] ('the Cross-Border Regulations') and the Civil Procedure (Amendment) Rules 2011[9] (which added section III to Part 78 of the CPR). The Cross-Border Regulations can also be found on the Online Resource Centre for this text. These rules only apply to cross-border disputes, where the mediation was commenced on or after 6 April 2011. The mediation starts on the date that the agreement to mediate is entered into by the parties and the mediator.[10]   **17.07**

Main provisions of the EU Directive

The Directive includes provisions directed at ensuring the quality of mediation, setting standards for the training of mediators, ensuring that mediation settlement   **17.08**

---

[5] See Article 2. A cross-border dispute is defined in Article 2(a).
[6] See Recital 8.
[7] See Recital 11 and Article 2.
[8] SI 2011 No 1133.
[9] SI 2011 No 88.
[10] Regulation 4 of the Cross-Border Regulations.

agreements can be easily enforced, upholding the confidentiality of mediation and ensuring that parties using mediation do not find themselves subsequently prevented from litigating their dispute by the operation of a limitation period.

Ensuring the quality of mediation

17.09 Member states are required 'to encourage, by any means which they consider appropriate, the development of, and adherence to, voluntary codes of conduct for mediators and organisations providing mediation services, as well as other effective quality control mechanisms concerning the provision of mediation services'.[11]

17.10 Member states are also required to encourage the initial and further training of mediators in order to ensure that mediation is conducted in an effective, impartial, and competent way.[12]

17.11 The systems in place for the regulation and accreditation of mediators in England and Wales and the work of the Civil Mediation Council (CMC), in particular by the operation of the Provider Registration Scheme[13] probably comply with this obligation, although further work may be needed in respect of individual mediators in private practice who are not members of a registered ADR provider, or ADR providers who are not registered members of the CMC.

Recourse to mediation

17.12 Article 5(1) provides that:

> A court before which an action is brought may, when appropriate and having regard to all the circumstances of the case, invite the parties to use mediation in order to settle the dispute. The court may also invite the parties to attend an information session on the use of mediation if such sessions are held and are easily available.

17.13 It is clear from Article 5(2) that national legislation can make mediation compulsory, whether before or after judicial proceedings have started, or subject to incentives, and that sanctions can be imposed on parties for failing to mediate.

17.14 Chapter 9 describes the various ways in which the courts in England and Wales encourage parties to use ADR processes, including mediation, to resolve their disputes and Chapter 11 sets out the sanctions that can be imposed if a party unreasonably refuses to use ADR. Although the courts of England and Wales have not gone so far as to make the use of mediation compulsory, recent

---

[11] Article 4(1) of the Directive.
[12] Article 4(2) of the Directive.
[13] See Chapter 13 at 13.45–13.47.

developments have required parties to undertake mandatory consideration of mediation.[14]

Enforceability of agreements resulting from mediation

Member states should ensure that the parties are able to request that a written agree- **17.15** ment resulting from a mediation is made enforceable by a court, by a judgment or decision, or other means in accordance with national law, unless the content of the agreement is contrary to national law.[15]

In relation to cross-border disputes where the parties, or one of them with the **17.16** explicit consent of the others, wish to apply for a mediation settlement to be made enforceable, an application can be made either under Part 23 (if proceedings have already been issued) or by using the Part 8 procedure (as modified by CPR r 78.24 and PD 78) for a Mediation Settlement Enforcement Order (MSEO).[16]

Provided the requirements in CPR r 78.24 and PD 78, para 22.1 and 22.2 are **17.17** satisfied, the court will usually make a MSEO without a hearing.[17] In the event of default, the parties can then apply for this order to be enforced in the same way as any other judgment or order of the court.

If the conditions for obtaining a MSEO are not satisfied or the parties choose not **17.18** to make an application for such an order, and they are not otherwise able to record their settlement agreement as a consent order in existing proceedings, the agreement reached in mediation can be enforced by suing for breach of the terms of the settlement agreement, obtaining judgment in that claim, and then enforcing the court order. However, using the procedure set out in CPR r 78.24 will enable the parties to proceed to enforcement by a quicker and more cost-effective route.

Where a person applies to enforce a MSEO which is expressed in a foreign cur- **17.19** rency, the application must contain a certificate of the sterling equivalent of the sum remaining due under the order at the close of business on the day before the application.[18]

Confidentiality

The circumstances in which the confidentiality of mediation can be overridden are **17.20** narrower under the Directive in relation to cross-border disputes than in domestic

---

[14] See Chapter 13 at 13.17(iii).
[15] See Article 6(1) and (2) of the Directive.
[16] See CPR r 78.24 and PD 78, para 22.1 and 22.2 for the procedure for applying for a MSEO.
[17] CPR r 78.24(8).
[18] CPR r 78.25.

cases where confidentiality in mediation can be overridden where the interests of justice require it.[19]

17.21 In cross-border disputes, the general rule is that a mediator or a mediation administrator has the right to withhold mediation evidence in civil and commercial proceedings and in arbitration.[20] Mediation evidence is defined as 'evidence arising out of or in connection with a mediation process'.[21]

17.22 However, the general rule is subject to some exceptions, which provide that a court may order that a mediator or a mediation administrator must give or disclose mediation evidence where:

(a) all the parties to the mediation agree;

(b) the evidence is necessary for overriding considerations of public policy; or

(c) the evidence relates to the mediation settlement, and disclosure is necessary to implement or enforce the mediation settlement agreement.[22]

17.23 Where a person seeks disclosure or inspection of mediation evidence, an application is made by a Part 23 application if proceedings have already been issued or by Part 8 Claim Form if they have not. The mediator must be made a respondent to the Part 23 application or a party to the Part 8 Claim Form.[23] The evidence in support must establish one of the grounds set out in (a), (b), or (c) above. The court has power to require the mediator to disclose or permit inspection of documentary evidence under CPR r 78.26. The court may also order the mediator to give oral evidence by any of the means prescribed by CPR r 78.27.

17.24 The provisions in CPR r 78.27 and 78.26 do not apply to proceedings that have been allocated to the Small Claims Track. If a party wishes to rely on mediation evidence in proceedings that are allocated to the Small Claims Track, that party must inform the court immediately.[24]

17.25 To ensure the privacy and confidentiality of mediation, no document relating to an application for a mediation settlement enforcement order may be inspected by a person who is not a party to the proceedings (under CPR r 5.4C) without the permission of the court.[25]

---

[19] See Chapter 13 at 13.49–13.58.

[20] Regulation 9 of the Cross-Border Regulations.

[21] See Regulation 8 of the Cross-Border Regulations and CPR r 78.23(2).

[22] See Regulation 10 of the Cross-Border Regulations and CPR r 78.26–78.28 which implement Article 7(1) of the Directive.

[23] CPR r 78.26(2).

[24] CPR r 78.28.

[25] See PD 78, para 22.3.

Effect of mediation on limitation and prescription periods

Member states are required to ensure that parties who choose to attempt to settle **17.26** their dispute by mediation are not subsequently prevented from initiating judicial proceedings or referring a dispute to arbitration by the expiry of limitation or prescription periods during the mediation process.[26]

The Cross-Border Regulations added a new provision to the Limitation Act 1980, **17.27** namely s 33A. This provides that where a time limit under the Limitation Act applies, in whole or in part, to a cross-border dispute, and a mediation in relation to the dispute starts before the time limit expires and, if not extended by s 33A, the time limit would expire before the mediation ends or less than eight weeks after it ends, then for the purposes of initiating judicial proceedings or arbitration, the time limit expires instead at the end of eight weeks after the mediation ends. Section 33A(6) and (7) define when a mediation is deemed to start and end.

By the operation of s 33A(4), if a time limit has been extended under s 33A, but a **17.28** second mediation starts before that extended time limit expired, and if not extended by s 33A(2) and (3), the extended period would expire before the second mediation ends or less than eight weeks after it ends, then the time limit will expire instead at the end of eight weeks after the second mediation ends. There are no restrictions on the amount of times the limitation period could be extended by virtue of the operation of s 33A(2), (3), and (4).

Similar amendments are made to the limitation periods set out in the Prescription **17.29** Act 1832, the Equal Pay Act 1970, the Sex Discrimination Act 1975, the Foreign Limitation Periods Act 1984, the Employment Rights Act 1996, the Land Registration Act 2002, and the Equality Act 2002 and also to specified secondary legislation made under some of those Acts.

Publicity

Member states should encourage the provision of information to the general public **17.30** on how to contact mediators and organizations providing mediation services, in particular on the internet (Article 9). They should also encourage legal practitioners to inform their clients of the possibility of mediation (Recital 25).

The government has improved the level of information offered to the public about **17.31** dispute resolution options and in particular mediation.[27]

---

[26] See Article 8.
[27] See <http://www.gov.uk>. The Legal Services Commission has also published a booklet on 'Alternatives to Court' at <http://www.communitylegaladvice.org.uk/media/808/FD/leaflet23e.pdf>.

Application of the EU Directive to domestic mediations

17.32 The EU Directive and CPR Part 78 Section III have no application to domestic mediations, which continue to be governed by the law described in Chapters 13 to 16.[28]

Implementation of the EU Mediation Directive in other Member States

17.33 The EU Directive has now been implemented in almost all of the member states. Some states (eg, Belgium, Greece, and Italy) have implemented a system of compulsory referral to mediation. Some states (eg, Spain), unlike the UK, have extended the scope of the Directive to domestic disputes. Other states (eg, Bulgaria) have provided financial incentives to the parties to use mediation.[29]

C European Code of Conduct for Mediators

17.34 The European Code of Conduct for Mediators has been approved by the Justice Directorate of the Commission. It sets out a number of principles to which individual mediators can voluntarily decide to commit, including competence, independence, and impartiality, the procedure for the mediation, fairness of the process, confidentiality, and the termination of the process. The Code therefore falls short of laying down a uniform set of principles which mediators across member states are obliged to follow. The CMC has endorsed the Code as laying down minimum standards which its members should observe.[30] The text of the Code can be found on the Online Resource Centre for this text.

D Enforceability of International Mediation Settlement Agreements

17.35 If arbitration or litigation proceedings have already been commenced, a mediated settlement reached during the course of those proceedings could be reflected as a

---

[28] The Ministry of Justice has consulted on the need to introduce similar measures for domestic mediations (Consultation Paper CP6/2011, 'Solving Disputes in the County Courts: Creating a Simpler, Quicker and More Proportionate System'). The Civil Mediation Council's response to the consultation, which can be viewed on its website at <http://www.civilmediation.org>, showed that 84.6 per cent of those surveyed agreed that provisions required by the EU Mediation Directive should be similarly provided for domestic cases. However, the government, in its Response to the Consultation, indicated that it intends to review the operation of the provisions implementing the Directive before deciding whether to introduce similar provisions for mediations in domestic disputes.

[29] For an overview of how the Directive has been implemented in other member states see the European Parliament's Resolution of 13 September 2011 on the implementation of the Directive on Mediation in the Member States, its impact on mediation, and its take-up by the courts (2011/2026(INI)).

[30] The Code of Conduct is discussed in more detail in Chapter 13 at 13.29–13.42.

consent order in the litigation or an agreed award in the arbitration proceedings. For cross-border disputes, the parties may also be able to obtain a MSEO. Such orders could then be enforceable in the same way as a court order or arbitral award.[31]

If the consent order or MSEO is made in the courts of an EU state, reciprocal **17.36** enforcement arrangements exist by virtue of the Jurisdiction and Judgments Regulation (Regulation (EC) No 44/2001). Consent orders of a court in an EU state which is a party to the Jurisdiction and Judgments Regulation can be registered for enforcement in the courts of England and Wales pursuant to CPR Part 74.

---

[31] See Chapters 18 and 19 for the options for recording settlement and Chapter 20 for enforcement.

PART 5

RECORDING AND
ENFORCING SETTLEMENT

18

RECORDING SETTLEMENT—
PRIVATE AGREEMENT

A Reaching a Clear Outcome

18.01 When settling a dispute it is important to ensure there is sufficient certainty and clarity over the terms agreed so that there is a legally enforceable compromise contract.[1] It is also desirable that the agreed terms are sufficiently detailed and comprehensive to cover the matters the parties intend to compromise. Once a settlement has been agreed it needs to be recorded.

18.02 The relative informality of some ADR processes compared to litigation can lead to less central issues being overlooked. Particularly where the agreement is essentially oral, as in negotiation or mediation, there may be a tendency to leave some points a little vague to achieve an agreement, or each party may have a slightly

---

[1] *Chitty on Contracts* (32nd edn, Sweet and Maxwell, 2015), paras 2-147 ff. Generally in relation to compromises, see Sir David Foskett, *Law and Practice on Compromise* (8th edn, Sweet and Maxwell, 2015). When dealing with a litigant in person, best practice is set out in *Litigants in Person: Guidelines for Lawyers* (Law Society, CILEX and Bar Council, June 2015), especially at paras 38–40.

different understanding of what has been agreed. Legal representatives need to address rather than ignore such problems as they may lead to a breakdown in the agreement.

Recording a settlement is the final part of the ADR process, and the lawyer has several responsibilities in ensuring that the process is completed properly. They should ensure: **18.03**

- the terms are comprehensive;
- each term is clear and sufficiently detailed;
- the client understands the agreement;
- the client accepts the agreement. Where the agreement is subject to client consent, the lawyer must provide the client with sufficient information and advice to ensure that the client takes an informed decision as to whether to accept the agreement;
- the terms are appropriately recorded. Private agreements are dealt with in this chapter, and court orders in Chapter 19;
- the terms are appropriately enforceable, for which see Chapter 20.

Funding arrangements and reasonable offers

Ultimately, it is the client's decision whether to accept a compromise, and the lawyer's role is to advise the client rather than imposing their own views on the client. Solicitors and barristers[2] are under professional obligations to protect their client's interests when advising on a settlement, without regard to the lawyer's own interests or any consequences for the lawyer. If there is disagreement between the client and their legal representatives over whether compromise terms should be accepted, careful consideration must be given to the lay client's interests. This can be particularly difficult in cases where under the terms of the client's funding arrangements the lawyers are entitled to withdraw from the case if the client will not approve a reasonable settlement. This may be appropriate if, for example, the client had misled the lawyer about the strength of the case. **18.04**

A lawyer acting for a publicly funded client who does not accept an offer of settlement should warn the client that there must be a report to the Legal Aid Agency,[3] which may lead to funding being withdrawn. **18.05**

---

[2] Under the Solicitors Regulation Authority Code of Conduct 2011 and the Bar Standards Board Code of Conduct respectively.
[3] Under the Civil Legal Aid (Procedure) Regulations 2012, SI 2012/3098, r 40(3).

B Forms of Recorded Outcome

18.06   The form used to record the outcome of an ADR process is often governed by the original agreement to enter ADR. For example, arbitration should result in an award, and early neutral evaluation should result in a report from the neutral third party. Successful mediations and negotiations normally result in an oral agreement. It is here that most potential issues arise with regard to ensuring that what is agreed is properly recorded. To avoid uncertainty, it is not uncommon for mediation agreements to include terms that any settlement reached in the mediation will only be binding if made in writing.[4] The same result is achieved by using the phrase 'subject to contract'.[5]

Compromise agreements

18.07   A successful non-adjudicative ADR should result in a contract compromising the dispute. The compromise agreement will take effect and be interpreted in the same way as other contracts.[6]

Full and final settlement

18.08   Where the whole dispute is settled the compromise agreement will normally be stated to be in 'full and final settlement' of the dispute. Care must be taken to ensure this is what the parties intend. It will mean the whole of the old dispute can no longer be litigated, and is replaced by the terms of the compromise. Use of the words makes it difficult to obtain a court order rectifying the agreement.[7] If the words are not used it may not be clear that the dispute has been fully settled, and one of the parties may then start or continue proceedings.

18.09   Care needs to be taken in defining the 'dispute' that has been settled. There have been cases where parties have been held to have settled claims they did not know existed.[8] Whether other related claims between the parties will be barred on the

---

[4] Such a clause was upheld in *Brown v Rice* [2007] EWHC 625 (Ch), and was said to have the same effect as a 'subject to contract' term. It will apply unless the parties have expressly or impliedly agreed to vary or waive it, or if there is an effective estoppel or collateral contract (*Brown v Rice* at [25]).

[5] This is generally taken to mean that no legal consequences flow from the communications, so that a binding compromise will only be reached when the parties make a subsequent written contract (*Avonwick Holdings Ltd v Webinvest Ltd* [2014] EWCA Civ 1436 at [19]; *Chitty on Contracts* (32nd edn, Sweet and Maxwell, 2015), para 2-125).

[6] For the approach to finding the parties' objective contractual intentions, see *Investors Compensation Scheme Ltd v West Bromwich Building Society (No 1)* [1998] 1 WLR 896; *Chartbrook Ltd v Persimmon Homes Ltd* [2009] UKHL 38; and *Rainy Sky SA v Kookmin Bank* [2011] UKSC 50.

[7] *Ondhia v Ondhia* [2011] EWHC 3040 (Ch).

[8] For example, *Brazier v News Group Newspapers Ltd* [2015] EWHC 125 (Ch).

basis they are included in a full and final settlement depends on the proper construction of the compromise agreement.[9] A settlement may even affect related claims by other persons. For example, in *Jameson v Central Electricity Generating Board*[10] a settlement of an asbestosis claim between an employee and his employer was expressed to be in full and final settlement. It was held to bar a subsequent Fatal Accidents Act claim by the employee's widow brought after the employee died. A party who wishes to preserve their right to sue on other causes of action should expressly reserve that right in the compromise agreement.

C Records Made During the ADR Process

It is good practice to keep a clear record of what is being agreed or provisionally agreed during a negotiation or mediation. It is also necessary to check what is agreed—it is all too common for different parties to have a slightly different understanding of what is being agreed. **18.10**

At the end of a mediation or negotiation it is crucial for all the parties to take time to agree a written version of the terms agreed. It is advisable to do this on a laptop or similar device, or at least to write up the terms with as few deletions and amendments as possible. Normally one lawyer will draw up the terms agreed, sometimes in the presence and with the assistance of the other lawyers, and all the parties will then check the document for accuracy. When a final draft is agreed it will be signed by each party and copies are then made. **18.11**

An alternative is for the lawyers for one side to produce a draft in the form agreed, and to send it to the lawyers of the other parties for agreement. There may be an advantage to the side that agrees to do the draft as they will have some control over the written detail, although the side drawing up the document will also bear the costs of doing so unless it has been agreed that the costs be shared. In addition to agreeing who should produce the draft it should be agreed when the draft will be sent to the other parties and who should pay the costs. **18.12**

D Forms for Recording Settlement

Any form of written or oral statement can set out the terms of a settlement. If the dispute is settled by an explanation, a clarification, or an apology then nothing further may be needed. However when a dispute relating to legal rights is settled it will **18.13**

---

[9] *Henley v Bloom* [2010] EWCA Civ 202.
[10] [2000] 1 AC 455.

normally be in the interests of both parties to record the outcome in a form that is legally enforceable. The following options are not mutually exclusive. For example, it may sometimes be appropriate for some of the terms agreed to be put into a formal written contract and others separately recorded, for example in covering or side letters.

Oral contract

18.14 Non-adjudicative ADR processes often lead to oral contracts.[11] Once there is an agreement and the basic requirements of a contract exist (the terms are sufficiently certain; there is some form of consideration, etc) there will be an enforceable contract.[12] Once a contract is made it may be difficult or impossible to vary it or to challenge it in court. If the agreement is conditional, for example on the approval of the client, that condition must be stated at the time, and will need to be fulfilled.

Exchange of letters

18.15 A simple and cost effective way of recording a settlement is for the solicitor for one side to write a letter setting out terms of settlement, with the solicitors for the other side replying to indicate agreement. This is appropriate for a wide range of settlements in non-adjudicative ADR where there is no particular need for any more formal document. It is commonly used where proceedings have not been issued so a court order is not an option. It can also be used after proceedings have been issued if there is no particular need for a court order. A typical exchange of letters settling a dispute can be seen in the Online Resource Centre for this handbook.

18.16 An exchange of letters can form a contract in itself without any face-to-face ADR process where there is an appropriate offer and acceptance. A chain of letters on a single issue does not necessarily amount to a settlement.[13] If there has been a face-to-face process then the letters will evidence the oral agreement that was reached.

Formal written contract

18.17 Non-adjudicative ADR processes commonly lead to a formal written contract, either because the process was wholly or partly conducted in writing, or because the oral agreement is reduced to a written contract. For example, an oral arrangement under which the parties state they will only be bound on signing a written agreement only becomes binding when the contemplated document is signed.[14]

---

[11] Unless there is an effective 'subject to contract' term, see 18.06.
[12] *Chanel v FW Woolworth* [1981] 1 All ER 745.
[13] *Jackson v Tharker* [2007] EWHC 271 (TCC).
[14] *Investec Bank (UK) Ltd v Zulman* [2010] EWCA Civ 675.

Although there is no essential legal difference between a contract formed or evi- **18.18** denced in letters and a contract recorded in a separate document, there are circumstances where it may be preferable to have a separate signed contract. A contract may be appropriate where the terms are complex, or where the outcome is particularly important and the parties want a formal separate legal document for later reference. A contract may be particularly appropriate where there will be an ongoing commercial relationship. Some contracts have to be evidenced or made in writing by law. Examples where writing is required include consumer credit agreements,[15] legal assignments,[16] guarantees,[17] and contracts for the sale or disposition of land.[18]

In a formal written contract it is common to include a preamble setting out that the **18.19** contract is to resolve a dispute, summarizing the matters that were in dispute and are covered by the agreement. This is for clarity on the issues resolved by the settlement, but it is not essential if it is not appropriate for the contract envisaged. This is followed by the agreed terms. An example can be seen in the Online Resource Centre for this handbook.

Other legal documents

The terms of an agreement can be wholly or partly incorporated into some other **18.20** appropriate form, such as a deed or conveyance. A deed may be more appropriate than a contract in relatively limited circumstances where formality is important (eg, as regards rights over land), or where it is not clear that one party is providing consideration, so there might otherwise be doubts over validity.

If there is already a contract between the parties, for example where there is an exist- **18.21** ing commercial relationship, it is necessary to decide whether that contract will be varied or replaced, and to make that clear. If the original contract is being varied, there will be two agreements: the compromise and the variation.

E Drafting Terms of Settlement

Some points will apply to all forms of written settlement document. **18.22**

- The terms must be comprehensive and accurate—once the terms have been reduced to writing and agreed it will be difficult or impossible to argue that any additional oral term is part of the final agreement.

---

[15] Consumer Credit Act 1974, ss 60, 61, and 65.
[16] Law of Property Act 1925, s 136.
[17] Statute of Frauds 1677, s 4.
[18] Law of Property (Miscellaneous Provisions) Act 1989, s 2.

- All practical details should be included such as dates by which actions such as payment should be carried out.
- Court powers to award interest and make orders as to costs only apply to court orders. Both matters should be dealt with specifically in a contract.[19] If there is no mention of costs, each side will have to bear their own.
- Some expressions used in settlements make it difficult to avoid further proceedings, and should be used with care. For example, a term in a settlement agreement that one party would pay 'damages for trespass' to be determined by a chartered surveyor acting as an expert almost inevitably resulted in further court proceedings over what that expression meant, being something not within the professional expertise of a surveyor.[20]
- Some enforcement options can be built in—for example that a payment will carry interest if it is not made on time. Care should be taken to avoid the term amounting to an unforceable penalty clause.[21]
- Agreed terms need to be enforceable. For example, this will be a problem if they seek to affect third party rights, unless the third party agrees to be bound.
- The terms may usefully provide for any relevant foreseeable future events, so that the agreement covers and is not undermined by foreseeable change.

---

[19] *President of India v La Pintada Cia Navegacion* [1984] 2 All ER 773.
[20] *Thorne v Courtier* [2011] EWCA Civ 460.
[21] *Cavendish Square Holding BV v Makdessi* [2015] UKSC 67.

19

RECORDING SETTLEMENT—
COURT PROCEEDINGS

A Settlements in Existing Court Proceedings

Where proceedings have been issued, terms of settlement of a dispute following an **19.01**
ADR process can be wholly or partly incorporated into a court order or judgment.[1]
There are some restrictions in CPR Part 2, over which judges have jurisdiction to
make certain orders, and the judge may not be prepared to make an order in the terms
sought. Settlements restricted to common law relief (money, delivery of goods), the
stay or dismissal of the case, and costs, can be made as consent orders without involving a judge.[2] Where a compromise is incorporated into a court order or judgment the
terms can normally be enforced by returning to court within the existing proceedings
(see Chapter 20).

B Methods of Recording Settlements in Court Proceedings

Where there are existing court proceedings there are several different ways of record- **19.02**
ing a settlement:

- settlement agreement, which may take any of the forms described in Chapter 18;
- judgment for immediate payment of an agreed sum together with costs. Often
  this form is used where a settlement is reached at the door of the court, with the
  judgment being pronounced when the case is called on before the judge;
- judgment for the agreed sum (and costs), subject to a stay of execution pending
  payment by stated instalments, see 19.04. Often the stay is agreed because the
  defendant cannot afford to pay the whole amount immediately;

---

[1] CPR Part 40, and *Blackstone's Civil Practice* Sir Maurice Kay (ed) 2016 (OUP); *Civil Procedure*
Sir Rupert Jackson (ed) 2015 (Sweet and Maxwell). When dealing with a litigant in person, best
practice is set out in *Litigants in Person: Guidelines for Lawyers* (Law Society, CILEX and Bar Council,
June 2015), especially at paras 48–53.
[2] CPR r 40.6.

- informing the court that the case has been settled upon terms endorsed on counsels' briefs, see 19.05;
- informing the court that the case has been settled on terms recorded in a contract. This is appropriate where the terms are detailed, or where signed writing is required. The outcome of the proceedings must still be dealt with;
- entry of a consent order setting out the agreement in the form of undertakings. This is more suitable where the dispute is about non-monetary matters, such as a claim for injunctive relief, or specific performance, whether as final or interim relief, see 19.06;
- consent order staying all further proceedings upon the agreed terms, see 19.07;
- consent order providing for 'no order' save as to costs, but setting out the agreed terms in recitals. This is more appropriate for non-money claims, and brings the proceedings to a conclusion other than quantifying costs;
- recording the agreement in a Tomlin Order, see 19.10 to 19.12. This is particularly useful where the agreed terms go outside the scope of the litigation, and in cases where the parties wish to keep the settlement terms confidential.

19.03 The fact that a settlement is reached after proceedings have been issued does not mean that the terms have to be recorded in a court order. Agreed terms can be recorded in an exchange of letters or a contract or the other methods described in Chapter 18. However once proceedings have been commenced, in addition to dealing with the terms of settlement, it is important to agree how to dispose of the proceedings and the costs of the proceedings. It is not unusual for a dispute to be settled by a written agreement, with a clause in the agreement (say) requiring the parties to consent to a Tomlin Order staying the court proceedings while the terms of the compromise are put into effect, and another clause in the agreement requiring the parties to consent to an order to dismiss the proceedings once the terms have been complied with.[3]

Judgment for immediate payment or by instalments

19.04 Immediate payment means within 14 days,[4] so is not suitable if the judgment debtor needs time to pay. In such cases enforcement may be stayed provided the judgment debtor keeps up to date with agreed instalments. A judgment in either of these forms may not be appropriate if the defendant wants to avoid an adverse judgment for credit-scoring purposes (because it will go onto the register of judgments if it is not adhered to).

---

[3] A compromise agreement in this form was used in *Starlight Shipping Co v Allianz Marine and Aviation Versicherungs AG* [2014] EWCA Civ 1010.

[4] CPR r 40.11.

Endorsement of settlement on backsheets

Barristers who negotiate and reach a relatively simple agreement may write the **19.05**
agreed terms onto their backsheets.[5] The endorsement on the brief or instructions
is evidence of the oral agreement. It would be normal for the lawyer for each party
to sign the other's endorsement signifying agreement. The parties may also sign to
signify their agreement, which is useful if the client has been reluctant to agree. It
is necessary to ensure the same wording is used on both briefs. Although a solicitor
may write a letter to confirm the agreed terms, no additional written record of the
agreement is needed. It should only be used where there is a final agreement, and
not where the terms are still subject to client approval.

Interim consent order

Interim orders can be used to record compromise agreements once proceedings have **19.06**
been issued, and if there has been a pre-commencement application for an interim
order. Where the parties reach agreement on the terms of an interim application,
these may be recorded as undertakings or in a consent order. A court cannot make a
consent order without the valid consent of the parties.[6]

It is not uncommon for negotiations prior to interim applications to result in the **19.07**
settlement of the whole case rather than just the interim application. In this situation, when the application is called on before the judge, an order may be made
staying, adjourning, or dismissing the claim on the basis of the terms agreed by the
parties. The terms may be recorded in the court's order, or as a schedule, or by a
separate agreement such as a contract.

True consent orders and submission to agreed terms

There is a distinction between a consent order based on a real contract and a simple **19.08**
submission to an order.[7] A consent order will be based on a real contract if the essential requirements for a contract are present, such as consideration passing from each
side. A true consent order can only be set aside on grounds which would justify the
setting aside of a contract.[8]

Where a consent order is simply based on one or more of the parties 'not objecting' **19.09**
there is no real contract between the parties.[9] Such an order can be altered or varied

---

[5] *Green v Rozen* [1955] 1 WLR 741.
[6] *Sharland v Sharland* [2015] UKSC 60 at [29].
[7] *Siebe Gorman and Co Ltd v Pneupac Ltd* [1982] 1 WLR 185.
[8] *Roult v North West Strategic Health Authority* [2009] EWCA Civ 444 at [19].
[9] *Siebe Gorman and Co Ltd v Pneupac Ltd* [1982] 1 WLR 185.

by the court in the same circumstances as any other order that is made by the court without the consent of the parties.[10]

Tomlin Order

19.10 The Tomlin Order is a form of consent order, and an example is shown in the Online Resource Centre for this handbook. They were named after Tomlin J.[11] In a Tomlin Order the court orders that further proceedings in the claim be stayed, except for the purpose of carrying out the terms of the compromise, those terms being set out in a schedule to the order. The order will also provide for each party to have liberty to apply to the court if necessary to compel compliance with the scheduled terms. This means that only three things are normally dealt with on the face of the order:

- a stay of the proceedings, except for the purpose of carrying out the terms of the compromise as set out in the schedule;
- each party to have liberty to apply to the court if necessary to compel compliance with the terms;
- the payment and assessment of costs.[12] If the amount of costs has been agreed, this can be included in the schedule.

Advantages and disadvantages of Tomlin Orders

19.11 Tomlin Orders have the following advantages:

- the schedule to the order does not have to be made public, so can include terms which the parties wish to keep confidential;
- the schedule, unlike the order itself, is not limited to those orders that a judge has jurisdiction to make in the case;[13]
- the schedule is better suited to record long or complex terms, as it can be worded in a more flexible way than the order itself.

19.12 A possible drawback of a Tomlin Order is that enforcement powers for the terms of the schedule are more limited than for the court order itself (see Chapter 20). Also, any application to vary the terms of the provisions on the face of the order will be governed by the CPR, which means the court can vary those terms if there has been

---

[10] CPR r 3.1(7) and *Blackstone's Civil Practice* (OUP), paras 42.39–42.42, and in particular where there has been a material change of circumstances, *Edwards v Golding* [2007] EWCA Civ 416.
[11] *Practice Note* [1927] WN 290.
[12] PD 40B para 3.5.
[13] *E F Phillips and Sons Ltd v Clarke* [1970] Ch 322.

a material change of circumstances. The terms in the schedule, however, are contractual, so can only be varied on the same grounds as any other contract, such as fraud, misrepresentation, or undue influence.[14]

Restrictions on consent orders and judgments

Any order or judgment, including those entered by consent, has the following restrictions:

19.13

- The court can only make an order that is within its jurisdiction, such as an order for damages or costs, or a declaration, even if the relevant term has been agreed by the parties.[15]
- The court can only make an order based on the issues, causes of action, and claims for relief pleaded in the statements of case. If this is a problem the parties may ask for permission to amend the statements of case to provide a basis for the order sought.

If the compromise includes matters outside the powers of the court or the issues in the case, the options are to use a Tomlin Order or to record all or some of the terms in a contract.

C Dealing with the Proceedings

The options for the future of the litigation are as follows:

19.14

- *Entry of judgment*: this ends the litigation with a clear winner. This is unlikely to reflect the intentions of the parties to a compromise.
- *Discontinuing the claim*: this ends the claim, but the claimant is required to pay the defendant's costs unless specific provision is made to the contrary.[16] Also, the claimant is not necessarily barred from commencing fresh proceedings.[17]
- *Dismissing the claim*: this ends the proceedings, but implies that the claim should never have been brought.
- *Staying the proceedings*: a stay is normally made for a set period, though it can be indefinite. This means that no further steps can be taken, but does not end the case. It may be appropriate where there is concern there may be problems in implementing the agreement.

---

[14] *Community Care North East v Durham County Council* [2010] EWHC 959 (QB).
[15] *Hinde v Hinde* [1953] 1 All ER 171.
[16] CPR r 38.6.
[17] CPR r 38.7, which says that court permission is required for subsequent proceedings.

D Drafting of Consent Orders

19.15 An example of a consent order can be seen in the Online Resource Centre for this handbook.

- Consent judgments and orders must be expressed as being 'by consent',[18] and must be signed by the legal representatives for each party.
- Care should be taken to ensure that the wording used reflects the parties' intentions, especially where the order is enshrining an existing oral contract.
- The order should state whether the claim is being stayed, discontinued, etc.
- The terms should cover costs.

E Terms as to Costs

19.16 It is very important to include a provision relating to costs in any settlement, whether a court order or a contract. If the case is a complex one, or has gone on for some time, then the costs may be substantial, quite possibly exceeding the claim for damages. In litigation, costs usually follow the event,[19] so that the unsuccessful party is ordered to pay the costs of the successful party. The default position in ADR is that each party will pay their own costs, so if there is no costs provision in the compromise contract or court order then each side will bear its own costs.

19.17 Terms as to costs should comply with the requirements of the CPR in order to ensure they are effective. This typically means the relevant term should provide for payment of costs on either the standard or indemnity basis,[20] to be agreed (ie that the sum payable should be agreed between the parties if at all possible), but, if the parties cannot agree, with the amount of costs to be determined through a detailed assessment by the court.[21] Possible agreements are that:

- each side bears its own costs;
- one side contributes a stated sum towards the costs of the other side;
- one side pays a percentage of the other side's costs, or costs on specific issues, the precise sum to be agreed or subject to detailed assessment;
- one side pays the costs of the other side, the precise sum to be agreed or subject to detailed assessment.

---

[18] CPR r 40.6(7)(b).
[19] CPR r 44.2(2)(a).
[20] CPR r 44.3.
[21] CPR Part 47.

F Administrative Consent Orders

In limited circumstances a consent order can be entered by a purely administrative **19.18** process, and sealed by a court officer without the need for the approval of a judge.[22] This can be done to order the payment of money, the delivery up of goods, the dismissal of all or part of the proceedings, an order to stay on agreed terms, and some other cases. The order should be drawn up and sent to the court together with letters expressing the consent of the parties.[23]

G Informing the Court of Settlement

Once a trial date or trial window has been fixed, there is a duty to inform the court if **19.19** settlement is reached, even if the court is not being asked to make a consent order.[24] The solicitor will normally do this, unless the settlement is reached at the door of the court, in which case the advocate will inform the judge. Any order giving effect to the settlement should be filed with the listing officer.[25] If the court is informed of a settlement at least seven days before the trial, all or part of the hearing fee is refunded.[26]

---

[22] CPR r 40.6.
[23] PD 23A para 10.
[24] PD 39A para 4.1; *Blackstone's Civil Practice* (OUP), para 61.15.
[25] PD 39 para 4.2.
[26] Civil Proceedings Fees Order 2008 SI 2008 No 1053, fee 2.1: there is a 100 per cent refund if more than 28 days' notice is given, 75 per cent if 15–28 days, and 50 per cent if 7–14 days.

20

ENFORCEMENT OF SETTLEMENTS

A Introduction

20.01 Entering into a compromise agreement as a result of negotiation or mediation, or obtaining an award through arbitration or adjudication, produces a solution to the underlying dispute between the parties. In most cases, the fact that the parties have agreed to use an ADR process, and that they will have agreed to the terms of the settlement in a non-adjudicative process, will hopefully mean that the parties will willingly honour the terms of settlement. Unfortunately, there are many cases where there are difficulties with enforcement. Obligations may not be honoured on time, or in the correct form, or at all. In these cases the party with the benefit of the compromise or award will need to consider how to enforce compliance by the other side.

B Methods of Enforcing Compromise Agreements

20.02 The approach taken to enforcement of compromises in large measure depends on the nature of the process used to resolve the original dispute. Essentially:

- in adjudicative procedures such as arbitration the tribunal will make an award. Enforcement will often be through registering the award with the courts of the state where enforcement is to take place, and then enforcing the award as a civil judgment (see 25.24 and 25.25);
- an exception is construction industry adjudications (Chapter 25), where the decision is not itself registrable. Instead it may be enforced through bringing court proceedings and entering judgment;
- in most non-adjudicative procedures, if the parties have resolved their dispute, they will have entered into a contract of compromise. Enforcement is through suing on that contract;
- alternatively in a non-adjudicative procedure the parties may agree to record all or part of the compromise agreement in a court judgment or order, and then enforce that judgment or order;

- settlements in ACAS-administered employment conciliations are enforceable in the county court as if they were county court orders;[1]
- failure to comply with binding decisions in expert determinations and other ADR processes is enforced by suing on the contract where it was agreed the determination would be binding.

C Discharge of Original Obligation by Compromise

In each of the situations set out in the previous paragraph it will be seen that enforcement is of the compromise, decision, or award, rather than the original dispute. In other words, settling a claim results in an accord and satisfaction,[2] or having it arbitrated results in the original cause of action being merged in the award. In fact, as a result it is no longer open to either party to sue on the original cause of action, and their rights and obligations are now defined by the compromise or award. **20.03**

There are three apparent exceptions to this rule, namely where:

- there is an express term reviving old obligations in the event of non-performance;[3]
- the compromise is based on performance of the agreed terms.[4] In such a case the party who has agreed to perform on the compromise agreement remains liable on the old cause of action until performance is completed;
- the compromise is ineffective, for example where an apparent compromise agreement does not comply with the requirements for the formation of a valid contract.[5]

D Enforcement of Compromise Contracts

Effect of endorsements on briefs

Where an agreement endorsed on counsels' briefs relates to an interim matter, it may be possible to go back to court if there is a change of circumstances. Where the agreement is a settlement of the dispute, enforcement is by bringing new proceedings for breach of the compromise agreement.[6] **20.04**

---

[1] Employment Tribunals Act 1996, s 19A(3); CPR r 70.5 and PD 70 paras 4.1–4.4.
[2] *Jameson v Central Electricity Generating Board* [1998] QB 323.
[3] *Smith v Shirley and Bayliss* (1875) 32 LT 234.
[4] *British Russian Gazette and Trade Outlook Ltd v Associated Newspapers Ltd* [1933] 2 KB 616.
[5] *Chitty on Contracts* (32nd edn, Sweet and Maxwell, 2015), chs 2–5.
[6] *Green v Rozen* [1955] 1 WLR 741.

Enforcement by civil proceedings

20.05 Where a compromise relates to the whole dispute, because the old cause of action is replaced by the compromise agreement, enforcement is by suing on the compromise contract. If a party fails to comply with the agreed terms, in most cases there will be an obvious breach of the compromise contract. In most cases there will be no defence, and it would be expected that entering judgment should be a matter of either:

- entering judgment in default[7] if the defendant does not respond to the particulars of claim within 14 days of the deemed date of service; or
- applying for summary judgment[8] if there is a response, on the basis that the defendant has no real prospect of defending the claim.

20.06 Once judgment has been entered, the claimant can use the normal court enforcement processes. These include execution against goods, warrants of delivery and of possession, charging orders, third-party debt orders, attachment of earnings orders, and receivership orders.[9]

Bankruptcy and winding-up

20.07 Insolvency is often an alternative to enforcement by proceedings in the civil courts. Breach of a compromise agreement may well be evidence that the other party is unable to pay its debts as they fall due (or any of the other grounds set out in the Insolvency Act 1986), which may make use of bankruptcy[10] or winding-up[11] procedures attractive. Bankruptcy is used in the case of individuals, and winding-up for companies and partnerships. They are not inexpensive alternatives to litigation, and operate as relief on behalf of all the creditors of the individual or company rather than specifically for the person bringing the proceedings. These insolvency procedures are swift, and can be very effective in obtaining payment from a reluctant payer. However, if the individual is made bankrupt or the company is wound up, the petitioning creditor is extremely unlikely to receive more than a small percentage of the amount owed.

---

[7] CPR Part 12.
[8] CPR r 24.2.
[9] *Blackstone's Civil Practice* (OUP), ch 79.
[10] *Blackstone's Civil Practice* (OUP), ch 83.
[11] *Blackstone's Civil Practice* (OUP), ch 82.

E Challenging Compromise Contracts

There are limited grounds for challenging the terms of a settlement: **20.08**

- A settlement can only be set aside in limited circumstances, for example if it was obtained by fraud or misrepresentation,[12] mutual mistake, unilateral mistake encouraged by the other side,[13] mutual mistake of law,[14] or for economic duress or undue influence.[15] It is unlikely that it can be argued that the agreement should be rectified[16] if it was drawn up by lawyers.
- It is not normally possible to appeal against a consent order, or to apply to court to vary its terms.[17]
- The court may decline to enforce a compromise if there is an equitable reason for not doing so, or if it can be argued that the terms of compromise have been frustrated.[18]
- One side may not be bound by the terms of a settlement if they can argue that the other side has repudiated it.[19]
- A court may refuse to enforce a consent order for someone who is not abiding by its terms.[20]

F Enforcement of Court Orders

Table 20.1 sets out, for each type of court order that might be used for recording a **20.09** settlement agreement, whether enforcement is either a one-stage or two-stage process, and the nature of the procedure to be followed.

---

[12] *Dietz v Lennig* [1969] 1 AC 170. There is a distinction between cases of fraud, where there is a right to rescind, and cases of negligent or innocent misrepresentation, where the court has the power to award damages in lieu of rescission (*Sharland v Sharland* [2015] UKSC 60 at [31], which concerned family law consent orders). Setting aside on these grounds is not straightforward, see *Hayward v Zurich Co plc* [2015] EWCA Civ 327.

[13] *Huddersfield Banking Co Ltd v Henry Lister & Son Ltd* (1895) 2 Ch 273. Establishing a mistake where a settlement is reached with the benefit of legal advice is difficult, see *Garnham v Millar* [2014] EWCA Civ 1168.

[14] *Brennan v Bolt Burden (a firm)* [2003] EWHC 2493 (QB).

[15] *D & C Builders v Rees* [1966] 2 QB 107.

[16] *Chitty on Contracts* (32nd edn, Sweet and Maxwell, 2015), paras 3-057 ff.

[17] *Peacock v Peacock* [1991] Fam Law 139.

[18] *Chitty on Contracts* (32nd edn, Sweet and Maxwell, 2015), ch 23.

[19] *Chitty on Contracts* (32nd edn, Sweet and Maxwell, 2015), ch 24.

[20] *Thwaite v Thwaite* [1981] FLR 280.

Table 20.1 Enforcement of the different types of court order recording settlements

Type of order	Enforcement procedure
Judgment entered for immediate payment of the sum agreed together with costs.	Enforcement proceedings (by execution against goods, charging order, etc) can be taken 14 days after judgment.
Judgment entered for the agreed sum (and costs), subject to a stay of execution pending payment by stated instalments.	If the instalments fall into arrears, the stay will be lifted, and the judgment creditor can then bring enforcement proceedings.
Consent order setting out the agreement in the form of undertakings.	If any of the terms are not complied with, enforcement may be possible immediately or on application to the court depending on the nature of the term in question.
Tomlin Order	• Substantive terms in a Tomlin Order take effect and are enforceable as they stand without the need for any further court order. • In the event of the scheduled terms being breached, enforcement is a two-stage process. First, the claim must be restored under the 'liberty to apply' clause, and an order obtained to compel compliance with the term breached. A failure to comply with that order may be a contempt of court.
Consent order staying all further proceedings upon agreed terms.	The courts are very unwilling to remove the stay imposed by this type of order, so enforcement can usually be effected only by bringing fresh proceedings for breach of the compromise contract.
Consent order providing for 'no order' save as to costs, but setting out the agreed terms in recitals.	Recitals in such a consent order may be enforced without the need to bring a fresh claim.[21]

---

[21] *Atkinson v Castan* (1991) *Times*, 17 April.

PART 6

OTHER ALTERNATIVE DISPUTE RESOLUTION OPTIONS AND THE INTERNATIONAL PERSPECTIVE

21

ONLINE ADR AND ODR

A Overview

The use of information and communication technology (ICT) in relation to all forms **21.01** of dispute resolution has developed substantially over the last decade, and further significant development is proposed. In saving time and money in resolving disputes, ICT has much to offer, especially in dealing proportionately with lower value cases. The use of the RTA PI Claims Portal to manage and potentially settle low-value road traffic accident personal injury claims proved successful and was extended. Computer-based ADR systems are widely used in relation to small-scale commercial transactions, in particular e-commerce, and this has been extended across the European Union, see 21.21–21.22. It has been proposed that online dispute resolution (ODR) be developed for potential use in all civil claims up to a value of £25,000, see 21.15–21.16.

While litigation and ADR have traditionally been seen as paper-based processes, **21.02** with face-to-face meetings, it is increasingly important to distinguish what really needs hard copy and physical presence from what can be managed electronically and using processes such as video-conferencing. Several factors are driving the use of online options for dispute resolution:

- A dispute can be resolved quickly because of the flexibility offered by online interfaces.
- A dispute can be resolved cost-effectively where conventional processes can be reduced and streamlined through online management of electronic documents.
- Online resolution may be useful where face-to-face meetings are unnecessary, or may be expensive, difficult, or inappropriate.
- Software can provide sophisticated analysis of figures and risks. Algorithms can assist with calculations and assessing offers, and provide objectivity.
- The provision of information online can speed up fact collection and analysis, with human intervention built in at appropriate points.

21.03 There are some potential problems in the use of online ADR:

- An online interface or shared drive, while subject to the same rules of confidentiality and privacy as any other ADR process, may give rise to privacy issues.
- Where an online service is used to settle a dispute, there may be procedural or jurisdictional issues as to how and where a settlement might be enforced, especially where a process is not clearly subject to a particular legal jurisdiction.

21.04 The use of software has focused primarily on facilitating existing ADR processes. However software is increasingly being used to develop new dispute resolution options, most commonly referred to as online dispute resolution (ODR), see 21.11–21.14. The importance of increased use of ADR in litigation and dispute resolution was emphasized in the Jackson Review of Costs.[1]

B The Use of Portals for Claim Management and Settlement

21.05 Online portals have been developed in England and Wales to deal with the early stages of certain types of civil claim. For road traffic accidents occurring after 30 April 2010, resulting personal injury claims are initiated through an online process for filing and managing documents.[2] The process is designed to facilitate settlement

---

[1] 'Review of Civil Litigation Costs: Final Report' Chapter 22 and Recommendations 22 and 23. Thirteenth Implementation Lecture 'Reforming the Civil Justice System—the Role of IT' at <http://www.judiciary.gov.uk/publications-and-reports/review-of-civil-litigation-costs/lectures>.

[2] Pre-action Protocol for Low Value Personal Injury Claims in Road Traffic Accidents and <http://www.claimsportal.org.uk/>.

through online exchanges where liability is accepted, and lawyers are remunerated through fixed fees. From 31 July 2013 the use of the portal was extended to cover claims with a value up to £25,000. A further portal to deal with Employers' Liability and Public Liability Claims was added on the same date.[3]

Although there are problems with claims that cannot easily be managed through the standardized system, and with avoiding fraudulent claims, the system essentially works well in providing a standard approach and supporting settlement in an area where costs could easily become disproportionate. **21.06**

C The Use of Online Resources to Support ADR Processes

While face-to-face meetings may be important for negotiation or mediation, many ADR processes are to a significant extent paper-based. The use of ICT can substantially facilitate processes through communication by email, and exchange and storage of documents and information electronically, sometimes using a shared site. The websites of many ADR providers are a very valuable resource providing pro formas,[4] and a number provide online options for initiating or managing ADR processes. Sample mediation or arbitration agreements can often be wholly or partly completed and submitted online. Online facilities may include exchanging evidence and opening statements, and sometimes exchanging drafts of a settlement. There are potential issues in relation to the enforceability of an online mediation clause,[5] or pre-dispute arbitration clauses.[6] **21.07**

It is quite possible for most ADR processes to be carried out entirely online. This is most likely to be appropriate where a dispute is based on documents, and/or can be captured with relative ease in written statements. Online ADR is less likely to be appropriate where there are a number of disputes of fact. Some ADR providers offer an online service for example to deal with financial issues on divorce where an impersonal computer screen may help to diffuse emotions that might arise in face-to-face meetings. **21.08**

A mediation may be conducted wholly or partly online using the services of various providers. A telephone or conference call mediation may be supported by **21.09**

---

[3] Pre-action Protocol for Low Value Personal Injury (Employers' Liability and Public Liability) Claims.
[4] For example <http://www.cedr.co.uk>.
[5] *Rosaalba Alassini v Telecom Italia SpA* (C-317/08).
[6] *Mostaza Ciaro v Centro Movil* (C-168/05); *Asturcom Telecomunicaciones SL v Christina Rodriguez Nogueira* (C-40/08); *Allen Wilson v Buckingham* [2005] EWHC 1165 (TCC).

documents exchanged electronically.[7] There may also be virtual meetings via web-cam conferencing facilities, including Skype.[8]

21.10 An arbitration may be carried out wholly or partly online, so long as this is what the parties agree in the arbitration agreement. A number of arbitration providers offer a paper only service where an award is made on the basis of written submissions and evidence only, and this is often done using electronic exchange of documents.[9] As noted in 21.19, UNCITRAL is involved in the use of online arbitration and their website is a useful source of information.

D The Development of ODR Options

21.11 It is quite possible for software to carry out all or part of an ADR process without the need for human intervention. Information can be captured online, for example through drop-down menus for cause of concern and remedy sought, and can then be processed using appropriate algorithms to propose solutions. More intricate software is starting to create distinct forms of ADR in which the whole process is automated, using innovative techniques and advanced technologies. Such options are commonly referred to as online dispute resolution (ODR), but alternatives such as internet dispute resolution (iDR) or electronic ADR (eADR) are also used.

21.12 Software for 'automated negotiation' has been primarily developed and used in the United States, particularly in relation to settling insurance claims. Programs for 'blind bidding' or 'double blind bidding' can assist in deciding on a figure for damages after liability is agreed. Essentially the parties agree parameters for how a final outcome may be reached, then each party makes a settlement offer in secret, and the software calculates whether the offers meet the agreed parameters. It can also carry out any further agreed computation to produce a possible settlement figure. If the offers do not meet the parameters, each party can make a further secret bid and the software will again see if they meet the parameters. As settlement offers are hidden, if the figures do not meet the agreed parameters the parties will simply know that their figures are too far apart for settlement, without knowing any detail of what figures the other side provided.

---

[7] For example <http://www.lawworks.org.uk>.

[8] For example the Mediation Room (<http://www.themediationroom.com>), Cybersettle (<http://www.cybersettle.com>), the Online Ombudsman Office (<https://www.ombudsman-services.org/>), Online mediators (<http://onlinemediators.com/>), and Online dispute resolution (<http://www.mediate.com/odr/>).

[9] For example <http://www.net-arb.com>, <http://www.onlinearbitration.net>, and <http://www.oanlive.com>.

Software for 'visual blind bidding' may be used where there are more issues and par- **21.13**
ties. If the parties agree to this, each provides a defined optimistic outcome for each
issue. The software makes all of these optimistic outcomes visible, as they define the
highest and lowest possible outcome. The software then generates a range of outcomes that all fall within the range of these outcomes. A party may also contribute
options that fall within the outcomes, but it will not be clear from the screen which
options are machine or party generated. The parties may agree on one of the possible
outcomes generated, or each may choose a different option from those generated, in
which case the software will use an algorithm to combine those options. A sophisticated algorithm can take into account matters such as which party moves into a
potential settlement zone quickest. Such software is potentially attractive as only a
best case outcome has to be revealed.[10]

Software may provide or support mediation through 'automated mediation' which **21.14**
mimics some functions a mediator might perform. Online mediation services
linked to sites such as eBay and PayPal have assisted in resolving many disputes
between sellers and buyers.[11] The process gathers information through web-based
forms and automatic email generation, then guides the parties to a constructive dialogue through reply options, limited free text boxes, and set deadlines. If the dispute
is not resolved, the parties are given the option of the services of a live mediator for
a low fee. The type of system has been successful in resolving millions of disputes
across many countries in several languages, with high success rates.

The Civil Justice Council's Online Dispute Resolution Advisory Group published a **21.15**
report on Online Dispute Resolution for Low Value Civil Claims in February 2015,
recommending the establishment of a new internet-based court service known as
HM Online Court to assist in resolving civil disputes of a value less than £25,000.[12]
The proposed court would have three tiers:

- The first tier would provide online evaluation to assist a user in categorizing a
  potential claim and understanding options.
- The second tier would provide facilitation, where papers and statements
  could be reviewed to support negotiation or mediation, with some automated
  negotiation tools.
- The third tier would provide online decisions, with judges working online to decide
  suitable cases on the basis of online submissions and telephone conferencing.

---

[10] See for example <http://www.cybersettle.com>.
[11] See <http://www.modria.com>.
[12] <www.judiciary.gov.uk/online-dispute-resolution/odr-report-february-2015/> (see the site for
supporting papers and videos).

21.16 The model is intended to provide a new approach to providing flexible and cost effective access to justice rather than simply supporting existing court services electronically. It is envisaged this approach would improve access to justice and save costs, following models already in place in countries such as Canada, Holland, and Germany. The paper and accompanying website provide interesting examples and background information. It was recommended that there be piloting with a view to launch in 2017, though this time line may be ambitious. The Civil Courts Structure Review being carried out by Lord Justice Briggs is considering the creation of an Online Court for civil claims that would include dispute resolution options.

E International Developments

21.17 Online ADR may be particularly attractive for resolving a dispute where the parties are in different jurisdictions, especially in relation to low-value claims. Fully agreed national and international standards are still being developed. As ADR processes are based in contract law, matters such as validity and enforcement are decided by where the contract was made and what law governs the contract, and in an online process these matters may not be straightforward. It is important to clarify any issues with an ADR provider. However trans-jurisdictional ODR processes are emerging which do not follow conventional models and the situation may be more complex.

21.18 In non-adjudicative ADR enforcement may rarely be an issue because the parties agree to the outcome, or an international seller or service provider has a reputation to protect, but if a party settles for tactical reasons knowing that enforcement may be difficult, problems can arise. As regards adjudicative ADR, there may be a challenge if a party does not like the award made. While provision for the international enforcement of arbitration awards has been in place for many years, the position as regards other forms of adjudicative ADR and ODR is still evolving.

Principles for international ADR and ODR

21.19 A body that has played a major role in the development of ODR is the United Nations Commission on International Trade Law (UNCITRAL), a body which has also been particularly concerned with the development of arbitration. For more than a decade UNCITRAL has been developing draft procedural rules for the use of ODR to be followed by guidelines for minimum requirements for services, legal principles, and enforcement and it provides a wide range of relevant documents, reports, and links to a range of national and international schemes and resources.[13] UNCITRAL has also set up a Working Group on Online Dispute Resolution.[14]

A further body of importance for international online ADR is the National Center **21.20** for Technology and Dispute Resolution. It has a website which provides access to a wide variety of information and resources relating to the international development and use of online ADR.[15]

European Union regulation

The European Union is developing a common approach to dealing with disputes **21.21** relating to goods and services purchased online to support the development of a common commercial market. The E-Commerce Directive was adopted in 2000, setting up a framework for electronic commerce.[16] On 29 November 2011 the European Commission published a Communication on Alternative Dispute Resolution for consumer disputes in the Single Market. This was followed in 2013 by a Directive intended to ensure all consumers within the EU have access to ADR options meeting set quality principles,[17] and a Regulation setting up a trans-European ODR platform linking consumers and traders with ADR-providing entities.[18] The British Government consulted on these proposals.[19]

The Regulation and Directive have been implemented. The new regulations apply **21.22** to all businesses in the UK selling goods, services, or digital content to consumers (except for health professionals, public sector providers, and contracts for the sale of land/tenancy agreements). Thus lawyers are covered by the new provisions. In summary, the main developments are:[20]

- There are new statutory obligations for businesses to provide information to consumers regarding the availability of certified ADR schemes.[21] Since 1 October 2015 a business that uses an ADR provider must provide information on their

---

[13] See <http://www.uncitral.org/uncitral/publications/online_resources_ODR.html>.
[14] See <http://www.uncitral.org/uncitral/commission/working_groups/3Online_Dispute_Resolution. html>.
[15] See <http://www.odr.info>, <http://www.odrexchange.com>.
[16] EU Directive 2000/31/EC.
[17] Directive 2013/11/EU, see <http://eur-lex.europa.eu/LexUriServ/LexUriServ.do?uri=OJ:L:20 13:165:0063:0079:EN:PDF>.
[18] See Regulation (EU) No 524/2013, <http://eur-lex.europa.eu/LexUriServ/LexUriServ.do?uri= OJ:L:2013:165:0001:0012:EN:PDF>.
[19] <www.bis.gov.uk/consultations>.
[20] Alternative Dispute Resolution for Consumer Disputes (Competent Authorities and Information) Regulations 2015 (SI 2015/542), Alternative Dispute Resolution for Consumer Dispute (Amendment) Regulations 2015 (SI 2015/1392).
[21] A list of certified ADR providers can be found at <http://www.tradingstandards.uk/ADRbodies>.

website and in their contractual terms. If a dispute is unresolved, all businesses must provide information about an appropriate certified ADR provider and whether the business is prepared to use ADR. From 9 January 2016 all businesses that sell goods or services online must provide on their website a link to the new ODR platform (see below).

- The Trading Standards Institute has been appointed as the competent authority within the UK to monitor ADR providers in non-regulated sectors. Areas such as financial services already have provision in place.
- An eight-week extension to the six-year limitation period may apply in cases covered by the Directive where ADR is ongoing at the end of the period, and the Limitation Act 1980 has been amended to this effect from 9 July 2015.[22]
- A new EU-wide residual ADR scheme is being created to fill current gaps in ADR provision. Since 9 January 2016 a new cross-EU online dispute resolution (ODR) platform has allowed parties throughout the EU to initiate ADR in relation to consumer complaints relating to online transactions. This platform is free to use, interactive, and multi-lingual.[23]

---

[22] Limitation Act 1980 s 33B.
[23] <http://ec.europa.eu/odr>.

22

EARLY NEUTRAL EVALUATION

A Introduction

Early neutral evaluation (ENE) is a non-binding assessment and evaluation of the **22.01** facts, evidence and/or the legal merits of one or more of the issues in the case or of the case as a whole. It is usually undertaken on behalf of the parties jointly, although in some cases it can be undertaken at the request of one party only in relation to their own case. The parties will usually appoint a neutral third party to evaluate the facts, evidence, and law in relation to the issue or case and provide an opinion on the merits.

ENE differs from mediation in that mediation is essentially a *facilitative* process. **22.02** ENE is an *advisory* and *evaluative* process. However, there is a close similarity between ENE and evaluative mediation. In this book, the term ENE is used when a neutral third party is asked to evaluate a dispute, without themselves becoming involved in any way in the negotiations between the parties. It is this disengagement from the negotiation process that distinguishes ENE from evaluative mediation.

ENE can take place within the court system, in which case the evaluation is usually **22.03** carried out by a judge. ENE can also take place outside the litigation process, but parallel with it, and even before litigation has been commenced at all.

Like mediation, it is a private and confidential process, and the evaluator must be **22.04** impartial. If the evaluator is appointed using an ADR provider, he or she will operate under a code of conduct that may be the same or similar to the code of conduct that governs the conduct of mediators.

B At what Stage should ENE be Employed?

ENE is usually employed in the early stages of a dispute (hence its name), but in fact **22.05** it could be utilized at any stage. Neutral evaluation employed at the early stages of a case can assist settlement by mediation, and can be carried out before or even during the mediation, and before or at any time during the process of litigation. ENE can also be used to settle disputes that arise during an assessment of costs after the main proceedings have been included, and the Costs Alternative Dispute Resolution Service (CADR) offers ENE, or a non-binding paper assessment of costs.[1]

C When should ENE be Used?

22.06   The rationale for ENE is that an unbiased evaluation of one or more issues in the case and/or the likely outcome by a neutral party, such as a judge or expert, will help the parties subsequently to settle the dispute by negotiation or even mediation. It can be particularly useful where one or more of the parties has taken an unrealistic and entrenched view of one or more of the issues, or the case as a whole, and would benefit from an assessment of the particular issue or the case by an independent person. It is particularly useful if the issues depend more on analysing or applying law, technical or specialist processes, or evidence to a given set of facts, rather than opposing factual evidence.

22.07   The process can be useful in that it enables each party to appreciate the strengths and weaknesses of the case and this in turn can encourage and lead to settlement, even if the parties do not agree to settle on the basis of the evaluation.

D Choice of Evaluator

22.08   The choice of evaluator will depend on the issues presented by the case. It may be that the case raises issues of a specialist or technical nature which would benefit from an evaluation by an expert.

22.09   The parties may privately appoint the neutral evaluator. Alternatively they may enlist the assistance of an ADR provider[2] to help them select and appoint a suitable person. Several ADR providers operate ENE schemes for the evaluation of particular types of cases, in particular, personal injury.

E Procedure

22.10   The manner in which the evaluation is conducted will be primarily decided by the evaluator, although the evaluator will usually fix the procedure after

---

[1] See <www.costs-adr.com>.
[2] See the Online Resource Centre for a selection of ADR providers.

consultation with the parties. The process is flexible, and the parties can tailor it to meet the needs of their case. The parties can control the amount and form of the information that is placed before the evaluator, and they can identify the issues of fact or issues of law or both that they want the evaluator to evaluate. The evaluator will usually be instructed by both parties (although, as stated above, it is possible for one party only to seek an evaluation of some or all of the issues in their case). Where the evaluator is instructed by both parties, they will both agree the terms on which he or she is instructed and the ambit of the instructions. The parties can also agree that the evaluator should carry out his or her own investigations independently of the parties, and make a recommendation based on those investigations. Once appointed, the evaluator may wish to hold a preliminary meeting with the parties to agree the ground rules, the documentation to be provided, whether a hearing is required, and to set time limits for each stage of the process.

22.11 The procedure usually provides for each instructing party to make written submissions to the evaluator, together with such evidence and supporting documents as they see fit. It is also possible to agree that each party should present some or all of their case at an oral hearing. The evaluator may also wish to hold a meeting with the parties (instead of or in addition to a formal hearing) to obtain further information about the issues in dispute.

22.12 The evaluator will evaluate the evidence (oral and/or written) and the law bearing in mind the submissions of each party and produce a recommendation setting out his or her assessment of the merits of the dispute and the likely outcome of it. The recommendation may or may not contain detailed reasons for the decision depending on the agreement reached between the parties and the evaluator.

22.13 The evaluation is non-binding and the parties do not have to accept it, although they can agree subsequently to settle their dispute in accordance with the recommendations in it.

F Neutral Fact-Finding

22.14 A variation in the process is to require the evaluator simply to investigate and evaluate the facts in dispute between the parties (but not the underlying issues of law or quantum) and reach a decision on those facts. It can be useful to appoint an expert to carry out a non-binding neutral fact-finding evaluation of one or more of the technical issues in the case to assist the parties in reaching a settlement.

G Judicial Evaluation

22.15   ENE can be carried out by a judge, in any court, with the aim of helping the parties to settle the case.[3] The judge will consider the legal and factual issues, evaluate the evidence and any submissions of the parties, and issue a non-binding recommendation or evaluation. If the parties ask a judge to express a provisional view on the whole case or issues in it, then it is part of the judicial function for the judge to agree to do so.[4] This gives the parties some indication of the likely outcome at trial. Judicial evaluation can have a strong persuasive effect on the parties, who may then adopt the judge's recommendations in settling the dispute. It is particularly useful if the case raises limited areas of factual dispute. It is also useful if there is a significant difference of opinion between the parties about the value of the claim, or where they have differing perceptions of the strength of the claim or specific issues. An ENE hearing, conducted by the judge, can provide the parties with guidance on the court's view of quantum.

Judicial evaluation in the Commercial Court

22.16   The Commercial Court may, with the agreement of the parties, in an appropriate case, provide ENE of a dispute or of some of the issues in the case. The approval of the judge in charge of the Commercial List must be obtained before ENE is undertaken. If, after discussion with counsel, it appears to the judge that ENE will aid the resolution of the dispute, the judge will, with the agreement of the parties, refer the matter to the judge in charge of the list. The judge in charge of the list will, if the state of business in the list permits, nominate a judge to conduct the ENE. The judge conducting the ENE will have no further judicial role in respect of the case, either at interim applications or trial, unless the parties agree otherwise.

Judicial evaluation in the Technology and Construction Court

22.17   Judicial evaluation can also take place in the Technology and Construction Court and in the Mercantile Court, although the parties must agree that a TCC judge should evaluate the whole case or some of the issues in it, and if they do agree, they will usually seek an order at a case management conference for an ENE to be carried out by the Court. The judge assigned to the case may carry out the evaluation him or herself, or it may be assigned to another TCC judge. The judge carrying out the evaluation will usually carry out no further judicial role in relation to the case.

---

[3]   CPR 3.1(2)(m).
[4]   *Seals v Williams* [2015] EWHC 1829 (Ch).

At the conclusion of the evaluation, the judge will produce a written report with conclusions and brief reasons. Unless the parties otherwise agree, the report will not be binding on them.[5]

22.18 The judge will usually evaluate the case based on a summary of information provided to him or her. The judge undertaking the ENE will issue directions for the preparation and conduct of the ENE. These will usually include dates for the exchange of submissions and documents (which may include exchange of witness statements and expert evidence), a direction that the ENE will be conducted entirely on paper or alternatively he or she may direct that there be an oral hearing (with or without live evidence being called). If an oral hearing is required, it will usually only last one day. The judge may also require the parties to jointly instruct an expert to help him or her reach a determination of the technical issues in the case (if expert evidence has not already been obtained).[6]

Judicial evaluation in the Chancery Court

22.19 ENE has also been recognized as a valuable tool for encouraging settlement in range of chancery cases in the Chancery Modernisation Review: Final Report by Lord Justice Briggs, published in December 2013. He reports that in some chancery regional trial centres, a form of judicial ENE takes place in the context of inheritance, contested probate, and cases decided under the Trusts of Land and Appointment of Trustees Act 1996.[7]

---

[5] See para 7.5.1 of the *Technology and Construction Court Guide*.
[6] Sample orders providing for judicial ENE can be found on the Online Resource Centre.
[7] 'Chancery Modernisation Review: Final Report' by Lord Justice Briggs, paras 5.6, 5.23–5.30, and 16.19.

23

CONCILIATION, COMPLAINTS, GRIEVANCES, AND OMBUDSMEN

A Introduction

23.01 Conciliation is a facilitative dispute resolution process in which a neutral third party seeks to assist the parties to a dispute to reach a settlement. As such it is virtually indistinguishable from mediation. Grievance, complaints, and ombudsman schemes are designed to provide effective and speedy relief where problems arise between a customer and an organization. It is recognized that the customer often wants no more than an explanation or an apology (such as in relation to medical care). These schemes seek to provide a local or inhouse solution when a problem arises. However, complaints procedures have themselves grown in sophistication, and increasingly they provide for 'appeals' to national bodies where a matter cannot be resolved by the local organization.

Definitions

23.02 This is an area where there is a lack of generally agreed definitions for the processes dealt with in this chapter, but Table 23.1 contains a number of working definitions.

B Conciliation

23.03 While conciliation is in most respects identical to mediation (see Chapters 13 to 17), the most important conciliation processes (ACAS conciliation and in-court conciliation in family cases) have a statutory basis, and involve conciliators who are appointed by an outside body rather than the parties. Other conciliation schemes include the Disability Conciliation Service and the Furniture Ombudsman Conciliation Scheme. Like mediation, conciliation is a non-adjudicative, facilitative process. It is conducted on a confidential, without prejudice basis. If it is successful it will result in a compromise agreement, which, like mediation, can cover issues and interests going outside the scope of the original dispute. If it is unsuccessful, the parties can revert to other forms of legal redress, typically through the courts or tribunals.

Table 23.1 Conciliation, complaints, etc definitions

Term	Definition
Conciliation	A non-adjudicative, facilitative dispute resolution process
Complaint	A problem raised in the context of a one-off transaction or incident, typically raised by a customer or the user of a service
Anonymous complaint	Where a complainant either does not give their name or refuses to permit their name to be communicated to the respondent
Formal complaint	Typically a written complaint. Whether the complaint needs to be signed depends on the terms of the relevant complaints procedure
Informal complaint	Typically an oral complaint, but also where a complainant asks for a written complaint to be treated as an informal complaint
Grievance	A complaint that arises in the context of a continuing relationship, particularly that between employees and employers
Ombudsman	Independent umpire who deals with complaints brought by individuals against certain public bodies and commercial entities, usually as a second tier process (similar to an appeal)

Employment conciliation

The Advisory, Conciliation and Advisory Service (ACAS) was founded in 1974, and **23.04** provides arbitration, conciliation, and mediation services for all forms of employment issues in the UK. Workplace mediation and mediation in employment disputes are considered at 16.27–16.29. ACAS also publishes guides and rules, which are available on the ACAS website,[1] to support these schemes.

ACAS has a discretion to offer conciliation services for parties who are considering **23.05** making a claim to an Employment Tribunal in any type of workplace dispute; and a statutory duty to do so after a claim has been made to an Employment Tribunal.[2] The service is free of charge to the parties.

In discretionary cases, the ACAS conciliation service is only available if: **23.06**

- the parties have already tried to resolve the dispute (perhaps through a grievance or complaints procedure);
- there are grounds to believe that a valid tribunal claim is likely to be made by a party eligible to make the claim;
- providing a conciliation service will not interfere with good employment relations in the employer's organization, such as collective agreements and procedures.

---

[1] See <http://www.acas.org.uk>.
[2] Employment Tribunals Act 1996, s 18.

23.07 Mandatory ACAS conciliation is only 'mandatory' in the sense that ACAS is under a duty to offer the service, rather than the parties being obliged to take it up. When an Employment Tribunal claim is made the Tribunal will send a copy of the claim form and all other relevant documents to an ACAS conciliation officer[3] and will notify the parties that the services of a conciliation officer may be available to them.[4]

- If all parties to the dispute agree to use the conciliation service, then ACAS will set up a conciliation meeting with the parties and the conciliator to explore settlement of the dispute. The parties have no choice over the selection of a conciliator.
- At the meeting, the conciliator will explain the process, his or her role, and explore each party's case and discuss proposals for settlement with each party.
- It is not the function of an ACAS conciliator to ensure that the terms of settlement are fair to the parties, and nor should the conciliator advise the parties about the merits or likely outcome of the case.[5]
- If settlement is reached, it will be recorded on an ACAS settlement form and be signed by both parties. It is enforceable in the county court.
- ACAS will inform the Tribunal that settlement has been reached.

C Complaints and Grievance Procedures

23.08 Government agencies, companies, and organizations that offer goods or services to the general public commonly have internal complaints and grievance procedures to look into and respond to any problems raised by their customers of a formal nature. It is seen to be good for customer relations for problems to be investigated by someone within the organization and for the problem to be resolved with the customer quickly and before it escalates into a contentious dispute. Having a complaints system may be a regulatory requirement, such as in relation to the provision of legal and medical services. Efficient and effective complaints and grievance procedures also form part of an organization's quality control or quality assurance procedures, which are aimed at ensuring that high levels of service are maintained, with any weaknesses being addressed swiftly before other customers are affected by similar problems.

---

[3] Employment Tribunals Act 1996, s 19; Employment Tribunals (Constitution and Rules of Procedure) Regulations 2004 SI 2004 No 1861 reg 21.

[4] Employment Tribunals (Constitution and Rules of Procedure) Regulations 2004 SI 2004 No 1861 reg 2(2)(d).

[5] *Clarke v Redcar & Cleveland Borough Council* [2006] IRLR 324.

Raising a complaint or grievance

Complaints and grievances are usually the first stage of resolution for many disa- **23.09**
greements that members of the public have with companies or government departments. Good complaints handling should be reasonable, fair, and proportionate, as
well as accessible and responsive to an individual's needs. Under many complaints
schemes there is a fairly short time limit for lodging the complaint. In some schemes
an official complaint form must be used, but others can be accessed by raising the
complaint by letter or email. Most schemes will require a written, formal complaint.
Most organizations refuse to investigate anonymous complaints, particularly when
they relate to the conduct of staff. This is because it is grossly unfair to the person
identified in such a complaint, who cannot reasonably be expected to respond to an
incident involving an unidentified person.

Complaints handling

Many complaints procedures are handled at a local level, often informally. How the **23.10**
complaint will be dealt with depends on the procedures laid down by the relevant
complaints policy and the circumstances of the particular case. The organization
will typically acknowledge receipt of the complaint in writing, and indicate a period
over which it is intended that the matter will be investigated and a decision reached.
A person (the 'investigator'), or sometimes a panel, typically of three people, will be
designated by the organization to investigate the matter. Some procedures give the
investigation and decision-making responsibilities to a single person. Others desig-
nate one person to investigate, who reports to a more senior person, who makes the
decision on the basis of the report. A great many complaints are dealt with entirely
on the basis of written materials. In others the complainant, and possibly employees
of the organization, will be interviewed, followed by a decision. In others there will
be a meeting where the facts relating to the complaint will be raised and considered.
Most complaints and grievance policies say very little about the investigation process, leaving a great deal to the discretion and good sense of the investigator or panel.
Where the policy sets out a specific procedure, that of course should be followed.

Most investigators or panels will tailor the amount of time spent in investigating a **23.11**
matter and the degree of formality to the nature of the complaint and its serious-
ness. The guiding principles are the rules of natural justice. These mean that anyone
who may have an adverse finding against them must be notified of the nature of the
allegations being made, and be given a reasonable opportunity to respond to them.
Most investigators will also want to ensure that the real complaint is looked into, so
will often communicate with the complainant to ensure they have fully understood
what lies behind the complaint.

23.12 Meetings and hearings take a variety of different forms. They usually start with the person chairing the meeting asking each person to introduce themselves, and then explaining the nature of the investigation. The complainant is often asked to say what they are seeking from the investigation. The meeting can then take a number of different courses, from a general discussion to something more resembling a court hearing with questions being put to the different people in turn. Whatever form it takes, each person directly involved must be given a fair chance to state their case.

Acting for a party in a complaint

23.13 When acting for either a complainant or the person against whom a complaint is raised, it is first necessary to get the full story, both from the person involved and from the relevant documents. This may involve some investigation of what documents are or should be available. It may also become clear that other people may need to be contacted to find out what they know. It is vital to obtain a copy of the relevant complaints procedure or policy, together with any of the company's written procedures or guidance notes that may be relevant. It may be that a meeting or hearing will have been already convened by the company or organization but, if not, consideration should be given to whether this would be helpful in conveying the case of the person who is being represented. Sometimes they will be best advised to have a matter considered on the papers, but in many cases, particularly serious matters, they will only have their side of events fully considered at a meeting or hearing.

Decisions in complaints and grievance investigations

23.14 The primary decision that needs to be made is whether to uphold or dismiss the complaint or grievance. This may be done at the meeting, or by letter shortly afterwards. It is best practice to give reasons for the decision, although these are usually short. Some complaints are dismissed after initial fact-finding. Organizations should keep records of successful and unsuccessful complaints, and good practice is to take appropriate action to rectify problems identified by the process for the benefit of future customers and employees. Typical outcomes that may be available in an individual matter under different complaints and grievance processes include:

- an explanation;
- an apology;
- compensation;
- reduction of a bill or a refund;
- disciplinary action.

Information following exhaustion of complaints procedures

A trader who has exhausted its internal complaint handling procedure in a com-   **23.15**
plaint made by a consumer must inform the consumer,[6] in a durable form:

- that the trader cannot settle the consumer's complaint;
- of the name and website address of an ADR entity or EU listed body that would be competent to deal with the complaint[7]; and
- whether the trader is obliged or prepared to submit to such ADR process.

D Ombudsmen

Ombudsmen act rather like umpires in complaints brought by individuals and   **23.16**
public or private organizations. If an organization is a member of an ombudsman
scheme, it should make this clear in a brochure or on its letterhead. Most ombudsmen belong to the Ombudsman Association,[8] which can provide information about
the available public and private sector ombudsman schemes.

Important ombudsman schemes include the Local Government Ombudsman   **23.17**
(England),[9] which deals with complaints about services provided by local authorities
in England, and the Parliamentary and Health Service Ombudsman,[10] which deals
with complaints about services provided by government departments and the NHS
in England. There are also ombudsman schemes for a range of different consumer
services, including many professions, public utility companies such as energy, water,
and telephones, and financial services such as banks and insurance companies.

Complaints handling by ombudsmen

Ombudsmen are independent from the organizations they investigate. Ombudsman   **23.18**
schemes usually provide that reference to the ombudsman is only permitted after
attempting to resolve the complaint through an organization's internal complaints
procedure. According to the Ombudsman Association's *Guide to Principles of Good
Complaints Handling* ombudsman schemes should be designed to comply with the
following seven principles:

- *clarity of purpose*, with a clear statement of the role of the ombudsman and the aims of the scheme;

---

[6] Alternative Dispute Resolution for Consumer Disputes (Competent Authorities and Information) Regulations 2015, SI 2015/542, reg 19, as amended by SI 2015/1392.
[7] See SI 2015/542 regs 4 and 10, and Chapters 17 and 21.
[8] Its website is <http://www.ombudsmanassociation.org>.
[9] See <http://www.lgo.org.uk>.
[10] See <http://www.ombudsman.org.uk>.

- *accessibility*, so that the scheme is free and open to anyone who needs to use it;
- *flexible procedures*, which can be adjusted to meet the requirements of each case. The *Guide* makes the point that it is important that each complainant is made to feel they are being treated as an individual with their complaint being dealt with on its own merits;
- *transparency*, so that information is readily available;
- *proportionality*, so that the process used is appropriate to the complaint;
- *efficiency*; and
- *quality outcomes*, with the process leading to positive change.

Procedure on references to ombudsmen

23.19 Most ombudsman schemes use a 'documents-only' process. They may be started by a letter or the completion of a complaints form. The depth of any particular investigation will depend on the nature and complexity of the complaint. In some cases the primary function of the ombudsman is to explain the decision-making process or to provide other information to the complainant. This may be the case where the complaint is essentially one where the complainant does not understand what has been done because it has not previously been clearly explained. In most other cases the ombudsman has to enter into detailed correspondence with the complainant and the organization in an attempt to identify exactly what lies behind the complaint, and to get the organization's explanation for what it has done.

Grounds on which ombudsmen make their decisions

23.20 Under the legal ombudsman scheme decisions are based on what the ombudsman considers to be fair and reasonable in all the circumstances of the case. This can include reference to how a court might have decided the case, the relevant code of conduct, and what the ombudsman considers to have been good practice at the time of the act or omission. Public sector ombudsmen normally only review how a decision was made, not whether it was right, and uphold a complaint if there was 'maladministration' that resulted in an injustice. Maladministration can include:

- a public body not following its own policies or procedures;
- rudeness;
- taking too long;
- failing to act;
- treating the complainant less fairly than other people; and
- giving wrong or misleading information.

Private sector ombudsmen may come to a decision against the organization on any **23.21** of the above grounds, and also if it is felt that the organization's conduct was unfair or unreasonable when compared with industry standards of good practice.

Relief available

Compensation is usually only available in private sector schemes. Compensation, **23.22** interest, limitation on fees, and putting right specified errors are among the remedies available to the Legal Ombudsman. The primary relief in public sector schemes is the review of a decision or act of a government department or local authority, with a changed decision being the ultimate goal of the complainant. There are a number of cases where an apology will be the primary relief given.

Can a complainant bring court proceedings?

Pensions Ombudsman Scheme decisions are binding, which means that while **23.23** they can be enforced, the parties cannot subsequently sue on the original dispute. Generally, other ombudsman schemes are not binding, but they might be depending on the rules of the scheme, and the circumstances of the case. A decision of the financial ombudsman has been held to be final and binding once the complainant accepted the decision where the complaint amounted to a legal cause of action.[11] The same should apply to decisions of the legal ombudsman, as both schemes have similar relevant provisions.[12]

---

[11] *Clark v In Focus Asset Management and Tax Solutions Ltd* [2014] EWCA Civ 118.
[12] 'Res judicata and ADR', Sime [2015] CJQ 35 at 49.

24

EXPERT (OR NEUTRAL) DETERMINATION

A What is Expert Determination?

24.01 Expert determination is a process in which an expert (or a neutral) is appointed to make a determination on the issues referred to him or her by the appointing parties. Expert determination is a determinative process, rather than a facilitative process (mediation) or an advisory evaluative process (early neutral evaluation). It is most commonly employed in cases of a technical nature where the parties are likely to benefit from a determination by an appropriate expert such as an accountant, surveyor, or engineer. However, it is not always the case that an expert needs to be appointed to carry out a determination. In appropriate cases, the parties can agree that the determination is carried out by an independent third party, or even by a panel consisting of a number of neutral third parties and a lawyer.

24.02 The parties may contractually bind themselves, in advance of any dispute arising, to use expert determination to resolve a dispute about one or more specified issues or all issues arising out the contract between them. Alternatively, after a dispute has arisen, the parties may select expert determination as the most appropriate ADR process to resolve the dispute and this can take place, before or after the issue of proceedings.

24.03 The relationship between the parties and the expert, the obligations of the expert, and the circumstances in which the decision will be final and binding on the parties will be primarily governed by the terms of the contract by which the expert is appointed.

24.04 Where the parties use expert determination to resolve the dispute, they usually agree that the determination is final and binding on them, and typically this is recorded in the contract. 'Final' means that the decision cannot be reviewed or appealed. 'Binding' means that the parties must comply with the determination. If this is not expressly stated in the clause, the court may imply such a term.[1] The parties may also

---

[1] *Cott UK Ltd v FE Barber Ltd* [1997] 3 All ER 540 at 549[B]; *Baber v Kenwood Manufacturing Co Ltd & others* [1978] 1 Lloyd's Rep 175.

agree that the determination is only binding on them for a temporary or interim period (although this is less common).

Expert determination (unlike arbitration) is not subject to the supervision of the **24.05** court. However, the court may be involved if a dispute arises as to the jurisdiction of the expert, or one or both parties wish to challenge the determination. A court order may also be necessary if there is a need to enforce the determination in the event of non-compliance by one party.

Where the determination is to be final and binding on the parties, the contract may **24.06** provide for some exceptional circumstances in which the determination can be challenged, such as a manifest error on the part of the expert. Additionally, other grounds of challenge may exist even if they are not specifically set out in the contract.[2]

Expert determination should not be confused with the rules relating to expert **24.07** evidence that can be adduced under the CPR Part 35. In an expert determination, the expert is acting as the decision-maker, not as a witness. In court proceedings, an expert acts as a witness, and the ultimate decision-maker will be the judge. Where the court ordered the parties to appoint an expert accountant pursuant to a mediation settlement agreement they had reached, the expert was being appointed under the agreement and was not a court-appointed expert under CPR Part 35. Therefore, the court was not entitled to examine the approach of the expert under CPR Part 35 or 40.[3]

Expert determination is also very different from arbitration because expert determi- **24.08** nation is subject to little review or intervention by the court, there is no award or judgment, there is no right of appeal, and the rules of natural justice and the strict rules of evidence do not apply unless the contract contains terms to the contrary. An expert has no immunity from suit, unless this is conferred by contract, unlike an arbitrator who has statutory immunity. An expert does not act in a judicial capacity and so can use his or her own expertise to inform his or her decision.

B Cases Suitable for Expert Determination

Expert determination is a very useful and cost-effective way of determining disputes **24.09** of a highly technical nature. It can be used in a wide range of commercial cases such as rent reviews, company, asset or share valuations, construction disputes, real property disputes, land valuations, and energy disputes. Relevant factors governing

---

[2] See 24.30–24.51 for the grounds on which an expert determination can be challenged.
[3] *Beauty Star Ltd v Janmohamed* [2014] EWCA Civ 451.

selection will include the extent to which the parties want a cost-effective, speedy, conclusive determination of the matters in dispute, within a relatively informal process, with control over the selection of an appropriate expert. The parties can also use expert determination to settle disputes that arise during assessment of costs when the main proceedings have been concluded.[4]

C Contractual Nature of Expert Determination

24.10 Expert determination is most commonly used where the parties agree in advance in the underlying contract between them to use expert determination to resolve a specified or any dispute arising out of the contract. A separate contract will also come into existence between the parties and the expert when the matter is referred to the appointed expert for determination. In the event of a dispute between the parties, the court may be asked to construe the contract, and if it is clear and unambiguous, the court is likely to give effect to it.

24.11 The parties should give consideration to the following matters when drafting the contractual provisions relating to expert determination:

- the type of dispute that may be referred for expert determination; this may be confined to narrow technical issues which are within the expert's field of expertise, or relate to all disputes arising under the contract. If the clause is clear, the court is likely to give effect to an 'all disputes' clause,[5] even if the matters go beyond the expert's area of expertise;
- the qualifications of the expert;
- the need for the person so appointed to act as an expert and not an arbitrator;
- the machinery for appointing the expert;[6]
- the procedure that should be followed for the determination;[7]
- the extent to which the parties are to be bound by the determination;[8]
- the extent to which there may be exceptions to the final and binding nature of the award. The parties can agree that the determination is final and binding on them except in the case of manifest error by the expert, or fraud, or collusion. This is

---

[4] Costs Alternative Dispute Resolution (CADR) offer expert determination or a binding paper assessment of costs which is quicker and cheaper than assessment of costs through the court process. See <www.costs-adr.com>.

[5] *Thames Valley Power Ltd v Total Gas and Power Ltd* [2005] EWHC 2208 (Comm); *Sunrock Aircraft Corporation Ltd v Scandinavian Airlines System* [2006] EWHC 2834 (Comm), reversed by the Court of Appeal on other grounds [2007] EWCA Civ 882.

[6] See 24.12.

[7] See 24.13–24.16.

[8] See 24.04.

important. The court will construe the contract to determine whether and, if so, what contractual grounds of challenge exist. In the absence of any contractual grounds of challenge, an expert determination can be challenged on only a small number of grounds;[9]

- whether or not reasons should be provided for the determination;[10]
- the time for payment of any monetary sum which the expert determines should be paid by one party to the other, and whether the expert has power to award interest and, if so, at what rate;
- the fees of the expert and the costs that the parties may incur in relation to the determination, and whether power is conferred on the expert to award costs between the parties;
- whether the expert is to have immunity;
- time bars for challenge or time bars for referring the matter for determination.

D Selection of the Expert

The parties may agree on the identity of the expert they wish to appoint. Alternatively, **24.12**
they may enlist the help of a professional body or an ADR provider that offers an expert determination service. In the event of deadlock between the parties, or defects in the appointing machinery, in certain circumstances, the court may be able to intervene to resolve the deadlock.[11]

E Procedure

If the parties have spelt out the procedure that should be followed in advance in **24.13**
the substantive contract, or in the contract appointing the determiner, then this procedure should be followed. However, it is more usual for the parties simply to agree in advance to refer disputes to an expert for determination, leaving the parties and the expert to agree on the appropriate procedure once the referral to the expert has been made.

The parties can retain a degree of control over the process and the appointed expert **24.14**
will usually seek to agree any appropriate procedural directions with the parties. The determination can be done in a relatively informal way, with both parties

---

[9] See 24.33–24.46 for contractual grounds of challenge, and 24.47–24.51 for other grounds of challenge even in the absence of an express or implied provision in the contract permitting a challenge to be made on those grounds.
[10] See 24.20–24.22.
[11] *Sudbrook Trading Estate Ltd v Eggleton* [1983] 1 AC 444.

simply making submissions on paper, and the expert providing the determination in writing.

24.15 The procedure that is typically agreed will provide for each party to send to the expert:

- written submissions setting out their case on each of the issues;
- copies of all relevant documents (the parties should cooperate to produce an agreed bundle of documents if possible);
- in some cases, the parties may agree that the parties or their lawyers should make submissions at a meeting or hearing and, although this is usually not required, the attendance and cross-examination of witnesses;
- the parties may also agree that the expert can conduct his or her own lines of inquiry.

Implied duty to cooperate

24.16 The parties are under an implied duty to cooperate with each other and with the expert in relation to the determination.[12] Where an expert's proposed terms of engagement are reasonable and are consistent with the rights and obligations in the agreement between the parties, the implied term to cooperate is likely to require the parties to accept the expert's appointment on those terms.[13]

F Confidential Information

24.17 The parties may agree that they can each provide information to the expert on a confidential basis. If they do so, and the expert is obliged to give reasons for his or her determination, the expert should summarize any confidential information relied upon so that both parties can ascertain what the expert took into account in reaching the determination.[14] This is particularly important if the parties have agreed that the determination can be challenged on the grounds of manifest error.

24.18 To avoid any suggestion of bias in favour of one party, it is preferable if the parties openly exchange any information that is placed before the determiner, and that any hearings or meetings are held in the presence of all parties. However, there is

---

[12] *Panamena Europea Navigacion (Compania Limitada) v Frederick Leyland & Co Ltd* [1947] AC 428 at 436. Also, see *Yan Seng Pte Ltd v International Trade Corp Ltd* [2013] EWHC 111 (QB) and *Bristol Groundschool Ltd v Intelligent Data Capture Ltd* [2014] EWHC 2145 (Ch).

[13] *Cream Holdings Ltd v Davenport* [2011] EWCA Civ 1287.

[14] *Halifax Life Ltd v Equitable Life Assurance Society* [2007] EWHC 503 (Comm) (per Cresswell J at [48]).

unlikely to be any bias or breach of the rules of natural justice if a meeting takes place with one side alone, but in circumstances where it is recorded and transcribed and the other party is given an opportunity to respond.[15]

G Nature of the Decision

In expert determination the parties will usually agree that the decision will be bind- **24.19** ing on them and, where this is so, the court will uphold the decision unless there are grounds for setting it aside.[16] The decision does not take the form of an award or an order, unlike arbitration.

H Reasons for the Decision

The parties can agree whether written reasons should be provided for the determina- **24.20** tion. If the contract by which the expert is appointed does not require reasons for the determination, then the expert is not obliged to provide them.

However, if the parties agree that the expert should give reasons for the decision, and **24.21** the expert fails to do so, the court may order that reasons be provided by enforcing the contractual provisions, or under its inherent jurisdiction.[17]

Where reasons are to be given, they should be intelligible and adequate in all the **24.22** circumstances. The reasons can be stated briefly, but they should explain the basis for the expert's conclusions on the issues he or she was asked to determine.

I Issues that can Arise in Expert Determination

The following issues can arise in expert determination: **24.23**

- One or both parties may decide to ignore the expert determination provisions in the underlying agreement and instead commence court proceedings to resolve the dispute.
- One party may dispute the expert's jurisdiction to determine a particular issue or the dispute.
- One or more of the parties may challenge the expert's determination.

All of these matters are discussed in the remainder of this chapter.

---

[15] See *Rydon Maintenance Ltd v Affinity Sutton Housing Ltd* [2015] EWHC 1306 (Ch).
[16] *Thames Valley Power Ltd v Total Gas & Power Ltd* [2005] EWHC 2208 (Comm).
[17] *Halifax Life Ltd v Equitable Life Assurance Society* [2007] EWHC 503 (Comm).

J Ignoring an Expert Determination Clause

Breach of contract

24.24 Expert determination clauses, if clearly and unambiguously drafted, will be upheld by the courts, and such clauses will generally prevent the parties having recourse to the courts to resolve their dispute.[18] If one party refuses to comply with an expert determination clause in the contract, the other party may be entitled to damages for breach of contract.[19]

Applications to stay court proceedings pending expert determination

24.25 The court also has discretion to stay court proceedings issued by a party who failed to use the contractually agreed machinery in the contract to determine the dispute.[20] The burden will be on the party seeking to litigate the dispute to show grounds why the claim should not be stayed so that the parties can invoke the contractually agreed method of ADR.[21] In exercising its discretion to enforce such clauses by staying proceedings commenced in breach of the clause, the court may consider the following factors:[22]

- the extent to which the parties have complied with the requirements in any pre-action protocol;
- whether the dispute is suitable for determination by the ADR process the parties have contractually agreed to use;[23]
- the costs of that ADR process compared to the costs of litigation;
- whether the dispute could be resolved more quickly by court proceedings than by requiring the parties to use the contractually agreed ADR machinery;[24]
- whether a stay would accord with the overriding objective;
- whether an element of the claim was not subject to expert determination so that the proceedings relating to that part could not be stayed, and having parallel litigation and expert determination proceedings is likely to increase costs and time, and be contrary to the interests of justice.[25]

---

[18] *Harper v Interchange Group Ltd* [2007] EWHC 1834 (Comm).
[19] *Sunrock Aircraft Corporation v Scandinavian Airlines System* [2007] EWCA Civ 882. Also, see *Union Discount Company Ltd v Zoller* [2001] EWCA Civ 1755.
[20] *Channel Tunnel Group Ltd v Balfour Beatty Construction Ltd* [1993] AC 334.
[21] *Cott UK Ltd v FE Barber Ltd* [1997] 3 All ER 540.
[22] *DGT Steel and Cladding Ltd v Cubitt Building & Interiors Ltd* [2007] EWHC 1584 (TCC).
[23] *Cott UK Ltd v FE Barber Ltd* [1997] 3 All ER 540.
[24] *Thames Valley Power Ltd v Total Gas & Power Ltd* [2005] EWHC 2208 (Comm).
[25] *Abbas (t/a AH Design) v Rotary (International) Ltd* [2012] NIQB 41. See also *Turville Heath Inc v Chartis Insurance UK Ltd (formerly AIG UK Ltd)* [2012] EWHC 3019 (TCC).

A temporary stay of the proceedings, for a stated period, does not debar a party **24.26** from pursuing its claim in court. A stay merely halts proceedings for a few weeks, until after the determination. If, following the determination, there is still a residual dispute, the court proceedings can be reactivated.[26]

K The Extent of the Expert's Jurisdiction

Some expert determination clauses may provide that the expert is to have exclusive **24.27** jurisdiction to determine the extent of his or her own jurisdiction in the event of a dispute between the parties. However, the court will be the final decision-maker as to whether the expert has jurisdiction to determine the dispute, even if a clause purports to confer that jurisdiction on the expert in a manner that is final and binding.[27]

The court can be asked to determine the extent of an expert's jurisdiction: **24.28**

- before the matter is referred to the expert;
- during the expert's determination but before the decision is reached;
- after the determination, where one party alleges that they are not bound by the determination because the expert has exceeded his or her jurisdiction.

If an application is made to the court to determine the jurisdiction of the expert **24.29** before the expert makes the determination, the court will assess whether the dispute is real and not hypothetical and, if it is real, whether it is in the interests of justice and convenience for the court to determine the matter first, particularly if it would be wasteful of time and costs if the expert determined a dispute when he or she had no jurisdiction to do so.[28] An independent accountant appointed to determine a dispute about the treatment of liabilities in company accounts misinterpreted his jurisdiction in considering himself bound to follow an erroneous policy which was adopted in earlier accounts and his determination was therefore not valid and enforceable; the court ordered a fresh determination to be carried out based on the correct principles.[29] The court will not always determine a dispute about the extent of the expert's jurisdiction in advance of the determination. It may be that the obvious and convenient forum for arguments to be raised about jurisdiction is in the expert determination in the first instance and that can be done without prejudice to a party's contention that the expert had no jurisdiction.[30]

---

[26] *DGT Steel and Cladding Ltd v Cubitt Building & Interiors Ltd* [2007] EWHC 1584 (TCC).
[27] *Barclays Bank plc v Nylon Capital LLP* [2011] EWCA Civ 826.
[28] *Barclays Bank plc v Nylon Capital LLP* [2011] EWCA Civ 826.
[29] *Shafi v Rutherford* [2014] EWCA Civ 1186.
[30] See *Wilky Property Holdings plc v London & Surrey Investments Ltd* [2011] EWHC 2888 (Ch). See also *MP Kemp Ltd v Bullen Developments Ltd* [2014] EWHC 2009 (Ch).

L Grounds for Challenging the Decision

24.30   The court will give primary consideration to the terms of the contract in ascertaining whether the determination can be challenged. If the parties agree that their dispute should be resolved by expert determination and that the expert's decision is to be conclusive and binding for all purposes, then provided the expert has done exactly what he or she was instructed to do, the report, whether or not it contained reasons for the decision, can generally not be challenged by seeking to set it aside in court proceedings.[31]

24.31   However, *contractual* grounds for challenge may exist, on one or more of the following grounds:

- failing to provide reasons for the determination when the contract requires reasons to be given;
- manifest error;
- an error of law;
- lack of procedural fairness;
- the determination was not intended to be final and binding in relation to matters of construction.

24.32   Alternatively, even in the absence of contractual grounds for challenge, other grounds of challenge may exist as a matter of law, namely:

- material departure from instructions;
- fraud;
- partiality.

M Contractual Grounds for Challenge

No reasons for decision

24.33   Reasons need only be given for the determination if the contract so provides.[32] If the expert fails to provide reasons for his or her decision, despite having agreed to do so, then the decision can be challenged. However the court is likely to order that the expert should provide reasons within a specified period of time, rather than set the decision aside.[33]

---

[31] *Jones v Sherwood Computer Services plc* [1992] 1 WLR 277.
[32] See 24.20–24.22 above.
[33] *Halifax Life Ltd v Equitable Life Assurances Society* [2007] EWHC 503 (Comm).

Manifest error

The parties may agree in their contract that the expert's decision will only be binding **24.34** on them in the absence of manifest error. If there is such an error the decision may be set aside.[34] However, even if the expert has clearly erred, in the absence of any contractual term enabling the parties to challenge the decision on the grounds of a manifest error, the decision will be binding on the parties.[35]

The meaning of 'manifest error' has been defined in a number of different ways: **24.35**

- 'oversights and blunders so obvious as to admit of no difference of opinion';[36]
- an error which is 'obvious or easily demonstrable without extensive investigation';[37]
- 'an error which was so obvious as to be beyond reasonable contradiction for it to be manifest'.[38]

A manifest error does not import a condition that the error has to be manifest at **24.36** the time the determination is given. Where the determination issued by an expert was based on the terms of the original contract between the parties, which had subsequently been varied, the determination could be set aside on the grounds of manifest error because the amount certified was that due under the original agreement instead of the amount due under the agreement as varied.[39]

If the expert's reasoning is not apparent from the determination itself, the court can **24.37** look at other material that was available to the expert to determine if a manifest error has been made and any subsequent reasons the expert may have given by way of clarification.[40]

An error of law

There is no rule of public policy preventing the parties from conferring on the expert **24.38** the right to be the sole arbiter of a question of law, and a provision effectively ousting the court's jurisdiction to decide questions of law is not void on the grounds that it

---

[34] *Veba Oil Supply and Trading GmbH v Petrotrade Inc* [2001] EWCA Civ 1832. See also *Walton Homes Ltd v Staffordshire County Council* [2013] EWHC 2554 (Ch), where the parties disagreed about the interpretation of words in the contract, and the expert relied upon an opinion from counsel in reaching his determination. It was held that the expert had not made a manifest error, because matters of interpretation of this kind do not admit of no difference of opinion.

[35] *Jones v Sherwood Computer Services plc* [1992] 1 WLR 277.

[36] *Conoco (UK) Ltd v Phillips Petroleum Co UK Ltd* (unreported, 19 August 1996).

[37] *IIG Capital LLC v Van Der Merwe* [2007] EWHC 2631 (Ch) (per Lewison J at [52]). This definition was upheld and approved on appeal (see [2008] EWCA Civ 542 at [35]).

[38] *Macdonald v Livingstone* [2012] CSOH 31.

[39] *North Shore Ventures Ltd v Anstead Holdings Inc* [2011] EWCA Civ 230.

[40] *Homepace Ltd v Sita South East Ltd* [2008] EWCA Civ 1.

is contrary to public policy. If the parties agree to refer to the final and conclusive judgment of the expert an issue that consists of a question of law, the expert's decision will be final and conclusive and therefore not open to review by the courts on the ground that the expert's decision on construction was erroneous in law, unless other grounds for challenge exist.[41]

24.39 However, Lord Neuberger has recently cast doubt on the decision in *Nikko Hotels (UK) Ltd*, in *Barclays Bank plc v Nylon Capital LLP*.[42] The court did not have to decide the issue of whether the expert could be the sole decision-maker on a question of law on the facts of that case. However, Lord Neuberger observed that in his view *Nikko Hotels (UK) Ltd* could not be safely relied upon in relation to this issue.[43] In *Premier Telecom Communications Group Ltd v Webb*, however, Moore-Bick LJ pointed out that it is necessary to remember that Lord Neuberger's comments were *obiter*, and that neither of the other members of the court agreed with them. He noted that whilst the parties might define the terms of the expert's mandate in such a way that any error of law on his part rendered his decision invalid, to do so in many cases would risk undermining the whole purpose of the reference. Ultimately, whether an error of law invalidates the determination will depend on the construction of the contract.[44]

Failure to act lawfully or fairly

24.40 In an expert determination, if the procedure is set out in the contract, and the expert has not followed this, it may be possible to challenge the determination on the basis that the expert failed to act fairly.[45] However, in the absence of any agreement between the parties and the expert about the procedure that should be followed, an expert determination cannot be set aside on the basis that the expert failed to follow a fair procedure in accordance with the notions of natural justice.[46]

---

[41] *Nikko Hotels (UK) Ltd v MEPC plc* [1991] 2 EGLR 103 (Ch) where Knox J departed from *Re Davstone Estates Ltd's Leases, Manprop Ltd v O'Dell and Others* [1969] 2 Ch 378, where Ungeod-Thomas J held that clauses, which purported to make the expert the final arbiter of questions of law, were void on the basis that they were contrary to public policy because they purported to oust the jurisdiction of the court in relation to questions of law. *Nikko Hotels* has been followed in subsequent cases such as *Brown v GIO Insurance Ltd* [1998] Lloyd's Rep IR 201 at 208 and *Immarsat Ventures plc v APR Ltd* [2002] Lawtel, 15 May 2002.

[42] [2011] EWCA Civ 826 at [65]–[69].

[43] [2011] EWCA Civ 826 at [69].

[44] *Premier Telecom Communications Group Ltd v Webb* [2014] EWCA Civ 994, per Moore-Bick LJ at [9].

[45] *John Barker Construction Ltd v London Portman Hotel Ltd* [1996] 83 BLR 31.

[46] *Bernard Schulte GmbH v Nile Holdings Ltd* [2004] EWHC 977 (Comm) at [95]; *Owen Pell Ltd v Bindi (London) Ltd* [2008] EWHC 1420 (TCC).

Where the parties agree on the procedure or the machinery by which the determina- **24.41**
tion is to be carried out, the court can intervene and provide its own machinery if
the procedure agreed has broken down.[47] Likewise, if one party fails to follow the
contractual machinery, for example by failing to disclose relevant documents to the
expert, having agreed to do so, the court may order him or her to do so.[48]

However, if the parties have not spelt out the procedure in the contract, the pro- **24.42**
cedure should be left to the expert and the court will not intervene in advance of
the determination and give directions as to the manner in which the instructions
should be given to the expert, that the expert should have specific expertise, or that
the expert should be supplied with particular documents.[49]

The decision is not intended to be final on matters of construction

Questions as to the role of the expert, the ambit of his or her instructions, and **24.43**
the nature of his or her instructions (namely whether he or she had exclusive
jurisdiction to determine the matters referred to him or her or whether his or
her jurisdiction was concurrent with that of the court) are to be determined as a
matter of construction of the agreement. If the agreement confers on the expert
the exclusive remit to determine the matter, then the jurisdiction of the court to
determine that question is excluded. It is irrelevant whether the court would have
reached a different conclusion or whether the court considers that the expert's
decision is wrong, for the parties have, in either event, agreed to abide by the decision of the expert.[50]

However, if it can be said that, by the terms under which the expert was appointed, **24.44**
the expert's determination was not intended to oust the jurisdiction of the court in
matters of interpretation of the terms of the underlying contract between the parties, then the court can intervene if the expert issues a determination based on an
incorrect interpretation.[51]

Recent decisions demonstrate that the courts will not readily accept that the parties **24.45**
intended an expert's decision to be final and conclusive in respect of the construction of the contract, in the absence of a clear and express provision in the contract

---

[47] *Sudbrook Trading Estate Ltd v Eggleton* [1983] 1 AC 444; *Cream Holdings Ltd v Davenport*
[2011] EWCA Civ 1287. See also *Furlonger v Lalatta* [2014] EWHC 37 (Ch).
[48] *Bruce v Carpenter* [2006] EWHC 3301 (Ch).
[49] *Vimercati v BV Trustco Ltd* [2012] EWHC 1410 (Ch).
[50] *Mercury Communications Ltd v Director General of Telecommunications* [1994] CLC 1125;
British Shipbuilders v VSEL Consortium plc [1997] 1 Lloyd's Rep 106 and *National Grid Co plc v M25
Group Ltd* [1999] 1 EGLR 65.
[51] *Mercury Communications Ltd v Director General of Telecommunications* [1996] 1 WLR 48, and
Homepace Ltd v Sita South East Ltd [2008] EWCA Civ 1.

that the expert was to be the sole decision-maker in relation to questions of construction, particularly where the expert could not be expected to have professional expertise in determining issues relating to the construction of the contract.[52] This is so even if the clause provides for any difference between the parties in relation to the interpretation of the contract to be referred to the expert and his or her decision was to be final and binding.[53]

24.46   Where the court retains jurisdiction to decide questions of construction, the court has a discretion whether to determine a dispute about the proper construction of a clause in a contract *in advance* of the expert determination but it is likely to do so only in an exceptional case so as to avoid unnecessary litigation which could be a waste of time and costs.[54] Where both parties reached different views on the meaning of a clause in the contract and it was likely that one or other of them would seek to challenge the expert's interpretation of the meaning of the phrase, then the court may find that it is in the best interests of the parties to clarify the position before the expert begins the determination.[55]

N Other Grounds on Which an Expert's Determination can be Challenged

Material departure from instructions

24.47   The decision can be challenged if the expert has departed from his or her instructions in a material way. This could be established if, for example, the expert was mistaken about the terms of his or her instructions, or he or she addressed the wrong question or did not do what he or she was appointed to do; for example, if he or she valued the wrong number of shares, or shares in the wrong company, or failed to carry out a test by a contractually stipulated method.[56] An expert who failed to value shares in a company in accordance with the books and records of the company including 'any handwriting takings' had materially departed from

---

[52] See *Menolly Investments 3 Sarl v Cerep Sarl* [2009] EWHC 516 (Ch); *Thorne v Courtier* [2011] EWCA Civ 460.

[53] *Persimmon Homes Ltd v Woodford Land Ltd* [2011] EWHC 3109 (Ch).

[54] *Mercury Communications Ltd v Director General of Telecommunications* [1996] 1 WLR 48; *British Shipbuilders v VSEL Consortium Plc* [1997] 1 Lloyd's Rep 106 at 109. See also *MP Kemp Ltd v Bullen Developments Ltd* [2014] EWHC 2009 (Ch).

[55] *Thorne v Courtier* [2011] EWCA Civ 460.

[56] *Jones v Sherwood Computer Services plc* [1992] 1 WLR 277; *Veba Oil Supply and Trading GmbH v Petrotrade Inc* [2001] EWCA Civ 1832. Also, see *In Kollerich & Cie SA v The State Trading Corporation of India* [1980] 2 Lloyd's Rep 32 where certificates of quality were set aside because they did not comply with the terms of the expert determination clause in the contract.

instructions and the determination was set aside.[57] Any decision reached on an issue that was not within the expert's terms of reference is also liable to be set aside on this basis.

Any departure will be material unless it can be said to be trivial or de minimis. **24.48** Once any departure is material, it has, until recently, been the position that it is not necessary to show that it affected the result and the determination will not be binding on the parties.[58] However, in *Ackerman v Ackerman*,[59] Vos J held that where a departure from instructions would have made no difference to the determination, the departure was not a material one and the determination was therefore binding on the parties. The Court of Appeal granted leave to appeal on this single issue, and Moore-Bick LJ, granting leave to appeal considered that the decision of Vos J may have been wrong on this point.[60]

In the absence of a material departure from instructions, the decision will be binding **24.49** even if the expert has made a serious mistake of fact or of law or professional judgment (unless, as explained above, the terms of the contract permit a challenge on one of these grounds).

Fraud

If the expert is guilty of fraud or has colluded with one party in reaching his or her **24.50** decision, then it can be set aside.[61] If the expert is misled by fraudulent misrepresentation by one party, this may also entitle the innocent party to bring proceedings against the wrongdoers.[62]

Collusion

In the case of partiality, it must be shown that the expert actually was biased. A mere **24.51** possibility of bias will not suffice.[63] Meetings or telephone conversations with one

---

[57] *Begum v Hossain* [2015] EWCA Civ 717.
[58] *British Shipbuilders v VSEL Consortium plc* [1997] 1 Lloyd's Rep 106; *Veba Oil Supply and Trading GmbH v Petrotrade Inc* [2001] EWCA Civ 1832.
[59] [2011] EWHC 3428 (Ch).
[60] [2012] EWCA Civ 768 at [19]–[22]. See also the decision of the Court of Appeal in *Begum v Hossain* [2015] EWCA Civ 717, where Roth J, setting out the relevant principles [at para 9(vi)], noted that 'Once a material departure from instructions is established, the court is not concerned with its effect on the result. The position is accurately stated in para 98 of Lloyd J's judgment in the *Shell UK* case [1999] 2 ALL ER (Comm) 87 at 108–109; the determination in those circumstances is simply not binding on the parties.'
[61] *Campbell v Edwards* [1976] 1 WLR 403.
[62] See *Bruce v TTA Management Ltd* [2015] EWHC 936 (Ch).
[63] *Marco v Thompson (No 3)* [1997] 2 BCLC 36.

party may enable a challenge to be made on the grounds of bias or collusion if the existence of those communications is not disclosed to the other party.[64] However if the communications with one party are recorded in writing and then disclosed to the other parties, a claim on the grounds of bias or collusion is not likely to succeed.[65] The potential for bias exists if an expert acts as mediator and then subsequently takes on the role of determiner.[66]

O Procedure for Making a Challenge

24.52 A challenge to the decision in an expert determination will usually be made by issuing Part 8 proceedings. Part 8 proceedings may also be issued in advance of an expert determination to decide any disputes about the interpretation of the expert determination clause, or to resolve disagreement about matters that should be referred to the expert pursuant to the clause. If the decision is set aside, the court may, in some circumstances, make the determination itself, if necessary after considering expert evidence adduced by the parties, or it may direct a new expert to be instructed to determine the matter.

P Enforcing a Decision

24.53 A decision reached by expert or neutral determination cannot be enforced in the same way as if it were a court decision. A failure by one side to honour the decision amounts to a breach of contract and proceedings can be issued in relation to the breach. In those proceedings, the court can make an order giving effect to the decision of the expert, and if there are no valid grounds for challenging the decision, summary judgment is likely to be granted to enforce the decision.[67] The court's decision can then be enforced in the same way as any other judgment.[68] Winding-up or bankruptcy proceedings could also be brought against an individual or company or partnership that refused to pay a monetary sum awarded by an expert determination.

---

[64] See, for example *Paice v Harding (t/a MJ Harding Contractors)* [2015] EWHC 661 (TCC) (a case involving adjudication).

[65] *Rydon Maintenance Ltd v Affinity Sutton Housing Ltd* [2015] EWHC 1306 (Ch).

[66] See *Glencot Development & Design Ltd v Ben Barrett & Son (Contractors) Ltd* [2001] BLR 207 (TCC).

[67] *Rydon Maintenance Ltd v Affinity Sutton Housing Ltd* [2015] EWHC 1306 (TCC).

[68] See Chapter 20 for further detail about enforcement.

Q Suing the Expert

An expert or neutral person carrying out a determination is not immune from suit **24.54** in the same way as a member of the judiciary. An expert can be liable in negligence or breach of contract if he or she is negligent in the determination that he or she reaches or fails to act in accordance with the contract.[69] Many experts seek to secure immunity by inserting clauses in the agreement by which the parties agree that they will not hold the expert liable in respect of the determination or call the expert as a witness in any proceedings. These clauses may be unenforceable if they are unreasonable under the terms of the Unfair Contract Terms Act 1977.

R Disputes Review Panels

This can be a hybrid form of determination, which may or may not involve an **24.55** expert. They can take a number of different forms, but typically they will allow for each party to appoint an independent party to the panel, and the independent parties will then choose a chairman. The chairman or the independent parties may or may not be an expert, depending on the nature of the dispute that is being referred to the panel. Decisions made by the panel will usually be binding on the parties unless they agree that they will refer the decision to arbitration within a specified time limit. A disputes review panel was used in the Channel Tunnel litigation.[70] They are commonly set up under construction contracts and provide a speedy, relatively cheap solution to interim problems that can arise during lengthy construction projects, so that the overall project is finished on time.

---

[69] *Sutcliffe v Thackrah* [1974] AC 727; *Arenson v Casson Beckman Rutley and Co* [1977] AC 405.
[70] *Channel Tunnel Group Ltd v Balfour Beatty Ltd* [1993] 1 All ER 664.

25

ARBITRATION

A Introduction

25.01 Arbitration[1] involves an impartial arbitrator or tribunal considering both sides of a dispute and making a decision on the issues raised by the parties. There is no statutory definition of the term 'arbitration', probably because it can take a wide variety of forms and can arise in a wide variety of legal contexts. It is based on an agreement between the parties to refer their dispute or difference to arbitration. That agreement may be made before or after the relevant dispute has arisen. This means that there may be a pre-existing arbitration agreement which, when a dispute arises, one of the parties wishes to evade. There is a strong public policy in favour of upholding arbitration agreements, which is supported by the idea that an arbitration clause in a contract is separable from the rest of the substantive contract[2] (and so continues to apply even if the substantive contract is avoided), and by the jurisdiction to stay court proceedings[3] that are commenced in breach of an arbitration agreement.

25.02 A key question in arbitration law is the extent to which domestic law should prescribe how arbitrations should be conducted, and the extent to which the parties should be allowed to devise their own procedures. This is reflected in the distinction in the Arbitration Act 1996 between mandatory and non-mandatory provisions.[4] These provide a highly developed set of procedures for arbitrations, in keeping with this country's status as a leading venue for international arbitrations. The intention is that the mandatory provisions cover only the matters that are essential for the effective resolution of disputes referred to arbitration, with everything else covered by non-mandatory fall-back provisions, which the parties can change if they wish.

---

[1] See *Russell on Arbitration* (24th edn, Sweet & Maxwell, 2015); *Redfern & Hunter on International Arbitration* (6th edn, OUP, 2015).

[2] Arbitration Act 1996, s 7.

[3] Arbitration Act 1996, s 9. The court can use its jurisdiction to stay insolvency proceedings to similar effect where the parties have agreed to arbitrate (*Salford Estates (No 2) Ltd v Altomart Ltd* [2014] EWCA Civ 1575).

[4] Arbitration Act 1996, s 4.

B Fundamental Concepts in Arbitration

Arbitrations governed by the Arbitration Act 1996 are subject to three general principles that are set out in s 1, as follows: **25.03**

(a) the object of arbitration is to obtain the fair resolution of disputes by an impartial tribunal without unnecessary delay or expense;

(b) the parties should be free to agree how their disputes are resolved, subject only to such safeguards as are necessary in the public interest; and

(c) ... the court should not intervene except as provided by [the Arbitration Act 1996].

Where the parties have agreed to refer their dispute to arbitration, that implies they want their dispute decided:[5] **25.04**

- by a tribunal they have chosen;
- in a neutral location (this is of particular importance in international arbitration) and with neutral arbitrators;
- in privacy;
- speedily and efficiently; and
- with light but efficient supervision by the courts.

C Requirements

In order for there to be an effective reference to arbitration the following requirements must be met: **25.05**

- there must be a dispute or difference;[6]
- the dispute must be 'arbitrable'. This means there needs to be a private law dispute rather than a dispute relating to public law or legal status;
- there must be an agreement to arbitrate;

---

[5] *Fili Shipping Co Ltd v Premium Nafta Products Ltd, sub nom Fiona Trust and Holding Corp v Privalov* [2007] UKHL 40 (per Lord Hoffmann at [6]). This case establishes that in interpreting arbitration clauses the courts work on the principle that sensible business people do not want their disputes determined partly by arbitration and partly by the courts. This 'one-stop adjudication' principle is a starting point in interpreting what the parties have agreed rather than a presumption (*Trust Risk Group SpA v Amtrust Europe Ltd* [2015] EWCA Civ 437). The same principle is applied in interpreting other dispute resolution clauses, and also jurisdiction clauses (*Starlight Shipping Co v Allianz Marine and Aviation Versicherungs AG* [2014] EWCA Civ 1010).

[6] Arbitration Act 1996, ss 6(1) and 82.

- for the Arbitration Act 1996 to apply, the agreement to arbitrate must be in writing;[7]
- the nature of the dispute must come within the terms of the arbitration agreement;
- the parties must have had legal capacity to enter into the arbitration agreement;
- any contractual condition precedent to arbitration must be complied with;
- the parties must find an arbitral tribunal willing to act and decide the dispute; and
- the dispute must come within the terms of the particular reference to arbitration.

Contractual foundation of arbitration

25.06 Almost any type of dispute can be referred to arbitration, regardless of the legal classification of the underlying cause of action. That said, arbitration is most commonly used for resolving disputes arising out of a contract between the parties, frequently with the agreement to arbitrate being found in a clause in the substantive contract. Where such a dispute is referred to arbitration, from a technical legal point of view there will often be four contracts:

- the underlying substantive contract on which the dispute is based ('the substantive contract');
- the agreement to arbitrate, which is separable from the substantive contract;
- the agreement between the parties and an arbitral institution referring the dispute to arbitration under the aegis of that institution. Often the parties agree that the institution's arbitration rules will apply to the arbitral proceedings; and
- agreement(s) appointing the arbitrators, made between the parties and/or the arbitral institution and the individual arbitrators.

Mandate of the arbitral tribunal

25.07 The jurisdiction of an arbitral tribunal depends on the mandate given to it by the parties. An arbitral tribunal will not have jurisdiction unless the dispute comes within the terms of the particular reference to arbitration. This will be limited by the terms of the arbitration agreement (which may be a standard clause in the substantive contract, or an agreement after the dispute has arisen to refer that dispute to arbitration), and the separate agreement between the tribunal and the parties appointing the tribunal. It means, for example, that the arbitrators cannot make a decision against a person who is not a party to the arbitration agreement, or on matters not covered by the arbitration agreement, or on matters not covered by the parties' agreement with the arbitrators.

---

[7] Arbitration Act 1996, s 5; New York Convention 1958 Art II.

D Stay of Legal Proceedings

To prevent a party from breaching an agreement to arbitrate by bringing court **25.08** proceedings, s 9(1) Arbitration Act 1996 allows the other side to apply for a stay of those court proceedings. A stay can be sought whether the legal proceedings said to breach the arbitration agreement are brought by way of claim or counterclaim,[8] and include unfair prejudice petitions under s 996 Companies Act 2006,[9] as well as ordinary Part 7 claims. A stay under s 9 imposes a halt on the legal proceedings,[10] and in practical terms usually has the consequence that the dispute will be referred for final determination by arbitration.

The main question under s 9 Arbitration Act 1996 is whether the dispute raised in **25.09** the litigation is a matter 'which under the [arbitration] agreement is to be referred to arbitration'. If it is the court 'shall' grant a stay (so this is mandatory rather than discretionary), unless the court is satisfied that the arbitration agreement is null and void, inoperative, or incapable of being performed.[11]

E Commencement

Arbitrations are commenced by sending a notice of arbitration and then appoint- **25.10** ing the members of the arbitral tribunal. A notice of arbitration (also known as a notice to arbitrate) has to be in writing and must comply with the requirements[12] for appointing the arbitral tribunal. These requirements can be met by a reasonably simple letter. In practice the letter tends to include additional details in order to comply with further requirements set out in any relevant institutional arbitral rules.

The parties are free to agree on the procedure for appointing the arbitrator or arbi- **25.11** trators, including the procedure for appointing any chairman or umpire.[13] Where the parties agree to a three-member tribunal, the usual position is that each party appoints one arbitrator, and these two arbitrators then appoint a third member who acts as the chairman.[14] Arbitrators may be chosen because they are known profes- sionally by, or recommended to, the appointing parties, or may be nominated by an

---

[8] Arbitration Act 1996, s 9(1).
[9] *Fulham Football Club (1987) Ltd v Richards* [2011] EWCA Civ 855, but not winding up relief, which is not arbitrable (*Salford Estates (No 2) Ltd v Altomart Ltd* [2014] EWCA Civ 1575).
[10] CPR r 3.1(2)(f) and CPR Glossary.
[11] Arbitration Act 1996, s 9(4); New York Convention 1958 Art II(3).
[12] Which are set out in Arbitration Act 1996, s 14(3)–(5).
[13] Arbitration Act 1996, s 16(1).
[14] Arbitration Act 1996, s 16(5).

arbitral institution. Alternatively, arbitrators may be nominated by the President of a professional body. In the absence of contrary agreement, there are default provisions for different types of arbitral tribunal.[15]

F Procedure in Arbitrations

25.12 The complexity of the procedure adopted in an arbitration will depend on what the parties have agreed, which will be influenced by the nature and importance of the dispute.[16] Relatively simple procedures tend to be adopted in consumer arbitrations, whereas in commercial arbitrations procedures can closely resemble those used in commercial litigation. The overall aim is the fair resolution of the dispute without unnecessary delay or expense.[17] Different stages in the process may be heavily prescribed by the rules of an arbitral institution as chosen by the parties. In the absence of agreement the default provisions of the Arbitration Act 1996 will apply.[18]

Preliminary meeting

25.13 A preliminary meeting will often be convened shortly after the tribunal is appointed. It is an opportunity for the parties and arbitrators to meet, but its main purpose is as a forum for the tribunal to discuss jurisdictional matters and to make procedural directions for the preparation of the evidence needed for deciding the reference. There is no set agenda for preliminary meetings. It may well be possible for directions to be agreed between the parties, which will make a preliminary meeting less necessary. It is becoming increasingly common to hold preliminary meetings by conference telephone calls or through video-conferencing.

Directions on procedure and evidence

25.14 It is for the arbitration tribunal to decide all procedural and evidential matters that have been referred to it, subject to the right of the parties to agree such matters between themselves.[19] Procedural matters to consider may include:[20]

- when and where to hold the proceedings;
- the languages to be used and whether translations are required;
- whether written points of claim and defence will be used, and their form;

---

[15] Arbitration Act 1996, s 16.
[16] Arbitration Act 1996, s 33(1)(b) requires arbitrators to adopt procedures suitable to the circumstances of the particular case.
[17] Arbitration Act 1996, s 1(a).
[18] Arbitration Act 1996, s 4(2).
[19] Arbitration Act 1996, s 34(1).
[20] Arbitration Act 1996, s 34(2).

- whether documents should be disclosed and produced, and at what stage;
- whether to apply the strict rules of evidence;
- whether expert evidence is required, and the time, manner, and form in which such evidence should be exchanged and presented;
- whether the tribunal should take the initiative in ascertaining the facts and the law; and
- whether and to what extent there should be oral or written evidence or submissions.

The tribunal may fix the time within which any directions are to be complied with, **25.15** and may if it thinks fit extend the time so fixed (whether or not it has expired).[21]

Pre-trial hearing/conference

If the arbitration is of some complexity it may be sensible to hold a pre-trial hearing **25.16** or conference. This will usually take place a number of weeks before the expected start of the hearing. The main purpose is to review what has been done in preparation for the hearing, to assess whether the parties are going to be ready for the hearing, and to make directions.

Bundles

Directions are usually made for the compilation of bundles for the hearing. They **25.17** will usually contain the documents dealing with the reference to the arbitration and the appointment of the tribunal. They will then usually have the statements of case, and any procedural orders and directions. It may well be that separate bundles will be required for the evidence. These files should be divided into the contemporaneous documentation, the witness statements of the factual witnesses, and the expert evidence. A further file is likely to be needed to contain the written opening submissions or skeleton arguments and authorities.

No right to an oral hearing

Subject to contrary agreement between the parties, the tribunal can decide whether **25.18** and to what extent there should be oral or written evidence or submissions.[22] In deciding whether to deal with the dispute on the documents or after an oral hearing the tribunal must bear in mind the need to act fairly, giving every party a reasonable opportunity of putting its case and dealing with that of the other side, and the need to avoid unnecessary expense and delay.[23] While it might be unwise to proceed

---

[21] Arbitration Act 1996, s 34(3).
[22] Arbitration Act 1996, s 34(2)(h).
[23] Arbitration Act 1996, s 33(1).

without a hearing in an arbitration where a substantial amount of money is at stake, arbitrators have the power to do so.[24] A number of institutional rules reverse this position, and give the parties the right to insist on an oral hearing.

The hearing

25.19 Arbitrators can choose to adopt either an adversarial (the traditional English court method of conducting hearings) or inquisitorial (civil law system) approach to the hearing.[25]

Closing of proceedings

25.20 The arbitrators will include a mechanism for closing the proceedings. This may be a date designated in the tribunal's directions, or a set period after a stage in the process, or after the last closing submission at the hearing. After the closure of proceedings the usual rule is that no further evidence or submissions can be given to the tribunal (although sometimes tribunals give permission for further material to be advanced even after the close of proceedings).

G Privacy and Confidentiality

25.21 There are long-established principles of arbitration law that arbitral proceedings are private[26] and confidential.[27] See Chapter 5 for more details.

H Awards

25.22 There are four different types of awards and orders that are available to arbitrators, namely:

- *procedural orders*, which provide procedural directions and measures designed to preserve evidence or the subject matter of the dispute ('conservatory measures') while an arbitration is proceeding;[28]
- *interim (also referred to as partial) awards and awards on different issues*, which finally dispose of one or more of the substantive issues in the arbitration, leaving the other issues to be decided later;[29]

---

[24] *Boulos Gad Tourism and Hotels Ltd v Uniground Shipping Co Ltd* (2001) LTL 21/2/2002.

[25] Arbitration Act 1996, s 34(2)(e) and (g), which provide that the arbitral tribunal can decide whether and to what extent it should take the initiative in ascertaining the facts and the law.

[26] *Oxford Shipping Co Ltd v Nippon Yusen Kaisha* [1984] 3 All ER 835.

[27] *Ali Shipping Corp v Shipyard Trogir* [1999] 1 WLR 314.

[28] Arbitration Act 1996, ss 38 and 39.

[29] Arbitration Act 1996, s 47.

- *final awards*, finally disposing of the arbitration;[30] and
- *costs awards*, which provide for the payment of the costs incurred in the arbitration between the parties.[31]

Usually, once an order or award is made it is binding on the parties. Most sets of **25.23** institutional arbitral rules include provision for parties making suggestions for the correction of clerical mistakes in orders and awards.[32]

I Enforcement of Awards

A domestic arbitral award may be enforced either by bringing an ordinary civil **25.24** claim on the award in the High Court, or by using the summary procedure under s 66(1) Arbitration Act 1996. This section allows the court to grant permission to enforce an award of an arbitral tribunal in the same manner as a judgment or order of the court. Permission is sought by issuing an arbitration claim form in the High Court, which is considered without notice.[33]

Cross-border enforcement of arbitral awards can usually be achieved through the **25.25** New York Convention 1958,[34] which applies to arbitral awards made in the territory of a state other than the state where the recognition and enforcement of such awards are sought.[35] In deciding whether the Convention applies, an award is treated as made at the seat of the arbitration,[36] regardless of where it was signed, despatched, or delivered to any of the parties.[37] A party seeking the recognition or enforcement of a New York Convention award must produce the duly authenticated original award or a duly certified copy, and the original arbitration agreement or a duly certified copy.[38] Where permission is given, judgment may be entered in terms of the award.[39]

---

[30] Arbitration Act 1996, ss 46–58.
[31] Arbitration Act 1996, ss 59–65.
[32] Also, see Arbitration Act 1996, s 57.
[33] CPR r 62.18.
[34] New York Convention 1958 on the recognition and enforcement of arbitral awards. This is an extremely successful international convention, and has been ratified in more than 140 countries. Ease of enforcement under the New York Convention is one of the most compelling reasons for using arbitration.
[35] New York Convention 1958 Art I.
[36] Where the Arbitration Act 1996 applies, the seat of the arbitration is designated or determined in accordance with s 3.
[37] Arbitration Act 1996, s 100(2).
[38] Arbitration Act 1996, s 102(1).
[39] Arbitration Act 1996, s 101(3).

J Appeals

25.26 In accordance with the principle of limited court intervention in arbitrations,[40] there are only limited grounds for seeking judicial review of arbitral awards. Under s 68 it is possible to challenge an award on the ground of serious irregularity, and, unless the parties agree to exclude the right, under s 69 it is possible to appeal on a point of law. Both provisions are applied restrictively. There are also restrictions on appeals within the court system in the limited cases where court applications can be made in arbitration claims.[41]

---

[40] Arbitration Act 1996, s 1(c).
[41] See for example *Itochu Corporation v Johann MK Blumenthal GmbH & Co KG* [2012] EWCA Civ 996.

26

CONSTRUCTION INDUSTRY ADJUDICATION

A Introduction

Construction industry adjudication[1] was introduced by statute and requires all construction contracts, as defined, to have a provision for adjudication.[2] The statutory requirement is for adjudication by an independent third person who produces a decision on the dispute which is binding on an interim basis until finally determined, as appropriate, by the court, arbitration, or agreement. The adjudicator must reach a decision within a 28-day period (subject to any agreed extensions).[3]   **26.01**

B Requirements

Construction contract

A 'construction contract' is an agreement for the carrying out of construction operations, either directly or through others such as by subcontracting, or by the provision of labour.[4] 'Construction operations' covers the construction, alteration, repair, maintenance, extension, demolition, or dismantling of buildings or structures forming, or to form, part of land, and also various other defined activities, and with some exclusions.   **26.02**

Dispute

The parties to a construction contract have the right to refer any 'dispute' to adjudication.[5] The dispute must have crystallized. This is defined to include any difference, and so has the same meaning as 'dispute' in relation to arbitration.   **26.03**

---

[1] See *Coulson on Construction Adjudication* (3rd edn, OUP, 2015) for a detailed explanation of the subject.

[2] Housing Grants, Construction and Regeneration Act 1996 ('the Act') as amended by Part 8 of the Local Democracy, Economic Development and Construction Act 2010.

[3] Section 108(2)(c) of the Act.

[4] Sections 104(1) and 105 of the Act.

[5] Section 108(1) of the Act.

C Contractual Right to Adjudication

26.04 Under the Act[6] a construction contract must include written terms that:

- enable a party to give notice at any time of its intention to refer a dispute to adjudication;
- provide a timetable with the object of securing the appointment of the adjudicator and referral of the dispute to him or her within seven days of such notice;
- require the adjudicator to reach a decision within 28 days of referral or such longer period as is agreed by the parties after the dispute has been referred;
- allow the adjudicator to extend the period of 28 days by up to 14 days, with the consent of the party by whom the dispute was referred;
- impose a duty on the adjudicator to act impartially;
- enable the adjudicator to take the initiative in ascertaining the facts and the law; and
- permit the correction of clerical or typographical errors in the decision.

If the contract does not include such a clause then the appropriate terms of the Scheme for Construction Contracts are implied.[7] The Scheme provides terms dealing with all the main features of adjudication required by an express clause complying with s 108 of the Act.

D Commencement of the Adjudication

Notice of adjudication: the commencement of adjudication

26.05 An adjudication is commenced by the referring party giving a notice of adjudication to all the other parties to the contract. This is a notice in writing, either in a letter or a formal notice, stating the referring party's intention to refer a stated dispute arising out of the construction contract to adjudication.

Ambit of the reference

26.06 It is for the party making the reference to adjudication to define the issues to be adjudicated, and it is the notice of adjudication that achieves this. This means the adjudicator has no jurisdiction to decide matters outside these issues in the absence of agreement to vary by the parties.

---

[6] Section 108 of the Act.
[7] Section 108(5) of the Act.

Nomination of adjudicator

An adjudicator needs to be appointed within seven days of the notice of adjudica- **26.07** tion. The adjudicator may be named in the construction contract, or else will have to be appointed in accordance with the machinery in the contract (which may adopt the institutional rules of a dispute resolution service provider) or the Scheme for Construction Contracts. These may provide for an adjudicator to be selected by a nominating body, such as AICA, RIBA, RICS, or TeCSA. Most appointing bodies have a five-day turn-around time for making appointments and aim to make the appointment within the seven-day deadline. The adjudicator has two days to confirm whether they are available to act.

Referral notice

A written referral notice needs to be sent by the referring party to the adjudicator **26.08** not later than seven days from the date of the notice of adjudication. These seven days run in parallel with the seven days for appointing the adjudicator. The adjudicator is required to inform the parties of the date of receipt of the referral notice. Referral notices are in effect formal statements of case.

E Procedure

Timetable for procedural steps

The adjudicator is required to establish the timetable and procedure for the adjudi- **26.09** cation, which may include the consideration of any documentary or oral submission of the parties, site visits or inspections, and meeting the parties. The adjudicator may seek expert advice. There is a general duty to avoid incurring unnecessary expense,[8] and the need to make a decision within 28 days of referral (or any extended time) means that the adjudication has to be conducted expeditiously. All documents and information provided to the adjudicator must be made available to all the parties.[9]

Response to referral notice

The adjudicator will consider whether the responding party should be allowed to **26.10** put in a response to the referral notice, and when. Usually a direction is given providing for the response within a short time after the submission of the referral notice.

---

[8] Scheme for Construction Contracts (England and Wales) Regulations 1998 SI 1998 No 649 as amended by SI 2011 No 2333 para 12(b).

[9] Scheme for Construction Contracts, para 17.

Subsequent statements of case

26.11   The adjudicator may direct that there are further rounds of submissions or request parties to address particular issues. Obviously the time for providing such responses or information is likely to be short given the limited time to make the decision.

F Adjudicator's Decision

26.12   Adjudicators are required to act impartially in carrying out their duties, and must decide the dispute in accordance with the relevant terms of the contract and in accordance with the law applicable to the contract.[10] There is no obligation to have a hearing, although the adjudicator may decide to hear oral evidence or representations.

26.13   Reasons for the adjudicator's decision are only required if one of the parties makes a request. Interest may be awarded in addition to the principal sum if payable under the contract. There is usually provision for the adjudicator to apportion his or her fees and expenses between the parties and there may be an express provision for the adjudicator to apportion and assess the costs of the parties, otherwise the adjudicator cannot do so.

G After the Adjudication

26.14   Should the losing party fail to comply with the adjudicator's decision, the winning party can enforce the decision through the court by way of summary judgment. On an application for summary judgment the losing party can challenge the adjudicator's decision only on limited grounds such as lack of jurisdiction or breach of the rules of natural justice, but not on the merits.

26.15   The underlying policy of adjudication is 'pay now, argue later'.[11] A claimant who receives less than they expected can sue for the balance through the courts or by arbitration. A party who disputes the sum found due in an adjudication can bring proceedings to recover any overpayment either by virtue of a contractual implied term or by virtue of an independent restitutionary right.[12]

---

[10] An adjudicator who fails to produce an enforceable decision is not entitled to any fee from the parties, *Systech International Ltd v PC Harrington Contractors Ltd* [2012] EWCA Civ 1371.

[11] *RJT Consulting Engineers Ltd v DM Engineering (Northern Ireland) Ltd* [2002] EWCA Civ 270.

[12] *Aspect Contracts (Asbestos) Ltd v Higgins Construction plc* [2015] UKSC 38. Limitation runs from the date of the overpayment.

INDEX